A Concise History of Intern

Ever since the financial crisis of 2008, doubts have been raised about the future of capitalism. In this broadranging survey of financial capitalism from antiquity to the present, Larry Neal reveals the ways in which the financial innovations throughout history have increased trade and prosperity as well as improving standards of living. These innovations have, however, all too often led to financial crises as a result of the failure of effective coordination among banks, capital markets, and governments. The book examines this key interrelationship between financial innovation, government regulation, and financial crises across 3,000 years, showing through past successes and failures the key factors that underpin any successful recovery and sustain economic growth. The result is both an essential introduction to financial capitalism and also a series of workable solutions that will help both to preserve the gains we have already achieved and to mitigate the dangers of future crises.

LARRY NEAL is Emeritus Professor of Economics at the University of Illinois at Urbana-Champaign, Research Associate of the National Bureau of Economic Research, and Visiting Professor at the London School of Economics (2006–2014). Specializing in financial history and European economies, he is author of *The Rise of Financial Capitalism: International Capital Markets in the Age of Reason* (Cambridge University Press, 1990). His recent publications include editing *The Cambridge History of Capitalism* (Cambridge University Press, 2014); and *"I am not master of events": The Speculations of John Law and Lord Londonderry in the Mississippi and South Sea Bubbles* (2012).

NEW APPROACHES TO ECONOMIC AND SOCIAL HISTORY

SERIES EDITORS
Barry Doyle (University of Huddersfield)
Debin Ma (London School of Economics and Political Science)
Larry Neal (University of Illinois, Urbana-Champaign)

New Approaches to Economic and Social History is an important new textbook series published in association with the Economic History Society. It provides concise but authoritative surveys of major themes and issues in world economic and social history from the post-Roman recovery to the present day. Books in the series are by recognized authorities operating at the cutting edge of their field with an ability to write clearly and succinctly. The series consists principally of single-author works – academically rigorous and groundbreaking – which offer comprehensive, analytical guides at a length and level accessible to advanced school students and undergraduate historians and economists.

A Concise History of International Finance

From Babylon to Bernanke

LARRY NEAL
University of Illinois at Urbana-Champaign

CAMBRIDGE
UNIVERSITY PRESS

University Printing House, Cambridge CB2 8BS, United Kingdom

Cambridge University Press is part of the University of Cambridge.

It furthers the University's mission by disseminating knowledge in the pursuit of education, learning and research at the highest international levels of excellence.

www.cambridge.org
Information on this title: www.cambridge.org/9781107034174

© Larry Neal 2015

First published 2015

Printed in the United Kingdom by TJ International Ltd. Padstow Cornwall

A catalogue record for this publication is available from the British Library

ISBN 978-1-107-03417-4 Hardback
ISBN 978-1-107-62121-3 Paperback

Contents

Figures

Boxes

x

Tables

Preface

For many years, I offered a graduate seminar in "Financial History" at the University of Illinois. The course always began with an overview of the most recent financial difficulties confronting the international economy. The first time I offered the course, I worked backwards from the present and ended as far back as student interest or my knowledge base allowed. It soon became clear, however, that instead of re-tracing a supposed evolutionary trail of financial development and disorders, I should skip back to "how it all began," and then take the narrative arc forward to the present. But how far back was it necessary to go? That question was answered at first in terms of my limited knowledge. When I became fascinated by the events of 1720 with the Mississippi and South Sea bubbles in Paris, London, and Amsterdam, that was where I would begin the rest of the course.

When I took these ideas to the graduate students at the London School of Economics in 2006, there was definitely an air of triumphalism about the "Great Moderation" and the ongoing globalization of finance, but this changed rapidly over the course of the next five years as the "Great Recession" began in 2007 and kept unfolding. Increasingly, I had to explain how difficult it was to get different national financial systems coordinated effectively while financial innovations occurred. While trying valiantly to keep up the morale of the students, who increasingly came from the corps of continuing layoffs in the financial sector, I also had to go farther and farther back to begin a new, more nuanced, and much longer "narrative arc" for the material. The variety of international backgrounds and experiences of the LSE students, reflected in their research papers, helped greatly to expand my knowledge base back in time. To date, it only goes back to Babylon based on the ongoing work of ancient archaeologists. The intervening millennia suffer from lack of surviving written documentation comparable to clay tablets and *bullae* until the parchment records of medieval Europe appear. Even so, there are enough examples of successful financial innovations in the past to restore my faith that this crisis, too, shall pass.

The research papers from the students in my courses at the University of Illinois, California Institute of Technology, London School of Economics and Political Science, Sciences Po, and the University of California at Los Angeles has improved my grasp of the historical record. Seminar participants at CalTech, Cambridge, Chicago, Harvard, Michigan, Northwestern, Oxford, Toronto, and Yale over the years raised valid points. Continued interchanges with my colleagues at Illinois – Lee Alston, Jeremy Atack, Charles Calomiris, Virginia France, and Charles Kahn, as well as my work with Lance Davis and Eugene White, kept up my enthusiasm for the project over the years. Careful reading of earlier drafts by Richard Steckel, Mira Wilkins, and David Wishart will benefit readers of this book.

1 | *Introduction*

Someday you guys are going to need to tell me how we ended up with a system like this ... we're not doing something right if we're stuck with these miserable choices.[1]

Ever since the financial crisis of 2008, doubts have been raised about the future of capitalism. Certainly, seven years of doubtful recovery from the recession of 2007 and then another recession in 2012 in several European countries generated pessimism about the ability of capitalist economies to deal effectively with the persistent instability of the global financial system. At the heart of this pessimistic outlook is a deeper concern over the perils of international finance, compounded by confusion over the proliferation of exotic financial products marketed by hedge funds, venture capitalists, and assorted niche firms that make up the "shadow banking" community. No wonder new studies appear almost daily that try to explain to the wider public, as well as overwhelmed policy makers, what went wrong and what should be done now and in the future to avoid a repeat disaster. As President Bush remarked to his top economic policy makers, Henry Paulson, US Secretary of the Treasury, and Ben Bernanke, chairman of the Federal Reserve System of the US, at the height of the crisis in September 2008, "Someday you guys are going to need to tell me how we ended up with a system like this ... we're not doing something right if we're stuck with these miserable choices."

This book joins a long list of historical works designed precisely to explain to former President Bush (and the rest of us) just how we ended up "stuck with these miserable choices." Most studies to date provide detailed indictments of the apparent perpetrators of the crisis,

[1] President George W. Bush to Ben Bernanke, chairman of the Federal Reserve System, and Henry Paulson, Secretary of the Treasury, as reported by James B. Stewart, "Eight Days: The Battle to Save the American Financial System," *The New Yorker*, September 21, 2009, p. 72.

beginning with the prime movers – variously profligate politicians, indifferent regulators, or opportunistic financiers – then move on to the propagators of the crisis – rampant greed, ignorance, or indifference of the general public. Few note the international elements; most prefer to focus outrage on the villains near at hand or, most persuasively, on the US with its complex financial system and overwhelming wealth at the center of the international financial system since the Second World War. Even fewer try to suggest ways to resolve the crisis internationally, preferring instead to deal with the domestic issues of concern to their national audience. Most end with a depressing conclusion that there will be a crisis next time, perhaps sooner than later and probably worse if policy makers or the public do not take the lessons of history or the prescriptions of the author to heart.[2]

In contrast to those works, the present one takes both an international view and a very long historical background. This author tried to instill the various lessons of financial history in an increasing number of international graduate students at the London School of Economics during the years the crisis was unfolding, 2006–2010. Chastened by the experience of repeatedly mis-forecasting the next episode, I resolved to take both a broader and deeper perspective on the financial innovations that accompany economic expansion and then, all too often, lead to financial crises with disruptive effects. To encourage the youth of the world that their future promises better times than their parents are living through at present, I emphasize the benefits of financial innovations throughout history that have increased trade, enabled technical progress, and improved standards of living in general. Historians as well as contemporary observers often overlook the real benefits of financial innovations while dazzled by the extraordinary fortunes created for a favored few. Before the general benefits of financial innovations can be realized in the real economy, however (and they have been realized repeatedly and especially over the past three centuries), some method of coordination among the various elements of a financial system must be found. Effective and mutually beneficial coordination among banks, capital markets, and governments while dealing with a financial innovation occurring somewhere in the economy turns out to be hard for all concerned.

---

[2] Useful overviews of the literature are Kindleberger and Aliber 2011, Chapter 1; Neal 2011b; Lo 2012.

Often enough, the problems of coordination overcome the financial system and some kind of crisis ensues. More interesting, and the reason to write this book, is that solutions are found occasionally. When solutions are found, good things happen for the entire economy, at least until the next financial innovation disrupts the system. Other histories of finance devote much effort to cataloguing various crises of the past and identifying common elements among their respective causes and consequences (e.g. Reinhart and Rogoff 2009). Very little, however, has been done to identify effective solutions to crises and to determine their common elements to see if a similar solution could be found to the current crisis. Solutions, when they do occur, seem to take a very long time to unfold; or to depend on some exogenous shock such as a major war; or to simply abandon the particular financial innovation that is blamed for the crisis. A closer look at particular successful recoveries, however, may reveal common strategies that can be applied generally, due allowance being made for the changing historical contexts of financial crises. That is the ultimate goal of this book. The years of global prosperity prior to 2008 generated billions of stakeholders in the benefits of global capitalism and international trade. The ultimate purpose of this work is to help meet their desire to find solutions to the financial crisis, workable solutions that will both preserve the gains already achieved and also mitigate the dangers of future crises.

How to keep up with developments in international finance

The elements of the international financial system that led up to the global crisis of 2007–2012 are well documented in the official publications of international organizations such as the International Monetary Fund (IMF), the Bank for International Settlements (BIS), and the Organisation for Economic Cooperation and Development (OECD). The different perspectives they offer are instructive, not just for understanding the complexity of the financial crisis but also for revealing the divergent interests at play in resolving that crisis. The IMF, while acting as an international bank and lender of last resort in many cases since it was established in 1944, tends to reflect the views of the finance ministers from the 188 member states. The BIS, established earlier than the IMF in 1930, but with a much smaller membership (60 central banks in 2012) provides a separate forum for central bankers to discuss common issues and organize concerted responses to particular matters of international concern. Monetary and financial conditions are the main concern of central banks in the modern world, all of them jointly responsible for issuing the fiat currencies that currently make up the world's money supply. The OECD, created in 1960 to continue the work of the Organisation for European Economic Cooperation (OEEC), which began coordinating Marshall Plan expenditures in 1949, monitors the overall economic conditions for each of its 34 member countries as of 2012, but these are the richest and most open economies in the world, accounting for most of the global output and trade. One can expect differing viewpoints from the fiscal authorities (expressed in the IMF's semi-annual *World Economic Outlook (WEO)*, the central bankers (given by the annual reports of the BIS (BIS *Annual Report*), and the governments of the major players in the global economy, whose overall appraisals of both domestic and international economic issues appear in the semi-annual *OECD Economic Outlook*.

The IMF *Global Financial Stability Report (GFSR)* of the IMF's Department of International Capital Markets, issued semi-annually since March 2002 and supplemented quarterly with updates, is especially useful for the topics covered in this book. The *GFSR* takes an international perspective on capital markets, summarizing the state of both bond and equity markets among member countries with graphic displays of the current state of the four risk elements and two conditions that the IMF believes affect the overall stability of the financial system. The risk elements consist of macroeconomic risks, emerging market risks, credit risks, and market and liquidity risks; the conditions affecting stability are the investing public's appetite for risk and monetary and financial conditions as set by central banks and regulators. While the *GFSR* for April 2012 claimed that risk conditions had moderated since their previous two reports in January 2012 and September 2011, monetary and financial conditions were unchanged but the public's "appetite for risk" had risen (meaning stock market indexes globally had risen). Provided that central banks maintained ease of monetary and financial conditions, something they had been doing to an unprecedented extent since 2008, the global economy could slowly recover. Later events in May and June, however, forced the IMF to reduce their forecasts of economic growth for the coming year, especially for Europe, although they maintained their optimism for 2014 if policy makers held to their course.

The June 2012 BIS report explained in detail, however, why central banks had reached the limit of their resources and it was now up to fiscal authorities around the world to come to the rescue. How? Mainly by tightening their budgets, whether by reducing subsidies or increasing taxes, and by introducing "structural reforms" in their regulation of labor, capital, and product markets. The deregulations implied by the phrase "structural reforms" are supposed to unleash pent-up energies that will generate rapid economic growth. Critics of the central banks point out that implementing any of their recommendations comes at a political price, which explains why they have not been implemented even after thirty years of exhortation by central bankers the world over. If forced to do more to facilitate realization of the global public's appetite for risk, the central banks would have to implement and expand new policies of massive investments in long-term securities, so-called "quantitative easing" (QE). According to BIS economists, the emerging problem with quantitative easing, when combined with financial liberalization, is that such "financial elasticity" creates extended buildups of balance sheets, both domestically and on international capital accounts. When these bloated capital account positions are readjusted, longer and more severe recessions occur in the real economy (Borio 2014; Borio, James, and Shin 2014).

The consensus of the finance ministers of the world then was that central bankers should do more to bring the global economy out of the crisis, but central bankers agreed that finance ministers should take up the burden as their tool kits had been exhausted. No wonder widespread pessimism continued unabated. While both the IMF and the BIS draw on the expertise of a large staff and a bevy of well-paid consultants and so provide excellent analyses of the ongoing crisis backed up with official statistics, both are obsessed with the idea that policy makers should maintain stability in the financial system, whether by preventing financial excesses or by cleaning up the mess left when a financial bubble collapses. The idea of promoting economic growth presumably lies in the domain of other experts charged with determining taxes and subsidies. The implicit assumption is that finance is simply the handmaiden of industry, not a prime mover, even if long-run investment in durable capital is necessary for technical progress to take root and continue. Nevertheless, the two organizations nicely convey the conventional wisdom of the economics profession within the government bureaucracies of the member countries.

The conventional wisdom is faithfully transmitted to the public by media such as *The Financial Times* and *The Economist* magazine. (*The Wall Street Journal* typically elects to discredit the bureaucracies in general, both domestic and international.) At the root of the ongoing crisis, according to the conventional wisdom, is the continued imbalance of trade patterns and consequent pressures among the major economies of the world to finance these imbalances, leading in turn to excessive financial elasticity.

How we got to this mess: the conventional wisdom

Villain #1 is the US, which persisted in running large current account deficits even after the end of the Bretton Woods System in 1971–1973, which was designed to help the rest of the world recover from the economic losses of the Second World War by providing a market in the US for their exports. The intent of the Bretton Woods system, which was overseen by the IMF and the World Bank, was to stabilize macroeconomic conditions in the member countries. It did this first by encouraging countries to remove quantitative restrictions on trade in goods and services, substituting instead transparent and reliable tariff barriers, which in turn were subject to reciprocal reductions by trading partners. Further, countries committed to fixed exchange rates with the US dollar in pricing both their exports and imports, making the tariff barriers to be surmounted by foreign suppliers fixed and clear as well. In compensation for opening their economies to foreign suppliers and displacing less efficient domestic producers, member state governments could control their money supply and protect domestic finance from foreign capital movements. They could subsidize firms and workers who were displaced by foreign competition until they could find alternative niches to fill in the growing economy.

In terms later made popular among international macroeconomists, governments signing on to the Bretton Woods System committed to fixed exchange rates and monetary sovereignty while giving up access to international capital markets. This was one way to solve the "trilemma" of not being able to pursue all three goals simultaneously. The Bretton Woods solution contrasted with the nineteenth-century solution of the classical gold standard, which committed countries to fixed exchange rates and open capital markets while giving up monetary sovereignty. From the perspective of trade imbalances that obsess the IMF analysts, however, the classical gold standard worked well as long as the British economy exported capital on a large scale. Economic historians now agree that the Bretton Woods System also worked fine as long as the US economy exported capital on a large scale, something it had done only briefly, from 1924 through 1928 in the period between the First and Second World, and again during the Bretton Woods era, 1944–1973.

The original treaty was signed at the Bretton Woods resort in New Hampshire in June 1944 after Allied victory in the Second World War seemed assured with the success of the D-Day invasion earlier that month. While the Bretton Woods system lasted formally from 1944 until its formal abandonment in 1973 after failed attempts to reach agreement on realignment of fixed exchange rates among the member countries, its effective term of operation was from 1958, when the European Payments Union (EPU) was wound up and the western European countries made their currencies convertible with each other and the US dollar for current account dealings, until August 15, 1971. On that date, the US government unilaterally pulled the rug out from under the system by refusing to redeem US dollars held by foreign central banks into gold at the agreed rate of $35 per ounce of gold. This action, a unilateral abrogation of the basic terms of a long-standing international treaty, adhered to by 125 countries at the time, could be considered from some perspectives an act of war, or at least an act that would lead to severe sanctions or reprisals by the other countries. For our purposes, however, it was just a very dramatic example of "financial innovation," this time by a government rather than by private banks or by market operators.

Moreover, it is an excellent example of a crisis created by a financial innovation, as the effects were immediate, international, and required adjustments by bankers, market operators, and regulators. These systemic effects were overshadowed by the oil shocks that were to follow in 1973 and 1978, but those shocks in turn were set off by the effect of the sharp fall in the international value of the US dollar that followed the end of the Bretton Woods Agreement to keep the dollar pegged at $35 per ounce of pure gold. The oil shocks of the 1970s were not the first or the last time that it became obvious that disruptions in finance could lead to serious and prolonged disruptions in the real economy. Only later, and only among a few academic specialists, did it seem that the creation of the Bretton Woods System was also a financial innovation, and one that helped create and sustain the prosperity of the real economy for the leading members of the IMF. The connection between the gradual implementation of the full Bretton Woods System and the "golden age of growth" during the period 1950 to 1973 was too obvious to miss, even as it has become increasingly impossible to reconstitute the virtuous cycle of increasing trade, increasing prosperity, and steady, high rates of economic growth that occurred for many countries (Bordo and Eichengreen 1993).

With the breakup of the Bretton Woods System came an extended period of experimentation with new financial innovations, catalogued under the general rubric of financial disintermediation for the US, but extending into Europe and then beyond, affecting even Communist China and eventually the Soviet Union. For economic historians and especially for financial historians, the world is still adjusting to the end of the Bretton Woods System, still seeking a new system of coordination among the operating elements of a financial system itself in order to generate growth in the real economy on a continuing basis with benefits widely distributed. In that unfolding perspective, the sub-prime crisis that began in the US in 2007, culminated in September 2008, and then reappeared in 2010 with the sovereign debt crisis within the European Union, represents the persistent failure to date to create an effective financial system that encompasses all trading nations (the IMF now has 188 members) and facilitates economic growth for all.

A post-Bretton Woods System, or Bretton Woods II?

The economists of the IMF have tried to work out a post-Bretton Woods System that would allow the free movement of capital internationally. They first argued that countries should try to maintain fixed, or at least tightly bounded exchange rates, thereby limiting their monetary sovereignty. The hope was that investments by the advanced economies in the less-developed (or "developing") countries within the IMF would generate sufficient economic growth that national politicians would be willing to forgo control over the national currency, having sufficient largesse from the accumulation of foreign capital at their disposal. Indeed, the experience of the European common currency, creating the euro as a new currency at fixed conversion rates with the legacy currencies of the member countries, created exactly this benefit for all concerned. Capital importing countries, mainly the southern and western periphery (Greece, Italy, Spain, Portugal, and Ireland) prospered from the employment opportunities created by foreign capital while capital exporting countries, mainly the northern periphery (Germany, Finland, Netherlands, Austria) prospered from their strong exports.

The problem that bedeviled this possible solution was that governments in developing countries had to issue debt denominated in the currencies of their creditors, which meant in US dollars, German *Deutsche Marks*, or Japanese yen. This created the so-called "original sin" problem of having to keep the borrowing country's exchange rate fixed to the currency of the creditor country, as any devaluation would make the debt burden worse. That is exactly what happened during the 1980s, especially for Latin American countries that had borrowed heavily from US banks, often with their encouragement, which were seeking higher interest rates abroad. Eventually, starting with the Latin America countries, governments did decide to issue bonds in their own currency, but also making provisions for redemption among the various creditors in case of delays in interest payments or outright default, the so-called "collective action clauses."

At this point, IMF consensus changed in recognition of the political reality that national governments would always fall back on control of the domestic money supply in case of financial difficulty. Hence, the new framework for post-Bretton Woods arrangements to resolve the trilemma would be (1) allow free international movement of capital, (2) maintain monetary sovereignty, but (3) permit flexible exchange rates. Meanwhile, the euro-zone solution seemed ever more appealing as the capital importing countries were able to issue government debt in euros and, with the support of the European Central Bank (ECB), pay interest rates as low as those paid by the German government on its bonds. So the EU part of the developed world remained convinced that their resolution of the trilemma was still best for them, namely to forsake monetary sovereignty within the European Union in favor of open capital markets and fixed exchange rates within the European System of Central Banks (ESCB), but with flexible exchange rates of the euro with the rest of the world.

The "Asian tigers," by contrast, having suffered the problems of issuing debt in foreign currencies and then confronting adverse exchange rates that increased their debt burdens to unsustainable levels in 1998, moved to their version of the original Bretton Woods System. This was to allow some movement of capital inward, but keep tight control on the export of capital; fix exchange rates on current account for trading purposes with the US dollar, or possibly a basket of widely used foreign currencies including the euro and yen; and keep monetary sovereignty. The China solution basically replicates the way West Germany and then Japan exploited the original Bretton Woods System during their golden ages of growth, in effect creating a second Bretton Woods System, BWII (Dooley *et al.* 2003, 2009). China's efforts have been imitated to greater or lesser degrees by other countries in Asia and Latin America. Each has experienced its own growth miracle as a consequence, according to this analysis. The key is to maintain export-led growth for long enough to raise productivity and living standards in the exporting country up to the levels of the leading economies. To do this, however, requires another country or set of countries to maintain import deficits during the growth spurt of the country catching up. The US, with its increasingly open economy after the Second World War, managed to provide this service for Japan and Germany during Bretton Woods I and then for Korea and China during Bretton Woods II.

Global imbalances: how sustainable are they?

Sustaining this global imbalance, which dominates the thinking of the IMF and *The Financial Times*, requires China to finance its continued export surpluses to the US by investing in US assets. Given the reluctance of the US authorities to allow Chinese control over productive assets in the US, China's export surpluses are invested in US government debt, just as Germany and Japan's export surpluses in the 1960s were largely invested in US government debt. But, just as the German and Japanese export-led growth miracles ended with the end of the Bretton Woods System in 1973, economists predict that the Chinese experience, begun in 1978, will end eventually, but when and with what repercussions no economist dares predict. (The authors of the Bretton Woods II argument, however, make a convincing case that it did not end with the financial crisis of 2008. That had separate causes, and requires distinct solutions, which we deal with in the final Chapter 14.)

Seeking some kind of international agreement comparable to the Bretton Woods treaty that established the IMF in the first place is clearly desirable for all countries concerned. The sovereign debt crisis in the European Union that began in 2010 demonstrates the limits to which monetary sovereignty can willingly be ceded by national governments to an international regime, even one so benign as the European Union and its institutional commitment to "soft power." Maintaining the euro as the common currency in the future will necessarily mean allowing market forces to determine the relative value of each government's debt. Whether EU governments will respond to the pressures of international capital markets to keep their obligations to service their debt in line with the revenues they can obtain from their tax base will determine the success of the euro as a financial innovation.

Meanwhile, the austerity programs enacted in the UK and the European Union in response to the financial crisis that began in the US and the UK have had wider repercussions, dampening the success of the export-led growth policies for China, which foresees the danger of a property market meltdown, much as Japan suffered at the end of its spurt of export-led growth in the 1980s. The leading prophet of doom, Professor Nouriel Roubini, drew the logical conclusion in July 2012 that the world economy was headed for "a perfect storm," a financial crisis worse than 2008 (*Daily Telegraph*, July 18, 2012). He argued that central banks and government treasuries had run out of bullets, having exhausted their resources in vain attempts to deal with the 2008 crisis. He and more economists are concerned that globalization of the world's economies, essentially since the end of the Bretton Woods System, has engendered a spate of financial innovations that are misconceived and doomed to fail, wreaking havoc on domestic economies when they collapse. Only a concerted change of policies by the two largest economies in the world – the US and China – can lead to a more stable and prosperous economic situation globally, according to Roubini. By the end of 2014, however, neither country had changed policy and no further crisis had yet occurred, even if both economies faced diminished prospects for economic growth.

This time is different, but there are historical parallels

As dire as the current situation appears, it resonates with financial historians who have studied past crises. Many of the studies that have appeared draw the parallel with the events that transpired leading up to the Great Depression that plunged the US into economic distress starting in 1929, becoming widespread and very severe in 1931, and ultimately led directly into the disaster of the Second World War. No one wants to see that sequence of events replicated, but some of the dysfunctional policy responses that occurred in 1930 and 1931 have been eerily replicated in Europe. Weimar Germany's Chancellor Heinrich Brüning's insistence upon government austerity in 1931, including reduced salaries for government officials, especially university faculty and teachers, have been replicated in 2011 at German insistence upon Greece, Portugal, and Ireland and willingly imposed by governments in Spain and Italy, and indeed, by a number of state governments within the US.

Even the dramatic changes in financial regulations by the New Deal government in the US, which included the separation of investment banking from commercial banking along with establishment of deposit insurance for commercial banks (the Glass–Steagall Act of 1933) and then establishment of the Securities and Exchange Commission (SEC) (also in 1933), were taken up again by the Sarbanes–Oxley Act of 2002 (in response to the Enron collapse in 2001), and the Dodd–Frank Act of 2010 (in response to the September 2008 crisis on Wall Street). Like the earlier regulatory legislations in the US, legislators took action before a full analysis of the existing crisis was available to them. For example, the report of the Financial Crisis Inquiry Commission (FCIC), a bipartisan committee established by Congress to answer President Bush's question to Paulson and Bernanke, was published in 2011, well after the Dodd–Frank Act had been signed into law. Not surprisingly for economic historians, the law of unintended consequences was again validated by subsequent events.

Legislators and economic analysts viewing the effects of the Great Depression of 1929–1933, for example, drew upon their assessments of what had gone wrong during the previous panic of 1907, one that also began in the US but quickly spread to first the UK and then on to the European Continent. Policy makers in Britain at the time drew upon their sense of history and tried to avoid replicating the events that had led to the Baring Crisis of 1890, one that eventually cut short the expansion of the classical gold standard within Europe, removing Portugal and Italy from the club, and keeping Spain out. The response organized by the Bank of England at the time, however, eventually brought about the adoption of the gold standard in the "newly-indus-trializing countries" of the time, Japan (1895), Russia (1896), India (1898), the US (1900), and even Argentina (1899). Much of the reasons for adopting, or abandoning, the gold standard after the Baring crisis of 1890 were lessons of history drawn from the various experiences of France, Germany, and the US after the American Civil War and the Franco-Prussian War of 1870.

There again, lessons were drawn, either correctly or incorrectly, from the various experiences of countries in the decade following the conclusion of the Napoleonic Wars in 1815, which included a financial crisis in the US in 1819 and a major stock market crisis and widespread bank failures in the UK in 1825. Commentators at the time referred to the lessons of the South Sea bubble of 1720. One major policy maker heavily influenced by the repercussions of 1825 and its analogy with the South Sea bubble of 1720 was US President Andrew Jackson. In 1836, near the end of his second term, he refused to renew the charter of the Second Bank of the United States, thereby removing the equivalent of the Bank of England from the US economy, leading to the worst depression of the nineteenth century in 1837.

Commentators savaging the progenitors of the Mississippi and South Sea bubbles of 1719 and 1720, in turn, drew upon the apparent follies of speculators during the Tulip Mania of 1636–1637 in the Netherlands. A major work, the *Groote Tafereel der Dwaasheid* (translated as The Great Mirror of Folly), appeared in various editions in Amsterdam in 1721. So the search for historical analogies is as much a feature of financial crises as the condemnation of financiers held responsible for the collapse in asset values and the consequent regula-tory responses by public authorities.

How did it all begin?

Rather than continue this pursuit of cataloguing episodes of apparent human folly through the recorded ages, let's try to go even farther back to get a fresh start from as close to the beginning of the rise of finance as currently possible. We shall see how various attempts were made to facilitate the improvement of economic conditions through finance, given the technology, markets, and governments of the time. Again and again we shall see crises occurring, but every once in awhile they were resolved in an effective way and both finance and economic growth resumed. We will focus on those examples of successful recoveries, which will prove to have some common elements, some of which are possibly relevant even to the crises at the beginning of the twenty-first century.

Again and again, we shall see common elements of financial innovations that allow great projects undertaken by human hands, but conceived by human minds, to come to fruition, and then hijacked by more opportunistic operators to end in crisis, bringing ruin to friend and neighbor. More often than not, the key to success was, and no doubt will remain, the ability to mobilize resources on a large scale, a scale sufficiently large to require impersonal exchanges. Avoidance of disaster meant an accompanying set of personal commitment devices to assure distant participants that their efforts or investments would be suitably rewarded. Successful commitments in the long run implied typically some form of legitimate governance of contracts along with public monitoring, delegated in some manner as the information and communications technology of the time enabled. Unsuccessful commitments also had common elements, typically due to the accumulated expense of maintaining coercive force to exclude access to the governance structure.

Our story could no doubt begin with a conjecture of primitive family units emerging from the Great Rift Valley of northeastern Africa and spreading out along the coasts and up the various rivers in search of sustenance and shelter to survive the rigors of the early Ice Ages, but we will constrain our narrative to the existence of written records as analyzed endlessly by subsequent generations of historians. The story of international, i.e. impersonal, finance makes its first striking appearance precisely in the cuneiform incisions found in the clay *bullae* of ancient Babylon.

2 | Distant beginnings: the first 3,000 years

Two factors have led to the rise of finance historically: long-distance trade and long-lived productive assets. Markets for goods and services and markets for assets both require some form of finance to bridge the time between when agreement on a trade is reached and when actual delivery occurs or when the structure is completed. Expanded trade and improved standards of living that result from the beneficial uses of finance, however, more often than not have led to increased conflict with outsiders or even with traditional power elites inside an economy. Preserving the benefits of finance in the long run, therefore, is and always has been very hard. Ultimately, the operations of finance through institutions (banks) or through markets (stock exchanges) have to be supported by and meet the approval of government authorities (regulators). Coordination of the innovations that arise spontaneously in banking, capital markets, or government powers is necessarily difficult. While these observations seem painfully obvious to observers of the ongoing financial travails after the crisis of 2008, they also help to clarify our understanding of the rise and fall of ancient civilizations and the vagaries that afflicted pre-industrial societies.

Rise of cities and the beginnings of finance

The archaeologist and historian of the ancient Near East, Marc Van de Mieroop, begins his history with the establishment of Uruk, the first city known to history, around 3000 BC (Van der Mieroop 2005, p. 23). The location of Uruk on the lower Euphrates River just north of the marshes that extend into the Persian Gulf probably arose after thousands of preceding years of settled agriculture and villages scattered throughout the alluvial plain known as the Fertile Crescent. These early residents had access to a variety of fish and shellfish, primitive grains, and possibly domesticated animals. They had developed pottery, along with permanent dwellings usually arranged

15

around a central temple (or market or meeting place). The creation of an impressive stepped temple (ziggurat) with its surrounding precincts covering over 100 hectares by 3000 BC, clearly implied a central authority with the ability to sustain a population large enough to have specialized functions. These surely included soldiers and priests, but also construction workers, boatmen, farmers, shepherds, craftsmen for textiles and pottery, and trade. The location of Uruk enabled it to receive shipments by water, either from the lands along the Gulf or from the mountains to the north at the headwaters of the Euphrates or to the east accessed by the Tigris or river valleys leading to Iran. There is evidence that Uruk was the hub of an extended network of trade in all directions, including not only the Persian Gulf but also the Mediterranean, the high lands of Anatolia, and even the mountains of Afghanistan.

Most important for our understanding of this distant civilization were the scribes, men trained in the language used to maintain courtly records and legal contracts. In his early work, Van der Mieroop discovered hoards of financial records in the form of clay tablets and *bullae* in a close-knit neighborhood found in the ruins of ancient Uruk. The records of one businessman, Dumuzi-gamil, as translated by Van der Mieroop (1992) indicate that he flourished by financing long-distance trade and local agriculture until the king, Rim-Sin, issued an edict declaring all debts null and void in 1788 BC, our first record of a financial crisis. The business was ruined and the remaining records deal only with continuing law suits, a recurring theme throughout financial history!

These records provide clear evidence of financial entrepreneurship and private enterprise by an individual who was not a warlord, palace courtier, or priest.[1] He kept his records in his own hand, not using the skills of a scribe, which was unusual given the difficulty of recording contracts and inventories on wet clay tablets using sharpened reeds to incise the various cuneiform symbols that comprised the Sumerian language. Some of the contracts arranged partnerships among as many as thirty other individuals in financing substantial trade with other ports on the Persian Gulf. The liability of each partner was limited

---

[1] William N. Goetzmann provides more analysis of the significance of these records on his web site at Yale School of Management, available at: http://viking.som. yale.edu/will/finciv/chapter1.htm.

to the amount originally invested, as remains the case today with private ventures organized to undertake risky ventures with uncertain, but potentially high returns.[2] Dumuzi-gamil's ventures, however, were cut short by the royal decree, which was unusual in that it negated all merchant debts as well as private household debts. Later rulers of Babylon would periodically declare jubilees on the occasion of a victory or ascending to power, but maintain enforcement of commercial contracts. Even Hammurabi, for example, took care to maintain existing property rights after he conquered Rim-sin's capital of Larsa (Charpin 2012, p. 192).

The evidence of trade at long distances for the Bronze Age economy of the Middle East, which required long-term finance, continues to be uncovered by archaeologists. While early archaeologists focused on valuable artifacts deposited with burials or in temples, explorations of shipwrecks with modern sonar and aerial and satellite imagery to detect ancient waterways and settlements have led to increasing appreciation of the scale of economic production and trade. The oldest shipwreck to date, found off the Greek island of Dokos, contained a cargo with hundreds of pottery items dating from 2500 to 2000 BC. During the tumultuous transition to the Iron Age around 1200 BC, another ship foundered off the coast of Turkey, with a cargo of ingots of copper and tin, and scrap bronze tools to be re-cycled. While Cyprus was the main source for copper, tin had to come from the mountains of Anatolia or southern Spain, with Phoenician sailing ships providing the bulk transport (Glausiusz 2008, p. 709). The *Uluburun*, another shipwreck dating from 1300 BC, was discovered in 1982. It continues to provide fascinating material for researchers, with 17 tons of cargo including ostrich eggs, ebony, ivory, resin, spices, weapons, jewelry, and textiles as well as ingots of copper, tin, and glass. The artifacts

---

[2] In the 1980s, for example, a group of 161 businessmen in Columbus, Ohio put up varying sums amounting to $12.7 million to finance the potential recovery of the "ship of gold," the *SS Central America* that sank in a hurricane off the North Carolina coast in 1857 with up to 21 tons of gold from California. The entrepreneur in charge of the recovery efforts, Tommy Thompson, did discover the ship and recovered the gold in 1988, but as of 2013 his company, Columbus Exploration Limited Partnership, had not paid back anything to the investors, or even the crew who helped recover the gold, or a group of another 90 investors who put up an additional $9 million for future explorations (*Columbus Dispatch*, May 29, 2011).

came from eleven different cultures with jewelry from Egypt, copper from Cyprus, and tin from central Asia (Marchant 2012, p. 426).

While it is evident from these tangible artifacts that the individuals responsible for carrying out such complicated and diverse commerce had finance and contracts for ongoing business relations, little documentation is available to tell us how they arranged their affairs. Most evidence of Old Babylon comes from temple and palace archives and deals with administrative routines. Juridical texts that specify contracts yet unfulfilled or resolutions of disputed contracts are most valuable for the financial historian. Unfortunately, even then the bulk of contracts that had to be drawn up and recorded due to the value of the transaction are lost. Once a transaction was satisfactory, the creditor returned the tablet to the debtor, who then destroyed it. But the details of the contracts retained show how personal details were imprinted to facilitate what would become impersonal exchange. Dumuzi-gamil's partners relied on the merchants in Dilmun (modern Bahrain) to reciprocate with valuable cargo on a ship's return to Ur. A formal contract was inscribed on a clay tablet, which was then left in the sun to dry, after which it was covered with a thin layer of clay on which a copy of the text was again written. Then cylinder seals of the person receiving or transferring the goods were rolled along the edges of the envelope while it was still wet, along with the seals of some of the witnesses. Charpin writes, "This meant that if there was ever any dispute, the envelope would be broken open and reference would be made to the original text of the tablet, which could not have been modified" (Charpin 2010, p. 11).

An example from 1820 BC reads:

One and one-sixth shekels silver (i.e. 9.33 grams) to which the standard interest is to be added, Ilshu-bani, the son of Nabi-ilishu, received from (the god) Shamash and from Sin-tajjar. At harvest time he will repay the silver and the interest. Before five witnesses (their names are listed). In month seven of the year that ApOil-Sin built the temple of Innanna of Elip. (Van der Mierop 2005, p. 21)

In the Temple of the Sun God in Sippar, about 1750 BC, a tablet records fourteen loans of silver paid out to various individuals with the terms of interest, demonstrating that it was serving as a bank (Cribb 2004, p. 92). Most likely, this temple, as was the normal case later in neo-Babylonian times, was advancing payments to agents who would collect rents or goods demanded by the temple staff, while earning a commission for their services sufficient to cover the interest. Interest then varied, but was normally taken as 20 percent, regardless of the duration of the loan (Jursa 2010, pp. 76, 490 ff.). Moreover, the tablets dealing with property transfers were kept as evidence of title, to be transferred intact to the next purchaser or heir to maintain continuity of contract and proof of ownership. The tablet described the precise cadastral location of the property and its qualities, and recorded the purchase price, usually in shekels of silver, with the names of the witnesses at the time of sale (Charpin 2010, Chapter 4). Properties of large landowners, when divided up among the heirs, would also have the accumulated tablets divided up among them, in at least one case documenting the successive owners of one property for two hundred years. While these tablets were preserved, those for one-time business transactions were destroyed at the end of the deal. Only those that were still outstanding were kept, but those allow us to note rates of interest and prices of goods, including the difference between spot and time prices.

As early as the beginning of the second millennium BC, the long-distance trade overland in Old Babylon led to merchant organizations that persisted for several generations, based on cities located along major intersections of trade routes. The northern Assyrian city of Assur on the upper reaches of the Tigris river was one such merchant-controlled city. The merchants of Assur maintained regular offices within designated market districts in numerous outposts along the major trading routes. Given that overland trade required large numbers of donkeys for pack animals, and that some of the goods were bulky – tin, copper, barley, and woolen textiles – Assurian merchants formed joint-stock companies to finance the repeated caravans. Individual merchants, as well as wealthy officials or landowners, paid in gold or silver to the individual holding the *naruqqum* or "money bag" for a share of the profits of the enterprise, which typically lasted for ten years (Veenhof 2010, p. 55). The representatives of Assur at the trading cities along the caravan routes then monitored the affairs of each company. In each way-station, the merchants from Assur had their own quarters or *kārum* where they kept a permanent presence with facilities for safekeeping of goods in transit. The records of the Assur representatives in the Central Anatolian city of Kanesh give remarkable detail on the organizations created by the merchants headquartered in Assur.

Assur itself was governed by a city council, members of which were chosen from among the leading merchants, and oversight of the city's finances was given to an annually elected official, a *līmum*. All this was initiated by an enlightened ruler, one Erishum I, around 1950 BC, but the success of the continued trade and its importance for the various warlords who rose and fell each generation within Mesopotamia and its environs meant that the Assurian commercial network was maintained for several hundred years. One document asserts that all the merchants in the Mesopotamian system were given free passage even through areas at war and they were exempted from typical service obligations imposed on farmers and craftsmen (Veenhof 2010, pp. 42–43). All in all, the clay tablets discovered by modern archaeologists in modern Iraq, Syria, and Turkey document the existence of long-lived and sophisticated forms of private finance, profitably tolerated by the political authorities. Indeed, the institutions of the merchants of ancient Assur uncannily presage those of the merchant-bankers of Genoa nearly 3,000 years later. There can be no doubt that all organized merchant efforts along the trans-Eurasian and trans-Mediterranean trade routes in the intervening centuries adopted similar techniques to those first documented by the Assurians.

Despite the documentation of contracts and promissory notes, with details of market-determined prices and fluctuating rates of interest, coinage had not appeared, so some form of central assessment of values was useful to sustain long-distance impersonal exchange. Nevertheless, silver was used as a standard of payment for the Assurian trade, and later in neo-Babylonian times, and the shekel was defined as a uniform weight. Prices in units of silver of six basic commodities – barley, dates, mustard, cardamom, sesame, and wool – were faithfully recorded on the astronomical diaries maintained by the priests of the Temple of Marduk in Babylon. Published by Slotsky (1997), there are more than 3,000 observations covering five centuries (from 568 BC to 72 BC). For the earlier period in Babylon, from 626 BC to 539 BC, Jursa (2010) has compared prices for three basic commodities – barley, dates, and sesame – taken from a variety of mainly private archives that are most likely market prices. They show a sharp rise in prices, especially for barley toward the end of this period, which covers the conquest of Babylon by the rising Persian empire.

Finance and economic progress interrupted

Why the sophisticated financial arrangements already evident in the Bronze Age, which facilitated the economic growth of cities, leading to specialization of labor and undoubted accumulations of wealth by the most fortunate merchants whose trading networks extended from central Asia to the farthest shores of the Mediterranean, did not survive into later ages remains an issue among ancient historians. The volcanic explosion of Thera (on the island of Santorini) around 1628 BC, one of the largest ever known in the northern hemisphere, clearly wreaked havoc on the Minoan civilization, and likely disrupted its extensive trading networks to the north and east as well. Frequent earthquakes along the numerous fault lines that run north–south through Egypt and east–west through Turkey and Iran, certainly caused disastrous floods along river courses as well as tsunamis threatening ancient seaports.

More telling, however, is the evidence of repeated military invasions, whether by Hittites armed with iron weapons from the north, or sea-peoples marauding the eastern shores of the Mediterranean, all of which led to population losses, widespread destruction of cities, and the end of the Bronze Age by 1000 BC. We have no archaeological or documentary evidence comparable to that for the merchants of Assur to inform us how these military forays were financed, but it appears they relied on booty from occasional raids or tribute levied on a regular basis from a merchant-city. By the sixth century BC, for example, Jursa (2010) shows that the neo-Babylonian civilization had recovered from the devastation at the end of the Bronze Age, and its rulers financed large-scale public works, including major canals to connect the Tigris and Euphrates. These projects required paying workmen on a large scale, using the booty regularly taken from the Phoenician cities on the Mediterranean and merchant enclaves in Bahrain and on the eastern trade routes to India and Afghanistan. Eventually, the Persians under Cyrus the Great put an end to this source of revenue and imposed their own regular tributes upon the conquered cities of Mesopotamia. War finance would appear again and again as first a destabilizing shock to the system of private commercial finance, before becoming a source of insurance for the protection of private commerce, a process still ongoing in the twenty-first century.

Perhaps the earliest example of private finance providing the necessary sinews of war for military success occurred in Persia in 423 BC.

Darius II managed to seize the throne by borrowing large sums from the wealthy Murašû family to hire an armed force to escort him into the capital city of Persepolis and depose his half-brother Sogdanus, who had claimed the throne on the death of their father (Stolper 1985). The archives of this family contain hundreds of tablets recording various business deals, almost all dealing with the terms of leasing particular plots of land owned by the king or temple to tenant farmers, identified by name, and witnessed by several unrelated individuals. In many cases, copies of the tablets were also given to the tenants or representatives of the king or temples to maintain verifiability of the contract. Strikingly absent are tablets describing partnerships or commercial ventures such as found in the earlier archives from Ur or Assur.

The incorporation of the Mesopotamian "fertile crescent" into the Persian empire apparently stifled further economic progress there, according to the analysis by Jursa (2010). Consolidation of imperial control required constant tributes to support an ever-larger standing army, whose defense of an ever-expanding frontier became increasingly burdensome. By contrast, the increasing number of independent Greek city-states that began to proliferate throughout the Aegean Islands and the littoral of the Mediterranean provided a different political structure, one that ultimately was supportive of continued economic progress driven by expanding trade opportunities and support of the resulting trade network.

Innovations in war finance and international trade

Greek city-states first invented coins, what we even now identify as money, readily exchanged for goods and services wherever the coin was recognizable as a legitimate unit of account. Grecian cities eventually numbered over 1,000 spread throughout the Mediterranean and Black Seas, and all were engaged in maritime trade to greater or lesser degrees. Rather than defining units of payment by weight of a standard grain or metal as found in the cuneiform tablets of Mesopotamia, the kingdom of Lydia located in Anatolia along one of the several caravan routes from central Asia to the Mediterranean, began around the seventh century BC to stamp standard weights of electrum, a naturally occurring mix of silver and gold found locally. The innovation may have been intended to assert Lydia's independence from the chaos of the empires collapsing around it, but the usefulness of coined money for sustaining trade led to widespread imitation by other states. By the time of the Classical period for Athens, many of the Greek city-states had taken up coinage using silver, gold, or copper. The coins, stamped with symbols of the king or city, and often dated, provided traders with standard units of value that could be readily identified and accepted as payment even by foreign merchants without the trouble of weighing and assaying.

Coins as a form of money then greatly facilitated impersonal exchange throughout the Mediterranean and, given the evidence of coin hoards found in India, central Asia, and the British Isles, well beyond the Mediterranean by Roman times. The proliferation of mints throughout the Mediterranean world in later centuries, moreover, led to the rise of bankers equipped with scales to weigh the various coins and with the expertise to determine their quality, and then assure the seller that full value had been paid by the buyer. For long-distance or long-period transactions, the verified value of coins could be sealed in a purse, and inscribed with their value, attested by the sign of the banker (Goitein 1967, pp. 231–235). Only if the local government would accept the coins in payment of taxes could the local coinage be accepted at tale (face value), without weighing and assaying to determine its intrinsic value as a metal, and even then acceptance at face value of the coins was only within the locality of the mint. Impersonal exchange financed by coins, then, required governmental taxing authority that spanned both time and space of the transaction and that was not easily acquired, much less sustained.

Millett (1991) documents the importance of banking in ancient Athens for financing the long-distance trade necessary to sustain their prosperity while Cohen (1992) also relates how markets were used to raise money in case of war, our first recorded example of the complementarity between banks and markets for providing finance. Cohen emphasizes the conscious separation of public activities in the service of the Greek city-state from the private activities in pursuit of profit by individual Greek citizens. The regular demands for military support in defense of trade routes, upon which the city-states relied for provisions, were met by giving the residents equal opportunity to share in whatever spoils of war might be obtained. The wealthiest elites were expected each to provision one or more triremes, the classic Greek warship, the middle class to equip themselves with the arms necessary to serve as hoplites, and the lesser citizens to man the oars, all to share

capped at 12 percent per annum in Roman times, as had been the case earlier in Mesopotamia, and most recorded loans were at this legally enforceable level, there is evidence of variable interest rates below 12 percent. And there is other evidence of interest rates above the legal limit, which were justified by lending to foreigners, who were not subject to Roman law. Temin concludes that Roman banks were spread throughout the empire, sometimes loaning out tax receipts locally before remitting them to Rome, sometimes providing payment services for officials and merchants, but all in all providing the financial basis for sustained expansion of trade and empire.

Later, shipments of silk, tea, and precious stones by the Sogdian traders along the fabled Silk Road required large-scale organization and military protection, but were carried out by private entrepreneurs, who relied on their confidential means of finance backed by the tribute they collected on behalf of their military masters (de la Vaissière 2005). Their trade, as well as the extensive trade of the Mediterranean in the Middle Ages, was financed by shipments of cash equivalents – standard rolls of silk, sealed purses of gold coins with their total value inscribed on the outside, or paper credits. These could be *suftaja* (written orders to give the bearer the same value at his destination as he paid at his start, for which he had paid a fee), which were not negotiable, or *riba*, a promissory note of a given sum in units of account to the bearer, which were negotiable (Goitein 1967, pp. 242–245). Interest could be paid if the creditor and debtor were not coreligionists, otherwise it was concealed in the form of commissions or fines for late repayment. In each case, however, the name of the creditor and date and place of the issue were clearly stated, which was also the case for the sealed purses containing various quantities of specific coins. In this way, impersonal exchange over long distances taking months and sometimes years to complete could be contracted and financed on the basis of personal assurances.

Collateral for such debt contracts was sometimes specified, but usually was implicit in the pledge made by the creditor. Only much later could merchants and merchant bankers use public issued debt as collateral for their private debts; that would appear to be the transforming financial innovation made by the merchant-controlled city-states that emerged in Italy from the remains of the former Roman Empire of the West. Temin (2013) notes that while Rome clearly had private banks, and private long-term securities in the form of mortgage bonds, there was no public debt to be traded as such, and the same held for imperial China. Oddly, while the maritime empires of the early Phoenicians and Greeks maintained the complementary roles of public markets for government debt and private banks for private enterprise, the land-based empires of Persia and later of Rome and China all eschewed the idea of state debt. Instead, these "balanced-budget" empires relied on forced conscription of soldiers or laborers to meet emergencies arising from local rebellions, foreign invaders, or natural disasters. But even Venice and Genoa, the Italian city-states given credit for initiating the instruments of modern finance – stable currencies, bills of exchange, and long-term public debt – owed the success of their innovations to bureaucratic and legal initiatives that came even earlier, and not from Rome but from Avignon and the papal court residing there in the twelfth century.

3 | *The Italians invent modern finance*

All Italian scholars insist that the origins of modern international finance arose among the Italian city-states that eventually established self-rule during the centuries following the collapse of the Roman Empire in the West (Fratianni and Spinelli 2006). Italian merchants perfected the foreign bill of exchange to finance trade throughout medieval Europe into the North and Baltic Seas, as well as with the ancient ports of the Mediterranean and Black Seas. Their home cities also developed the precursors of sovereign debt in the form of perpetual annuities. Both financial instruments – the bill of exchange and perpetual annuities – have been studied in terms of the way they circumvented the religious prohibitions on usury in Christian Europe (de Roover 1963; Munro 2013), but our emphasis here will be on the way they interacted to create viable and effective markets in international finance. The innovative pressures of war finance for the Italian city-states throughout the Middle Ages were critical for the development of new financial instruments and techniques. Their usefulness in promoting the expansion of trade and production in non-military pursuits after the religious wars of the sixteenth and seventeenth centuries led to the further rise of financial capitalism, first in the Low Countries and then in Great Britain (Chapter 4).

But which of the several Italian city-states that emerged on the peninsula after the demise of the Roman empire and then the division of Charlemagne's Holy Roman Empire should claim pride of precedence? Florence has long held sway, thanks to the stunning art and public monuments financed by the fabulous Medici family during the Renaissance, and whose bank was extolled by de Roover (1963). Later economic historians have asserted the greater importance of Venice, which remains a comparable tourist attraction to Florence (Lane and Mueller 1985; Mueller 1997; Pezzolo 2013a, 2013b). The role of Genoa's *Casa di San Giorgio*, however, has recently taken pride of place (Felloni 2006; Fratianni and Spinelli 2006; Marsilio 2013).

While acknowledging its significance, this chapter will make an argument for the financial innovations made by the crusading popes of the Middle Ages (cf. Caselli 2008, 2013).

The papal revolution and separation of church and state

The papal revolution began when Pope Gregory VII proclaimed his spiritual authority over that of the Holy Roman Emperor Henry IV in 1077 (which Henry affirmed on his knees in the snows under the papal castle at Canossa in January 1078). This was the defining moment that launched the legal tradition that has guided Western politics, philosophy, and economics ever since (Berman 1983). Not only did Gregory's successors mobilize Western European believers to undertake the large-scale efforts of the Crusades into the Near East over the next two centuries, they also followed his lead in centralizing collection of revenues from all of western Christendom and remitting them regularly to the papal Curia in Rome. Key to the success of both papal initiatives of expansion and centralization was mobilizing international finance, exchanging currencies collected in one part of Europe into means of payment acceptable in another.

Throughout western Europe, agents of the papacy collected Peter's Pence and various tithes from the scattered churches and remitted them to Rome. Within the Mediterranean, they enlisted experienced merchant-sailors to support the pilgrimages and the intermittent Crusades to the Holy Land and the Levant. Both the remittances and the logistical support required by the papal court were essential for the merchants based in northern Italy who had established secure bases and trading posts throughout western Europe and the Mediterranean Sea. Each city in northern Italy – Florence, Genoa, Milan, and Venice – successively took pride of place in dealing with papal finances depending on the origin of successive popes.

For the remittances, typical recourse was made to the foreign bill of exchange, especially as the English kings and later the French monarchs explicitly forbade the export of gold or silver, even for religious purposes. Exports of wool or wine purchased with the local currencies could serve as well, however, once sold they were sold at a profit in Italy or elsewhere. The woolen manufacturers in Florence and later Antwerp, for example, benefited from the continued supply of English wool, which was financed by bankers based in those cities. They used

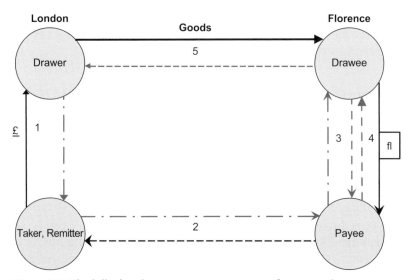

Figure 3.1 The bill of exchange as an instrument to finance trade

the foreign bill of exchange as their favored financial instrument for intra-European trade. Figure 3.1 shows how an Italian banking firm could collect the papal dues in England, purchase a bill of exchange from a wool merchant in London, who would send the equivalent quantity of wool to Florence, where the weaving firm would pay for it in Florentine ducats to redeem the bill presented to them by the bank's representative in Florence. At the end of the transaction, the weaver in Florence paid for the English wool in ducats, extinguished the bill, and then sent it back to the wool merchant in London. Meanwhile, the banking firm in Florence credited the account of its partner (or factor) in London for the payment.

There was nothing particularly novel about this use of the bill of exchange to convert payments in kind into currency that would be more useful to the papacy. Indeed, Postlethwayt in his classic work, *The Universal Dictionary of Trade and Commerce* (1971 [1774]), argues that such means of payment were used in ancient times for much the same purpose. He cites verses from the Book of Exodus, which describe how payments to the temple in Jerusalem were made in various ways by the citizens of Judea and bankers in the temple made the necessary exchanges so they could pay their tax in silver. As argued in Chapter 2, such techniques were used whenever long-distance trade was established on a continuing basis. The use of the *hawala* by Arab traders as well as the *hundi* by India traders on the sub-continent dates back to ancient times, and all of them used the personal connections illustrated in Figure 3.1 among the financiers and traders within each trading city, and the personal connections maintained between the financiers in the respective cities. In the case of the papal remittances, the Medici popes could rely upon family relations to carry out the collection of tithes in England, convert them to bales of wool that were exported to Florence or Flanders, where they would be sold for local currency that would be credited to Rome. The point here is that what appeared to be large-scale impersonal exchange between wool producers in England and weavers of fine woolens in Florence was financed by virtue of very close personal relationships within the Italian banking firm.

While the foreign bill of exchange served also for financing aspects of the various pilgrimages and crusades, raising an army sufficient to attempt recapturing the Holy Land from the grasp of its Moslem conquerors required funding on a scale that was unprecedented. Raising these funds required a completely different initiative, one that took almost two centuries to develop and then only under desperate circumstances. Following Gregory VII, various efforts were made by the succeeding popes to incite the faithful to join in the various crusades that the popes promulgated to demonstrate their authority, whether to regain control of the sacred sites in the Holy Land or to maintain independence from the current aspirant to be Charlemagne's successor as Holy Roman Emperor. Promises of remission of sins proving insufficient for the task, various expedients were employed to guarantee the provisioning and expedition of armored knights from various parts of Catholic Europe by sea to the eastern Mediterranean. Most crusades failed in their ultimate purpose, as did the financial expedients devised by the various popes. These proved increasingly inadequate as the expenses of transport rose and the power of the Turkish occupiers increased throughout the Levant (Grossman 1965). Further, military success in a crusade diverted attention from maintaining papal authority *vis-à-vis* the Emperor. Only in 1264, under the frenetic efforts of Urban IV, did a viable system of papal finance emerge (Padgett 2012).

While the improvements in papal finance failed ultimately to regain control of the eastern Mediterranean, the papal financial innovations set examples for Italian bankers from northern Italy, generically known as Lombards, to imitate and perfect. They dominated European banking over the rest of the Middle Ages and through the Renaissance, but as the historian of papal revenues stated: "The prominent position held by the Italian banker in European financial affairs must be attributed in no small degree to the business and the protection of the papacy" (Lunt 1934, 1, p. 56). For example, as creditors to the church, Italian banks could call upon papal officials to sanction delinquent debtors, measures especially effective against visitors to Rome or participants in pilgrimages or crusades. To carry out the large-scale, long-term funding required for the crusades, however, Italian banking firms had to put their operations at exchange places spread across Christian Europe on a more permanent basis. Urban IV (1261–1264), was the key innovator who established the legal sanction for his favorite bankers to have a permanent position at key sites for collecting and then remitting papal revenues.

Urban had managed church finances as Patriarch in Jerusalem during previous, failed, crusades and was originally from Troyes in France, one of the major sites for the Champagne fairs where merchant accounts were settled at the quarterly accountings in each fair. Urban IV became pope at a desperate time for the Roman papacy, when attempts of the Holy Roman Emperors to control Tuscany and Lombardy in addition to Naples and Sicily and then control the papacy as well appeared close to success. Urban's predecessor had tried to mobilize the king of England in his defense against the emperor, but Henry III found it impossible to raise the taxes required from his subjects while his barons confirmed their independence from his prerogatives. Urban IV then turned to Charles of Anjou and by promising him continued funding – as well as the kingdom of Sicily – brought his armies into play. He promised to finance the French armies with a papal tithe, which his agents collected regularly once they were put in place permanently. To anticipate these revenues with immediate funds for the troops in the field, Urban IV used the existing Florentine bankers who had been allied with the preceding popes, and who were exiled at the time from Florence, due to the temporary victory of the Ghibelline faction. Urban knew that the Genoese merchant bankers dominated the exchange fairs in Champagne and were better situated to arrange the funds necessary for the French troops, but at the time the Genoese were arranging the finances for the Emperor. The Genoese bankers would be aligned with either France or Milan until one of their own families became pope (Francesco della Rovere as Pope Sixtus IV in 1471).

To solidify the role of the Florentine banking firms, Urban encouraged them to become organized as joint-stock companies with specific charters rather than as occasional partnerships, while arranging that they would have permanent rights for staying in both France and England in order to collect the papal tithes. Unlike partnerships, which had been the typical practice previously, the *societas* formed by the pope's bankers had a legal personality distinct from that of the individual partners, as well as transferable and heritable shares. The new structure made the firm more permanent than a partnership, which had to be re-organized every time one of the partners left the firm. They now had a unitary *corpo* (capital stock) that outlived the individual partners and initial investors as well as permanent *filiali* (branches) abroad. They also had a permanent presence in Rome with regular accounts kept with the pope's *camera,* which in succeeding centuries was generally headed by a close relative or former partner of one of the banking firms. With the solid base of financing established, the pope's surrogate armies prevailed against the emperors in Italy. More important for financial history, the more formal and institutional structure of the Italian banks was sustained, due to its capacity to expand capital by adding new shareholders (called the *supracorpo*) and eventually attracting large-scale, long-lived deposits from wealthy nobles and merchants (Sapori 1970). This was to become a model for the rest of Europe and eventually for modern banks in general.

Establishing the foreign bill of exchange for profit

Under the tutelage of the papacy now fully independent from the Emperor, Lyons in France became the primary focal point for facilitating the finance of intra-European trade, trade that rose with population increases and technological advances in during the high Middle Ages, roughly 1000 to 1300 AD. Trade was financed among knowledgeable merchants along the European trade routes via the foreign bill of exchange, which under European practice became the basic financial instrument that transformed personal exchange between local individuals bound by multiple bonds of mutual interaction into impersonal exchange between trading partners separated by distance, religion, culture, and legal regimes. To see how the Italian bankers were able to transform the payments mechanisms developed to finance intra-European trade into a profitable business of finance, we need to see how the simple exchange of one local currency for another to finance, say, the woolen trade between London and Florence, as shown in Figure 3.1, could turn into a method for "making money from money," receiving interest effectively on short-term commercial bills. The key was to re-exchange the first bill at its destination and demand repayment in the original currency back at the original point of origin – "change–rechange" as it became known.

A great deal of confusion over the origin and purpose of the bill of exchange arises over the observation that the proliferation of the use of the bill in financing trade necessarily meant a delay in the time from when the bill was first purchased to when it was finally paid out, which implies that a rate of interest must have been charged. Indeed, Postlethwayt's discussion of the bill of exchange begins by distinguishing four forms: common exchange, real exchange, dry exchange, and fictitious exchange (Postlethwayt 1971, I, *Bill of Exchange*). In the case of "dry exchange" the financier becomes the "taker" of the bill by lending a sum to the drawer, which he expects to have repaid in due course. Figure 3.2 shows how the circuit of obligations is now

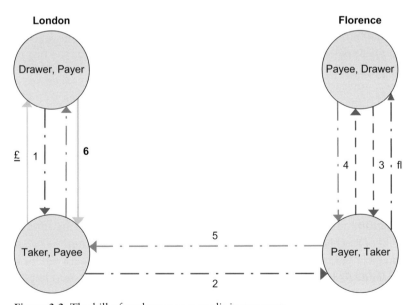

Figure 3.2 The bill of exchange as a credit instrument

completed by a re-exchange of a new, reciprocal bill rather by the delivery of goods. At the end of the two circuits of payment by bills, the original receiver of cash in London must pay back a specified sum to the original taker.

Step 1 reprises the roles of the merchant and the financier with the financier paying the merchant in pounds sterling for the bill he has drawn; in step 2 the financier sends the bill to his correspondent in the foreign city, who accepts it, but holds it until it is due for payment in Florence. Rather than make payment in ducats, however, he writes a "rechange" bill demanding payment of the stated amount of ducats in pounds sterling back in London. If the exchange rate of pounds/ducats is the same in both cities, then the borrower in London would just be asked to repay the same amount of pounds he borrowed originally. But, due to the normal difference in exchange rates between the two cities, depending which city is quoting the rate, the amount of pounds demanded in London by the "rechange" bill coming back from Florence will typically be more than the amount originally paid.

An example will clarify the process, as presented in the 2013 paper by Bell, Brooks, and Moore (2013). They found a bill bought in Venice by the company of Cosimo di Medici for 150 ducats in Venice on September 27, 1442 from the Venetian merchant, Francesco Venier and Bros. The exchange rate in Venice for English currency was 1 ducat = 44½ pence. So the bill, payable in London at three months from its arrival there, was for £27 16s 3d (6,675 pence). When presented to Venier's counterparty in London by the Medici representative, however, it was protested and sent back to Venice. On March 31, 1443, then, Venier repaid the Medici firm the amount of the protested bill. But, in London, the sum of £27 16s 3d was converted to Venetian ducats for repayment at the exchange rate then ruling in London on Venice, 41¼ pence = 1 Venetian ducat. So the 6,675 pence in London purchased a bill on Venice in the sum of 161.82 ducats, 11.82 ducats more than Venier had paid originally. The extra ducats finally repaid by Venier to the Medicis represented a profit of 7.9 percent over six months, an annual return close to 16 percent (Bell, Brooks, and Moore 2013, p. 3).

The reason for the lower exchange rate of the Venetian ducat in London than in Venice was apparently due to the time difference in payments implied by the three-month usance period allowed for fulfillment of the exchange in each direction. So, it would imply that the three-month interest rates expected by merchants in each city would be the same, implying a marvelous unity of short-term capital markets in early modern Europe. Contemporary analysts, indeed, suspected an international conspiracy among the professional dealers in foreign exchange, the much-reviled exchange dealers. An English royal commission in 1564 explained:

There is good reason why the Exchange at Antwerp goeth about 4d Flemish lower at usance then the price of the Exchange is in Lombard street, for by the Exchange at Antwerp the pound English being the valuer as not paid for and answered until a month after the delivery of Flemish money for the same, and by Exchange in Lombard street the pound English being the valuer is paid a month before the delivery of his value in Flemish money for the same. So that when the English pound is paid for a month before hand, then the price thereof in reason ought to be the less; and when the English pound is not paid for in Flemish money until a month after hand, then the price in reason ought to be the more. But hear you perceive that this necessary and fair name Exchange might be truly termed by the odious name of buying and selling of money for time, otherwise called usury. (Memorandum prepared for the Royal Commission on the Exchanges, 1564; reproduced in Bell, Brooks, and Moore 2013, pp. 2–3.)

Dry exchange might well have been thought of as usury, as the interest rates gained by such change–rechange were substantial, and well above what was available to long-term investors in sovereign debt or landed property.

But a more plausible explanation for the continued possibility of such profiteering in the selling and re-selling of bills of exchange can be found in the cost of re-minting the coins obtained in Venice into coins used for ordinary commerce in London, and then re-minting the coins obtained in London back into coins for final use back in Venice. Re-minting costs varied depending on the seigniorage fees levied by the local authorities and the brassage charges by the mint, but as long as one of the localities charged for minting, there was a normal profit to be made by the financiers carrying out change–rechange operations or "dry exchange" in general. Indeed, when we look at rates between London and Amsterdam for the early eighteenth century, while the rates fluctuated within much narrower bands than was the case in medieval or Renaissance times, the difference was always a constant 2 groot per pound, reflecting not the seigniorage charges at this later date, but the standard commissions charged for entering payments into accounts at the Bank of Amsterdam (see the work by Eagly and Smith 1976).

The change–rechange between Medina del Campo and Lyons from 1578 to 1596 typically generated returns of 8 percent annually, a figure that was also cited as the expected rate of return in the period by the Florentine author, Bernardo Davanzati (Boyer-Xambeu, Deleplace, and Gillard 1994, p. 84). Calculations for an earlier period (*c.* 1437–1481) between Bruges, London, and Venice, indicate much higher rates were normal, ranging from 15.6 percent to 20.9 percent, and rising as the length of the loan rose from one month to six months (Bell, Brooks, and Moore 2013, Table 1, p. 7 and Table 4, p. 17). These were all well above the rates paid by Venice and Florence on their respective long-term debts, much less those paid by Genoa's *Casa di San Giorgio*.

Establishing the legitimacy of sovereignty, from the papal revolution to city-states

Possibly even more important than the specific financial instruments created by the papacy or the individual city-states, however, was the idea that the Church had a separate corporate identity from the State, with its own legal system and authority over its members and, moreover, that the Church had this authority and identity in perpetuity, or at least until the Second Coming of its Lord. Entrenching this independence within a *corpus* of canon law, and then asserting it repeatedly in different regions and in response to different challenges was a drawn out and fitful process that lasted centuries, but it was a process sustained by the frequent election of new popes, even surviving the contested election at the beginning of the fourteenth century that led to the removal of the papal court from Rome to the French city of Avignon (1309–1378).

Indeed, the spread of self-governing city-states in northern Italy was a direct consequence of the papal revolution, as the pope's independence from the Emperor encouraged the various towns of Lombardy to assert their own independence from the German emperor on the other side of the Alps. In the century from 1050 to 1150 AD, hundreds of self-governing communities were created throughout northern Italy. Initiated by Milan, the largest city on the Lombardy plain, in 1057, where the townspeople revolted against the bishop appointed by the emperor to assert their freedom from external authority, capital levies and military obligations, urban independence quickly spread throughout Europe. The trajectory of independent cities tracked closely the so-called "Lotharingian axis," the arc of fragmented political units that emerged from the middle division of Charlemagne's empire in 855 and then was divided between East and West Francia by the Treaty of Meerssen in 870. (This arc across western Europe is better known now as the "Blue Banana," from the illumination created by the cities' lights at night.)

While the arc extended naturally into southeastern England to include London as well as the various cities of the Low Countries, and stretched along the Rhine into Switzerland and through the alpine passes, its base was firmly established across the Lombardy plain of northern Italy. Fourteen cities united in the Lombard League against Frederic Barbarossa in 1167 – Verona, Venice, Vicenza, Bergamo, Treviso, Ferrara, Brescia, Cremona, Milan, Lodi, Piacenza, Parma, Modena, and Bologna – to assure the pope they were united in their determination to resist the demands of the emperor. Each city formed a system of communal self-government by consuls, elected for fixed terms by popular assemblies, so consuls appear for Pisa in 1084, Asti in 1093, Arezzo in 1098, Genoa in 1099, Pavia in 1105, Bologna in 1123, Siena in 1125, Brescia in 1127, and Florence in 1138 (Berman 1983, p. 388, citing D. P. Waley in *Encyclopedia Britannica*). The number of consuls varied, usually between four and twelve, but always had fixed terms of office to forestall entrenched power by a ruling clique. Although the subsequent histories of Milan, Florence, and Venice show how difficult it was to withstand the corruption of power, their charters served as models for later developments of republican constitutions that could prove more enduring.

The popular assemblies in each Italian city had legislative power, but with limits enshrined in written charters that established a code of laws, and the judicial offices to interpret the laws and to limit the authority of the consuls. Admission to citizenship after a year of residence carried with it the responsibility to join in common defense of the city which, when funds had to be raised to hire *condottiere* or equip the citizen militia, meant liability to contribute proportionally according to one's wealth. The independent authority to issue municipal debt by the city authorities led to the first written evidence of long-term sovereign debts, which arose in each case to consolidate the outstanding short-term debts that the city had accumulated while raising armies or dispatching armadas.

Venice created such a consolidated debt in 1262, called a *Monte*, but promised to pay annually 5 percent, a "just price" for the rent of the capital collected by common consent among the citizens. Genoa followed with its version of a long-term consolidated debt as a *compera*, or joint-stock company, in 1274 (Pezzolo 2013a). Siena was not far behind Venice or Genoa when it imposed a *presta generalis* (general loan) in 1287 on both the capital city and the surrounding rural communities (Pezzolo 2008, pp. 18–19). Florence, Pisa, and Lucca followed by the mid fourteenth century. The curious result, given current economic theories about the term structure of interest rates on government debts, which generally show increasing yields as the length of maturity rises, is that each city found that it could succeed in paying lower interest rates on such long-term debt than it had been forced to pay on new issues of short-term debt. The driving motive was likely that the interest payments on the new long-term debt were regular and paid by a permanent organization established by the city fathers, as opposed to interest payments on the existing short-term debt, which depended on the arrival of fresh tax revenues, which could and did often fall into arrears.

The standard form for short-term debt was set by the city of Genoa when it created a formal loan in January 1150 in which the consuls of Genoa sold the income from municipal stalls for a term of twenty-nine years (Felloni and Laura 2004, p. 21). A secondary market for the exchange of shares in a company established to collect tolls dated January 22, 1214 appeared as well (Felloni and Laura 2004, p. 29). The shares in the successive *comperes* formed to collect various taxes paid out dividends regularly, but adjusted them to reflect the amount of revenue that had been collected in the preceding period. The other cities pledged to pay a fixed income, called a rent to avoid the charge that they were paying interest, annually, but payments were often delayed until sufficient taxes, tolls, or fees had been collected. Arrears could mount up for years, during which the re-sale value of the shares declined as well. Genoese shares, however, quickly reflected the varying payouts in their prices on the secondary market. The Genoese practice of adjusting payouts to reflect the irregularity of the revenue source backing the repayment of the loan to the city was later applied to the *asientos* they bought from the Spanish authorities in the sixteenth century, as discussed below.

The Italian city-states all restricted their issues of debt to their own citizens and kept public records of their claims, and only opened up their markets in government debt to outsiders when the rising expenses of war outstripped the resources of local citizens, as with Venice's participation in the War of the League of Cambrai in 1511 (Gilbert 1980). Even the first steps towards use of capital markets by government authorities maintained the essential marks of personal, bank-oriented, exchange through the *Banco di Rialto* in Venice or the *Casa di San Giorgio* in Genoa. In Avignon, however, the devastation of the surrounding countryside caused by the Black Death led Pope Clement VI to purchase the entire city from the king of France in 1348 – a cash purchase of 80,000 gold florins. The purchase assured the papal court's continued autonomy from the French kings or any secular authority, but it also created a substantial debt to the individuals and organizations that supplied the cash, who were not limited to the residents of Avignon and included religious orders and dioceses across Europe as well as cities within the Papal States, such as Bologna and Ferrara.

The officials of the Curia began at that time the careful and consistent recording of the amount of credit extended by individual persons or corporate bodies, and then insured that the annual interest payments were regularly remitted over the following years. Moreover, the election of successive popes then provided long-term continuity of the contract implied between the Church and the believers. The bureaucratic precision to the recording of the purchases of shares in the total debt and the regular payment of interest on the individual shares set an example of transparency and probity that could be imitated to the benefit of other corporate bodies established throughout Europe, but first in the city-republics established in in explicit or implicit imitation of the corporate governance example of the papal court.

The Casa di San Giorgio *sets the basis for modern finance*

The most interesting financial innovation to emerge among the medieval Italian cities was doubtlessly the *Casa di San Giorgio* in Genoa. Unlike Venice or Florence, which would both be dominated by powerful merchant families, Genoa seemed always wracked by family feuds, financed by the successes that family firms might have in securing trade privileges at any of the various ports around the Mediterranean, and eventually in the Black Sea. Recognizing the difficulties of sustaining debt service on debts accumulated by a feuding family liable to be deposed, and then to return or not to power, the company of St. George was created in 1408 in order to administer previous loans as a single debt offering a reduced rate of interest of 7 percent in place of the previous interest rates of 8, 9, and 10 percent (Felloni and Laura 2004, p. 35).

Briefly, the *Casa di San Giorgio* maintained general ledgers of the consolidated debt, but also collected the tolls and sales taxes that had been assigned by the city authorities to the earlier lenders. When new demands on Genoa's resources arose in later years in the course of the many wars waged in Italy, France, and the Holy Land, it became a matter of course for the city authorities in temporary office to assign new sources of revenues directly to the *Casa di San Giorgio*, which eventually included the islands of Corsica and Sardinia as well as the city of Caffa on the Black Sea. In effect, the *Casa* was a joint-stock corporation with a well-defined governance structure based on its shareholders, who held the sovereign debt of the city of Genoa. This corporation became a state within a state, taking the secular power of the consuls, and later of the single magistrate called the *podestà*, under its direct control. Hence, the famous assessment by Machiavelli:

This establishment presents an instance of what in all the republics, either described or imagined by philosophers, has never been thought of; exhibiting within the same community, and among the same citizens, liberty and tyranny, integrity and corruption, justice and injustice; for this establishment preserves in the city many ancient and venerable customs; and should it happen (as in time it easily may) that the *San Giorgio* should have possession of the whole city, the republic will become more distinguished than that of Venice. (Machiavelli, *History of Florence and the Public Affairs of Italy*, available at: www.gutenberg.org/files/2464/2464-h/2464-h.htm#link 2HCH0056, accessed March 15, 2013)

Regardless of the political consequences of the separation of financial control of a state's tax base under a corporate body with a separate structure of governance, the significance of responsible management of sovereign debt exemplified by the papal court and then the *Casa di San Giorgio* was profound. It initiated the symbiotic relationships among private banking establishments, public capital markets, and government ministries that led to the rise of financial capitalism and its eventual spread globally in the twenty-first century.

The symbiosis of sovereign debt and commercial credit

The symbiosis of sovereign debt and private finance stems from the usefulness of sovereign debt held in private hands as potential collateral against separate, shorter-term borrowing for commercial or personal purposes. The impartial registration of ownership of shares in the public debt by the papal Curia, the *Casa di San Giorgio*, or the city authorities allowed owners to assure their creditors that they could be reimbursed fully, even if the venture for which they had borrowed funds did not prove profitable. Creditors given such assurances then could lend more money and at better terms than without such assurances. The logic is clear, but the historical evidence to confirm such operations is difficult to uncover. It must be found in the account books kept by individual merchants or households, or in notarial records of contracts that might need third-party enforcement, or in court records of unresolved disputes over failed contracts. Even there the nature of such use of sovereign debt as collateral must be inferred from circumstantial evidence as successful ventures would end with the loan being repaid, presumably with interest, and the collateral reclaimed by the original borrower.

The circumstantial evidence, however, is compelling in favor of the use of emerging sovereign debt as collateral for private financial ventures. For the duchy of Milan, whose ruler consistently tried to enlarge the market that operated around Milan, especially after the devastation of the Black Death in 1348 (Epstein 2000), the interest paid on Milan's public debt fell over time, as did interest rates paid by private merchants for their shorter-term loans (de Luca 2008, pp. 62–63):

[In Milan] ... public bonds represented a large part, or the entirety, of the goods that *censi consegnativi* borrowers sold to the lenders (as a security) in exchange for the loan (and that is rented in exchange for another rent that represents the interest). In the *censi* stipulated by our merchant-entrepreneurs from 1575 to 1611, the total of revenues which were "temporarily" transferred with this function summed up to 379,580 lire ... For granting lenders the financial risks were considerably reduced. Therefore state securities not only represented an additional, non-taxable income, but were also used as a collateral of credit by the productive world and contributed to increase its changes to obtain more funds, playing a pro-cycle effect on private investments. The diffusion of this use of government bonds is also witnessed by the ordination of the Milanese merchant guild, dated 7 July 1572, in which it is specified that in order to constitute a *censo* on the "state revenues from which a yield is received," it is necessary to present a copy of Chamber records testifying how the borrower acquired them. (de Luca 2008, p. 63)

The Milan case, accordingly, is a clear example of the potential complementarity of public finance, private credit, and economic production, when continued coordination of all three spheres of activity can be maintained. Previously, it seems clear that banks dominated historically as the chief form of finance for powerful empires as in the cases of Rome and China, and even as late as the Habsburg empire under Charles V and Philip II. Banks also provided the financing of long-distance trade, typically in stages along the fabled Silk Road of central Asia, or in seasonal voyages in monsoon Asia or in the Mediterranean or North Sea littorals. But in medieval Europe, it was the open markets for public debt and then private debt of corporations, all emerging after and in response to the papal revolution of the eleventh century, that proved complementary and beneficial to existing banking practices. The process of discovering and then exploiting the possibilities of these financial innovations, however, took centuries and numerous financial crises before they could be accepted as the most desirable way for economies to operate. The contrasting experiments made by François I of France and Philip II of Spain amply illustrate the difficulties.

The king and the city make a deal, again and again

The competitive exigencies of war finance throughout the remains of the western Roman Empire during the Middle Ages kept driving the process of financial innovation in Europe. The Christian *reconquista* of the Iberian peninsula from the Moslem occupiers began almost immediately but only gained momentum in 1325 when the Catalan towns received permission from the king of Aragon to sell *censals*, the Spanish form of *rentes* in return for their consent to collecting new royal *aides* (sales taxes). Barcelona sold two forms: a *censal mort*, a perpetual heritable annuity paying 7.15 percent annually, and a *censal vitalicio*, a life annuity for two lives paying 14.29 percent annually (Munro 2013, p. 241). The huge difference in yields must have reflected on the demand side the superior liquidity of the perpetual annuities, which were easily transferred to third parties if the original lender needed cash, while the life annuities were committed to the original insuree.

From the supply side, the perpetuals could only be extinguished if the city managed to raise enough treasure to redeem all the annuities at once, while the life annuities would expire gradually on their own as the original insurees died off. Only the interest would have to be paid annually in each case. Only city-republics powerful enough to be confident that their independence would continue indefinitely would prefer the perpetual annuities to life annuities when the need for war finance arose.

To complete the *reconquista* in 1492, the joint monarchs, Ferdinand of Aragon and Isabella of Castile, sold a series of hereditary, perpetual, and redeemable *rentes*, the *juros de heredad* of Castile. Initially they paid 10 percent, but after the victory over Grenada they averaged around 7 percent, a nominal yield sustained through the end of the reign of Philip II in 1598. While the monarchs asked the provincial authorities, the *cortes*, for the resources to finance the war against Grenada, the sales taxes were enacted by the *cortes*, who assumed responsibility for collecting them and then using the proceeds to pay the interest on the *juros*. As the city and provincial elite held most of the *juros*, at least initially, and the taxes were collected from the commoners purchasing their consumption goods on the local markets, the commitment to pay the annual interest was credible and durable. Imitation of this successful combination of royal authority and city/ provincial corporate responsibility to create viable sovereign debt occurred shortly afterwards in France.

There, François I inveigled the city of Paris to levy new taxes on the basis of which the city could issue *rentes* as well – the *rentes sur l'Hôtel de Ville* (Vam Malle 2008, Chapter 2). Because the bourgeois merchants responsible for collecting the taxes and servicing the *rentes* also held many of them, and the *rentes* could be re-sold readily in case of need, they were a popular investment and commanded a high price. François and his immediate successors continued to support the system due to the low yields, 8.33 percent initially compared to the previous loans that required paying 16 percent annually (Vam Malle 2008, p. 61) Further, any excess of tax revenues over the amount needed to pay the interest payments were kept by the city in reserve or used for other purposes, generally paying themselves for the imputed expenses of collecting the taxes and disbursing the interest payments, but also improving fortifications, quays, and paving streets (Vam Malle 2008, p. 69).

The Parisian leaders naturally resisted raising the taxes that would be required if the quantity of *rentes* were to be increased to meet the monarch's rising demands for war finance, and as long as taxes were not raised and wars were won the system continued. When the wars became overtly religious conflicts later in the century, however, the monarch's demands increased, leading to an alteration in the system. In 1562, the *rentes* of the *Hôtel de Ville* were widely held, but to increase their volume the king persuaded the Parisian council to issue a new set of *rentes* based on the subsidies that the clergy pledged to pay Paris, representing the clergy's contribution to the king's efforts to stamp out religious heresy in France. The Parisian authorities agreed to issue these new *rentes*, despite losing the previous means of control over the collection of the revenues, partly to show support for the king's fight against the Huguenots but mainly to help the king recover control of the port of Le Havre, vital for the foreign trade of Paris and its hinterland, and therefore for the continued collection of tax revenues (Vam Malle 2008, p. 85, drawing on Cauwès 1896, p. 411). The war did not go well, and the clergy failed to make the promised payments in support of the new issue of *rentes*. Eventually, the city had to declare the *rentes* in default after several years of covering the shortfall in clerical subsidies by drawing down their reserves. So ended the first experiment in converting reputable city bonds bearing low interest rates and enjoying widespread public demand into truly national sovereign bonds.

Lending to the borrower from hell, again and again

The experience of the Genoese bankers in providing finance to Philip II of Spain demonstrates both the difficulties of implementing financial innovations and how they could be overcome. Philip II, the Habsburg monarch of Spain from 1556 to 1598, is known among financial historians as a serial defaulter on sovereign debts. His father, Charles V, had stopped interest payments on the debts he owed to a wide range of bankers and merchants throughout his extensive domains at the end of his reign in 1552. Philip's declarations of royal bankruptcy in 1557, 1575, and 1596 set a bad example for his successors, who declared bankruptcies as well in 1607, 1627, 1647, and 1653. In each case, the creditors of the Spanish monarchs were forced to accept long-term securities, *juros*, in place of the short-term securities, *asientos*, they had originally purchased. Why the same bankers, mainly from Genoa, continued to loan to the Spanish monarchs again and again on the basis of *asientos* after having dealt with the previous default has remained a puzzle for economists ever since. The most obvious reason is that silver continued to flow into Spain from the various mines exploited first in Peru and then in Mexico throughout the sixteenth century, carried on the well-organized and guarded treasure fleets of Spain. But for that precious metal to sustain long-term finance while it was dispersed throughout Europe and then Asia required financial engineering, built on previous experience with financing Mediterranean trade.

Two economic historians working on the archival records of the *asientos*, however, how managed to uncover more compelling and simpler explanations for the repeat business of Genoese bankers lending to Spanish monarchs (Drelichman and Voth 2014). Simply put, it was always a profitable business for the bankers, something discovered by economic historians plowing through the terms of thousands of the contracts still kept in the Spanish archives. The first loans by the Genoese were relatively short-term with very favorable rates for the lenders. The short-term debt contracts, the *asientos*, assigned a particular source of Philip's revenue denominated in Spanish silver currency to the Genoese banker in return for a future commitment by the banker to remit an equivalent sum in gold currency to Philip's armies or navies wherever they might be. Every *asiento*, however, made it clear that the banker's commitment, in turn, depended on the amount of revenue actually received. Frequently, specific alternative sources of funds were spelled out in case, for example, the treasure fleets did not arrive, or were delayed, or partially lost.

In short, the original loans to Philip were exactly as the Genoese *compere* had contracted to take up the rents from market stalls or tolls at the city gates or sales of salt as they had done for centuries in Genoa before all of the accumulated debts were combined into the single debt administered by the *Casa di San Giorgio*. Just as the Genoese *compere* had allowed explicitly for variations in the rents that might come from the use of market stalls, or the traffic coming through the city gates, or the revenues from the sale of salt, so the individual *asientos* specified "state-contingent" terms for the returns that would be paid to the lenders. Ultimately, the Spanish monarch relied on fresh shipments of silver arriving from the mints and mines of Mexico and Peru in the regular silver convoys that set out twice a year from Cartagena and Vera Cruz to reclaim the right to the revenue pledged by the *asiento*. Moreover, the terms of the loan to Philip II often included provisions to delay or cease remittances in the event of a shortfall in the revenues granted to the lender.

Collecting the data on each of the *asientos* administered by the monarchy over the period 1566–1600, which covered two of the largest "bankruptcies" by Philip II, and then analyzing the amounts laid out by the individual bankers from Genoa (there were 127 from 60 families) and comparing their disbursements with the eventual repayments, or settlements made in lieu of the contracted repayment, Drelichman and Voth find that nearly all Genoese family firms made handsome annual rates of return. They typically ranged around 20 percent and only rarely were less than the standard rate of 7.3 percent that the Spanish monarchs promised on the long-term *juros*, the basic long-term sovereign debt of the monarchy. These very favorable returns to the Genoese bankers account for the repeated use of their resources and financial engineering techniques whenever Philip II felt the need to mount yet another expensive military campaign. The most expensive, and ultimately most disastrous for his finances, was the Grand Armada of 1588. Yet, the Genoese willingly extended the resources needed to prepare the fleet and maintain the large invasion force in the Low Countries that was intended to land in England, and made an excellent return on their investment.

The major reason for the success of the Genoese financially was their canny writing of contingency clauses in the contracts they made with the Spanish court, clauses that often included the provision that the Genoese banker could receive *juros,* the Spanish version of long-term debt, at discounted prices in case of default. The Spanish *juros* had fixed sources of regular tax revenue assigned to the monarch by the *cortes* of Castile to back them and cover the fixed interest of 7.3 percent on their book value. Actual yields would rise if the market price fell, however, which it often did when payments of "rents" fell in arrears. Genoese bankers receiving them in lieu of the promised *asiento* revenues in default got discounts that ranged up to 50 percent, giving them a yield of over 14 percent.

No alternative lenders appeared to undercut the terms demanded by the Genoese, a tribute to the coherency of the Genoese cartel. The Genoese would punish any interloper who dared cut in on their lucrative business with Spain by cutting him off from the network of European commercial finance. Cartels, however, are inherently unstable, especially if the numbers rise into double digits. Maintaining solidarity among 60 families, who were among the most contentious of all Italian families in dealing with local affairs within Genoa, would have been impossible without the backing of the *Casa di San Giorgio* and its ultimate importance as the coordinating agency for the Genoese banking community. All of the Genoese families with representatives living permanently in Madrid also held varying amounts of the shares of the *Casa di San Giorgio*, valuable collateral for their repeated business with each other.

The Genoese create "virtual" foreign exchange

Lending to Spain was profitable indeed for the Genoese on the basis of the very favorable terms of the individual short-term loans. But the Genoese are famed in financial history for another source of profit, namely charging interest on the business of making the currency exchanges required to settle accounts among princes and merchants across Europe (see Spufford 2003). Their basic service to Philip II was to buy the silver he imported from the Americas, then re-sell it in north Africa and the eastern Mediterranean in return for gold, silk, and spices, which they then shipped overland via the "Spanish road" to pay the Spanish troops in the Low Countries. The Spanish road, in fact, ran the length of the Lotharingian axis, with Genoese outposts located within each self-governing city, avoiding French territory. Along this overland route, however, repeated payments in different local currencies would have to be made – indeed, the proliferation of mints along the Lotharingian axis came to be one of its distinguishing features. Coping with repeated exchanges, however, was something the Genoese perfected by creating a virtual foreign exchange market in 1535 at Besançon (in France), basically to avoid ecclesiastical censure for the practice of charging interest on loans made regularly among the merchant bankers operating along the length of the Lotharingian axis.

Payments of dry bills of exchange made quarterly at the meetings of the Genoese bankers at the Bisenzone fair, wherever it might be held in fact, were also made in terms of a virtual basket of five gold coins issued by the cities of Venice, Genoa, Naples, Castile, and Milan called the *scudo di marco*. Unlike the business of exchange described above, in which a comfortable but variable interest rate could be earned by writers of bills of exchange in foreign currencies, exchange of the *scudo di marco* was fixed in terms of the five currencies, so the element of seigniorage or even brassage necessary to generate the difference in exchange rates between two currencies in their respective mints was missing. Instead, the Genoese tied each bill of exchange written for the quarterly meetings of the Bisenzone fair to a bill of rechange, a *pactum di ricorsa*, which specified in advance the rate of re-exchange. The loans typically lasted a year, some longer, and yielded about 10 percent annually (Pezzolo and Tattara 2008, p. 1104). The Genoese argued, successfully, that the exchange of local coins into the virtual money of account, and then from the money of account back into local coins of identical value, was a transformation of kind as well as of place and therefore avoided the charge of usury.

The Genoese argument, a bit specious theologically, was all the more convincing as the fixed rates of conversion for *rechange* provided lower interest rates than existed elsewhere. Over the course of the sixteenth century and into the war-torn seventeenth century, the Bisenzone market changed physical location several times to stay under the control of the Genoese bankers, who nevertheless kept it named as the Bisenzone market, from its original location (Pezzolo and Tattara 2008).

The Genoese merchant bankers search for yield

Despite the continued profits the Genoese obtained from their short-term lending to Philip II and the significant returns they reaped from the offshore money market they managed for decades, the continued war losses of Philip and his successors led the Genoese to turn their attentions to other borrowers, especially the Papal States, while the yields on their own sovereign bonds remained the lowest in Europe. Figure 3.3 compares the yields on the sovereign debts issued by the various Italian city-states with the yields on debts issued in Barcelona, Holland, and Cologne (from Pezzolo 2013b). They confirm what Epstein (2000) had reported earlier, and that Stasavage (2011) has documented as well, namely that city-states in control of their own tax sources, without undue interference from either bishop or prince, could issue tradable debt at interest rates that typically ran around 5 percent per annum, much lower than the rates that foreign exchange bankers could make through the *change–rechange* process shown in Figure 3.2.

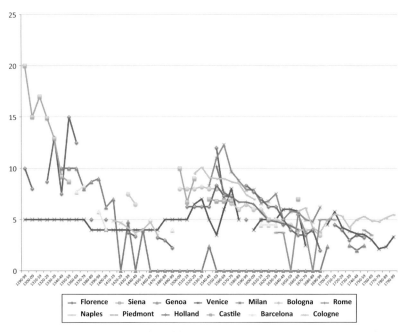

Figure 3.3 Sovereign bond yields in western Europe, 1290–1780 (from Pezzolo 2014, Figure 10.1, p. 300)

Clearly, Venice led the way at the end of the thirteenth century, while Florence and Siena carried on their intermittent warfare to establish hegemony over the Tuscan region, but all three major cities recovered solidly in financial terms from the devastation of the Black Death in the middle of the fourteenth century. By the end of the fifteenth century, just as Spain was completing its *reconquista* of the Iberian peninsula and Vasco da Gama and Christopher Columbus were permanently opening up the Atlantic trades, the Genoese bankers in control of the *Casa di San Giorgio* persisted in maintaining the lowest interest rates of all, right into the end of the eighteenth century. Part of the explanation was the retrenchment of the Genoese, as they were driven back from their possessions on the Black Sea, the Levant, and the eastern Mediterranean over the course of the fifteenth and sixteenth centuries, and sharply reducing their military expenditures as a result. But much of it came from finding profitable returns in financing the military adventures of the Spanish monarchs at very favorable terms. Indeed, Genoese investors start to show up as major holders of papal debt after centuries of supporting the German emperors in their contests with the Italian popes, and even invest in Venetian debt. The Genoese may have been the first to exhibit the classic search for yield by the rentiers of financial capitalism. This will occur repeatedly in later centuries, first with the Dutch, then the English, and eventually even the Americans. Before that story of the rise and spread of financial capitalism can be told, however, we have to deal with the tumultuous seventeenth century, starting with the revolt of the Low Countries against Philip II in 1568.

4 | *The rise of international financial capitalism: the seventeenth century*

The Eighty Years War between Spain and the Netherlands began in 1568, with resistance by the towns in the Low Countries to the increased taxes levied by Philip II's regent, and then continued off and on until 1648, when the seven northern provinces were recognized as an independent republic in the Treaty of Westphalia (1648). The intensity of the religious conflicts that motivated each side – Philip and his successors as defenders of the Catholic orthodoxy and styled as "Most Catholic Majesties" opposed to Protestants represented by a range of dissenters from pacifist Quakers to assertive Anabaptists – culminated with the Thirty Years War (1618–1648). Under the duress of war finance, the combination of corporate bodies issuing long-term debt and facilitating large-scale transfers of funds across multiple currency borders, a symbiosis that had begun in Italy under papal guidance, now spread into northern Europe. From there, the instruments and organizations for modern international finance would spread across the Atlantic, but with distinctive differences among the European imperial powers and within their colonies in the Americas.

The Thirty Years War completed the financial reorganization of western Europe and laid the basis for the rise of the modern nation-state. In the Treaty of Westphalia, the monarchies of the belligerents recognized the legitimacy of self-governing republics in the United Provinces of the Netherlands and the Helvetian Confederacy of Switzerland. The distraction of Spanish and Austrian rulers from maintaining authority over their overseas possessions allowed the Dutch, English, and French trading enterprises to expand across the Atlantic, making their well-to-do merchants and gentry aware of the possibilities of trade in sugar, tobacco, and slaves while holding out always the allure of possible silver and gold mines, given the Spanish success in Mexico and Peru.

Within the battlefields of central Europe, on the other hand, cities and towns learned to create their own municipal debts by forcing loans from their citizens to pay off the marauding armies who threatened otherwise to burn their wooden walls and dwellings. So-called "*brenn-geld*" became the basis of long-standing municipal debts thereafter known as "*Kontributionen,*" which were calibrated to the estimated replacement value of the buildings in the city (Redlich 1959). The Dutch government, however, found that such long-lived securities were not favored by their taxpayer citizens, who had become quite used to the ease of transfer of the short-term bearer bonds. These had become so popular, in fact, that the provincial authorities of Holland found they could simply roll over the bonds as they were redeemed at the offices of local tax receivers. Holland's total debt grew steadily throughout the remainder of the Eighty Years War, but was over-whelmingly in the form of short-term *obligatie* (Fritschy 2003).

The rise of Dutch sovereign debt

Before the full-scale outbreak of revolt in 1568 against the religious dictates of Philip II began, however, the towns of the Habsburg Netherlands had already successfully imitated the financial innovations of other cities in northern Europe by issuing long-term annuities ser-viced by the city's excise and customs taxes in response to the war finance demands imposed on them by Charles V in 1542 (Tracy 1985). Life annuities, issued for the duration of one or two lives, the names of which were designated by the purchaser, dominated. Life annuities were already a favorite investment for bourgeois families wishing to provide for their children, and had been issued by other corporate entities throughout Christian Europe for centuries. These securities, however, had no secondary market, and had to pay high interest rates as a result. The attraction to the city authorities of issuing such high-interest securities was that they were extinguished naturally as the annuitants died off and they required no lump sum repayment of principal.

Heritable annuities were also issued, but apparently in smaller quantities, perhaps due to the uncertain longevity of the sovereignty of the small cities in the Low Countries. They were always under pressure from the Counts of Burgundy and now from the Holy Roman Emperor as well, as Charles V acquired these titles as well as becoming king of Spain. As explained by Munro (2013), heritable annuities cleverly evaded usury limits on the interest that could be demanded by the annuitant because they paid out a share of the total rent earned from the property that the States-General pledged as their backing. Essentially, they gave the annuitant an equity position in the corporate property of the city. The perpetual annuities were heritable, transferable, and therefore suitable for re-sale, unlike the life annuities. A secondary market, therefore, was possible for these new securities, and the possibility of selling them in case of need for cash surely increased the willingness of citizens to purchase them in the first place.

Foretelling the rise of an international market for these securities, a large part of the annuities sold later by the County of Holland went to "foreigners," primarily residents of the surrounding provinces in the north. Opening the capital market to foreigners was a step beyond what had been initiated by the Italian city-states, but was consistent with the cosmopolitan reach of papal finance, described in Chapter 3. Cities in the southern Netherlands, generally more prosperous than those in the northern Netherlands, could limit the issue of their securities to their own citizens, in contrast to the practice of northern cities, who had to induce investors from farther afield if they were to meet their fiscal obligations to the royal authority. Central government finance remained in the form of the long-term *juros* and short-term *asientos* analyzed in Chapter 3, while the individual cities began to issue their annuities as either *liifrenten* (life annuities) or *losrenten* (heritable annuities).

The revolt of the Netherlands took a permanent turn against Spain with the loss of the Spanish Armada in 1588. Spanish attempts to interdict interlopers in their overseas possessions, which included those of Portugal from 1580 to 1640, proved increasingly futile, especially against the rising maritime powers of England and Holland. The closing of the Scheldt River by rebel Dutch forces in 1585 forced the international merchants to move from Antwerp, many relocating to Amsterdam as well as other Dutch, English, and French ports. The émigré merchants and sailors in these ports formed several joint stock companies and extended partnerships to initiate long-distance trade to the East Indies now that the previous Portuguese monopoly had become contestable. Philip II had acquired the crown of Portugal in addition to that of Spain, but concentrated his military and naval forces on maintaining his European domains, as did his successors. The Asian trade that had proved so valuable to Portugal now became accessible to others, if they could but muster the courage and finances needed. By far the most successful was the joint-stock corporation created by the Dutch in revolt in the northern half of the Low Countries.

The VOC and the Stock Exchange of Amsterdam

Various port cities in the northern Low Countries after 1595 had already organized individual ventures (*voorcompagnien*). They all required a larger number of investors to commit resources to construct and crew a large ship to make the all-sea voyage around the Cape of Good Hope and then wait a minimum of three years for its return. Only when "their ship came in" could the Asian goods be sold off and the profits divided proportionally among the investors. No fewer than sixty-six separate ships had left the various ports of the Netherlands in attempts to reach the sources of pepper and spices in the East Indies. Some tried the Northwest Passage through the Arctic Circle in Canada, some the northeast passage through the Arctic Circle in Russia, some the westward voyage through the Straits of Magellan and the South Seas, but only those that used the Cape of Good Hope route around Africa managed to return with profitable cargoes. Most of the ships using alternative routes failed to return at all. Enough of the returned ships, however, made such high returns that investors willingly put up their capital again for subsequent voyages and more merchant communities entered the competition..

Similarly, the French (1600) and the English (1601) organized to equip one or two ships to make the attempt. The possible returns were fantastic – with an initial investment of 144,000 *livres* for two French ships out of St. Malo in 1600, the one surviving a deadly encounter with the natives of Madagascar was returning with a cargo worth 2,000,000 *livres* when it was captured by a Dutch ship off the coast of Spain. Meanwhile, so many *voorcompagnien* were being financed in the northern Low Countries that the military leaders of the Dutch revolt, Prince Maurice of Nassau, the *stadhouder* of Holland, and Johan Oldebarnevelt, the advocate general of the States-General, decided to consolidate all of them into one united, chartered joint-stock company. In 1602, the *Vereenigde Oost-Indische Compagnie* (hereafter, the VOC) became the largest joint-stock company in the world for the next century and would maintain its monopoly of Dutch trade with Asia for nearly two centuries.

At the time, invidious comparisons of the VOC with the existing *Casa di San Giorgio* of Genoa were made, with the inference that eventually the VOC would envelop the finances of the emerging Dutch state just as the merchant-bankers of the *Casa di San Giorgio* had assumed the taxes and finances of Genoa and, increasingly, of the Spanish crown. The corporate governance structure of the VOC was deliberately designed, therefore, to forestall this possibility. Strategic decisions were made by a board of seventeen directors, the Heeren XVII, eight of whom were appointed by the city authorities of Amsterdam, four from Rotterdam, one each from the four smaller cities of Delft, Enkhuizen, Hoorn, and Middleburg. To serve as a tie-breaker and to keep Amsterdam from dominating the entire company, a seventeenth director was added, who rotated among the other five cities.

Two consequences followed for the remainder of the VOC's history to the end of the eighteenth century. First, as control of the company was in the hands of the directors, who were appointed by their respective cities and not by stockholders, any foreigner could become a shareholder and there were no restrictions on who could purchase shares. Unlike the *voorcompagnien* that preceded the VOC in exploiting the possibilities of the spice trade with Asia, the direction of the VOC was very much under the control of the city authorities and not of the major investors. True, each director was required to invest in at least 6000 florins (f) of VOC stock, but this paled by comparison with Isaac Le Maire's f85,000 or Pieter Lingtens' f60,000 in the Amsterdam chamber and f45,000 in the Zeeland chamber. Unlike *voorcompagnien* who financed their ships and cargo by selling shares in either bottomry or cargo, the VOC had to finance the outfitting of its ships by issuing medium-term debt, beginning the process of increased debt-leverage that would eventually spell its downfall at the end of the eighteenth century.

Second, however, any future increase in capital would have required a complicated change of political control among the six cities; so after an initial rounding up of capital from the original capital of f6,424,588 in 1602 to f6,440,220 in 1620, no further increases in capital stock occurred until the VOC was wound up in 1795. A problem arose when some ships had returned with cargo and the company directors failed to even declare a dividend, much less distribute the profits. The charter was for ten years, not for the return of any particular ship. In 1609, moreover, the directors declared the capital to be non-refundable, so disappointed shareholders from then on had no recourse but to sell their shares to someone else. So began the modern world's first recognizable stock exchange, as shareholders sought to find someone willing to buy some or all of their shares. Completing a transaction, however, required first a visit to the one of the six chambers of the VOC to confirm that the shareholder was fully subscribed, and then another visit to confirm the transfer in the stock ledger of the chamber. The official transfer cost was set at $f2.80$, $f0.60$ fee charged by the clerk and $f2.20$ charged for the stamp tax on the deed of transfer (Petram 2011, p. 18). Transfers were few, as most investors had put up only small amounts, some as little as $f20$, and large investors would find it difficult to come to an agreement with any comparably wealthy potential buyer, especially as no dividends had yet been declared. Most transfers occurred when new installments were due on the initial subscriptions.

This state of affairs led to the first documented "bear" operation, as Isaac Le Maire, the wealthiest investor of all with $f85,000$ stock in the Amsterdam chamber, organized a syndicate of ten stockholders to sell forward contracts of VOC shares at lower than current prices (Van Dillen 1930). Unfortunately for the success of the bear operation, the short sales were one-year contracts, coming due between June 1609 and January 1610. While VOC share prices did fall soon after the operation began, word got out what was transpiring and the directors had ample time to organize a counter operation. By raising the price of shares and demanding delivery of the shares promised by the members of the syndicate, they carried out the first "bear squeeze" recorded in history. The city fathers of Amsterdam then passed a statute forbidding short sales of VOC shares, which forced Le Maire to leave the Netherlands. In France, he then tried to organize another company for the East India trade, and actually had his son discover the alternative route to the Pacific around Cape Horn. All to no avail for Le Maire's fortune, however, as the VOC directors maintained that both routes were included in their monopoly.

Nevertheless, the VOC directors did begin distributing dividends, first in kind with quantities of mace priced to be 75 percent of the capital stock, and then the following year in amounts of pepper at set prices. By the time the original charter expired in 1622, the VOC was paying generous dividends every two years. A secondary market gradually developed, but according to the latest history

(Petram 2011, p. 27), it was informal and focused on forward trades of varying duration and carried out among a small group of merchants active in the trade of East India products, mainly spices. Using the notarial archives where some of the contracts were recorded, as well as court records when disputes required third-party enforcement by the city authorities, Petram finds that only after the conclusions of the Thirty Years War and the Eighty Years War were the fortunes of the VOC so well established, with regularly paid generous dividends, that all the apparatus of a well-organized secondary market in its securities had appeared due to the private initiative of a few specialists.

They gathered daily in the confines of the official Exchange building, where contracts for forward (*tijd handel*) contracts, options, and repos were made. When actual transfers of stock were made, they were done at the Amsterdam offices of the VOC. Usually, however, only the differences between current market price and the specified contract price were settled, so the legal transfers recorded in the ledgers of the VOC were but an unknown fraction of the actual trading that occurred. (This was to be true to an ever-increasing extent for secondary securities markets for the next four centuries.) Those differences, in turn, were easily settled either in cash or, in the event of large sums, by transfers within the respective accounts of the *Wisselbank*, or Exchange Bank of Amsterdam, established in 1609.

The Bank of Amsterdam

The timing of the establishment of the *Wisselbank* in 1609 was again a response to the exigencies of war finance that had cumulated over the past forty years. In the absence of an established market for sovereign government debt, and with the difficulties of reaching common accord among the separate provinces and independent cities in revolt against Spanish authority for sharing the expenses of defense, the debasement of the metallic coins constituting the money supply was inexorable. The strained finances of individual provinces led each of the fourteen mints in the Netherlands (eight provincial and six municipal) to follow its own policy in the timing and extent of successive debasements. The numerous mints in the adjacent areas of the Spanish Netherlands and Westphalia took advantage of the resulting confusion in circulating coins to produce their own variants. Foreign coins were introduced as well by merchants from the British Isles and the Baltic and German city-states. By 1610, moneychangers in Amsterdam had to keep track of nearly 1,000 different gold and silver coins. Bit by bit, but relentlessly, the price of silver rose on average 1 percent a year in terms of the unit of account, the florin decreed by Charles V in 1544 but which had long ceased to exist as a coin (Dehing and t' Hart 1997, p. 40).

During the Twelve Year Truce that followed peace in 1609, the city authorities of Amsterdam proposed that each trading city in the northern provinces establish its own exchange bank. Such a bank would assure merchants that they would be paid in a single, reliably valued currency, rather than in a welter of variously debased coins of uncertain origin or intrinsic value. As usual, the other provinces could not accept an initiative coming from Amsterdam and, as usual, Amsterdam went ahead and established its own Exchange Bank, the Bank of Amsterdam. Under the duress of war finance even before the Thirty Years War began in 1618, therefore, the Dutch had developed first their version of Genoa's *Casa di San Giorgio* in the form of the VOC and then their version of Venice's *Banca di Rialto* in the design of the Bank of Amsterdam. Regulation, however, of these two organizations was done according to uniquely Dutch devices.

Government regulation, Dutch style

For the VOC, regulation was split up among the city councils of the six participating cities, although each director was required to hold f6000 of VOC stock in order to have some pecuniary interest in the company's operations. For the Bank of Amsterdam, regulation was left to the city council of Amsterdam, which enforced its monopoly on wholesale payments. What, however, would be the equivalent of the perpetual annuities backed by earmarked taxes that had been the ultimate means of war finance for the Italian city-states and the papacy? As noted earlier, the individual Dutch cities had developed similar annuities in response to the pressure of Habsburg taxes early in the sixteenth century (Tracy 1985). Later work on the various expedients developed by the northern provinces during the course of the Dutch revolt, however, finds that the northern provinces by and large shunned such annuities (Fritschy 2003). After various expedients were tried and failed in the first years of the revolt, the province of Holland, by far the largest and most prosperous of the northern provinces, levied a wide range of excise taxes throughout the province and then issued short-term debt instruments (*obligatien*) backed by the taxes. Individual tax receivers scattered throughout the province were responsible for collecting the taxes and redeeming the notes when they came due. These "common means" taxes essentially extended the excise taxes long collected by cities throughout the province. Instead of using them to back long-term annuities (such as the Spanish *juros*), however, the States-General used them to back short-term debts (similar to the Spanish *asientos*).

Starting in 1574, these taxes funded the bulk of war expenditures, which rose sharply as the revolt became more and more successful. When the Twelve Years' Truce began in 1609, the States-General tried very hard to convert the outstanding mass of accumulated short-term debts into long-term annuities. They found, however, that the *obligatien* were so popular and widely held by the population that there was no demand for long-term *renten*. The easy redemption of the notes at the offices of the local tax receivers, combined with the ease of transfer, as they were payable to bearer, made this the predominant form of Dutch government debt thereafter, especially after war expenditures rose sharply again after 1621. It was left to the shares of the VOC to be the primary form of long-term, sovereign debt that could be widely held and usefully posted as collateral for medium-term private loans, necessary for financing the extended voyages now possible for Dutch merchants, who added the Mediterranean, Atlantic, Africa, and Asia maritime trades to compensate for the Spanish attempt to displace their previous dominance of the North Sea and Baltic trades (Israel 1989).

Consequences for Dutch financial capitalism

In the detailed accounts of one such medium-scale merchant in Amsterdam, Hans Thijs, Dutch scholars have found dramatic evidence of how a typical merchant could parlay a modest investment in VOC shares into an increasing number of profitable ventures, financed by medium-term loans from a wide variety of lenders and at lower interest rates (Gelderblom and Jonker 2004). Hans Thijs was a profitable merchant from the time he arrived in Amsterdam in 1595 until his death in 1611. Starting his career with his father in Antwerp, he had been sent to Danzig while his father moved to Frankfurt after the Spanish seized control of Antwerp. The family was part of the general exodus of international merchants who fled Antwerp after the closing of the Scheldt River access to the sea in that year. Developing trades with tanners, goldsmiths, and diamond dealers while in Danzig, Thijs expanded his dealings when he joined the cosmopolitan bourgeois already active in international trade in Amsterdam. He took part in several of the early *voorcompagnien* until he converted his part shares in several *voorcompagnien* into shares of the VOC in 1602. Until then, he financed his trading ventures by loans from family members, mainly his father at first. On these loans, he generally paid interest of 8–8.5 percent annually and sometimes 10 percent.

Like most investors, he paid up his shares in the VOC in four installments: one-fourth in 1603, one-third in 1604, one-third in 1605, and the final one-twelfth in 1607. As his holdings increased with each payment, the resale value of the shares increased as well (Figure 4.1), giving him ever-greater opportunity to use them as collateral to raise money for more ventures in more distant shores (Gelderblom 2003). As he deployed his VOC shares as collateral, he found a wider range of individuals willing to lend to him, and at

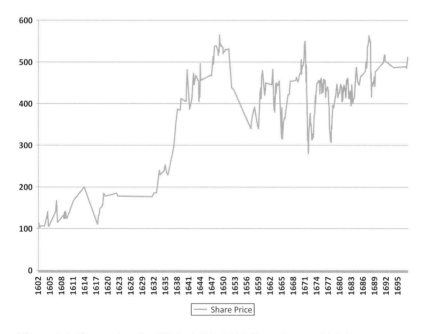

Figure 4.1 Share prices for VOC, 1602–1698 (from Petram 2011)

reduced rates, generally below 7 percent (Gelderblom and Jonker 2004, Table 1, Appendix, p. 668). More of his financing came from outside his family and professional circle, but when they did lend to him they had to meet the lower interest rates offered by other investors. With the formation of the VOC, therefore, Thijs (and no doubt hundreds of other like-minded merchants clustered in Amsterdam) was able to move from personal, close relationships' financing within the tight networks of artisans who would contract with him on a repeat basis, out to more formal and impersonal exchanges among a wider and looser network of potential investors. He accomplished this on the basis of VOC shares that were publicly traded and widely held, even by foreigners.

The Dutch coordination of banks, markets, and governments in finance: an appraisal

The huge, unprecedented scale of the VOC made its share capital the most widely available form of collateral that any merchant from any part of the world engaged in trade through Amsterdam or the other five port cities could usefully employ. This aspect made the VOC uniquely superior to the *Casa di San Giorgio* for facilitating international finance, as the shares of the *Casa* were kept closely under the control of managing directors from the Genoese merchant families. But the corporate governance of the *Casa*, with its annual election of seasoned merchants serving as "protectors" of its corporate interests, remained superior to the governance structure of the VOC, which remained entirely independent from the interests of its shareholders while serving the interests of the political elites of the six Dutch cities represented on the board of directors.

The secret to the success of Hans Thijs, and that of the many generations of venture capitalists who followed his example, was to use his VOC shares as collateral to his lenders. They, in turn, could follow the daily pricing of these shares in the Amsterdam market to reassure themselves or, if they did not want to bother with that effort, they could buy a "put" option that would allow them to sell the shares at a fixed price in the future in the event that Thijs could not repay the loan as promised. VOC shares, then, took the place of long-term sovereign debt as the main form of collateral for merchants in the newly formed Dutch Republic.

Gelderblom and Jonker (2004) laud the creation of the VOC as a case of private initiative by profit-oriented merchants to create a novel financial instrument that served much the same functions as English national debt when it finally came into existence at the end of the seventeenth century (see Chapter 5). Later work by the two scholars with a third author, however, reaffirms the case that the creation of the VOC as such was more the initiative of public authorities coordinating the overall military effort against Spain than of the private merchant groups scattered through the six cities in question. Indeed, it was clearly the intent of the authorities to make the VOC the overseas admiralty responsible for defending Dutch shipping in Asia, and its direction by city authorities was comparable to that of the existing five admiralties that had responsibility for defending the port traffic of the individual coastal provinces. From extolling the VOC as a private, rather than public, initiative, the same Dutch scholars have moved to excoriating it as a poorly structured corporation that set only a bad example for future Dutch enterprises (Gelderblom, de Jong, and Jonker 2013).

"Tulipmania": irrelevant for the history of finance

One of the most publicized speculative bubbles in history, the "tulip-mania" of 1634–1637, occurred in the midst of the Thirty Years War. While it took place mainly in the city of Haarlem, it had repercussions throughout the province of Holland. As explained by Garber (1989, 2000), the extensive movements of troops and their suppliers had led to an outbreak of the dreaded plague. European cities scattered along the Lotharingian axis connecting the Mediterranean ports of Italy to the North Sea and Baltic ports had long established strict rules of quarantine against traveling merchants, who were required to stay in specified quarters until it was clear they did not carry the plague. Garber argues that such merchants found themselves trapped in Haarlem as a result of the quarantine and passed the time engaged in the speculative trade that had arisen there on breeding exotic varieties of tulips. *Bloemists*, Dutch specialists in raising tulips, had discovered that infecting tulip bulbs of a given variety with a mosaic virus could generate mutations that sometimes produced spectacular new colors and shades. If one such mutant did appear, its bulb in turn could be divided up to reproduce a new generation of similar bulbs, all of which could be divided multiple times again, leading to a bonanza for the lucky owner of the initial bulb (Garber 1989).

The tulip trade had existed since the 1590s and the rise of Dutch trade with the Levant that also brought coffee into Amsterdam. An authoritative history of the tulip trade describes the complexities of dealing in tulips:

Tulips, depending on the type, bloom in April, May, or June, and last only for a short period, perhaps a week or two. After they had blossomed, it was thought imperative to lift the tulips out of the ground, dry them off, and keep them wrapped up indoors. Otherwise they might be damaged in the ground. When September came, the tulips were replanted, and they remained in the earth until after the next flowering season the following summer ... If a bulb was sold to another party, it would still stay underground until the summer, so that sometimes, if the bulbs were sold on, the tulips would be found in the gardens of third or fourth parties – and the same problem of immovability faced those who sold property where tulips where planted. (Goldgar 2007, p. 204)

The possibilities for either seller or buyer to renege on any given offer were manifold, given the difficulties of maintaining continuity of each contract on each bulb and the need for each party to trust the other's integrity in the absence of witnesses at the multiple stages of blooming, lifting, storing, and re-planting. Hence there arose the custom of pledging *rouwkoop*, or "grieving money," which a buyer who had reneged on his/her contract would offer to the disappointed seller when some plausible ground was found for reneging on the earlier agreement. The prevalence of plague and the enforcement of the quarantine within each city in 1636 created yet another layer of uncertainty in maintaining an intact chain of evidence for each contract. With this background of an exotic item available for speculative gambling by itinerant merchants forced to idle their time in the coffee-houses of Haarlem during the plague quarantine, what really did happen to the honest burghers of Dutch cities and their temporary guests delayed for a while from supplying the military and naval forces engaged in the Thirty Years' War?

Goldgar argues persuasively that previous analysts of the tulipmania really do not know, as they all relied on a series of pamphlets that ridiculed the speculative excesses in extravagant terms, but these were all published after the tulipmania had subsided. Most ignored dealing with any factual details and focused on the presumed foolishness of people thinking they could make a fortune by buying a forward contract on a tulip bulb. Goldgar states flatly that the prices listed by the classic articles on tulipmania by the Dutch economic historian Nicholas Posthumus (Posthumus 1926, 1927, 1929, 1934) cannot be trusted and are filled with transcription errors as well (Goldgar 2007, n. 9, p. 329). Instead, she pored through the notarial archives in Holland to find the contracts relating to tulips during the period before, during, and after the tulipmania. She found that in both Amsterdam and Haarlem (the center of the tulip trade) those engaged in the trade were all knowledgeable individuals, mainly merchants with long experience in either the tulip or related trades. These would be the middle-class professionals able to afford legal services. By contrast, Garber suggests that the speculators were transient peddlers, whose dealings would be informal and enforced only through peer pressure.

Thompson (2007) offers quite another perspective on the tulipmania, however. He rightly emphasizes the historical context of the Thirty Years War and the importance of news about the course of that long and involved conflict for the Dutch merchant community. Thompson suggests there were a third set of participants in the market for tulips, public officials who had superior information about events in the war that would affect the prices. He emphasizes the earlier spike and fall in tulip prices from 1632 to a collapse in the fall of 1636, all before the tulipmania. These price movements he ascribes to the apparent victory of the German Lutheran princes upon the death of Johan Tilly, leading commander of the Catholic imperial forces, in 1632. German princes were the leading demanders of tulips, apparently competing with each other in festooning their *Wasser-schlossen* (water castles) with ever more elaborate displays of flowers. The battle of Wittstock (1636), however, reversed the fortunes of the German princes with their defeat by the Swedish army in support of peasant revolts throughout central Germany. The German market for tulips was essentially terminated.

What happened then was a concerted effort by the public officials to limit their losses on their forward contracts for tulips, the prices of which had been steadily rising until news of the defeat of the German princes. To do this, they enacted a public decree that *rouwkoop* on the tulip contracts would now be set at 3½ percent of the contract price. With this announcement, forward prices were no longer determined by expected future spot prices plus interest rate, but were now, instead, option prices. Sellers of tulips for forward delivery were now confronted with the likelihood that buyers would renege and only pay 3½ percent of the contract price at its expiration when they would discover in turn how fundamental demand for tulips had fallen. To make this at all profitable to the sellers, they had to raise the strike prices. An odd twist on the arrangement was to make the *rouwkoop* payments effective at the end of November 1637, rather than October, the usual end of forward contracts. But what the legal regulation did, according to Thompson's argument, was to create a new set of prices, option strike prices that would climb sharply until the end of November 1637, when the *rouwkoop* default payments (option fees) came into effect.

To sum up: the tulipmania was a brief episode that had no lasting effect on the long-run development of the tulip industry, which continues to flourish in Holland to the present day. Nor did it have any real effect on the Dutch economy other than the few people who might have expected fantastic gains but had to deal with only the 3½ percent they actually received. Overall, in fact, the Dutch economy continued to prosper from supplying matériel to the forces arrayed against each other in the interior of Germany. Further, the markets for government debt were not affected in the least, as shown by the steady rise in issues of the *obligatien* and the continued low interest rates on them that satisfied the Dutch taxpayers. The only relevance of the tulipmania to the history of international finance that remains, therefore, may be the confusion that option pricing may have created among Dutch pamphleteers, who mistook inflated strike prices for fixed option fees on forward contracts as the normal forward prices for future delivery. We shall see this confusion again when we review some of the literature about the South Sea bubble, an actual financial crisis, in Chapter 5. Nevertheless, other financial histories still give it a major role in the development of financial markets, which is why we deal with it here.[1]

---

[1] Perhaps the reason for the long-standing role of tulipmania in the history of financial crises is that when the first actual *financial* crises occurred in the Fall of 1720, Dutch publishers rushed to print books excoriating the stockjobbers led by John Law in the Mississippi bubble, which had just collapsed. In their rush to print they found it convenient to use plates from the tulipmania pamphlets to make their points. See Goetzmann *et al.* (2014).

French financial innovations with no Stock Exchange or bank?

At the conclusion of the Thirty Years War, while the independence of the Netherlands and Switzerland were recognized, there remained issues between France and Spain, leading to War of the Pyrenees, and an expansion of French territory. This also led to a succession crisis in France, with the young Louis XIV confronting successive uprisings by cities and nobles called the Fronde. Thanks to Cardinal Mazarin imposing fresh taxes to finance the royal armies, each uprising was defeated and the king determined to rule thereafter as an absolute monarch, with lasting consequences for the French economy. When his brilliant minister, Jean-Baptiste Colbert, assumed control of the royal finances, first as finance minister and then as *Contrôleur général* in 1665, he created the system of royal tax farming (renting out for a fixed term the right to collect a given set of taxes to a consortium of private lenders) that sustained France's central government until the revolution of 1789.

Colbert first began to consolidate under one heading the taxes known as *aides* (excise taxes) (1663), then he did the same for the *gabelles* (salt taxes) and *traites* (internal customs duties) (1664). Finally, in 1668, he created a *Ferme Générale* (General Farms) lease that combined all the major tax farms. Along with the consolidation, however, he initiated major tax reforms, both unifying tax rates across the diverse regions of France and lowering the internal tariffs that had been collected by the main predecessor of the *Ferme Générale*, the *Cinq Grosses Fermes* (Johnson 2006, p. 979). While this increased the total cost of each tax farm, the result was to encourage the existing financiers of royal debts to combine as a general partnership, technically a *société générale*, much as had been done in Genoa through the *Casa di San Giorgio*. In the French case, however, it was the absolute monarch who protected the rights and privileges of the tax collectors, not the corporation as in the Genoese precedent.

The end result was to increase significantly the volume of tax revenues collected by the monarch after 1660, although in times of war recourse was still to collect the land tax assessments on the various cities, nobles, and clergy as well as make further demands on the General Farms to speed up advances on future tax collections. For international finance, however, the participation of financiers in the General Farms was limited to French citizens. For these wealthy individuals, the absolute monarch could commit credibly to maintain their tax collection privileges, but clearly could not commit to foreign investors. (Note that this aspect continued the limitation of the previous device used by French monarchs in the sixteenth century, borrowing from the city of Paris, which in turn issued securities (the *rentes sur l'Hôtel de Ville*) to its residents, as discussed in Chapter 3).

British financial innovations: ahead of their time?

After the defeat of the Spanish Armada in 1588 and the death of Elizabeth I in 1603, the Stuart kings of England and Scotland, James I and Charles I, attempted to imitate the revenue devices of the Spanish and French monarchs, but without the economic resources those rulers had at their disposal. Their only option was to auction off charters of overseas corporations, the one royal prerogative remaining to them. Even with this potential source of revenue, it took some effort for them to devise techniques to commit credibly to sustain the privileges of the purchasers of the each charter for the entire term of the charter, typically fifteen years, as with the original charter granted to the East India Company (EIC) by Elizabeth I (Harris 2013). James I, however, made it a point to re-confirm the EIC charter, and over time there evolved a set of commitment devices to facilitate, if not absolutely guarantee, the credibility of royal charters. These included interpretations of English law that distinguished between the English crown as an eternal corporate body and its current occupant's living body, so one monarch's commitment became binding on his/her successors, according to the judiciary. The Statute of Monopolies in 1624 actually represented a consensus among the crown, the parliament, and the judiciary about which existing monopolies were legitimate and could continue as authorized.

With the outbreak of the Civil War in 1642 between the Parliament based in London and Charles I based in Oxford, however, the Long Parliament had to devise a new set of ideas to justify its authority, while denying the authority of the living monarch. The key financial innovation was to create excise taxes collected throughout the kingdom (initially only in the areas controlled by Parliament). These taxes were justified as necessary expedients to finance the standing army led by Oliver Cromwell. But they then had to be legitimized in practice by the way they were assessed, collected, and recorded regularly by standing committees. The documentation of the regular flow of revenues collected by local Justices of Peace throughout the country allowed at least short-term securitization of the excise to occur, much like the *asientos* that had been used so effectively by Philip II in his wars against the Dutch and English earlier, and like the *excijsen* collected by the revenue collectors in Holland in 1642.

The English excises were collected centrally by Parliament throughout the area under control of its armies, which meant the entirety of England and Wales. Moreover, they continued to be collected in the same manner, by the same officials, even after the Restoration of the monarchy and the return to power of Charles II in 1660 (Coffman 2013). Regular receipts of the land taxes also arose under the authority of the Long Parliament, as Cromwell insisted they be collected in monthly installments. This created another revenue flow that could have been securitized, although it was not at the time. Instead, the lands expropriated from the Royalists were sold off to supporters of Parliament to secure their immediate and permanent allegiance to the new regime.

Coffman (2008) documents in detail the extent of financial services that developed from the Long Parliament's initiatives, financial developments that continued thereafter. In summary:

A robust money market grew up around this system. Revenue commissioners collected the duties from taxpayers, who could only pay in coin or specie (but not in the regime's paper – its publike faith bills, military debentures, or warrants). In principle, the commissioners then turned those monies over to the parliamentary fund. More often than not, the commissioners had already made advances to the fund sufficient to cover the monies received. Alternatively, if they held additional monies, they might be ordered to have their clerks pay the regime's creditors directly. After April 1646, when these debts became assignable, goldsmith-bankers began to syndicate their loans and to buy up, at a discount, debts held by common creditors. (Coffman 2013, pp. 84–85)

By 1648, the Protectorate established by Cromwell had cemented the excise as the main source of central government revenue and regularized the collection of the land tax, along with the external customs. Flush with control now over Ireland, Scotland, Wales, and England, Cromwell determined to protect the British Isles by raising a standing navy to complement his standing army, which had no more domestic enemies to confront. So began in 1651 the first of the Navigation Acts that were to define British naval and foreign commercial policy for the next two hundred years. The immediate effect was to instigate the First Anglo-Dutch War (1652–1654), which ended by transferring about 1,200 merchant ships from the Netherlands (8 percent of their total) to the British, doubling their merchant fleet in turn and launching the continued rise of British naval and shipping supremacy thereafter.

One of the financial sidelights of this war, minor and short-lived by comparison with the Thirty Years War that preceded it, was Cromwell's decision to allow Sephardic Jews, mainly from the Netherlands, to immigrate to England, bringing with them substantial amounts of funds in the first generation. The religious motivation for Cromwell's decision was supposedly that he bought the argument put forth by Menasseh ben Israel that the second coming of Christ would not occur until the Jewish diaspora had covered the entire world. The substantial funds offered to Cromwell by the Dutch Jewish community, however, was certainly an economic motivation. Another Cromwellian precedent, therefore, was to establish the willingness of British authorities to import foreign capital.

Conclusion

To sum up, by the second half of the seventeenth century, the three dominant mercantile powers of Europe were:

France, ruled by an absolute monarch and committed to national independent monetary policy.

The **United Netherlands**, ruled alternatively by the pensionary of the States-General in times of peace and by the *stadhouder* from the House of Orange in times of war but always committed to fixed exchange rates with silver.

The **British Isles**, an emerging power that combined Parliamentary legislation with constitutionally constrained monarchy, but remained committed to the international mobility of capital.

When the Dutch *stadhouder*, William of Orange, became William III of Great Britain in 1688, there followed a variety of joint-stock companies chartered by Parliament to help finance the continuation of wars against Louis XIV of France, but each new chartered company, starting with the Bank of England in 1694, explicitly allowed foreigners to own stock. While foreigners could not become directors, they could vote in the annual meetings of major shareholders (Dickson 1967; Neal 1990, Chapter 1). Thereafter, financial innovations flourished. Bank-oriented innovations moved from Genoa and Venice through Amsterdam, leading to public banks throughout Europe, ending eventually with the European Central Bank in 1999. Meanwhile, market-oriented innovations were led by the Bisenzone "virtual market" that Italian bankers created in the sixteenth century, moving to Antwerp, then London's Royal Exchange, and eventually to London's Exchange Alley, culminating with the global securities markets after the collapse of the Bretton Woods System in 1973. Both types of innovations proved complementary in the long run, and together they provided the basis for modern economic growth after 1700.

Lurking always in the background, however, was the credibility of the commitment by the ruling authorities to sustain payment of interest or dividends on the financial assets they had created, as well as to facilitate full repayment of the principal of the debt if the public so demanded. Moreover, authorities had to maintain the commitment of commercial bankers to fulfill their fiduciary responsibilities to their depositors without disrupting private finance by imposing arbitrary financial demands when meeting the challenges of revolution or war. These issues were still in the process of being worked out by the respective governments when the "financial revolution" finally arrived in England.

5 | The "Big Bang" of financial capitalism: financing and re-financing the Mississippi and South Sea Companies, 1688–1720

The accumulated expenses of the War of the Spanish Succession (1701–1714) left each of the great powers of Europe with unprecedented burdens of government debt. The overlapping Great Northern War (1700–1721) also encumbered Sweden and Russia with pressing financial problems. The competitive experiments with ways to deal with their amassed debts among the emerging nation-states of Europe over the next decade ended with Britain alone holding the key to success in war finance. Spain retreated from European expansion to focus on its increasingly productive colonies in Latin America while strengthening mercantile ties with France and allowing provincial elites to regain their local authority over both taxes and coinage. Austria focused on exploiting the trade and finance possibilities through its acquisition of the remaining provinces of the southern Netherlands, which meant renewing the privileges of the city authorities there as well. The Netherlands found that the resources of Holland no longer sufficed to maintain its role among the Great Powers, and the Dutch merchant capitalists turned instead to invest in emerging powers, first Britain, then Germany, Russia, and finally even the new republic calling itself the United States of America. France, having dallied with an attempt to imitate the financial successes of the Netherlands and Great Britain under the tutelage of John Law during the years 1716–1720, reverted to its previous reliance on domestic financiers to sustain both royal authority and provincial aristocracy.

Britain alone among the contesting military powers of Europe in the eighteenth century succeeded in convincing a large and diverse number of individuals to hold onto their claims against the government. Especially important were the foreigners holding British sovereign debt, which included not only the expatriate community of French Huguenots and Sephardic Jews settled in London after the Acts of Toleration in 1689, but also Dutch and German merchant elites, and even the Swiss city of Basel. In the first generation of British financial innovation after 1688, Parliament created a unique combination of chartered corporations to hold most of the national debt created by war finance. Each of the "Three Sisters" – the Bank of England (chartered in 1694), the United East India Company (completed in 1709 with the merger of the Old and New East India Companies), and the South Sea Company (chartered in 1711) – held or managed large chunks of the government's funded debt, as did the Bank of Scotland (chartered in 1695). Further increases of debt required to finance the following wars (War of the Austrian Succession and the Seven Years War) were left to the management of the Bank of England. By the middle of the eighteenth century, the Three Sisters held or managed 97 percent of the vastly increased national debt of Great Britain.

In 1752, the government consolidated the Three Per Cent Annuities previously issued to finance the War of the Austrian Succession into one security – the Three Per Cent Consol. This perpetual annuity was backed by Parliament's commitment of specific taxes to ensure continued payment of its dividends, and it proved so successful that it has been the mainstay of British public finance until the late twentieth century. By 1757 the consolidation was completed, culminating the "financial revolution" in British public finance that began in 1688 (Dickson 1967) and initiating the means to confront France successfully in the Seven Years War and eventually the French Revolutionary and Napoleonic Wars. But did it really begin in 1688 with the Glorious Revolution, or were there other, less dramatic but possibly more durable factors that accounted for the long-term success of the British financial innovation?

The "Glorious Revolution" (or Dutch coup d'état)

It has become a "stylized fact" in the economics literature that the Glorious Revolution of 1688–1689, so-called by later generations of Whig historians, laid the political basis for the financial revolution that followed (North and Weingast 1989; Acemoglu and Robinson 2012). In late 1688, William III of the House of Orange in the Netherlands landed in England with his Dutch troops and in February 1689 he and his wife Mary were formally crowned as king and queen of England. For the Whig majority in Parliament, William was a legitimate successor to James II as his wife Mary was James' daughter. But for the

Jacobite supporters among the Tory minority in Parliament his success in claiming the thrones of England and Scotland was due only to the military forces he commanded as *stadhouder* in charge of military affairs of the province of Holland. While he brought his Dutch advisers with him, who played important roles in helping to finance his wars, William also placated the English Parliament by acceding to its Bill of Rights, essentially forgoing royal prerogatives in favor of joint governance with Parliament.

Dickson (1967) saw this agreement as the basis for the "financial revolution" in English public finance that followed, but he also emphasized the Dutch financial practices that William's advisors brought to bear in Great Britain. The Dutch precedents with their East India Company (VOC) and its method of assuring investors of ease of transfer and transparency of the market value of its shares appealed to Dickson as a key feature of the English financial revolution. Neal (1990) noted the clean features of the English adaptation of the Dutch model, and argued that by stripping the VOC model of the encumbrances that provincial Dutch political concerns had placed on the marketability of VOC shares, the English had hit upon a formula that would launch the "rise of financial capitalism."

Later, economic historian Douglass North and political scientist Barry Weingast accepted Dickson's conclusion about a financial revolution but emphasized the political institutions arising from the Bill of Rights as the essential constitutional commitment by the British monarch that allowed not only the financial revolution to occur but set the stage for market-driven enterprise in the private sector that would eventually culminate in the Industrial Revolution by the nineteenth century (North and Weingast 1989). The constitution set constraints on the king, constraints that could not be loosened without Parliament's consent and, moreover, constrained Parliament from replacing the Crown so it could not become a predatory ruler in turn. That these double commitments were effective in establishing private property rights more generally, North and Weingast argued, was demonstrated by the vastly improved marketability of the public debt. This was the evidence Dickson had presented on the enormous increases in the central government debt with the war expenses incurred by William III, first against James II in Ireland and then against Louis XIV in the Nine Years War with the League of Augsburg (1689–1697). Dickson showed that each new issue of debt could be offered at lower nominal yields, and the new issues were huge increases over the debts incurred under the Stuarts from 1660 to 1688. While North and Weingast acknowledged that the initial constitutional settlement was tenuous, the confidence shown by the public in the constitutional commitment by absorbing willingly the huge increases in war debt meant that future administrations could build on this foundation while private enterprise could prosper.

North and Weingast focused on the commitment mechanisms that were put into place by 1690 and which were sustained afterward, the persistence of which they ascribed to the importance of the constitution agreed upon by both Parliament and the Crown. Political historians since have challenged the solidity of the constitutional arrangement, given the emergence of contesting Tory and Whig parties within Parliament and the recurrent threat of a Jacobite rebellion that might restore the Pretender, or his son (Bonnie Prince Charlie) to the Crown (Hoppit 2000). Economic historians have challenged the solidity of the commitment mechanism for the finances of the Crown as well, noting the continued high interest rates required to market the short-term debt, which also meant that long-term annuities with modest interest payments promised to investors had to be issued well below par, so that yields remained high (Sussman and Yafeh 2006). Repeated threats of Jacobite invasions and restoration of the Stuart dynasty also created sharp falls in the prices of government debt and rises in interest rates, demonstrating the fragility of the constitutional commitment emphasized by North and Weingast (Wells and Willis 2000).

Whatever the apparent fragility of the constitutional commitments and their effects on the credibility of public debt, however, the commitments remained in place through very turbulent times. One reason may be that the succeeding monarchs were more interested in foreign affairs and sustaining the military and naval expenditures they required than in asserting control over Parliament (Hoppit 2000). Another reason may be that the range of political conflicts within England allowed for some workable compromises to occur. As in the cities of the European Continent, there was the conflict between landed and mercantile interests in England; and as in the kingdoms of Europe there was a conflict between Parliamentary and royal power. But England also had a third issue of religious conflict that opposed the established Church of England against the various Protestant sects as well as the remaining Catholic minority, an issue that bridged the two parties, Whigs and Tories, who were at odds over the other two arenas of economic and political power (Stasavage 2003). A more compelling reason, however, may well be the long history of Parliamentary procedures that had been established precisely to collect taxes and administer them fairly and transparently, beginning with the precedent of the Long Parliament described in Chapter 4.

For financial precedents that could help explain the staying power of the financial revolution once begun in England, one can point to a uniquely English quality of financing private commerce. Van der Wee noted that the transmission of financial innovations along the Lotharingian axis of cities running from Antwerp to Florence in Europe made a distinct disjunction at the English Channel. He argued that "[t]he revitalization of financial methods in the 15th and 16th centuries followed two distinct paths of development: one inspired by Italian procedures and passing from Geneva–Lyons–Genoa to Amsterdam; the other, more independent of Italian influence and more innovative, went from Antwerp to London" (van der Wee 1993, p. 145). As explained in Chapter 3, Antwerp developed the foreign bill of exchange as a negotiable instrument through the process of serial endorsement, which provided increasing security for final payment of the bill to each successive endorser. Van der Wee expanded on the later significance of these innovations in Antwerp by noting that private circulation of negotiable bills of exchange was adopted in the seventeenth century by the British and further developed there. In contrast, clearing payments through a public bank became the basis for the Dutch payments system through the seventeenth century, setting the stage for the continued divergence of the two financial systems.

Antwerp's innovations had been driven essentially by the need to make use of private credit instruments to facilitate payments in its prospering market when silver from the mines in southern Germany were diverted to Lisbon by the Spanish rulers in order to finance the Portuguese trade with the East Indies. The Dutch revolt soon followed and eventually succeeded first in removing Spanish forces from what became the United Provinces of the Netherlands. By closing off the Scheldt River in 1585, the Dutch destroyed the international trade of Antwerp, which remained under Spanish control. The Amsterdam city fathers welcomed the flight capital of the Antwerp merchants, but they insisted on maintaining it within the confines of the Bank of Amsterdam, established in 1609 and explicitly modeled on the Rialto

Bank of Venice. In this way, the city fathers maintained their political authority while the Antwerp merchants sustained their overseas trading opportunities, but now directed them from Amsterdam (Lesger 2006). By forcing the deposit of the specie, silver, and gold earned from the expansion of overseas trade into accounts at the Bank of Amsterdam, the city authorities circumvented the problem of currency shortage that had driven the Antwerp merchants to make the financial innovations described by van der Wee.

By contrast, the joint kingdoms of England and Wales and Scotland under James I and VI had no public bank, or wealthy merchants, or sophisticated bankers, much less a stock of metallic money stored in a central secure place. As Kerridge (1988, p. 47) phrased it, "Banking was still without 'bankers' so-called." They were rather merchants or factors making payments from one inland trading city to another as part of their trading activities. It took foreign merchants, largely Italians and Netherlanders called "remitters," to negotiate foreign bills of exchange in Britain (Kerridge 1988, p. 47). By the mid seventeenth century, then, the same process that van der Wee described for Antwerp in the previous century was occurring in England – the *bills obligatory* issued person to person for extended periods of time were becoming transferable by endorsement and were virtually indistinguishable from inland bills of exchange. Persons wanting to receive immediate cash would go to the nearest commodity market and try to sell inland bills of exchange on London; sellers flush with cash, especially cattle drovers after disposing of their herds for cash, would want to buy inland bills of exchange, rather than carry back large sums of money. The bill on London became the standard means of payment, and the bill market in London then became the clearing process for the settlement of accounts in lieu of a public bank (Kerridge 1988).

While London had no centralized banking system or a broadly based and well-functioning market for long-term government debt before 1688, over the course of the seventeenth century it did develop a centralized market in company shares. The creation of the EIC in 1601 led to a secondary market in shares by the middle of the century. Unlike the Dutch or French competitors that soon followed, shareholders in the EIC ran the company and were elected annually. Indeed, this was to be the standard form for all subsequent chartered joint-stock companies in England and Scotland, demonstrating that company promoters in Britain had to appeal to a broad market pool of potential investors to have any success. As a result, British companies had more flexibility in decisions regarding increases in equity through new equity offerings and with stock splits. Relative to Amsterdam and Holland, London and England saw the chartering of a wide range of companies especially during the second half of the seventeenth century. Scott (1912) in his history of English, Scottish, and Irish joint-stock companies, lists over fifty separate companies created by 1688. Some of these were small and some did not last very long. But what is clear is that, prior to 1688, most sectors and a wide range of individuals had some experience with the equity market and the secondary market in shares. As a result, London had developed centralized brokers who dealt in company shares and stood ready to buy and sell (Carlos, Key, and Dupree 1998). It was this market that would grow exponentially in the last decade of the seventeenth century (Murphy 2009).

The pressing demands for war finance dominated the political powers in both Britain (Civil War and Interregnum 1640–1660) and the Netherlands (Thirty Years War, 1618–1648), and led to financial innovations in government finance for both countries in the seventeenth century, as described in Chapter 4. The differences in British and Dutch experiments in raising new sources of funds had consequences that made their respective paths to modernity diverge even farther. How each country tried to resolve the "big problem of small change" with their domestic coinage, for example, provides an instructive example of path dependence in the development of each country's financial system (Redish 2000; Sargent and Velde 2002). In contrast to the unification of mints undertaken in Holland, and the establishment of a virtual unit of account in the "*banco guilder*," Britain was unable to initiate comparable reforms in its coinage. This was partly due to separate coinages in England, Ireland, and Scotland, and the political difficulties of making reform in one kingdom without a corresponding reform in the other, a problem that plagued the British currencies even after the re-coinage of 1696.

The "big problem of small change" for Great Britain as a whole persisted until 1817, when the government finally minted token coins with fixed rates of convertibility to their large denomination coins and bank notes – the "standard formula," according to Sargent and Velde (2002). Only then were the thousands of token coins issued privately and locally over the previous two centuries displaced, as well as the country bank notes that had exploded during the suspension of convertibility of Bank of England notes from 1797 to 1817. The inability of the successive governments in Britain in this period to implement the "standard formula" already in place in the Netherlands and most of Continental Europe with respect to coinage meant that the differences between the two financial systems with respect to banks and capital markets were sustained as well.

The contrasting case of the goldsmith bankers in London with the *kassiers* in Amsterdam highlights why we can characterize seventeenth-century financial systems as bank-centered in Amsterdam and market-centered in London (Richards 1929; Quinn 1994), while acknowledging the overall superiority of the Dutch financial system. In London, the goldsmith bankers held their own reserves in gold or silver rather than turn all specie over to a central repository such as the Tower of London or the mint where it could be seized by the central authority. By issuing notes that gave the holder the right to withdraw the specie upon due notice, the goldsmith-bankers created an increase in the means of payment. Importantly for the security of the system as a whole, they held each other's notes in sufficient quantity to have a claim upon the reserves of other goldsmiths in case of a sudden demand for redeeming their own notes. These also served as a "poison pill" against a threat of a run on a bank's reserves by a competing bank. In this way, the goldsmiths created a mutually reinforcing payments network that laid the basis for further market interactions in the future when markets for new securities appeared (Quinn 1997). Maintaining the credibility of the network required multiple monitors, both among the goldsmiths in London and with their correspondents overseas (Neal and Quinn 2001). The dispersal of metallic reserves among multiple agents across the British network contrasted with the concentrated reserves maintained in the public deposit bank in Amsterdam – and this contrast drove financial innovation along separate paths in the two cities.

Neal (1990), following Dickson (1967), attributed much of the success of the financial reforms initiated under William III to his Dutch financial advisors, while acknowledging the unique way that some of the Dutch techniques were imported and improved. The importance of previous fiscal reforms under Charles II (Chandaman 1975) and even earlier under Cromwell (Ashley 1934, repr. 1966), however, have been extolled by Braddick (1996). Despite the appropriation of church lands by Henry VIII, the re-allocation of them to local gentry and nobles to support the Tudor dynasty meant that the English monarchy had very limited resources from which to maintain a prestigious court, much less to wage sustained warfare overseas. To increase their revenue meant increasing taxes, and the Civil War put control of taxes permanently in the hands of Parliament.

The Long Parliament (1640–1648) introduced the excise on the Spanish and Dutch models, but under centralized authority, unlike the provincial models of Spain and the Netherlands. Further, even the land tax was re-assessed by Parliament and then collected on a monthly basis. Both innovations went far beyond anything attempted in the Netherlands then or even later. Centralized collection of the excise continued under Cromwell and was followed by central control (and re-allocation) of the customs revenues as well under Charles II. Finally, the rationalization of Treasury accounts initiated by George Downing under Charles II meant that at least the Exchequer could monitor the flow of receipts and expenditures on a regular basis. Implicit in the increased pace of collection of tax revenues and improved monitoring of their flow was the possibility for securitization of anticipated future taxes, well before the regime change in 1688 (Roseveare 1991; Coffman 2008).

t' Hart (1991) took issue with Dickson over whether it was "the Devil or the Dutch" that were primarily responsible for the implanting the key elements of the Dutch city and provincial models of public finance in Britain after 1688. She concluded that it was more likely the Devil, given both the history of prior tax innovations and fiscal reforms in England and the ambivalence of William himself over becoming controlled by mercantile interests, whether in London or Holland. While the idea of a funded long-term debt was self-consciously based on the successes of the Dutch cities and provinces, the importance of annuities was declining for Holland after the mid seventeenth century. Even for Britain, short-term debt was far more important as a source of finance for William's wars (Sussman and Yafeh 2006). The importance of the prior rationalization of the Treasury as well was made clear in the work by Roseveare (1991), who also emphasized the importance of centralized collection of tax revenues and management of them at the Treasury before the establishment of the Bank of England.

By 1688, even before William assumed power, English government had already established a unique and compelling historical legacy of

Parliamentary power over the purse, one that would serve as a model for future imitators and competitors. For example, the pressures of war finance in 1705 during the War of the Spanish Succession finally led the province of Holland to initiate a state lottery loan, a direct imitation of the many lottery loans created earlier in England, a striking example of financial innovation in the opposite direction. According to a well-informed contemporary observer, the Dutch lottery was a failure until an expatriate Scot, John Law, told the authorities how to insure a minimum return to ticket holders. We will deal with John Law's magnificent experiment with French finance later. First, however, we need to take a closer look at the essentially British financial innovations that took place after 1688. These were three-fold: a public bank, a private stock exchange, and financial regulation by various laws and practices, typically with a light touch.

The Bank of England

The creation of the Bank of England in 1694 finally gave London a bank that could act on a scale as large as that of the Bank of Amsterdam. Unlike the Bank of Amsterdam, however, the Bank of England was a joint-stock company along the lines of the EIC, the Royal African Company, and the Hudson's Bay Company to name only a few of the already existing companies. It was not created by a merchant guild or by government. Subscriptions of capital came from a wide variety of persons: goldsmith-bankers, a larger number of small merchants and artisans in London, and a number of Dutch individuals, both naturalized and foreign. The governance of the bank set out in its charter was the same as that of the existing joint-stock companies. There was an elected, not appointed, court of directors, and each shareholder with £500 capital was entitled to vote for the directors. The Bank of England's corporate structure, therefore, made it far more responsive to the economic and financial demands of its customers and especially its shareholders than was the case for the Bank of Amsterdam, which was always subject to governance by the city authorities, or the VOC, which had to deal with six separate sets of city authorities that made up the Heeren XVII.

As was the custom for the existing goldsmith-bankers in London, the Bank of England could and did issue bank notes with a total redeemable value greater than the stock of silver and gold on hand. This made it a fractional reserve bank, unlike the Bank of Amsterdam. Moreover, it could discount bills of exchange in competition with the services provided by existing merchant houses, lawyers, scriveners, and gold-smiths. Book transfers among account holders facilitated payments, as in the case of the Bank of Amsterdam or the *Banco di Rialto* in Venice. In combination with the services already provided by the Bank of Amsterdam, then, the Bank of England enabled multilateral clearing of international payments among European merchants (Sperling 1962). In many respects, however, the English centralized financial market and the pre-existing secondary market in shares gave it an advantage over its Dutch counterparts in the eighteenth century.

The new coinage created in 1696 solved for the time being the difficulties of the Bank, but in light of the continued export of silver and import of gold, the official mint ratio between the two precious metals was set to make 16 ounces of silver equal to 1 ounce of gold. The 16:1 mint ratio put England effectively on a gold standard, while the Netherlands with its mint ratio of 15.5:1 was thereafter on a silver standard, although both were legally on a bimetallic standard. The consequence of having both gold points and silver points limiting the range within which exchange rates on bills of exchange could fluctuate was to narrow further the possible fluctuations in the course of the exchange rate on foreign bills of exchange between the two countries (Quinn 1994; Flandreau 2004). This unforeseen outcome of Isaac Newton's direction of the re-minting process served not only to facilitate further the payments for the growing trade between the two mercantile powers, but also to remove most exchange risk in capital movements between them. The monetary basis for the financial symbiosis of the two countries was therefore in place from 1697, when the English re-coinage was completed, to 1797, when the Bank of England was forced to suspend convertibility of its notes into gold or silver and the Bank of Amsterdam was falling under French control.

A further advantage of the corporate structure of the Bank of England, compared to that of the VOC, was the concentration of its capital stock in one city, London, instead of being divided up in fixed proportions determined by political considerations among the various port cities, as was the capital stock of the VOC. In the long run, this meant that the Bank of England (chartered in 1694), the New East India Company (chartered in 1698), and the South Sea Company (chartered in 1711), like all earlier English joint-stock companies, were all fully capable of increasing their capital stock in order to enlarge their activities when that met the interests of the stockholders. The VOC, by contrast, never increased its capital stock throughout the eighteenth century, even as trade between Europe and Asia continued to grow. Finally, the transfer books and stock ledgers of the Bank of England, modeled on those of the VOC, were kept available for transfers on all business days for the Bank. Those of the VOC, by contrast, were usually opened for transfers when dividends were to be paid out. Consequently, trade in Bank of England shares (as in all joint-stock companies in London) could be daily for spot transactions, while trade in VOC and West India Company (WIC) shares in Amsterdam had to be on a forward, time contract basis. Eventually, especially after the re-finance of the South Sea Company's shares in 1723, much of the business of Amsterdam's stockjobbers revolved around the enormous capital stock of the English companies and the increasing size of the British government long-term debt.

The capital market in Exchange Alley

The establishment of the South Sea Company in 1711, which imitated the earlier successes of the Bank of England and the New East India Company in re-financing depreciated wartime government debt, created more opportunities for cross-holdings. In 1712, the Scottish financier John Law, then resident in Amsterdam, bought shares in the South Sea Company through the agency of his friend and mentor, Lord Ilay, using the services of Ilay's goldsmith-banker in London, George Middleton (Neal 2012, Chapter 4). By the end of 1720, when more Dutch money came to London in pursuit of the speculative gains to be gained during the run up in price of South Sea stock, Dutch holdings in Bank of England stock amounted to nearly 20 percent of the new purchases of Bank stock from 1720 to 1725, a period when the Bank's stock increased by 50 percent (Carlos and Neal 2006, Table 9). Indeed, the success of the English system of joint-stock companies led, at least, this one Dutch man to emulate the model:

We have established a company to insure ships, for the perils at sea, war and piracy, which is necessary for the trade and maritime trade, and which have been successfully established likewise in England, and have fully secured the insurance by gathering a large pool of capital: as such the initiator of this company believes that it would be a good idea to establish such a company, by collecting capital, in Rotterdam, as has been successfully done in England, and proposes to subscribe under the following conditions. (From *Het Groote Tafereel der Dwaasheid*, Amsterdam, 1721, English translation kindly provided by Rik Frehen)

Pledging of shares of widely held corporations such as the VOC as collateral for private loans occurred almost immediately in the Netherlands at the beginning of the seventeenth century (Gelderblom and Jonker 2004). We know that this had begun to occur in England at the end of the seventeenth century from the accounts of Francis Child, a major London goldsmith-banker in London (Quinn 2001). While the Dutch innovation enabled Amsterdam merchants to obtain loans from a wider range of sources at lower rates of interest almost immediately, the accounts of Francis Child analyzed by Quinn indicate that lending rates to merchants in London actually rose while pledging various forms of government debt as collateral for their borrowings from Child. Quinn argues that the rise in interest rates was a response to increased post-war demand for loanable funds by the private sector, which was taking advantage of peacetime opportunities for investment in the period 1698–1705. Child's loans guaranteed by government securities became larger, much more numerous, and for longer periods compared to his practice before the accession of William III (Quinn 2001, pp. 604, 611). In terms of using Dutch techniques in the capital market in London, Murphy (2009) has demonstrated that at least one broker, Charles Blunt, in London had created an active business in options during the stock market boom of the 1690s.

The South Sea bubble, however, disrupted this business for a few years (Charles Blunt became bankrupt and committed suicide in 1720 after the collapse of the bubble). Despite the efforts of the South Sea Company to sustain the level of their overpriced stock with the Bubble Act of June 1720 and a series of ad hoc maneuvers, including borrowing from the Bank of England, the bubble collapsed and the South Sea Company was eventually re-structured under government supervision. Robert Walpole's government managed, with the self-interested help of the Bank of England, to restore the vitality of the London stock market by June 1723 by converting one-half of the South Sea stock into perpetual annuities offering 5 percent interest for five years, to be reduced then to 4 percent and eventually to

3 percent Thus, Walpole at a stroke created an enormous stock of homogenous, readily transferable, and fungible financial assets that were widely held by at least 35,000 individuals (Carlos, Neal, and Wandschneider 2007). This was the permanent basis for the continued rise of the London capital market for the next three centuries.

Regulatory role of government

As we should expect, William III's need for war finance and Parliament's determination to assert its authority over the new monarch set the stage for the government's subsequent regulations of the financial sector. Once the dogs of war had been unleashed, however, neither king nor parliament could be master of events.[1] William's demands for funds for his troops on the Continent had the effect of removing much of the silver coinage of Britain to Holland, where it commanded a higher price, leading eventually to the re-coinage of 1696 (Jones 1988). Parliament, faced with continued demands for remittances in silver to William's troops in Europe, and with a growing shortage of silver coins suitable for circulation domestically, ordered a Commission on the Coinage to examine the problem and propose solutions. Members included William Lowndes of the Treasury, Isaac Newton (soon named warden of the Mint in time to direct the re-coinage in 1696 and later made Master of the Mint in 1699 until his death in 1727), John Locke (a Commissioner of the Excise under William, having returned to England in 1689 from Holland on the same ship with Queen Mary), and Charles Davenant (then without official position when James II fled). Lowndes reported that weighing successive bags of silver coins at the Treasury showed that clipping had reduced the weight of the coins on average by 50 percent. One solution to the shortage of coins, therefore, would be to cry up the value of the standard coin, the crown, by 25 percent. The Parliament proposed a more modest devaluation of 9 percent, but Locke's insistence that the credibility of the new government depended upon restoring the full value of the silver coins convinced both William and Parliament to strike new coins at full value. The result was depression of trade as the entire domestic payments system was thrown into confusion, while

---

[1] For the political vicissitudes that followed, see Hoppit (2000). Only the highlights directly affecting the history of international finance can be covered here.

remittances continued to flow to Holland and the government's short-term debt mounted steadily.

Lowndes and Newton were left to deal with the technical problems created by the re-coinage: Lowndes with collecting the taxes and accounting for expenditures at the Treasury and Newton to establish five mints throughout the country to produce more coins in the next three years than had been minted in the previous thirty. Newton also was in charge of prosecuting clippers and counterfeiters, inflicting the death penalty on at least one hundred individuals found guilty. Both men, however, proved their worth as dedicated public servants, and both continued to serve ably and effectively in their respective roles through the turmoil created by successive political regimes culminating with the South Sea bubble. The emergence of dedicated, capable civil servants throughout these tumultuous years was essential for the continuation of the financial revolution, which at its heart depended on reliable accounting of the government's revenues, expenditures, and debt service.

While the re-coinage did accomplish the goal of asserting the legitimacy of the new government, the economic problem remained that while both Britain and the Netherlands maintained both silver and gold as the basis for their domestic currencies, they had different mint ratios for the two metals, as explained above. This difference in mint ratios, with silver more valuable in terms of gold in Amsterdam than in London, meant that Stephen Evance and other goldsmith-bankers regularly made a profit by drawing bills on Amsterdam in silver and then re-changing them in Amsterdam to draw on London in gold (Quinn 1996). It also meant that Britain suffered from recurring problems throughout the eighteenth century with its small change, due to the disappearance of full-bodied silver coins that were melted down and exported to Europe.

Regulation of the financial sector by the British government proceeded in a desultory manner thereafter, the main effects occurring in the usury laws, which set a legal maximum of 8 percent in 1624, reduced to 6 percent in 1651 and only reduced to 5 percent in 1713 at the end of the War of the Spanish Succession (Horsefield 1960, p. xv). There it remained into the nineteenth century, although the rates on short-term commercial credit proved lower than the legal maximum through the eighteenth century (Flandreau *et al.* 2009a). The "law merchant" that had governed contracts involving foreign bills of exchange for centuries in Europe was incorporated bodily into British common law by 1710, which raised the inland bill of exchange to formal standing, making it the dominant form of commercial credit in Britain for the next two centuries. By expanding its capital stock in 1708 by absorbing yet more of the government's debt accumulated during the War of the Spanish Succession, the Bank of England had both its charter extended for another twenty years and its monopoly affirmed as the one note-issuing bank based on joint stock ownership in England. The Act of Union with Scotland in 1706, where the Bank of Scotland had existed since 1695 and new joint-stock banks were being considered leading to the Royal Bank of Scotland in 1727, meant that the monopoly was confined to England. Later, the Bank of Ireland was created as well in 1783.

The regulation of the stock exchange was left to the City of London, which licensed a limited number of brokers who were entitled to bring buyers and sellers of securities in contact with each other. All of them were required to maintain full ledger accounts with each customer, suitable for legal deposition in case of dispute. As the securities market developed, especially after 1688, however, the excitement it created induced a large number of entrants eager to help first-time investors seek out profitable opportunities. Among these entrants to the London market in the 1690s was a young dandy from Scotland, the eldest son of an eminent goldsmith-banker in Edinburgh, eager to see what future lay before him with his father's inheritance, his good looks, and his brilliant mind. John Law was destined, indeed, to shake the kingdoms of Europe to their roots, as he personally proclaimed to the British Ambassador in Paris in August 1719 on the eve of the Mississippi bubble (Neal 2012, p. 75).

The "Big Bang" of financial capitalism

While the Bank of England opened up its subscription books in 1694, initiating the idea of funded national debt for an entire kingdom governed by a constitutional monarch, John Law observed the historic event from his cell in Newgate prison in London, a convicted murderer and soon sentenced to be executed. Law had also observed the operations of the Royal Exchange dealing in wholesale commodity trading and purchases of bills of exchange, both inland and foreign, as well as the burgeoning trade in securities carried on outside the Royal

Exchange in the coffee houses clustered along Exchange Alley. He was familiar with the dozens of proposals for expanding a "fund of credit" by creating a universally acknowledged backing for bills that would be issued by a new organization with government approval. These could be pawnshops (called Lombards or even "Lumbards" after the example of the *monts de piété* that had generated credit for citizens of the various cities in northern Italy), or they could be land banks holding the properties freshly expropriated from the Jacobite supporters of James II by the new government, whether in Cornwall, Ireland, or Scotland. Thanks to his family connections through his mother with the Scottish clan Campbell, supporters of William III in Scotland, Law's escape from prison was arranged after he was transferred to another, less secure prison.

It appears most likely that his escape from London in 1694 during the ongoing War of the League of Augsburg was accomplished by fleeing first to Holland and then to Paris. There it appears he lived well again among high society in 1702, and making a reputation as an expert banker at the gambling tables for faro and basset before returning to Scotland. By this time, he had solidified his ideas for promoting trade by expanding the money supply, publishing his classic work, *Money and Trade* (1705). He also prepared a proposal of his own for a land bank in Scotland, which he strongly urged the Whig leaders there – the Duke of Argyll, John Campbell, and his brother, Lord Ilay, Archibald Campbell – to create (Murphy 1997). The proposal was defeated in the Scottish Parliament, more interested at the time in laying the groundwork for the Act of Union with England, accomplished in 1707. As Law was still convicted of murder and sentenced to die in England, the Act of Union required him to flee to the Continent for a second time, this time to Genoa and Turin as well as Holland and Paris. In the course of his travels, he witnessed the financing of the War of the Spanish Succession from both Genoa and Amsterdam, before arriving again in Paris in 1714 at the conclusion of the war.

The French government under Louis XIV had succeeded in installing his grandson, Philip V, as king of Spain at the end of the War of the Spanish Succession, but at the cost of accumulating unsustainable debt. Whatever was the debt to gross domestic product (GDP) ratio for France, it was over 100 percent and likely over 200 percent, but worse was that the tax revenues were less than 50 percent of peacetime expenditures so the government still had to keep issuing more debt even in peacetime. It was a perfect position for Law to make his ideas for financial and monetary reform heard by a responsive audience, and his ideas now combined the successful experiences of England with those of Amsterdam, both of which he had witnessed at close hand and, it appears, by close collaboration with important Genoese merchant banking families. The image of the *Casa di San Giorgio* with its corporate structure designed to circumvent local political strife while maintaining effective control of the republic's tax revenues, organizing corporate control of Genoa's overseas trade, and maintaining important overseas ports monopolized by Genoese merchants, must have inspired Law and solidified his concepts how to implement monetary reforms.

Law persisted in presenting his ideas to the ministers of Louis XIV in 1714, supported by the British Ambassador, a fellow Scot, Lord Stair, who had been appointed by George I, the new king of England in August 1714. When Louis XIV died in September 1715, his great-nephew, the duc d'Orléans, became Regent for the next eight years until the great-grandson, the future Louis XV, reached his majority at the age of thirteen. Both George I in Britain and the Regent in France needed to solidify their positions of authority by restoring public finances to a sustainable pattern and to keep Philip V in check. For a while, the strategic interests of Britain and France converged, as both were committed to restrain Philip V of Spain from using Spain's resources to increase his power in Europe. Philip could try to assert rule over part or all of France by dint of his direct descent from Louis XIV, or he could push Britain back out of the Mediterranean if he regained Gibraltar, Sicily, or Port Mahon, strategic ports that the Royal Navy had captured during the war.

Consequently, Law had the tacit support of the British to help the Regent solve his financial problems, but he encountered resistance from the traditional financiers of France, the moneyed men holding lucrative offices with control over local tax revenues and tolls, the operators of the provincial mints, and the merchants engaged in overseas trade in the Caribbean, along all the coasts of Africa, and into Asia wherever the English, Dutch, Spanish, or Portuguese had not yet established a firm monopoly. Law's persistence in rising to power over the next five years is one of the great episodes in financial history, all the more poignant for his ultimate failure in France with historic consequences for the future of Europe – and of international finance.

His original schemes for reform of French finances rejected by the Regent's council, Law managed to obtain approval nevertheless to establish a private, joint-stock bank, the *Banque Générale*, in 1716. Modeled on the success of the goldsmith banks in London, especially the bank established by David Campbell in London in 1692, which eventually became the historic private bank, Coutts & Co. (Healey 1992), Law's bank issued bank notes backed by full value silver coins. Taking advantage of his numerous contacts throughout mercantile Europe acquired during his travels in the twenty years since his escape from the London prison, he offered favorable rates for foreign bills of exchange and quickly acquired a substantial banking business, much to the chagrin of the traditional French financiers. He offered the Regent especially good terms for making subsidies to Charles XII of Sweden, but his *coup de grâce* was financing the purchase of the fabulous Regent diamond from Thomas Pitt, governor of the East India Company's Madras station from 1698 to 1709, which he accomplished in successive payments from June 1717 to August 1719 (Neal 2012, Chapter 3).

When the Regent needed even more cash in a hurry to finance troops against the movements of Philip V's army in northern Spain in 1718, Law was able to meet his demands but took advantage of the situation to raise the stature of his *Banque Générale* to a state (Regent)-supported *Banque Royale*. The new bank had the advantage of its notes being accepted for tax payments throughout the kingdom, but at the cost of making them convertible into *écu*, the standard French silver coin, at whatever happened to be the current legal value of the *écu* in terms of silver. And this was subject to repeated changes as the Regent (and the moneyers in charge of the mints) took advantage of the needs of the population for coinage to call in existing coins and re-mint them with lower amounts of silver, or, more easily, to simply "cry up" the value of existing coins to be worth more in terms of the unit of account, the *livre tournois*. One unforeseen consequence, apparently, was that the final payment due to Thomas Pitt for the Regent diamond in June 1719 was made by means of a bill of exchange drawn by the *Banque Royale* on a merchant in Hamburg, who refused to accept it on grounds that the *Banque Royale* credits with him were not worth the amount drawn.

While Law set aside that problem of private finance for another year by making a sizable bet with Pitt's son in August 1719 (Neal 2012,

Chapter 4) the expanded *Banque Royale* became a stunning success for the Regent and in terms of public finances. Philip V's army maneuvers were thwarted in 1718, while the British had to deal with Spain's refusal to deal with the South Sea Company in 1718. Under the terms of the Treaty of Utrecht in 1713, Philip had been forced to turn the monopoly of the *asiento* for delivery of slaves to Spanish America over to Britain's South Sea Company. To help the government finance naval support of its claims on Spain, the South Sea Company re-financed outstanding debt of the government that was in arrears and costing 9 percent annually, and did it successfully in June 1719 (Neal 1990, pp. 94–96). Now a race began between the governments of France, led increasingly by the financial reforms of John Law, and Britain, still absorbing the consequences of the creation of the South Sea Company in 1711. The upshot was to be the famed Mississippi and South Sea bubbles in 1719–1720, the first stock market booms and busts in history.

The Mississippi bubble

Law's success in financing the regime of the Regent in 1718 with a ready expansion of the bank notes of the *Banque Royale* led him to take over other parts of the French financial sector, creating his *Système* that was completed in February 1720. He had already begun to imitate the English example of swapping depreciated government debt for equity in an overseas trading corporation by reviving the moribund *Compagnie d'Occident* in August 1717, familiarly called the Mississippi Company in the British press. When its shares were only 60 percent of par value, reflecting the depreciated value of the government *billets d'état* that were used to subscribe the new company, Law used the note issuing powers of the *Banque Royale* in early 1719 to pump them up. He then absorbed into the company in addition the monopoly of trade with Africa and then India, creating the *Compagnie des Indes* in May 1719 with an additional 50,000 shares with nominal values of 500 *livres tournois*. With formal decrees in mid August 1719, the Regent's government carried out the completion of Law's *Système* for restructuring French public finances.

The grand scheme was to re-finance all outstanding French government debt, meaning all the *rentes sur l'Hôtel de Ville*, the offices that had been sold to financiers in the previous decades to finance Louis

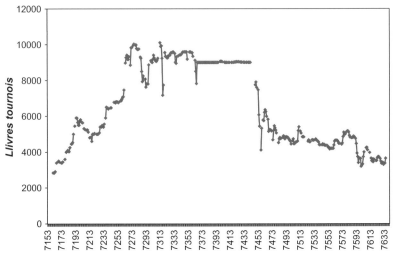

Figure 5.1 The Mississippi bubble, 1719–1720 (*livres tournois* per share) (from Murphy 1997)

XIV's wars, the debt held by the mint proprietors, and, most damaging to the vested interests of the traditional French financiers, the debt held by the *Compagnie de Fermes Générales*. To finance these successive acquisitions, Law had to expand the capital stock of the *Compagnie des Indes*, using at will the note-issuing power of the *Banque Royale* to sustain a continued rise in the market price of Mississippi stock until it reached his target of 10,000 *livres* per 500 *livres* nominal share (Faure 1977; Neal 1990, Chapter 4; Murphy 1997, Chapter 14; Velde 2009). This he had accomplished by the end of 1719, which was also when speculators who had been drawn in from all over Europe to invest in the new company began to realize their gains and try to repatriate their investments (Figure 5.1).

Law's attempts to counter these withdrawals were ingenious as well, albeit they failed at the end. First, he merged the *Banque Royale* with the *Compagnie des Indes* in February 1720, basically to eliminate all informal, over-the-counter trading in *Compagnie* shares. This eliminated the expertise of foreign stockjobbers and stockbrokers who had flocked to Paris from Amsterdam and London, and put into jeopardy all forward contracts they had made. The most knowledgeable of them had been selling out on forward contracts for some time (Neal 2012, Chapter 7).

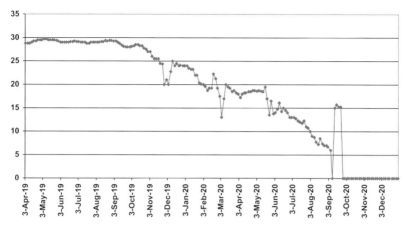

Figure 5.2 The French exchange rate, 1719–1720 (pence/*écu*, 2 months' usance) (from Castaing 1698–1908)

Second, he fixed the price of *Compagnie* shares at 9,000 *livres* in March 1720, payable only in notes of the *Banque Royale*. The remaining problem was that the exchange rate of the *livre* with the rest of Europe continued to fall and to fall ever more rapidly (Figure 5.2), reducing in real terms the capital gains of early investors in the *Compagnie*. Merchants dealing with France found that they no longer had the short-term commercial credit they relied on to finance their trade. Effectively, the mercantile payments system of Europe came to a halt until Law decided to soak up by decree the excess liquidity he had created by abusing the note-issuing power of the *Banque Royale*. The decrees of May 1720 first declared that the price of *Compagnie* shares would be cut from 9,000 to 5,000 *livres* by December 1, 1720, a reduction of 44 percent over the next six months, while the volume of *Banque* notes would be reduced month by month by a total amount of 50 percent.

According to the definitive account by Murphy (1997), Law had proposed this reduction in the value of both bank notes and company shares two months earlier, when the price of silver had been reduced to make French exports more competitive, but without altering the price of company shares or the amount of notes issued by the bank. Political considerations by the Regent, however, delayed the adjustment needed for the bank and company and when the decree of May 21, 1720 was rescinded on May 27, 1720, all confidence in the *Système* created by Law was lost. The price of company shares did not recover, however, despite the reprieve from the deflationary measures proposed by Law, and the company was forced to declare bankruptcy on July 20, 1720. Furthermore, the French exchange rate continued to fall, worsening the terms of trade for the country. The rest of the *Système* unraveled quickly and Law was forced to flee for his life in December. So ended the first major experiment in replacing precious metals as the basis for a country's money supply. It took 300 years after John Law's birth in 1671 for the world economy to give up on gold or silver as the basis for a currency when US President Nixon unilaterally abrogated the Bretton Woods Treaty and took the US dollar permanently off gold on August 15, 1971.

The South Sea bubble

Meanwhile, the British economy was experiencing the South Sea bubble, partly in imitation of Law's experiment, but with critical differences that made the outcome after the collapse of the bubble quite different. Given the apparent success of Law's restructuring of French finances by the end of 1719, and the evident success of the South Sea Company's earlier re-financing of the lottery loans of 1710 in June 1719, the South Sea Company proposed to convert the other annuities outstanding from financing previous wars into equity shares of expanded capital stock of the company. This was a more limited goal of its debt for equity scheme, which only extended to the government's long-term debt not already held by the Bank of England, the EIC, or the Million Bank, as opposed to Law's attempt to convert all French government debt, regardless of how it had been created or how it was currently held, into shares in the *Compagnie des Indes*. The South Sea directors, however, used much the same techniques perfected by Law to raise the price of existing shares. These consisted mainly of creating successive subscriptions with payments spaced out over several years to raise the price of existing stock. Higher-priced stock made it attractive to annuitants to trade in their high-yield securities for the new stock.

But the directors did not have the resources of a *Banque Royale* to finance the purchase of either its existing stock or its intended expanded stock. This restraint meant the South Sea had to divert cash from other uses in order to raise the price of its existing stock and to keep its price high as new stock was added from conversion of the outstanding annuities. Initially, the Company competed with the Bank of England for the privilege of converting roughly £25 million of both redeemable, medium-term annuities and irredeemable long-term (99-year) annuities into expanded capital stock. Thanks to widespread bribery of Members of Parliament (MPs) and a final sweetener of a promise to pay £7 million immediately to the Treasury upon conclusion of the conversion scheme, the South Sea Act was passed in February 1720, just as John Law's *Système* in France was beginning to show strain. After an initial success of raising money by a modest offering of new shares in March, the first and second subscriptions of new stock by converting existing annuities were issued. This opportunity for investing at the ground floor of a new bubble scheme, now that the French scheme was in peril, attracted more interest than the directors had thought possible. As the Mississippi bubble collapsed and uncertainty about Law's future increased, more money came into London and a rational bubble emerged, overwhelming the directors with the unexpected demand (Neal 1990, Chapter 4, Appendix; Kleer 2015). A third, unanticipated and poorly planned, subscription was then offered at even more favorable terms to holders of the 99-year irredeemable annuities. Taking stock of the situation, the company closed the transfer books in June 1720, which forced investors to take up forward contracts for either offloading their shares or for borrowing funds on the basis of shares pledged as collateral.

The forward premium on the forward contracts on the London Stock Exchange ranged from 40 to 100 percent annually, reflecting the shortage of ready cash for even normal business. Indeed, both the Bank of England and the EIC offered their shareholders the opportunity to mortgage some of their shares to get ready cash, with the Bank quickly mortgaging nearly 25 percent of its capital stock. The resulting shortage of tradable shares in the two companies created mini-bubbles in their share prices, mimicking at a much lower level the boom in South Sea Company share prices (Figure 5.3). As the European-wide credit crunch created by the collapse of Law's *Système* in France reverberated through the credit channels of Britain and Holland, the stock market booms ended in those countries as well, but with essential differences from France.

The Bubble Act of 1720 (6 Geo. I, cap. 4), enacted at the height of the speculative mania in London in June, differed significantly from the

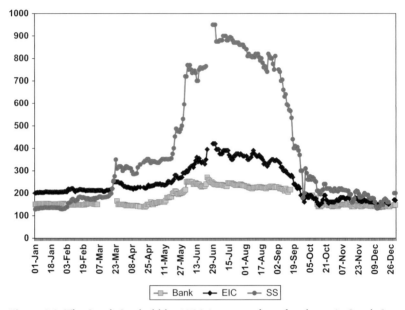

Figure 5.3 The South Sea bubble, 1720 (percent of par for shares in South Sea Company, East India Company, and Bank of England) (from Neal, 1990, Figure 4.5, p. 84)

regulations that Law and his successors had imposed on the Paris stock market. The Act's main intent was to charter not one, but two competing companies in marine insurance, but it also forbade any joint-stock company created under charter by Parliament from engaging in any other activity than that expressly defined in the charter. This did not prevent joint-stock companies created to finance public infrastructure such as toll roads, canals, port facilities, water works, gas works, and eventually railroads from being created in the future, but it did limit the enthusiasm for creating non-chartered companies, many of which had been proposed during the run up to the South Sea bubble in 1720 (Harris 2000). It was repealed, moreover, after the next major stock market crash in 1825.

Aftermath

More importantly, rather than declaring the company bankrupt and then carrying out a segmented default among the creditors, as the French did in 1721–1726, the British government led by Robert

Walpole re-organized and effectively re-financed the failed South Sea Company. It did this by transferring £5 million of the South Sea capital stock to the Bank of England, increasing the Bank's capital by 50 percent. Then the remaining £30 million capital of the South Sea was divided into two equal parts. One half remained as equity with the company, still getting interest on that part of the government debt it had acquired but enabled to carry out whatever profitable pursuits it might find in the South Seas – basically the Caribbean, South Atlantic, and Pacific Oceans on the west coasts of the American continents. The other half, split precisely for each of the shareholders, was a direct obligation of the government, a perpetual annuity carrying interest initially at 5 percent per annum. At one stroke, then, every shareholder had claims on two securities, one on the equity of a trading company with a defined monopoly and the other on the obligation of the British Parliament. Each shareholder could decide personally how to dispose of his/her corporate holdings and it appears that many took advantage of the opportunity to do precisely that (Carlos *et al.* 2013). In the process, the greatly expanded customer base for the stock market created lasting business opportunities for the specialists in Exchange Alley.

Later, when the furor from the re-organization of the South Sea Company had died down, Parliament did pass, at the bidding of Sir John Barnard, an act forbidding short sales of government debt (Barnard's Act, 7 Geo. II, cap. 8). The act was passed provisionally in 1733 during a prolonged lull in stock market activity in London and an unusually long period of peace so it was made permanent in 1736. While it explicitly did not cover short-term government debt such as the various Army, Navy, Victualling, and even Exchequer bills that government had to issue at the outset of any war, it did cover long-term debt such as the Three Percent perpetual annuities that had to be issued subsequently during the War of the Austrian Succession (1738–1744) and the Seven Years War (1756–1763). To finance these wars, the British government issued a veritable "ocean of annuities." An astute observer of the Amsterdam stock market, Isaac de Pinto (1771), argued that it was the stockjobbers in Amsterdam who provided the forward purchases of the new annuities that enabled the stockjobbers in London both to market the new issues of debt and to avoid violating Barnard's Act. The complementarity of the Amsterdam and London markets was surely at its height then, but the financial crises that hit both financial centers at the end of the Seven Years War, first in 1763 and then in 1772, put the relations on a different trajectory thereafter (Chapter 6).

The French financiers, back in power after the disgrace of John Law and his flight from the country, re-asserted their traditional authority over the government finances by checking the funding source used by each shareholder in the bankrupt *Compagnie des Indes*. No fewer than six different means of payment for the shares, corresponding to the initial debt conversions and then subsequent equity conversions from the companies that had been absorbed, as well as payments in gold or silver, were identified. Each form of payment was forced to take a percentage haircut when settling the claims, rising to 95 percent in the worst case – which the French financiers took to be foreign bills of exchange. These, of course, were the payments made by the multitude of foreign merchants and speculators that John Law had deliberately attracted to Paris, especially from Amsterdam, Edinburgh, Genoa, Hamburg, London, and Venice. Needless to say, foreign investors in French government debt were discouraged for the remainder of the century. Only Napoleon's troops were able to induce, by force of arms, foreigners in Europe to invest in French sovereign debt during the brief existence of his empire.

The various Dutch cities, which benefited greatly from the flight of capital out of France as Law's decrees took effect against the use of silver or gold coins for payments (Van Dillen 1925) also had some speculative activity, most of which occurred in late 1720, after the failures of Law's *Système* in France and the collapse of the South Sea Company's share prices were evident. The Bank of Amsterdam, in particular, saw its supply of foreign coins, mainly from France, deposited in unprecedented quantities to open accounts denominated in the Bank's special unit of account, *schellingen banco*. Nevertheless, some new companies were proposed that survived the recoil from the collapse of the bubbles in Paris and London. Most noteworthy was the marine insurance company launched in Rotterdam, Stad Rotterdam, which survived until absorbed by Fortis just before the collapse of that company in 2008. A slave-trading company out of Middelburg also continued its sordid business through the eighteenth century (Frehen *et al.* 2013).

Most interesting for its longer-term consequences, however, was the lock-in effect for Dutch investors in the English securities. Not only did they retain their investments in the South Sea Company, both the shares and the annuities, they also increased significantly their holdings of Bank of England stock. Neal (1990) explains this as a rational move to ensure that the directors of the Bank would play a constructive role in the re-organization of the South Sea Company (Chapter 4), a view that was substantiated by later research (Carlos and Neal 2006). Indeed, one Dutch scholar argued that Dutch investors in the English stock market in 1720 marked the start of Dutch foreign investment, a process that was to continue thereafter with only a brutal break during the French occupation of the Netherlands after 1795 (Groeneveld 1940). In the interaction of Amsterdam and London – the two financial centers of Europe in the eighteenth century – we can see already the basis for the financial capitalism of the nineteenth century.

6 | The rise and spread of financial capitalism, 1720–1789

The century covered in these chapters starts with the aftermath of the collapses of the Mississippi and South Sea bubbles in 1720 and ends with the legacy of Napoleonic war finance in 1830. The financial innovations in France, England, and the Netherlands after 1720 had international repercussions that proved important for the outcomes of the successive wars and revolutions that followed, right up to the Treaty of Vienna in 1815. They also created a number of financial crises, all minor in comparison to the famous bubbles of 1720, but instructive in showing both the benefits and risks of the new financial architecture that was taking shape. In the background of the political and military events that shaped the history of the eighteenth century in Europe were the ever-growing influences of international finance that accompanied both expanding foreign trade and more expensive warfare among competing powers. At the heart of the financial developments was the emerging symbiosis of the two financial centers of Europe after 1720 – Amsterdam and London. The merchant bankers of the other trading cities of Europe were important participants as well, especially along the historic Lotharingian axis stretching from the Low Countries into the Mediterranean ports of Italy, while new centers of finance were emerging on the other side of the Atlantic.

From 1720 right through 1815, a "cosmopolitan bourgeoisie" emerged who regarded Europe as their base but the entire world as their theater of operation (Jones 1988). These individuals made the best of the chaotic times of political upheavals and ever-wider military conflicts by taking advantage of the new financial instruments that had appeared in the aftermath of the collapse of the Mississippi and South Sea bubbles. In their historic ascent, they expanded trade to cover the entire globe for the first time in history, but they financed it increasingly from the new financial centers of Amsterdam and London while the merchant bankers of France looked on in envy. The logistics required to supply the ever-larger armies and fleets that the British and French periodically launched at each other (see Box 6.1, p. 109) also created larger-scale opportunities for the cosmopolitan bourgeoisie to provide the necessary finance for their personal profit (Hancock 1995). The resulting network of warehouses, port facilities, and merchant ships that had been required for each war remained in place afterwards, ready to be re-deployed in the service of peaceful commerce and industry.

The political consequences of each war also required more attention to ways for governments to make "credible commitments" to their debtholders and taxpayers that their wartime sacrifices had not been in vain. The combination of political awareness and economic opportunity enabled by the new instruments of finance led eventually, for the first time, to "the birth of the modern," as Johnson (1991) proposed to name the period 1815–1830. This was also when modern economic growth began according to Kuznets (1966) and the Industrial Revolution took shape according to the consensus of economic historians now. The secular nation-states that arose as Europe re-organized politically and economically after 1815 also re-structured their fiscal and monetary regimes, albeit reluctantly and with misadventures that will be the focus of Chapters 6–8 (cf. Cardoso and Lains 2010).

The secret of success for international finance over the course of the century from 1720 to 1815 lay in the complementarity that arose, more or less accidentally, between the financial instruments of payment used for personal exchanges (the foreign bill of exchange) and the financial instruments of debt issued to meet impersonal obligations by governments (sovereign debt). Coordination of the multiple uses of the two financial instruments required sustained benign neglect by government authorities, however, something that did not come easily to rulers, then as now, and especially during wartime. The British and Dutch were most successful throughout the eighteenth century and it was the symbiosis of London and Amsterdam as financial centers of Europe that assured the successful complementarity of bills of exchange and sovereign bonds in the long run. For the British, success was essentially due to the mutual standoff between monarch and parliament that persisted after 1688. For the Dutch, who abstained from the European wars as much as possible after 1713, parliamentary rule and provincial competition within the Republic combined to keep public finance directed toward peaceful pursuits until 1795, when they fell under French domination. France attempted various expedients

to imitate aspects of the British and Dutch success after the collapse of
John Law's *Système* in 1720, but only arrived at the parliamentary
solution for committing to sovereign debt after 1815. Even then,
commitment was initiated while under occupation by Wellington's
victorious troops.

The financial symbiosis of Amsterdam and London, 1720–1810

With its success in withstanding the shock of the collapse of the South
Sea scheme in the autumn of 1720, the Bank of England quickly
outstripped the Bank of Amsterdam thereafter as a focal point for
the international payments system of Europe. Even before the expenses
of the War of the Spanish Succession had exhausted the fiscal capacity
of the province of Holland to pay most of the cost of Dutch wars
as it had in the last half of the seventeenth century, the Bank of
Amsterdam had made its deposits irredeemable in 1700. Thereafter,
deposits could only be cashed out by transferring them to another
depositor willing to acquire them for their usefulness in settling
accounts with other bank customers. Nevertheless, this enabled them
to retain full value for settlement of debts denominated in bank money
in the first place, thus protecting creditors in Amsterdam from the
possibilities of debasement or paper inflation. This was an advantage
for Dutch creditors, and international merchants dealing through
the port facilities of Amsterdam, but the growth of the Bank of
Amsterdam's deposits in the future was limited by the slower expansion of trade and capital flows directed through Amsterdam.
The growth of London measured in terms of both trade and capital
continued to outstrip that of Amsterdam through the rest of the
eighteenth century. While the population of Amsterdam stagnated,
barely rising from 200,000 in 1700 to 217,000 in 1800, that of
London continued to rise from 575,000 in 1700 to 865,000 in 1800
(De Vries 2006, pp. 270, 271).

Moreover, with the eventual recovery of the London capital market
from the collapse of the South Sea Company's scheme in 1720, the
financial relationships of Amsterdam and London changed permanently. London's Bank of England continued to expand its capital stock
and its private business with the merchant community of London and
Europe and it soon overtook the Bank of Amsterdam as a center for

the international payments system of Atlantic trade. Nevertheless, Dutch investors remained committed to their ventures in the London capital market. Such was the case for Simon Bevel, a longstanding investor in English securities, who after 1720 had his agents in London remit to him dividends on Bank stock instead of on the Exchequer annuities that he had held previously (Dickson 1967, pp. 334–335). Dickson further states:

One aspect of "real" Dutch ownership was that English securities were increasingly used by Amsterdamers as collateral for short term loans. The index of loans recorded in the Amsterdam Notarial Archives compiled by Professor Hamilton shows that up to about 1719 the collateral used was mostly Dutch government securities, but that after this English government securities were increasingly used, and by the mid 1720s predominated. These loans were nearly all for periods from three months to a year, and the lenders were members of solid patriciate families. (Dickson 1967, p. 335)

The depth and liquidity of the English securities market, increasingly dominated by government debt in the form of the perpetual redeemable annuities, provided the bank-centered financial system of the Netherlands with an excellent basis for laying off the risks of short-term commercial loans, a basis that their own capital market failed to provide despite the "first-mover advantage" they had enjoyed from the venture shares of the Dutch EIC for over a century.

For the next sixty years of the eighteenth century the two mercantile powers had a financial symbiosis in government finance, one that sustained commercial expansion while allowing the remarkable rise of British national debt. The business of *actionistes* in the Stock Exchange of Amsterdam, first described in cynical detail by Joseph de la Vega in 1688 and then in admiring detail by Isaac de Pinto nearly a century later in 1771, gradually evolved from an active trade in shares of the VOC to a much more active trade in the Three Per Cent Consols created by the British government in 1751. The root of this generally maligned and much misunderstood trade was two-fold: first, the very size of the capital stock available in the secondary market and the large number of shareholders with manifold motives for holding shares created a large customer base for the services of the stock dealers; second, both Dutch and English joint-stock shares could be pledged as collateral for loans of varying length. Creditors accepting shares as collateral for their loans in case of future default naturally sought to protect their position by buying a put option for future delivery of the shares at a price sufficient to maintain their value as collateral for the loan. Selling put options and offsetting the consequent risk by buying call options became the specialized business of stockjobbers.

The business of dealing in options on securities was well understood and actively practiced in both Amsterdam and London by the end of the seventeenth century. De la Vega described it in his *Confusion de Confusiones* in 1688 in terms of creating artificially smaller divisions of the shares of the VOC, termed *ducatons*, and de Pinto elaborated on the various strategies that options provided to the stock dealers in Amsterdam. He noted that a purchaser of £1,000 of the British Three Percent Consols for forward delivery in Amsterdam at the next *rescounter* (settling) date, had four possibilities when the contract came due:

> *First*, he could pay then the agreed sum of money and have the full amount inscribed in his name in the books maintained by the Bank of England.
>
> *Second*, if he anticipated a rise in the price, he could pay an *actioniste* a modest sum to prolong the settlement of the contract another three or more months.
>
> *Third*, he could sell the contract to another individual and pocket the difference in price if the price of the Consol had risen in the meantime.
>
> *Fourth*, he could pledge the £1,000 Consol he had committed to purchase as collateral for a loan of cash to be used for another venture. (De Pinto 1771, p. 299)

Pledging a security not yet paid for as collateral for a loan (re-hypothecation as it is called today) was something that could not be done with French *rentes*, as de Pinto lamented. He considered this legal restriction on French government securities to be a fatal flaw for French finances. As discussed below, it had become illegal as well for British subjects in 1733, but they could take advantage of the Amsterdam facilities to avoid the costs of this restriction for them. And the British government could avoid as well the loss of access to war finance implied by restrictions on derivative contracts in Britain by allowing their financiers to use the escape valve of re-hypothecation provided by the Dutch stockjobbers.

While war finance was the source of the continued growth of the stock exchange business and the prosperity and number of its

professional middlemen, whether in London or Amsterdam, the inter-
ludes of peace during the eighteenth century allowed commerce among
the Europeans to flourish. The outbreak of war between revolutionary
France and the monarchies of Europe in 1793 disrupted the basis of
trade credit in foreign bills of exchange until peace was finally restored
in 1815. Until then, however, the increased negotiability of foreign bills
of exchange drawn on either Amsterdam or London allowed multilateral settlement of trade balances to occur in place of the previous
system of bilateral settlements. This meant that persistent payments
deficits by one part of Europe against another – for example, the
persistent deficit of England with the Baltic – could be settled by
surpluses earned in another part of Europe – for example, the English
re-export of sugar and tobacco produced in its American colonies to
Continental Europe.

    Multilateral settlement of differences in merchant accounts had
long been recognized as a more efficient way of organizing payments
systems. But in previous centuries, access to these giro services in
Barcelona, Florence, Venice, Genoa, or Lyon was limited to local
citizens and selected foreign merchants. Initiatives to encourage
trade through Antwerp and then Amsterdam broadened access to
the exchange banks there to include anyone willing to make a deposit
in silver or gold, coin, or bullion. Every increase in use of these
services by merchants from any part of Europe increased the potential
for trade as well. The result was to provide the basis for continual
improvements in the extent of the market within Europe for all
goods produced anywhere in the world. By 1720, manuals produced
for the benefit of European merchants instructed them on the
methods of drawing and paying bills of exchange throughout
Europe (Justice 1707).

    The network graphed in Figure 6.1 demonstrates the mercantile
connections among the major cities of western Europe in the eighteenth
century. Their intensity is indicated by the number of cities whose
exchange rates were listed in the commercial bulletins published in
each city, usually monthly, but at least semi-weekly in the case of both
Amsterdam and London. The relative importance of each city's merchants for financing intra-European trade is shown by the size of the
circles for each city. By 1720, the intensity of European trade had
clearly shifted to the north Atlantic port cities – Amsterdam, London,
Paris, and Hamburg – and away from the Mediterranean and Italian

Network (indegrees)

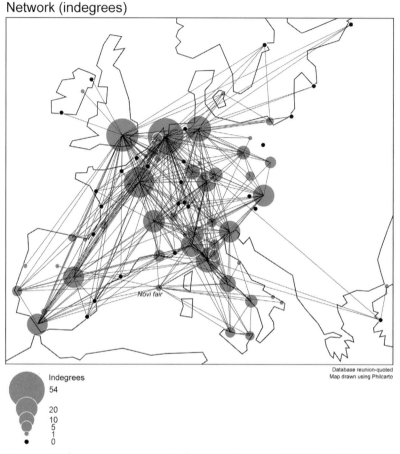

Indegrees
54

20
10
5
1
0

Figure 6.1 The payments network of western Europe, c.1720 (from Flandreau *et al.* 2009b, Figure 7, p. 161)

city-states. Tracing out the lines connecting each pair of cities, however, reveals that the Lotharingian axis was still present, thanks to the continued financial institutions of the Italian city-states, now joined by the Swiss cities of Geneva and Zurich.

Sugar, dye-woods, and tobacco from the Atlantic trades were bulk goods in heavy demand throughout Europe, adding to the already rising demand for pepper and other spices from Asia in addition to the continued demand for salt. The distribution channels created by the competing East Indies companies of the Dutch, English, French, Danes, and Austrians continued to expand into the rest of Europe over the rest of the eighteenth century, albeit with disruptions and dislocations during the various wars. Despite the increasing demands of war finance, however, commercial credit continued to be available at low interest rates. The self-regulating beneficence of the resulting system of international payments by bills of exchange within Europe and between Europe and the various mercantile outposts established by Europeans overseas was described and extolled by Isaac Gervaise in 1720 and elaborated by Abbé Condillac and Adam Smith, both in 1776.

The work of Flandreau *et al.* (2009a, 2009b) demonstrates that commercial credit was available to merchants with contacts in Amsterdam at rates from 3 to 4 percent annually throughout the period 1688 to 1789, despite the increasing presence of state finance throughout Europe. There were occasional spikes created by the uncertainties of war, especially at moments when the outcome of a lengthy war was uncertain. But because the increased debt issued by Britain (3 percent Consols) and Holland (bearer obligations) consisted of negotiable instruments easily transferred among merchants, war finance simply increased the possible means for settling their accounts with each other, regardless of nationality. Throughout the eighteenth century, London merchants enjoyed interest rates only slightly higher than in Amsterdam while Paris merchants had to endure higher rates, but still below those paid by merchants in Italy and Spain.

Figure 6.2 shows the varying course of short-term interest rates paid by merchants operating out of the main payments centers of Amsterdam, London, and Paris from 1723 to 1789. These are five-year moving averages of short-term interest rates converted to annual percentage as laboriously calculated by Marc Flandreau's team of graduate assistants from the various "price currents" that were printed up and distributed regularly to merchants both local and abroad in the three cities (Flandreau *et al.* 2009a). All sorts of interesting conclusions can be drawn from the resulting graph, but the most obvious is that the 5 percent usury limit on annual interest charged to individual borrowers, reduced from 6 percent by British statute in 1714, was never a binding constraint on British merchants actively engaged in the rapidly expanding commercial trade of Europe in the eighteenth century. True, in times of war when the financing needs of the British and French governments pressed hardest, interest rates rose, but never to the 5 percent usury limit until the end of the century. Then, Flandreau *et al.* argue, American independence and the trade readjustments that

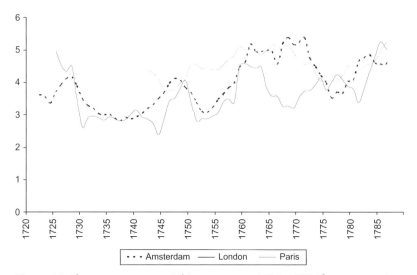

Figure 6.2 Short-term commercial interest rates, 1723–1789 (five-year moving averages of annual percentages) (from Flandreau *et al.* 2009a, Figure 6.5, p. 190)

followed induced a general tightness of European mercantile credit, a stringency not confined to Paris on the eve of the French Revolution.

The other striking feature is the lower interest rates for merchants in London compared even with Amsterdam after the collapse of the South Sea bubble, a phenomenon that persisted throughout the eighteenth century until the American war for independence. The infamous Fourth Anglo-Dutch War in 1780–1784, when British warships shelled Amsterdam with impunity, however, quickly reversed the situation. Rates remained higher in Paris than in either Amsterdam or London and were much more stable, for reasons that are not clear. The further analysis performed by Flandreau *et al.* to compare the seasonality of these commercial interest rates suggests to them that the efforts to finance the movement of crops throughout France into the main consumption center in Paris were less efficient than those that had been perfected by British and Dutch merchants by the beginning of the eighteenth century.

Flandreau *et al.* further suggest that the financial revolution touted by Dickson (1967) and extolled by North and Weingast (1989) as a reflection of the Glorious Revolution of 1688–1689 was really the imitation by the English monarchy of the way that rulers in the Dutch

Republic and the Italian city-states earlier had tapped into the pre-existing web of international commercial credit in western Europe. The interesting puzzle is how the British managed to do this without disrupting the private circuits of commercial finance as had been done in earlier centuries by the French monarchs and then the Spanish monarchs (as discussed in Chapter 4).

Impact of war finance, 1689–1815

The main effect of the wars of the eighteenth century (Box 6.1) on the financial systems of Europe was to demonstrate the surprising usefulness of the capital market for British government debt in peace-time as well as in war. As a result, Britain's national debt continued to expand with each war from 1700 through 1815 (Figure 6.3). Finance of the War of the Austrian Succession (1738–1742 for Great Britain) was done by issuing directly to the public the equivalent of the South Sea Annuities, now made perpetual and carrying a nominal 3 percent annual interest. The transfer books and stock ledgers for these issues were maintained by the Bank of England, which became necessarily a prime location for trading in the British funds. Thomas Mortimer's classic primer, *Every Man his Own Broker* (1761), argued in fact, that the transfer of ownership in any of the various public securities was so transparent that any one could do it on their own, without bothering to contact a self-styled broker.

Box 6.1 West European wars of the long eighteenth century, 1688–1815

War of League of Augsburg (also Nine Years War), (1688–1697)
First Jacobite Rising (1689–1692)
Great Northern War (1700–1721)
War of the Spanish Succession (1701–1714)
War of the Quadruple Alliance (1718–1720)
Anglo-Spanish War (1727–1729)
War of Jenkins' Ear (1739–1748)
War of the Austrian Succession (1740–1748)
Seven Years War (1756–1763)
War of American Independence (1775–1783)
Fourth Anglo-Dutch War (1780–1784)
French Revolutionary Wars (1792–1802)
Napoleonic Wars (1803–1815)

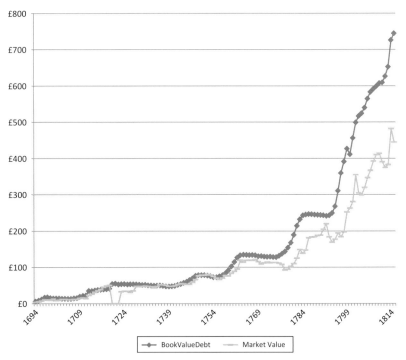

Figure 6.3 British national debt, 1694–1815 (million pounds sterling, current) (from Mitchell 1988, book value and Castaing 1698–1908, end of year market value)

The most enduring, and ultimately most controversial, piece of legislation to arise in the eighteenth century was Barnard's Act (7 Geo. II, cap. 8). The act was intended to eliminate time bargains in public securities altogether, the legislators thinking this would remove sudden movements in the prices of the various forms of government debt by eliminating the pernicious business of stockjobbing. Parliament passed the act originally in 1733 for a period of three years to see what effect it might have, and then made it permanent in 1736 after it appeared that the limited number of securities available had not suffered any adverse effects from the act. Even when the government began issuing its 3 percent annuities to finance the War of the Austrian Succession, no effort was made to repeal or even amend Barnard's Act.

The effect of Barnard's Act when the necessities of war finance arose a few years later with the War of the Austrian Succession was two-fold.

On one account, it gave a great deal of business to Dutch brokers, who only did business on time, and for quarterly accounts – February, May, August, and November. Isaac de Pinto (1771) asserted that Britain's success in raising war finance for the War of the Spanish Succession, the War of the Austrian Succession, and the Seven Years War was due to the ability of stockjobbers in London to sell their commitments to brokers in Amsterdam. The separation of broker and jobber functions, according to de Pinto, put brokers in London and jobbers in Amsterdam. De Pinto argued that Dutch stockjobbing in British annuities (namely Three Percent Consols) became essential and necessary for the British government because the latter borrowed increasingly large sums to wage each successive war in the eighteenth century. After borrowing 3 million in sterling to finance the War of the Austrian Succession, the British government borrowed at first 6, then 8, and finally 12 million pounds sterling as the expenses of the Seven Years War (1756–1763) mounted. The activity of stockjobbers, or *"actionistes"* in Amsterdam, he was convinced, enabled Britain to float these enormous sums at reasonable prices (see Figures 6.4a, 6.4b, Consols), while the huge quantity of tradable securities available to investors provided continued livelihood to the Amsterdam stock dealers. De Pinto, according to Wilson (1941, p. 160), was on the payroll of the English EIC and the scion of a family long associated with investments in English securities, as well as a major shareholder in both the Dutch EIC and Dutch WICs. He had advised the British delegation in Paris during their negotiations over ending the Seven Years War, so his testimony carries the authority of a well-established and experienced participant in the financial markets of both London and Amsterdam.

Dickson accepted de Pinto's argument and noted that some time in the 1740s the London stockjobbers had regular settlement dates for their accounts quarterly: on the fifteenth of the months of February, May, August, and November. These were the same days as the Dutch *rescounters*, but in fact occurred eleven days later until 1752, when Britain adopted the Gregorian calendar. This allowed settlements of the Dutch affairs in London to be drawn up and posted by the first mail packet to Amsterdam in time for the Dutch *rescounters*. Dickson concluded that Barnard's Act did push time bargains from London to Amsterdam, but had the unintended consequence of channeling London speculators into dealing on margins,

Figure 6.4a Prices of the British "funds," 1721–1763 (from Castaing 1698–1908)

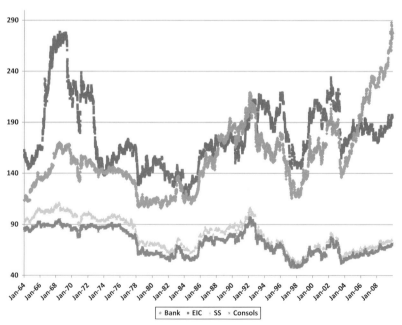

Figure 6.4b Prices of the British "funds," 1764–1809 (from Castaing 1698–1908)

"where the penalties on the broker were less severe, and harder to enforce" (Dickson 1967, p. 508)

For most historians (e.g., Wilson 1941), however, Barnard's act simply forced the group of London jobbers, whether they had business connections in Amsterdam or not, to deal only with each other in London, knowing that it was in neither party's advantage to report the other to the authorities. The reward for reporting a violation of the act to the authorities was only £500 and had to be split with the government. Whichever way the traders in London responded to Barnard's Act and the temptation of large new issues of prime government debt during the 1740s, 1750s, and 1760s, it is clear that their connections with Amsterdam were strengthened substantially. If Barnard's Act had little effect in practice on the London stockbrokers, then the rising interest of Amsterdam stockbrokers in English securities came from the demand of their Dutch customers for remunerative placements of their capital, not from displacement of stock exchange business in derivatives to Amsterdam. But whenever the London stockbrokers tried to organize more formally, the restrictions imposed by Barnard's Act and other statutory restraints on securities trading became binding (Neal 2011a). The testimony of de Pinto about the importance of Amsterdam's well-developed derivatives market with its experienced professionals for the initial placement of large blocks of British government debt cannot be dismissed.

The symbiosis of British war finance and trade finance

De Pinto and his peers dealing in the financial market of Amsterdam had already found other ways to benefit from British war finance by the end of the Nine Years War fought by William III against Louis XIV. They made full use of the well-established market for foreign bills of exchange routed through the giro facilities of the Bank of Amsterdam to finance British war efforts on the Continent, starting with the War of the Spanish Succession in 1701. William III raised money quickly at the outset of the hostilities by issuing new short-term sovereign debt in the form of Exchequer, Navy, and Victualling bills. These short-term government bills were used to purchase bills of exchange drawn by merchant bankers in London on their correspondents in Amsterdam. Once a bill was accepted in Amsterdam by the merchant banker, the Quartermaster of British forces used it to

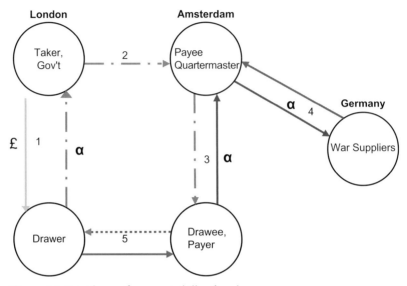

Figure 6.5 British war finance via bills of exchange

purchase in Amsterdam whatever the armies needed to wage war on
the Continent, whether it was supplies to Marlborough during the War
of the Spanish Succession or subsidies to Frederick the Great during the
Seven Years War. (This proved to be a very lucrative business for James
Brydges, the British Quartermaster during the War of the Spanish
Succession, as he became the Duke of Chandos and the wealthiest
man in Britain by the time of the South Sea bubble.)

When the extinguished bill was sent back to the London merchant
banker who had drawn it in the first place, it was typically used to
finance imports of consumer goods that were in high demand from
Britain into Amsterdam or other ports in Europe. Figure 6.5, adapted
from the bill of exchange diagrams in Chapter 4, depicts how this
process, first perfected during the War of the Spanish Succession,
ended up with Britain exporting consumer goods of all kinds to Europe
instead of soldiers to fight its wars on the Continent. Later, Adam
Smith referred to this as the process of transforming English woolens
into Hessian mercenaries, referring to the way George II and George III
raised troops in Germany during the Seven Years War.

Figure 6.5 compresses stage 3, which would take at least one to two
months between initial acceptance by the merchant banker in Amsterdam and final payout of the sum indicated to whomever ended up

holding the bill when it expired. In the meantime, the bill could be endorsed multiple times and used to pay for any number of goods and services provided by the markets of Amsterdam. Further, final payment would be made into the quartermaster's account with the Bank of Amsterdam, which would become very active during wartime. Each successive holder of the accepted and then endorsed bill would take it at a nominal discount from the amount stated to be paid at maturity by the drawee, earning a market rate of interest on the bill before cashing it in or passing it on.

Financial engineering takes off, financial crisis ensues, 1760–1763

Later, during the massive expenditures undertaken by both the British and French army and naval forces as well as by the German and Russian armies during the Seven Years War the mass of bills circulating through Amsterdam became enormous. The bills were typically written in relatively small amounts to improve their acceptability, which increased their number but also opened opportunities for merchant bankers at major ports to increase their earnings from dealing in them. They could anticipate potential earnings of commissions and interest payments by initiating acceptances ahead of actual deliveries of either consumer goods or military supplies. A merchant in Berlin, for example, eager to supply Frederick the Great with needed supplies from the Baltic granaries, North Sea fisheries, or Swedish smelters, could engage a merchant banker in Hamburg to draw a bill of exchange on his usual merchant banker correspondent in Amsterdam. When the bill was returned as accepted by the Amsterdam banker to Hamburg, the merchant banker sold it at a small commission to the Berlin merchant, while also endorsing it to add his liability for final payment to that already assumed by the Amsterdam banker. The Berlin merchant could then endorse it and send it to his suppliers in the Baltic or wherever, and they would readily endorse it on for eventual return to Amsterdam where it could be held or passed along until it matured in two to two-and-a-half months typically. The acceptance business thus created another early example of financial engineering, one that certainly helped Frederick the Great to prevail despite heavy losses initially during the Seven Years War and Britain ultimately to prevail over France in both the Americas and the Indies despite

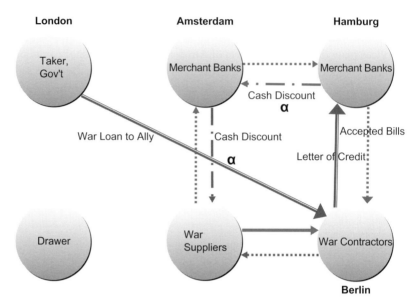

Figure 6.6 Acceptance bills from Amsterdam, through Hamburg to Berlin

initial setbacks. In the scenario depicted in Figure 6.6, a Berlin merchant such as Johann Ernst Gotzkowsky, eager to supply Frederick the Great's army with supplies at premium prices, commissions a merchant banker in Hamburg such as Johann Berenberg to use his connections in Amsterdam to get an accepted bill of exchange drawn on the merchant banker there. The Amsterdam banker does so for a small commission and the bill is passed back to Berlin, where Gotzkowsky uses it to pay for supplies ultimately coming from Amsterdam. The eventual holder in Amsterdam then turns it in upon expiration to get bank money credited to his/her account at the Bank of Amsterdam.

Meanwhile, if all has gone well for Gotzkowsky in Berlin, he has received ample payment from Frederick's quartermaster, paid the Hamburg merchant banker for the bill, and the Hamburg banker has paid off the Amsterdam banker before the bill has come due for him. Everybody is happy as long as the war goes on and Frederick's army wins battles. Indeed, when each acceptance bill comes due it can be replaced by a new bill, which will generate additional commissions and keep interest payments flowing through the system. Note, however, that the amount of actual cash flowing through the system is just the final amount of the bill when it is paid off, and even then it is just a

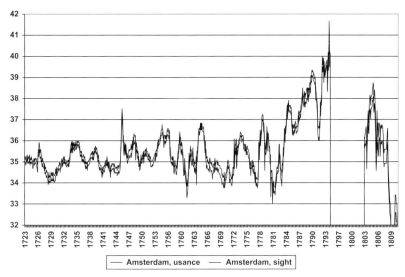

Figure 6.7 London exchange rates on Amsterdam, 1723–1810 (from Castaing 1698–1908)

transfer from one account in the Bank of Amsterdam to another. While the bill was outstanding, however, the contingent liability of all four parties involved in the process rose, meaning that leverage, the ratio of outstanding debt to actual cash assets in the system, also rose.

Any disturbance to the flow of goods through the logistical system set up to provide continuous supplies to the belligerent forces, however, would create a blockage in the circuits of short-term commercial finance. The time (two to two-ands-a-half months' usance) and spot (sight within three business days) exchange rates of bills of exchange drawn in London on Amsterdam were printed semi-weekly in Castaing's *The Course of the Exchange* from 1723 to 1811. Figure 6.7 shows that rates varied considerably in response to market demands for short-term finance throughout the eighteenth century, only occasionally breaking out of the band of 34–37 *schellingen banco* per pound sterling around the mint par of 35.5 *schellingen banco*, until the disruptions caused by the American War of Independence, followed by the Fourth Anglo-Dutch War led up to the massive disruptions caused by the French Revolutionary and Napoleonic Wars.

The larger and short-lived fluctuations in the rates reflect disruptions in credit flows more than changes in trade patterns, as identified by Ashton (1959). Even as late as the eve of the First World War in the summer of 1914, a break in payments routines for expiring bills of exchange would lead to a scramble for liquidity by merchants and increased demand for bills of exchange. If the scramble was in London, the price of bills of exchange was driven up and the market price for the pound rose. But if it was in Amsterdam, the market price for *schellingen* would rise and the pound fall. So peaks in the price of pound sterling in Figure 6.7 show a crisis in London and valleys a crisis in Amsterdam. Further, if the gap between the time price of foreign exchange and the spot price widens, the intensity of the crisis can be measured as well. The first mark of a scramble for liquidity in London, the sudden, but short-lived, spike in the price of the pound sterling, I called "the Ashton effect" (Neal 1990, p. 67). Sometimes a reaction followed quickly to produce an offsetting spike in the price of *schellingen banco* as merchants in Amsterdam scrambled for liquidity in response to the difficulties in London, and this I termed "the Kindleberger effect," as it was a clear marker of contagion for the crisis (Neal 1990, p. 67).

The standard stories of financial crises in eighteenth-century Europe show up clearly in the graph of London–Amsterdam exchange rates, as well as the occasional disruptions caused by news reaching Amsterdam or London of the outbreak of war, the result of particular battles, or the cessation of hostilities. So peaks in the price of pounds sterling drawn on Amsterdam in London occurred when short-term finance for trade was tight and interest rates high. The liquidity shocks also had marked effects on the prices of the English "funds," embodied in the share prices of the Bank of England, the EIC, the South Sea Company, and, after 1752, the Three Percent Consols. The interaction of these financial markets, one for long-term credit and collateral and the other for short-term commercial credit, can be seen in each crisis. The rise of the Amsterdam currency in 1725, for example, was a response to the final liquidation of the Law System in Paris and the devaluation of the *livre tournois*. The peak in London's currency in 1745 was due to the Jacobite rebellion in Scotland. A brief panic in London occurred in 1761 according to Ashton, but the follow-on effect was most severe in Amsterdam, as indicated by the exchange rates in Figure 6.7. But the increasing pressures on the Anglo-Dutch connection, and therefore on the entire European system of international finance, showed up most clearly in the financial crisis of 1763 at the end of the Seven Years War, which affected Amsterdam, Hamburg, London, and Paris. Thereafter, events of wars and revolutions with the economic and political

Box 6.2 West European financial crises of the eighteenth century, 1688–1789

1708–1710	London	Financing War of Spanish Succession
1709	Paris	Plague, famine, bank failures
1715	Paris	Standstill on French debt
1720	Paris, London, Amsterdam	Mississippi, South Sea, Dutch bubbles
1725	Paris	Liquidation of John Law's *Système*
1745	London, Amsterdam	Jacobite rebellion, War of Austrian Succession
1761	London	EIC speculation
1763	London, Amsterdam, Hamburg, Berlin	End of Seven Years War
1772	Scotland, London, Amsterdam	EIC speculation
1783	Paris, Amsterdam	End of American War
1788	Paris	Partial default on French debt

disruptions that ensued continued to shock the international financial system (Box 6.2). But it is worth looking at the event of 1763 in more detail, as not only the international connections of finance were laid bare during the crisis, but also the interactions of government regulations, markets for long-term sovereign bonds, and the money markets dealing in short-term commercial credit as the crisis unfolded. So the basic theme of Chapter 1, that coordination of government regulation, securities markets, and money markets is difficult, and easily undone by innovations or shocks in any one part of the troika of a functioning financial system, were nicely illustrated in the eighteenth century by the crisis of 1763.

The crisis of 1763

When the results of the Battle of Plassey (June 23, 1757) became known in Amsterdam and London, the price of the English EIC stock shot up spectacularly (Figure 6.4a). As some Dutch houses, notably the recently created firm of Gebroeders de Neufville, had sold English EIC stock short on the expectation that the French forces would prevail in India, a liquidity crisis unfolded. This affected a large number of firms throughout the Netherlands, Britain, and Germany, given the expansion of acceptance credit that had arisen with the improved fortunes of war for Frederick the Great. For a time, it even led to serious consideration of establishing a jointly funded insurance fund in Amsterdam to act as a lender of last resort for the participating merchant banks. As it became clear that the focus of the problem was the single firm of Neufville, however, the proposal was abandoned and the Dutch firms focused on working out their claims on Neufville, which eventually paid out 60 percent of its debts to the various creditors. Having successfully quarantined the toxic assets created by the Neufville firm, the remaining Dutch merchant bankers then resumed their profitable business in the expanded trade throughout Europe that ensued (Wilson 1941, Chapter 6).

Recent work on the 1763 crisis, however, highlights the international repercussions of the Neufville failure, while demonstrating the complexity of international finance on the European continent during the Seven Years War as well as the financial innovations that war finance stimulated for expanding the finance of trade afterwards (Schnabel and Shin 2010; Quinn and Roberds 2012). Further, the resolution of the 1763 crisis also helps explain the subsequent rise of London overtaking Amsterdam as a financial center thereafter.

When hostilities in Europe ceased in early 1763, Frederick decided to restore the pre-war value of the Prussian *thaler*, mainly to restore the value of his traditional tax revenues set in terms of the *thaler*. The re-valuation of the Prussian currency, however, meant that prices of supplies stocked up to meet wartime demands then fell sharply. That meant re-financing of existing commercial obligations became very difficult for all the merchants concerned, going back from Berlin to Hamburg to Amsterdam, and then to London. To put some names to the chief players in the resulting financial crisis, the leading textile manufacturer and army supplier in Berlin was Johann Ernst Gotzkowsky, who had committed large sums to buy the Russian grain supplies left by the retreat of the Russian army upon the death of their Empress Elizabeth. The bank he used in Hamburg was possibly Gebruders Berenberg, now acclaimed as the world's oldest private merchant bank, whose records still exist. The leading Amsterdam merchant banker who had accepted bills drawn by Gotzkowsky through the intermediation of Hamburg merchant bankers was, of course, Gebroeders de Neufville.

Neufville, along with several lesser houses in Amsterdam, declared bankruptcy at the end of July 1763. A series of Hamburg bankruptcies followed two weeks later, and Berlin bankruptcies would have followed in August, led by Gotzkowsky's obvious difficulties. Frederick, however, intervened to avert wider failures in Berlin by declaring a three-month moratorium on all outstanding commercial bills. This arbitrary exercise of sovereign judicial power staved off the economic effects of the general financial crisis for Prussia, but with long-run consequences that proved damaging to the Prussian economy. Gotzkowsky had to give up his huge collection of paintings, originally acquired during the height of his war profiteering, to pay the Russians for the grain stores he had committed to purchase. This collection laid the basis for the future Catherine the Great to expand the Hermitage's art treasures, but Gotzkowsky nevertheless had to declare bankruptcy in 1767.

Meanwhile, the giro banks in Hamburg and Amsterdam attempted to aid their leading merchant banks by lending short-term on the basis of deposits of silver coin or bullion. In Hamburg, the leading merchant bank of Paul & Johann Berenberg had to increase its borrowings from 58,400 *marks banco* in 1762 to 140,600 in 1763, before reducing it to more sustainable level of 75,900 in 1764 (Schramm 1949, p. 159). While this bank recovered, 95 other firms declared bankruptcy as the resources of the Hamburg *Wechselbank* were overwhelmed (Henderson 1962, p. 97). In Berlin, bankruptcies were averted in 1763 by the arbitrary suspension by Frederick the Great of commercial laws governing bills of exchange. But Berlin's special bankruptcy court set up in 1763 had to deal with mounting numbers of failure for several years after, much to Frederick's disgust (Henderson 1962, pp. 101–102). While the attempts in Hamburg proved inadequate, the intervention by the Bank of Amsterdam proved quite effective, according to the research of Quinn and Roberds (2012).

The leading merchant banks in Amsterdam – Hope & Co., Andries Pels & Zoonen, George Clifford & Zoonen, Vernede & Compagnie, de Smeth, Horneca Hugguer, and Cazenove, in addition to Gebroeders de Neufville – all used their access to the resources of the Bank of Amsterdam to cover payments on the outstanding bills they had already accepted. Initially, they deposited silver coins for short-term loans to be credited to their accounts, as silver coins were the only collateral on which the Bank was allowed to extend fresh bank money, and then only temporarily as the merchant had to buy back the coins at the end of the three-month loan. A shortage of coins ensued on the Amsterdam market, which elicited huge imports of silver bullion to be minted in Holland, as well as imports of coins (mainly Spanish) from London. De Pinto reported that Dutch merchants sold their British debt in London to purchase the silver (De Pinto 1771, pp. 19–20) in 1763.[1]

Figure 6.8 plots the semi-weekly exchange rates of London on Amsterdam (at two to two-and-a-half months' usance and at sight), Hamburg (two months' usance), and Paris (sight and usance). The usance rates in Amsterdam are consistently above the sight rates and the gap widens sharply in August and September 1763, reflecting the stringency in short-term finance that existed on the Amsterdam market. By October, however, the combined measures of the Bank of England, releasing vast stocks of silver coin, and the Bank of Amsterdam, lending on the deposit of silver coins brought in by the major investment banks, had restored the normal gap, reflecting a low rate of interest. The overall effect of the successful conclusion of the war from the British side shows up in the marked rise of the pound on both Amsterdam and Hamburg over the last six months of 1763. Meanwhile, the pound steadily strengthened on Paris from mid April on, again showing how the fortunes of war showed up in the mercantile relations of the leading maritime powers.

The Dutch response to the crisis, shown in Figure 6.9, was to allow the Bank of Amsterdam temporarily to accept bullion in addition to coins as collateral for repo loans. This access to temporary liquidity by the Bank was a new facility and was used only sparingly over the course of the crisis in Amsterdam (Quinn and Roberds 2012). Nevertheless, it proved effective in keeping the leading investment banks in business. Figure 6.9 shows that the influx of coin was sufficient to keep up the

---

[1] "En 1763 il y eut un si grand discredit à la Bourse d'Amsterdam, que les négociants les plus riches n'avoient pas le moyen de se prevaloir sur aucune place, pour faire face à leurs affaires; la vente de leurs fonds en Angleterre leur fut d'un grand secours. Ce moyen fut trouvé le plus prompt & le plus facile pour avoir de fortes sommes en especes; car le provenu de ces annuities fut envoyé en or & en argent. La bourse d'Angleterre vend pareillement souvent pour de grandes sommes d'annuitiés aux Hollandois." (De Pinto 1771, pp. 19–20.)

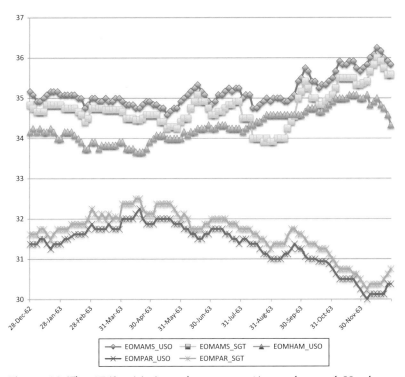

Figure 6.8 The 1763 crisis in exchange rates (Amsterdam and Hamburg, *schellingen banco*/pound sterling; Paris, pence/*écu* = 3 *livres tournois*) (from Castaing 1698–1908)

re-financing of bills of exchange until the end of July, when de Neufville was formally declared bankrupt. The influx of bullion helped marginally toward the end of the crisis, but did allow coins to be re-possessed by the bankers as the crisis abated. Presumably, this helped them meet the high demand for short-term credit that became evident in the market for bills of exchange drawn from London, as shown in Figure 6.8.

This period was also when the Bank of England saw the huge supply of silver it had acquired in the closing years of the Seven Years War disappear. Adam Smith even asserted that he had heard that the Bank indeed advanced "in one week, about £1,600,00; a great part of it in bullion. I do not, however, pretend to warrant either the greatness of the sum, or the shortness of the time" (Smith 1776, I, p. 303). Clapham could not verify this story in writing his history of the Bank, but did

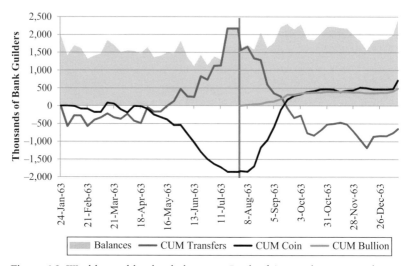

Figure 6.9 Weekly total banker balances at Bank of Amsterdam, 1763, showing accumulation by channel; CUM refers to the cumulated amounts from week to week (from Quinn and Roberds 2012, p. 28)

find a sharp reduction in the Bank's note circulation in 1763, which gave some credence to the story. Certainly, there was a temporary drop in the prices of the Consols (as shown in Figure 6.4a, p. 112). Clapham noted that "Consols fell from 96 to 82 in nine months and Bank stock … from 131 to 110" (Clapham 1945a, 1, p. 239), which also tended to confirm both the hearsay of Smith and the assertion of de Pinto. The superior flexibility of the British financial system over that of the Dutch was becoming evident.

Pressures on the Anglo-Dutch connection

A series of disruptions to the financial ties between London and Amsterdam ensued shortly after de Pinto's work was published in 1771. Revolutions, first in North America and then in France, strained the political ties between the UK and the United Provinces, and ultimately their financial ties as well. In the continued historical debate over the timing and causes of the relative decline of Amsterdam to London, it is clear that the expenses of the War of the Spanish Succession (1702–1714) had finally removed the Netherlands from further active participation in the great power politics of Europe. Thereafter, despite the strategic interests of Holland and Zeeland, which required open access to the high seas to maintain the prosperity of their long-distance merchants, the Netherlands maintained neutrality in the remaining wars of the eighteenth century. The long Anglo-Dutch connection came to a bitter end, however, either with the Fourth Anglo-Dutch War (1780–1784) according to Wilson (1941), or with the Batavian Republic created under French revolutionary pressure in 1795 according to Neal (1990), or with the incorporation of the Kingdom of Holland into the French Empire by Napoleon in 1810 according to Riley (1980).

During the previous wars of the eighteenth century, however, both Dutch and British stockjobbers could count on similar effects on the prices of their holdings of British sovereign debt. The threat of war generally caused a temporary fall in all British "funds," as in 1728, and actual war created sharper and longer falls in government debt prices, as in 1740 (War of the Austrian Succession) and again in 1756 (Seven Years War). When peace negotiations signaled the end of the war, however, prices would rebound. The certainty of an initial fall in price of British securities and an ultimate rise upon a successful conclusion of the war created obvious incentives for Dutch financiers to buy up British securities at the outset of a war and then sell them off at the conclusion.

As analyzed by Riley (1980), however, Dutch investors after the disruptions of the Seven Years War began to look for more attractive returns elsewhere. First they issued government loans to Austria and the neighboring states of Denmark and Sweden. They then moved beyond to Russia, Poland, Spain, and even to France, but especially the newly created United States of America (Riley 1980, Chapters 6 and 7). These individual loans were managed primarily by a leading merchant bank in Amsterdam, with each country's loans being the primary responsibility of a single house, whose reputation was the key to the marketability of the country's debt to Dutch investors. This initiated a process of merchant banking that eventually became the model for the British success in foreign lending, led by the Barings and Rothschilds in the nineteenth century.

The subsequent financial crisis in 1772 was more serious that even 1763 as it ended with the failure of Clifford & Sons, long one of the leading merchant banks in Amsterdam in their role as agents for the English EIC. Further, it was initiated from another peripheral banking firm, this time in Scotland, and, once again, as a result of a highly leveraged bet on the price of EIC stock going wrong. Alexander Fordyce had borrowed from his partners in the bank of Neale, James, Fordyce & Down to bet on a fall in the price of EIC stock, presumably because of the charge placed on the company to pay for escorts of Royal Navy warships. Somehow, Fordyce had also inveigled large acceptance bills from the Ayr Bank of Edinburgh, a new bank that from its creation in 1769 to 1772 had supplied 25 percent of the notes in circulation by Scottish banks, 25 percent of total deposits, and 40 percent of total Scottish bank assets, making it larger than the Bank of Scotland and the Royal Bank of Scotland combined. Fordyce's failure to repay his loans from the Ayr Bank led to their failure and pressure on London banks, forcing them to stop rolling over credits to their correspondents in Amsterdam, including the firm of Clifford & Sons (Rockoff 2009). As the main banking house for the EIC in Amsterdam, Clifford & Sons, which had been trying to keep up the price of India stock, owed such large debts to the banking community of Amsterdam and London that the mutual lending bank (*Stads-Beleeningkamer*) first proposed in 1763 was actually established at this time in Amsterdam.

The *Stads-Beleeningkamer* served its purpose well in supplementing the efforts of the Bank of Amsterdam to keep up the market for commercial credit by extending credit with municipal support to established banking houses on the basis of commodities and domestic debt as collateral. As in the crisis of 1763, however, the source of the systemic failure was quickly identified to be the one firm, and its creditors in London actually came to its rescue, while taking over its subsequent business. Accordingly, the nascent lender of last resort in the form of a mutual insurance fund among the leading merchant banks in Amsterdam was wound up in 1773. When the Fourth Anglo-Dutch War broke out in 1780, however, Amsterdam bankers were truly faced with a systemic crisis that was not focused on any particular banking house. The *Stads-Beleeningkamer* was resurrected and left in place, albeit not with enough funding to serve truly as a lender of last resort during the turmoil of the following decades.

Wider repercussions of the Seven Years War

The technique of war finance developed by the British after 1688, combined with William Pitt's implementation of the "blue water" naval strategy, worked well for the British forces and their allies during the Seven Years War on the continent. The successes of the British forces in India, however, and then in the wildernesses of North America, however, owed their success to quite different elements. Clive's success in India, following his decisive victory at the Battle of Plassey in 1757, came from immediate tribute from the Nawab of Bengal and then from the EIC continuing to collect the traditional taxes on Bengali peasants that had sustained the Nawab's luxurious life-style. The resulting fiscal regime simply replaced the traditional practice of Mughal emperors with more efficient administration by the EIC's clerks (Parthasarathi 2011). Eventually, the British government at home was able to collect in its turn an annual tribute of £10,000,000 (Neal 1990). In North America, by contrast, the pivot of British success was Wolfe's capture of Quebec City in September 1759, with British troops, rather than Hessian mercenaries or American colonial forces. Neutralizing the Indian tribes allied with the French south of the Great Lakes and in the Ohio River Valley, however, required yet a different strategy, one finally adopted by William Pitt. Noting both the difficulty of logistics to supply British forces in the American wilderness and the reluctance of local settlers to take orders from British officers, Pitt finally proposed that colonials could create their own militias with the promise of settling promising land in the Ohio country (Anderson 2001).

Pitt's policy of treating the colonials "like allies, offering subsidies to encourage their assemblies to aid in the conquest of New France" led to victory over French and Indian forces in the Ohio valley (Anderson 2001, p. 214). The promise of more land for the speculators of the thirteen colonies who had effectively mobilized colonial militias, however, was cut short by the royal Proclamation of 1763. This made clear that British imperial policy in North America now focused on Canada and its lucrative fur trade, long established by the Hudson's Bay Company (Carlos and Lewis 2010). The Ohio River Valley and the lands to the Mississippi were designated as Indian Territory, while British immigration to North America was funneled to Canada, to counter the weight of the long-established French settlers in Lower Canada. The new imperial strategy clearly undercut the visions of westward expansion that had motivated colonial support of the British military efforts in the French and Indian War.

Repeated efforts by the colonial leaders to repeal the British restrictions on possible westward expansion, promised in many of the colonial charters, proved most effective whenever they imposed trade restrictions with Britain. Consequently, non-importation acts, followed by export restrictions to the Mother Country, became the typical recourse by the American colonists to press their case to the British Parliament. Cutting off trade also cut off finance, which forced the British government to support occupation troops in the colonies directly by shipments of specie and supplies from England. The efforts of Britain to make the colonies pay at least some share of these expenses led eventually to the War of American Independence (1775–1783). While the mutual restriction of trade between Britain and the rebellious colonies simply forced Britain to increase direct shipments of soldiers, matériel, and specie in order to suppress the rebellion, the restrictions on trade, coupled to the effects of the Currency Act of 1764 (4 Geo. III cap. 34), which prohibited all the colonies from issuing their own coins or notes as legal tender, forced the colonial governments into a series of financial innovations, innovations that eventually evolved in the uniquely American financial system.

The Currency Act of 1764 did not prohibit the colonies from issuing paper credits in anticipation of future taxes or land sales when they were asked to raise supplies for British naval and army forces during conflicts with the French. Instead, "bills of credit" were regulated, with a maximum term of five years, to be redeemed by taxes collected (whether in kind or in specie), and then burned so they could not be re-issued, or stay in circulation beyond the fixed term. Widespread experience with such bills of credit among the various colonies during the French and Indian War was the basis for the financial innovation of the Continental Congress when it issued the infamous Continental Dollar on July 29, 1775 (Grubb 2013). Grubb insists that we should call these bills of credit, "zero coupon bearer bonds" rather than fiat currency. The importance of the distinction is that a zero coupon bearer bond with a fixed and certain expiration date should circulate immediately at a discount from its face value. A normal rate of interest, say 6 percent, would imply that a $1,000 Continental, payable in three years from date of issue, would be equivalent to $840 at the issue date, and then gradually increase in value until the maturity date, after which it would continue at $1,000 – unless there was rising uncertainty whether it would be redeemed at all once it had passed its expiration date. In that case, it would be subject to increasing rates of discount determined by the rate of price inflation created by the excess issue of paper credits. Grubb argues that the apparent inflation caused by the Continental initially was nothing more than rational discounting of the future value of the notes. That discount rate had to vary according to the probability that the states in revolt would prevail militarily.

All analysts agree, however, that the basic problem for the Continental Congress' finance of the revolution was its inability to tax on its own account, so it could not raise debt on its own (Bolles 1886–1892; Sumner 1891; Bullock 1895; Studenski and Krooss 1963). The Thirteen Colonies did not allow the Continental Congress to raise taxes on its own account, due to the rule of unanimity that had been self-imposed at the outset in 1775. There was always one colony to object to even a common external tariff (Rhode Island). So responsibility for redeeming the Continental dollars was allotted proportionally among the thirteen colonies, but with no enforcement mechanism available each colony's administration could become a free rider, especially if battles were taking place elsewhere. There were other problems, noted by persons at the time charged with administering the issuance of bills of credit and acquiring military supplies, persons such as Robert Morris, later to become the Superintendent of Finance for the Continental Congress in 1781. Morris worried especially about the failure of some states to redeem their allotments of bills by collecting taxes, but also about the issuance of competing bills of credit by some states and about the competition of counterfeit bills of credit introduced by the British, all problems stemming from the failure of the American politicians to provide a cash revenue for the service of public credit, which he proposed to remedy by establishing a funded national debt, sold primarily to foreign investors ("Report On Public Credit", July 29, 1782, Morris 1782).

The eloquence of Morris' arguments in favor of a funded national debt, backed by cash taxes collected regularly with interest paid faithfully, may have been due to the letters he had received earlier from Alexander Hamilton, but the forcefulness of his views stemmed from his long experience in dealing with the finance of international trade in the Atlantic economy as partner in the foremost shipping firm in the leading port of North America. The language and arguments in Morris' report are repeated faithfully in Alexander Hamilton's "First Report on the Public Credit" (McKee 1934, pp. 3–50), but the only part of Morris' vision that he could realize during his term of office was to create the Bank of North America (January 1782), modeled after the obvious success of the Bank of England.

Nevertheless, the ad hoc war financing by the colonies, coordinated but not enforced by the Continental Congress, worked sufficiently so that the initial military effort of the British was stymied by their defeat at the Battle of Saratoga in September and October 1777. This victory encouraged the colonies to greater efforts, but reduced the incentives to cooperate. While the rate of inflation from the circulation of the Continental dollars appears to have tapered off subsequently, it remained high and then picked up again when the British mounted victories in the southern colonies (Baack 2005). The Congress responded desperately with renewed and increasingly larger issues of bills of credit in later 1778 and through 1779, which caused higher and higher rates of inflation – rates that had effectively exhausted the possibility of raising more resources by issuing even larger quantities of bills of credit, even when they had been given the status of legal tender. But that status depended on the military capacity of the Congress to enforce it, and British victories made that capacity increasingly doubtful, especially in the south.

The alliance with France in 1778 after the colonists' victory at Saratoga and the diversion of the French fleet from the Caribbean to the Chesapeake in 1780 led to the defeat of Cornwallis at Yorktown, Virginia in October 1781. His defeat effectively ended the war and achieved independence for the new republic of the United States of America, just as its government finances were exhausted. But it did not end the trade embargo imposed by the British, so the American officials, led by Robert Morris during his term as Superintendent of Finance for the Continental Congress (1781–1784), had to create more financial innovations. Chief among these was to establish the Bank of North America, chartered in May 1781 and opened on January 4, 1782 with Thomas Willing, senior partner of Robert Morris, as president. Willing would later become the president of the First Bank of the United States, established in 1791. Morris managed to provide the bank with a temporary reserve of silver coins by convincing the commander of the French forces that this would preserve the value of bills of exchange drawn on France, the main source of his finance for local supplies. French credits to the US had to be paid in France, so bills of exchange on France were then sold to merchants in Philadelphia or New York, primarily through the services of Haym Salomon, who served as the local bill broker for French and Dutch bills of exchange on behalf of Morris and members of the Continental Congress (Peters 1911).

Financial capitalism, 1720–1789 131

One story of the course of inflation under the excessive issues of the Continental dollar then focuses on the outcomes of key battles that shaped expectations of the future issue of notes – American victories at Saratoga (September–October 1777) and Yorktown (October 1781) slowed the depreciation of the Continental, allowing the Congress to continue extracting an inflation tax (Baack 2001). But this overlooks the key efforts of the private merchant bankers in Philadelphia and Boston, who mobilized resources for the revolutionary war effort by tapping into the international network of trade credit that had arisen for entrepreneurs on both sides of the Atlantic after 1763. Foremost among them in the US was Robert Morris, who had become a junior partner of Thomas Willing's export–import firm in Philadelphia by 1763. By 1775, Willing & Morris were the largest shipping firm in Philadelphia but supported the call to arms by the Continental Congress and used their contacts to provide gunpowder to the Pennsylvania militia, and to acquire Spanish coins from Caribbean ports. Among the overseas contacts of Willing & Morris was the firm of Francis Baring, which had included Willing & Morris in its network of reliable contacts throughout the Atlantic trading world in the period before the War of American Independence (Hidy 1949, p. 14). After the war, personal relationships between the House of Baring and the Willing & Morris firm intensified, when Francis Baring sent his second son, Alexander, to the US in 1795 to examine the offer of land sales by Willing's son-in-law, William Bingham. Alexander bought a million acres for £90,000 and in 1798 added a strong personal tie by marrying Bingham's oldest daughter, Anna. Alexander Baring became the chief foreign agent for American public finance afterwards, dealing regularly with Thomas Willing, first president of the First Bank of the United States (1791–1807), Anna's maternal grandfather. Personal connections such as these certainly helped to solidify the basis for impersonal exchanges that rose exponentially in the nineteenth century between the two leading capitalist powers of the world.

Amsterdam and London part ways

The hostility of the British to Dutch investors for their continued financial support of American colonial aspirations throughout the American Revolutionary War did provoke the British attack on

Amsterdam in 1784. But even earlier, when Lord North commissioned an inquiry in to the extent of Dutch holdings of the British national funds in 1777, Dutch stockholders felt pressure to either withdraw or conceal their holdings in the British funds thereafter (Wilson 1941, p. 190). Opinions vary on the extent to which this occurred. Wilson argued that the Dutch felt little alternative to withdrawing, but Carter noted little change in the holdings of wealthy Dutch recorded in the Collateral Succession Tax records of the city of Amsterdam. Carter noted that while prices of British funds fell with the American and Dutch Wars, this made the yield on them, which rose to nearly 5 percent, all the more attractive (Carter 1953, p. 388). While holdings of French *rentes* by the wealthy Dutch increased in the 1780s as well, that did not require them to reduce their holdings of British securities.

Riley, like Carter, attributed Dutch investment in foreign government securities whenever and wherever it occurred to the continued search for reasonable returns on their surplus capital. Even after the establishment of the Batavian Republic under the watchful eyes of French armies in 1795, and the fleeing from Amsterdam of the wealthiest merchant bankers such as Henry Hope to join his correspondents in London, fresh Dutch investment in government securities continued. Only now this investment was in domestic Dutch government debt that was finally centralized into a combined national debt, replacing the scattering of annuities and bearer bonds previously issued by the cities and provinces. The debt was used to pay off the liberation forces of the French in the first instance, but thanks to the tax reforms of the Dutch Patriots, who had initially welcomed the French revolutionary ideals, the debt service was kept up faithfully. Later, under Napoleon's sterner rule, the Dutch found themselves providing funds to the various satellite kingdoms under French rule so they in turn could pay tribute to the French empire (Chapter 7).

De Pinto (1771) attributed Britain's success precisely to the useful role that Amsterdam's stockjobbers played in providing a liquid market for the new issues of British government debt that each war required. Increasing tensions between the Dutch and the British, however, cut off that symbiosis by the end of the American War, which culminated in the Fourth Anglo-Dutch War of 1780–1784. Thereafter, financial innovations in Britain relied more on importing financial talent and capital from the Continent, a process that was greatly facilitated by the French Revolution and its spread to the rest of Europe after 1793. The attraction of London as a destination for flight capital from the nobles and merchants in Europe who were subjected to the expropriations of Napoleon's forces brought fresh capital and talent into service for the British military and naval effort (Neal, 1990, Chapter 9, 1991). The Napoleonic Wars pitted not only French land power against British sea power, but also two different ways for using sovereign debt and merchant bankers in the service of war finance.

7 | Financial innovations during the "birth of the modern," 1789–1830: a tale of three revolutions

Had Napoleon fully understood the possibilities of Dutch finance for financing and provisioning his armies, he might have been able to establish his empire over Continental Europe. As it turned out, despite his brilliant efforts at re-shaping French public finances and re-organizing the French military, he failed to coordinate successfully banks, capital markets, and financial regulation for France and paid scant attention to the financial institutions in satellite kingdoms. To finance his imperial ambitions, however, Napoleon did appreciate the merits of Britain's financial innovations that had stymied the advances of the French revolutionary armies on the Continent. After assuming power in the *coup* of 18 Brumaire (November 9–10, 1799), he quickly imitated the essential features of British finance, at least as he saw them. He established the *Banque de France* in 1800, re-vitalized the *Caisse d'amortissement pour la dette publique,* and reconstituted the *Bourse de Paris*. With these three organizations, Napoleon mimicked the financial structure of Britain with its Bank of England, sinking fund (Commissioners for the Reduction of the National Debt), and London Stock Exchange. All of these had proven their worth in helping Britain finance its successful wars against France over the past century. But, like John Law nearly a century earlier, Napoleon felt that all these financial organizations would function even more effectively if he kept them under central control, whether by himself or by trusted civil servants. His constant intervention in the management of the national debt continually frustrated his minister in charge, Count Mollien. Further, his insistence on levying massive annual contributions from satellite kingdoms raised by new, heavier taxes undercut the legitimacy of the new regimes he created throughout Continental Europe.

Despite his incomprehension of the subtleties of British public finance, anchored in deeply rooted commercial finance both at home and abroad, Napoleon clearly understood the importance for the economic system he created on the European Continent of enforcing impersonal exchanges through constant monitoring by individuals connected to each other through a multitude of relationships. At the same time his armies occupied a country, he created a network of personal enforcers of exchanges. By installing members of his family or trusted generals as rulers of unified kingdoms throughout Continental Europe, Napoleon mimicked in many ways the networks of trusted correspondents that merchant bankers in Europe had established in previous centuries. Napoleon installed his younger brothers, Louis and Jérôme, as kings of Holland and Westphalia, his sister Elisa as rule of Tuscany, and his older brother Joseph as king of Naples and Sicily and then of Spain. Even the general he put in charge of Venice was a great-nephew of John Law, which is why Law's gravestone can still be visited there. Napoleon obviously had in mind a coordinated and authoritarian rule of the empire he created. Like Law in 1719, Napoleon felt that maintaining military control while imposing new institutions in place of the *ancien régime* would allow them to take root and become legitimate. The early success of the Napoleonic reforms, moreover, helped greatly by the declaration of peace by the Treaty of Amiens in 1802, sustained him in his mistaken belief.

In 1803, Napoleon directed the *Banque de France* to stabilize the *franc germinal* further by setting it equal to 290.32 mg of gold, a value it maintained until the First World War, over a century later. As the previous *franc* had been defined as 4.5 grams of silver, the bimetallic ratio was now set at 15.5:1. Meanwhile, the British pound had suspended convertibility into gold or silver as of February 1797, and it remained a paper pound floating against the French *franc* until 1819 when the British Parliament finally forced the Bank of England to resume convertibility of its notes at the pre-war standard in terms only of gold by 1821. Determined to finance his military campaigns by strictly old-style methods of levying contributions in kind from territories as he conquered them and raising tributes from previous conquests, all without issuing any new debt, Napoleon resumed his war plans. He obtained initial financing by selling off the vast extent of John Law's Mississippi scheme, known as the Louisiana Territory, to the US government for a bargain price of $15 million. This would have been equivalent to 72 million of the new *franc germinal* had the sum been paid in silver and gold to

the French Treasury.[1] In fact, while $11.25 million bonds bearing
6 percent interest for 15 years were issued in the US, Barings in
London and Hope in Amsterdam accepted them at 78½ percent of
par before paying out sums to Napoleon's Treasury and charging
their respective commissions. The remaining $4.75 million were paid
directly to French creditors in the US.

The successful conclusion of the Louisiana Purchase from a financial
standpoint depended first and foremost upon the fiscal capacity of the
young US government to pay immediate cash to France and French
creditors in the US and to make credible its commitment for servicing
the bonds issued to cover the remainder of the $15 million purchase
price. That fiscal capacity and credibility, in turn, was the result of the
brilliant fiscal reforms initiated by Alexander Hamilton as the first
Secretary of the Treasury and the continuation of his system by
Albert Gallatin, Secretary of the Treasury under Presidents Jefferson
and Madison afterwards. Hamilton's system, and its subsequent trials
and travails after proving its merits with the Louisiana Purchase,
deserve separate treatment later in this chapter. But our focus now
should be on the individual financiers who carried the silver coins from
one side of the Atlantic to the other. They were the actors whose
personal connections enabled the impersonal markets for this and
subsequent large-scale transactions to take place, during the war and
thereafter.

Personal exchanges and high finance during the Napoleonic era

The two merchant banking firms immediately responsible for the
actual payments to Napoleon for the Louisiana Purchase were Barings
in London and Hope in Amsterdam. Alexander Baring had been sent
years before to Washington by his father and founder of the firm
precisely to oversee the firm's financing of trade between the US and

---

[1] The official mint quantity of gold for the US dollar was 23.2 grains, while the
franc germinal was 4.7947 grains of gold. But calculations at the time put the
franc equivalent at 60 million FF, presumably taking into account the
transactions costs in transferring the funds, which could only be done through
Barings during the brief period of peace of the Treaty of Amiens. Also, the dollar
circulated at par with the Mexican peso at the time, while it took 5 French francs
for 1 peso (dollar) in the Americas but only 3.75 in Europe, implying that $15
million equaled 75 million francs in the Caribbean but only 56¼ million in
France.

Europe. Marrying the daughter of Senator Bingham of New York, a millionaire landowner in his own right, Alexander became the principal agent of the US government for their official transactions in England. James Monroe, when he came to London with the Louisiana bonds for the final payment, used Barings to exchange them for Three Per Cent Consols, which Barings then transferred to Hope & Co. in Amsterdam. There, the acting head of the firm, Pierre Labouchère, had married the third daughter of Francis Baring in 1796, which cemented the relationship between Hope & Co. in Amsterdam and Barings in London – and opened up financial flows between the two huge firms. The capital stock of Hope & Co. in Amsterdam grew from an unprecedented level of 4 million guilders in 1760 to over 7 million in 1770, when it exceeded the capital of the VOC, and then to over 15 million guilders by 1794, when its assets of 25 million guilders actually exceeded the assets of the *Wisselbank* (Jonker and Sluyterman 2001, pp. 121–122).

These personal connections for foreign exchange created more possibilities for Napoleon's war finance above and beyond allowing the US to purchase the Louisiana Territory from him. The leading French financier at the time, Gabriel-Julien Ouvrard, had been supplying the Spanish and French navies with supplies for their mutual war efforts against Great Britain in 1798–1802 while government payments to his *Compagnie des Négociants Réunis* fell farther behind despite the interval of peace in 1803. To recover his losses Ouvrard needed to help Napoleon's officers extract more resources from Spain, where he had personal relations. His father-in-law, Count of Cabarrús, was head of the *Banco Nacional de San Carlos* that Carlos III established in 1782 and which later became the *Banco de España*. Through Ouvrard's connections in Spain, especially with the prime minister, Manuel Godoy, he managed to obtain numerous drafts drawn by the Spanish treasury on silver held at the royal treasuries in Mexico. Further to these, Ouvrard also obtained numerous permits to import goods into Vera Cruz and to export the silver his agents would receive there from the Mexican mint. To complete these transactions while Napoleon went back to war in 1804, however, required the services of Hope & Co., who in turn prevailed upon Barings to cooperate in bringing the silver out of Mexico via neutral ships into European ports, where it could be credited to Ouvrard's company (Marichal 2007, pp. 161–167; Pearse 2009). Barings, in turn, prevailed upon William

Pitt early in 1805 to approve their role in the transfer of silver, arguing that after taking a handsome commission for themselves, they could divert one-quarter of the silver to British use, the result of applying an exchange rate of 5 francs per Mexican peso in Mexico but one of 3.75 francs in France, part of the arrangement made by Ouvrard (Wolf 1932, p. 104; Buist 1974, n. 4, p. 327). The British share of the silver could then replenish the silver stock of the Bank of England, pay Wellington's troops in Portugal, or ship to India for carrying on the now expanded trade with Asia, as the EIC had absorbed the trade of the VOC there.

The fortunes of war, however, disrupted all these plans so carefully made in the Spring of 1805 and forced the top financiers in Europe, the US, and Mexico to improvise repeatedly. In October 1805, the combined Spanish and French fleets that Ouvrard had already provisioned were destroyed off Cape Trafalgar by the British fleet led by Admiral Nelson. The Royal Navy thereafter was in control of the Atlantic shipping lanes as well as the Asian trade. The French defeat at Trafalgar created a financial crisis in Paris, which bankrupted many bankers and put Ouvrard's claims on the Spanish government on hold. Meanwhile, Napoleon was fully occupied with fighting the combined armies of Austria and Russia. With his decisive victory at Austerlitz in December 1805, however, Napoleon returned triumphant to Paris only to find his financial regime in total disarray. To set things right he took over the financial scheme that Ouvrard had so carefully constructed, first putting Ouvrard in prison and out of the picture. He then seized the drafts drawn by the Spanish treasury on Mexico that were still in Ouvrard's possession and sent them to the French consul in Philadephia. When the French consul in Philadelphia offered the drafts sent to him by Napoleon to American merchants who could still sail as neutrals to Mexico, however, they refused to accept them. Only the guarantee of merchant bankers like Barings or Hope & Co. could convince them that the drafts would be accepted in Mexico. Hope & Co., in turn, refused to return the drafts that Ouvrard had already given them.

While Ouvrard was languishing in prison and suffering the humiliation of a forced bankruptcy of his *Compagnie des Négociants Réunis*, the agents recruited by Hope & Co. to carry out Ouvrard's scheme were accepted readily by the leading merchants in the ports wherever they appeared: David Parish in Philadelphia and Baltimore, Vincent

Nolte in New Orleans, and Armand de Lestapis in Veracruz (Pearce 2009, p. 1329). By the beginning of 1806, they arranged a series of small, fast schooners that could outrun any British frigates in the Caribbean while they carried European manufactures to Mexico and returned with silver and tropical goods. The only competition for Hope & Co.'s schooners turned out to be British ships that were trading illegally while posing as neutral ships but with permits granted by the Royal Navy. These became even more important when Napoleon imposed his Continental Blockade after defeating the Prussian army at the Battle of Jena in October 1806.

Indeed, the Ouvrard–Hope–Baring scheme then flourished with British support. It was so effective that the Spanish government, still nominally neutral but compelled to remit an annual payment of 72 millions francs to France under the Treaty of Subsidies signed in October 1803, offered further permits to a competing set of British merchant firms – Gordon & Murphy and Reid, Irving. During the height of these shipments over the period 1805–1808, the British firms provided 27,820,000 of the total official silver export of 29,969,590 pesos, 93 percent (Stein and Stein 2000, p. 363). The sums were so large and so important for both the Spanish government and the British that both Spanish and British war ships were regularly used in addition to the private merchant ships sailing under neutral colors, mostly from the US. In 1807, the British warship *Diana* actually took on the largest single shipment, 3,679,835 pesos equal to £828,792, which was delivered safely to Barings in Portsmouth (Pearce 2009, p. 1326).

British war finance disrupted and resumed

The effectiveness of French military victories on the Continent, especially the occupation of Amsterdam and the establishment of the Bavarian Republic in 1795, had disrupted the traditional methods of British war finance, as described in Chapter 6. The result had been to force Britain to suspend convertibility of Bank of England notes in February 1797, and to seek peace by 1801. During the interval of peace, 1801–1804, Spain had taken advantage of renewed access to the silver supplies of Spanish America to import the record amount of over 70 million pesos, much of it carried by American merchant ships enjoying the privileges of neutrality. When war resumed in 1805, however, the British found that Vera Cruz could now substitute for Amsterdam as an outlet for British exports of consumer goods, mainly cotton textiles. Moreover, British quartermasters could now obtain silver directly from the Mexican mints, and on better terms than from Dutch merchants in Amsterdam as in previous wars of the eighteenth century. With this renewed access to Mexican silver, Britain could resume subsidies to Continental allies as well as renew the EIC's trade in Asia. William Pitt the Younger must have realized the value of this roundabout technique for financing Britain's renewed war efforts after 1803. Using the US and Mexican port as outlets for British exports of consumer goods allowed him to resume the method of war finance that his father, William Pitt the Elder, had used so effectively during the Seven Years War. He approved the Baring participation in Ouvrard's scheme shortly before his death in 1806.

Napoleon put an end to even this roundabout renewal of British war finance, however, by invading Portugal through the Basque territory of Spain in 1808, which led to the deposal of the Bourbon dynasty and the imposition of Joseph Bonaparte as the new king. The legitimacy of this new regime, however, was not recognized in Mexico and the supply of silver, now nearly exhausted by the excessive demands of the Spanish royal government over the previous decade of conflict, was cut off. Napoleon further tightened his Continental Blockade in 1810, but it was the refusal of Spanish American ports to pay for British exports that had been sent in large quantities in anticipation of further exports of silver that created a financial crisis in London.

Further disruption to the roundabout way of financing Britain's overseas wars by exporting textiles and housewares in order to pay for mercenaries came when the Jefferson Embargo took the US merchant fleet out of the trade flow. Enacted in December 1807 when Caribbean trade was offseason and New England ports were icebound in any case, the embargo only took effect for the year 1808 and was rescinded by Jefferson as he was leaving office in March 1809. Nevertheless, it was effectively enforced during its term and, whether intentionally or not, served to complement Napoleon's Continental Blockade and further impede British war finance. By cutting off the American market for British export goods, Jefferson's Embargo eliminated yet another reason for Atlantic merchants to accept the British Treasury's bills of exchange in order to access British export goods. Napoleon's Continental Blockade and Jefferson's Embargo combined to disrupt all Atlantic merchant shipping leading to a financial crisis in London in 1810, eventually the War of 1812 between Britain and the US, and Napoleon's ambition to conquer Tsarist Russia.

The innovations of financial capitalism again showed their importance in the diverse responses of the belligerents over the next five years. Napoleon's adventure in Russia, motivated to seal off the northern markets for British goods and tighten his Continental System, was financed by the traditional methods of invading armies, taking food supplies from cities and villages along the invasion route. Ouvrard, had he been back in favor, would have organized payments for such supplies along the invasion route in advance, offering commercial credits. Napoleon's defeat in Russia, of course, could be attributed to Russian determination as well as the primitive state of its rural market system and the brutal Russian winter, but the lack of financial support from a commercial network of merchants and suppliers spelled doom from the outset. On the other side of the Atlantic, President Madison of the US, totally enamored of Jefferson's foreign policy after having served as his Secretary of State, allowed the charter of the Bank of the United States to lapse in 1810. By discarding a vital element of Hamilton's system, over the objections of Gallatin, his Secretary of the Treasury, Madison eliminated a key source of war finance for the US when the War of 1812 did break out. While American forces managed to stave off total defeat by the minimal British forces diverted to the US from the war against Napoleon's European empire, Madison's war effort was clearly underfunded. In 1816, he authorized the charter of the Second Bank of the United States to make belated amends for his failure to keep Hamilton's original system of finance intact.

Alexander Hamilton had created the financial system of the new republic when he became the nation's first Secretary of the Treasury under President George Washington. Hamilton had served as Washington's aide-de-camp during the War of American Independence so he understood the importance of reliable sources of war finance. He had also served a term as one of Robert Morris' tax collectors for the state of New York in 1784. Further, as a lawyer in the city of New York dealing with the multitude of post-war claims between American merchants and British suppliers, he had detailed insight into the techniques that the British had used to finance their efforts in the war. It was Hamilton's genius to persuade the individual states with their different modes of finance and debts accumulated during the war to turn their individual debts into a consolidated debt of the Federal government, much as Morris had recommended back in 1782. In turn, states gave up their individual customs revenues, which were consolidated under the direction of Hamilton. The customs revenues thereafter formed the bulk of the Federal government's revenues, which proved more than ample to pay interest on the stock of Federal debt, right through successive wars until 1860 (Studenski and Krooss 1963, pp. 54, 68, 77, 92). Individual states had often paid their soldiers with claims on lands to be settled in their western territories, so Hamilton also consolidated these state claims, which often dated from their original charters, into Federal claims. Handling all the financial transfers involved was the Bank of the United States, chartered in 1791 for 20 years, but over the objections of Jeffersonian Democrats from slaveholding states. One of them objected that if Congress could take upon itself the power to charter a bank, why it could even emancipate slaves! Finally, Hamilton authorized the US mint in 1794 to produce coins at an official mint ratio of 15.13:1, slightly lower than the British ratio of 15.21:1. Hamilton's dollar was defined as either 374.4 grains of fine silver or 24.75 grains of fine gold (Officer 1996, p. 15). With a steady source of tax revenue, millions of acres of yet unclaimed land inland to be sold as needed, a stable currency, and a joint-stock public bank with branch offices in each state, the US Federal government began its life with an ideal template for a financial system after Hamilton's term of office.

Even Albert Gallatin, appointed as Secretary of Treasury by President Jefferson and charged with finding fault with the financial system set up by the Federalist party, reported that Hamilton's system was perfectly sound. As Hamilton's system was explicitly modeled on the British war finance system as recently improved under William Pitt's direction, however, it was inherently objectionable to Jefferson and his Republican party. While Gallatin certainly appreciated the flow of revenues from the customs duties levied on the expanding trade carried on by the American merchant marine under the flag of neutrality and the effectiveness of the Bank of the United States in collecting revenues and expediting expenditures, he worked assiduously to reduce the national debt and thereby eliminate the sinking fund that Hamilton had established. On that score, however, Jefferson repeatedly stymied Gallatin's efforts, first by taking on the entire Louisiana Purchase instead of just buying New Orleans as originally proposed, and then by imposing his ill-conceived Embargo in 1807. Further, Madison, when he succeeded Jefferson as President, let the charter for the Bank of the United States expire at the end of 1810 and then drifted into the War of 1812. That war effort required Gallatin, continuing as Secretary of the Treasury, to increase taxes and issue more debt on much worse terms than had been required to finance the Louisiana Purchase.

To sum up: the British system of public finance effectively proved its worth repeatedly throughout the remainder of the eighteenth century after recovering from the debacle of the South Sea bubble. It enabled British forces to prevail in each new confrontation with France, whether in North America or Asia, and to recover quickly from the shock of losing its American colonies as the benefits of the growing Atlantic trade and the military domination achieved in India by Cornwallis served to placate the imperial psyche. Hamilton in the new republic of the United States copied the best aspects of the British system, and even improved upon them by making the Federal government a major shareholder in the Bank of the United States, while keeping Federal lands in the west as an ultimate resource for finance of the new government. But his successors managed to undercut the best features of his system without financing the military power needed to maintain the independence of the new, and expanding government. Ultimately, Andrew Jackson, the "hero of New Orleans" who put the final seal of approval on the Louisiana Purchase at the end of the War of 1812, undid all of the Hamilton system when he refused to re-charter the Second Bank of the United States in 1836. Meanwhile, Napoleon's authoritarian intervention on the French imitation of the British system persistently undercut the incentives of private merchants and bankers to partake of the expanded profit opportunities that the British and American exploitation of the Atlantic trade had created. Ultimately, his failure to mobilize private finance effectively from either France or his satellite kingdoms meant that his military genius was repeatedly thwarted, first in Russia and finally at Waterloo.

Both the American and the French Revolutions at the end of the eighteenth century ultimately succeeded by making financial innovations that explicitly imitated the British system of finance as it had developed over the course of the eighteenth century. Testing both new systems in the crucible of war finance during the Napoleonic Wars, however, subjected both the American and French systems to stresses that undid their potential effectiveness, first in the US under Jefferson (1801–1809) and then in France under Napoleon (1803–1813). Meanwhile, the pathetic efforts of Spain's monarchy laid the basis for revolution in Spain and throughout the Spanish empire after 1808. The third revolution during this period, however, proved to be even more effective in creating the modern world, essentially by laying the basis for modern economic growth, growth that has persisted until now. This, of course, was the Industrial Revolution in Britain, based on the expansion of the British iron and coal industries, which were financed by the same techniques that had created the financial revolution much earlier. Rather than crowding out investment in the consumer goods industries that had been the key to Britain's export success when engaged in the wars of the eighteenth century, British government spending in the Napoleonic Wars actually funded investment in the capital goods industries and laid the foundation for the Industrial Revolution and modern economic growth that followed.

British war finance re-directed

The superiority of the British system of finance, however, was not obvious to observers on the spot in 1810. When the supply of silver from Mexico was cut off and the goods in transit were left unsold, the disruption in the chain of finance led to a severe financial crisis in London. The most dramatic evidence shows up in Figure 7.1, which shows the course of exchange rates against the British pound sterling. The sharp drop after Napoleon imposed the second Continental Blockade combined with Jefferson's Embargo provoked the famous Bullion Report of 1810. There, David Ricardo laid out the monetary orthodoxy of the so-called "bullion school," namely that the Bank of England's excessive note issue without bullion backing had created inflation, driving down the value of the pound sterling, inconvertible against silver or gold since February 1797. The collapse of the French *assignat* in the first throes of the French Revolution is the most obvious and dramatic change in European exchange rates and the London *The Course of the Exchange* did not resume quoting any French rates until peace talks began in 1801, when the strength of the *franc germinal* was evident with respect to both the Amsterdam and Hamburg bank moneys. In 1808, the British pound began to fall against all three, hitting bottom in 1811, prompting the investigation by Parliament.

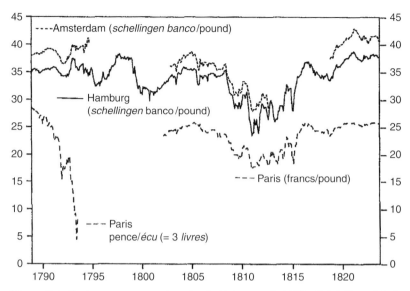

Figure 7.1 Exchange rates against the British pound, 1789–1825 (from Neal 1991, Figure 5, p. 76)

Thereafter, however, the pound continued to strengthen and stabilized after 1819 when Parliament put an end to the inconvertibility of the pound by restoring the gold parity at pre-war rates, effective in 1821. But would this be *prima facie* evidence of crowding out, due to excessive government reliance on inflationary finance? To dispel that fear, we have only to compare the market yields of the British Consols with those of the French *rentes* over the entire wartime period and post-war adjustment, as shown in Figure 7.2.

Clearly, Napoleon's reforms helped French public finances enormously compared to the disarray he found when he took power at the end of 1799, but even his efforts never managed to obtain the low yields enjoyed by his British opponents. Crowding out private capital formation by government expenditures on war was more a problem for Napoleon's France than Pitt's Britain, and crowding out was certainly a problem for the satellite kingdoms of Holland, Italy, and Spain under Napoleonic control. Further, the market value of the Bank of England, charged with supplying funds to Wellington's forces on the Continent as well as supplying the fleets of the Royal Navy throughout the world, held up throughout the war. Only the prospects of the EIC losing both the resources of the Dutch EIC as well as its monopoly of

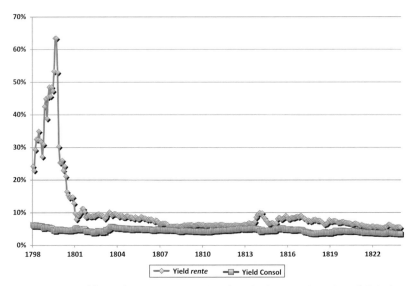

Figure 7.2 Yields on long-term sovereign bonds, France (*rente*) and Britain (Consol), 1798–1825 (from Castaing 1698–1908 and Courtois 1877, p. 11)

British trade with India at the end of the war created problems for investors in the British funds (Figure 7.3).

Figure 7.3 illustrates nicely how British government finance weathered the storms of war relatively calmly, riding the waves created by news of defeats and victories without too much turmoil. True, the Directors of the Bank of England were prematurely enthusiastic with news of Nelson's victory at Trafalgar in October 1805 when they raised the semi-annual dividend from £3½ to £8½ per £100 book value of a share. When they realized that Napoleon would continue his military offensives on the Continent, however, the dividend was brought back to £5 for the duration of hostilities and only lowered to £4 in April 1823. After Wellington's victory over Napoleon at Waterloo in 1815, however, all three ways to invest in British government debt – Three Percent Consols, Bank of England stock, or EIC stock – provided much the same market yield, until the disruptions of 1825. These, in turn, were created by the search for yield by holders of British sovereign debt as their passive income fell below the expected 5 percent yield that they had come to rely upon. The members of the London Stock Exchange responded by offering all sorts of new assets to their customers that bore higher yields, as well as significantly higher

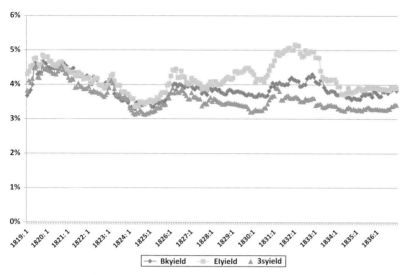

Figure 7.3 Yields on "The Funds" of Britain, 1819–1837 (from Castaing 1698–1908, Friday quotes)

risk, as it turned out. These were the bonds issued by various Latin American governments establishing their independence from imperial Spain even as the restored Bourbon monarchy in France managed to restore their cousins to power in Spain.

The yields for "the funds" shown in Figure 7.3 also highlight the problems created for the British government by the transition from wartime to peacetime finance. The price patterns of the three major securities available to risk-averse British investors changed their relationship from moving in synchrony during the restoration of the gold standard to diverging unpredictably, especially after the stock market crash in 1825. The capital stock of both the EIC and the Bank of England was invested in permanent government debt on which the government paid regular interest. Typically, the two monopolies passed through this interest payment to their shareholders plus some part of the profits obtained from their business activities. The dividends declared by the two had increased over the eighteenth century, but rose to all-time highs during the Napoleonic Wars. The Bank's business as the remitting agent for the government's war finance flourished. The EIC gained from absorbing all the Asian trade previously serviced by the French and Dutch EICs while the hostilities lasted. However, it was assessed a huge annual sum by the government, purportedly as compensation for the naval and military services the government provided for the protection of the EIC's trade, a sum that could be raised whenever the government felt the need.

The prices of Bank of England and EIC stock crossed over at the beginning of 1823 and the gap widened through 1824. Part of the decline in the Bank's stock was certainly due to its decision to drop its semi-annual dividend from £5 per £100, maintained constant from 1807 through 1822, to £4 per £100 in 1823, where it remained through 1838, before dropping again (Clapham 1945b, 2, p. 428.). The Bank was steadily withdrawing from its discount business, husbanding reserves, and fending off Parliamentary pressures to resume convertibility. The EIC, meanwhile, was in its final phases as a trading company in the period 1813–1833 and faced with a mounting problem of encroachment by non-Company English traders in the exports of Indian goods to Britain. To counter this, the Company was allowed to maintain its monopoly on all British trade with China. It was in the 1820s that the Company's import of trade goods from India began to feel the pressure of competition – in 1826–1827, they imported no goods whatever from India (Clapham 1945b, 2, p. 487). So it was the prospects of the continued China monopoly, and the earnings on monopoly pricing of tea for British consumers, that raised the market value of EIC shares in the early 1820s and the decline in Indian trade that lowered it in the mid-1820s.

All these relationships changed with the Resumption Act of 1819 to restore convertibility of the pound sterling to gold at the pre-war parity. After that act was passed, the market assessed the Bank's stock to be as risky as that of the EIC. The success of actual resumption in full in 1821 appears to have reassured the market initially that the Bank's stock was less risky than the stock of the EIC, whose fate was still a matter of intense discussion and dispute. At times, Bank stock even appeared less risky than Consols. The crisis of 1825, however, disrupted the price and yield patterns. Thereafter, Consols were clearly judged the safest security, EIC stock became priced with a higher risk premium yet, and Bank stock was priced with a risk premium that seems to have risen steadily toward the fateful year of 1833, when its charter was up for renewal.

The initial difficulty in returning to peacetime finance for the British government was doubtlessly caused by the repeal of Pitt's income tax in 1816, but then compounded by the decision in 1819 to return to the gold standard at the pre-war parity of the pound sterling, effective in 1821. The common element in all the problems of Britain's first return to gold arose from the pressures of coping with vastly increased informational uncertainties within the existing structure of English institutions that arose from these two policy decisions. These started with the Treasury itself, confronted by the difficulties of servicing the huge government debt accumulated during the Napoleonic Wars and deprived of its primary source of revenue, the income tax. These uncertainties continued within the Bank of England, forced now to take on new responsibilities while searching for new sources of revenue to replace its wartime profits. They were compounded by the response of the London capital market, which produced a bewildering array of new financial assets to its customers to replace the high-yielding government debt now being retired. All this left the London private banks and their corresponding country banks, as well as their customers in agriculture, trade and manufacturing, floundering in the resulting confusion. Financial disarray culminated with the stock market crisis of 1825, which contemporaries thought was just as dire as the South Sea bubble had been a century earlier.

Successive shocks in the transition from war to peacetime finance

To show how the British financial system recovered from these successive shocks to put together an improved financial system, one that proved its worth again and again over the following century, we analyze now, in turn, the shock to the financial system of shifting from wartime to peacetime finance in 1821, the financial crisis that occurred at the end of 1825, the efforts of the Bank of England to pick up the pieces, and, finally, the rise of a market in discounted commercial bills that put things right again – for a while. The lessons of each episode highlight the importance of appraising the financial system as a whole, rather than focusing on what appears to be its weakest link.

With Bank of England notes restored to convertibility in gold at prewar parity and a gold standard formally established in 1821, the British government was still faced with the loss of 20 percent of its total revenue from the income tax. To deal with the resulting budget shortfall the government turned to re-financing its existing debt at lower interest rates to reduce its debt service, which still accounted for 60 percent of total expenditures. This proved successful, especially as the deflationary effects of resuming convertibility in 1821 raised prices of new issues of sovereign bonds, so the overall effort of the government was successful, but with different effects on the three main funds. Statistical tests reported in Neal (1998) indicate that cointegration had existed throughout the wars between the three major stocks representing sovereign debt of the British government, but then broke down after 1821 – a statistical finding readily apparent in Figure 7.3 by comparing their yields over the period. The underlying reason for the separating paths of the three major "funds" available for individuals to invest in British sovereign debt was the separate policies the post-war government devised for each part of its long-term national debt.

The Treasury systematically retired its long-term debt in the form of the basic perpetual annuities, partly by using a small surplus due to reductions in the armed forces, especially the withdrawal of occupation forces from France after 1818. But by also making continued payments into the Sinking Fund, which purchased long-term debt at market prices and retired it, the Treasury was running open market operations that increased liquidity in the economy. Encouraged by the possibilities of retiring high-interest debt and reducing expenditures in this way, the government overreached in 1823. At the end of that year, the government converted £135 million of its 5 percent bonds to 4 percent bonds. It then continued to take advantage of monetary ease early in 1824 by converting £80 million of the 4 percent bonds to 3½ percent (Gayer, Rostow, and Schwartz 1975, 1, p. 185). This had a double-barreled effect, according to traditional accounts. On the one hand, British investors were disappointed to be receiving lower yields on their holdings in "the funds." "Even in that day 'John Bull could not stand two per cent'"(Clapham 1945b, 2, p. 487). On the other hand, the Bank of England was now obliged to buy back the "deadweight" part of the annuity yielding 3½ percent that the government issued to cover its expenditure on naval and military pensions, but had failed to sell to the public. The Bank had ample reserves to accomplish this, having accumulated bullion for minting into coins to replace the £1 and £2 notes it had issued during the paper pound period (1797–1821). In fact, as late as October 1824 the Bank's reserves amounted to fully one-third of its liabilities and by February 1825 it had increased its holdings of public securities by 50 percent from the low of February 1822 (Pressnell 1956, p. 480).

This meant that the Bank, like the Treasury, was also conducting open market operations, perhaps inadvertently and unwillingly. Nevertheless, the Bank added to monetary ease by placing cash in the hands of the public in exchange for the government securities they had previously held. This was done at the same time the Bank was drawing down its excessive gold reserves, a process that also increased the liquidity of the public. John Easthope, a Member of Parliament and a stockbroker, in his testimony to the Committee on the Bank of England Charter in 1832, argued that while the increase in the Bank's note issue before 1825 was not so large, it should have been decreased in light of falling gold reserves (Great Britain 1968, p. 469, item 57900). The episode he referred to was very likely the operations of Nathan Rothschild, who took advantage of the falling price of gold in Britain to borrow a large amount from the Bank to sell in France in November 1824.[2] Later, in mid 1825, when the Bank became concerned about its falling reserves and the fall of stock prices, Rothschild agreed to repay the loan, restoring the gold in installments spread over the months of June, July, August, and September.[3] The result was exceptional monetary ease in 1824 and into 1825, and then contraction in mid 1825, which brought on a payments crisis for country banks.

As Easthope argued, this was not the behavior one would want from a bank devoted to public service, although it was understandable behavior for a bank more concerned about the dividends it could pay to its stockholders than the general state of the monetary regime. On this point, the Bank's defense was that the exchanges had turned against Britain in 1825, so it was necessary then to contract its note issue and restore its gold reserves. Yet the evidence produced by the Bank itself for the Committee indicates that the exchange rate was never seriously threatened, at least no more than in earlier and later fluctuations that were not accompanied by financial panics. Indeed, such fluctuations as occurred created profit opportunities for the

---

[2] Bank of England, Committee of the Treasury Minute Book 29 October 1823 to 12th April 1826, fo. 117 Rothschild on November 30, 1824 requested a loan of £300 or £500,000 of Bar gold at 77/10 1/2 per oz. & will pay 3 ½ percent p.a. with collateral of Stock. "As I may require about £225,000 value of Bar gold tomorrow, I beg to mention it to you, in order to facilitate the delivery." The Bank's Court of the Treasury complied with this application.
[3] *Ibid.*, fo. 161, May 26, 1825.

House of Rothschild, which the Bank was only too happy to share in part without taking the risks incurred by Rothschild.

Country banks

The dysfunction of the financial system created at the top by the separation of operations and objectives between the Bank and the Treasury spread even further to affect the country banks. Confronted by the distress caused by severe and unanticipated deflation in 1819–1821, the Treasury did not wish to renew its reliance upon the Bank for buying Exchequer bills as it had done in 1817 in order to finance public works projects in the manufacturing districts and Ireland (Hilton 1977, pp. 82–87). Instead, it allowed the country banks to continue to issue notes of small denominations, deferring their elimination from circulation for ten years. Instead of disappearing from the money supply in 1823, as previously provided in legislation of 1816 (which mandated their termination within two years after the Bank resumed cash payments), they were allowed to continue until 1833.

The country banks, already providing necessary finance to manufacturing districts throughout England by the second half of the eighteenth century, found their business prospects greatly enhanced during the Napoleonic Wars. Part of the reason was the expansion of heavy manufacturing in the Midlands and South Wales, part was the growth of foreign trade from outports other than London, and much was due to the role of country banks in remitting to London the government's revenues from the land tax, the stamp tax, and the income tax while it was in effect. The end of the war reduced the basis for all these activities and eliminated the income tax. Moreover, the continuing threat of cash resumption by the Bank of England meant that the profitable note issue business would have to be wound up and replaced by some other form of revenue.

Into the breach stepped the stockjobbers and brokers operating in the London Stock Exchange. Their business, too, had been greatly enhanced by the incredible increase in government debt issued during the wars of 1793–1815. It was interrupted briefly by the crisis of 1810, which foretold the future difficulties the stock exchange traders would face when the war ended. In 1811, the response of stock traders was to enlarge greatly the list of securities they had available for investors in the London Stock Exchange. Canal stocks were especially favored, although a few other joint stock companies were listed – iron-tracked railways, docks, water-works and a few gas-works. Trading in most of these public utility stocks was quite limited, however, as most shareholders preferred to hold them as long-term assets and for their voting power. The various forms of government debt remained the most lucrative source of commission and speculative income for traders.

Latin American securities and the first Latin American debt crisis

The withdrawal of foreigners from the British national debt after the war, however, removed one class of customers who had been most active in trading, while the rise in the price of government bonds reduced their attractiveness as sources of interest income to the rentier classes. In response, the members of the London Stock Exchange began to develop a variety of new assets to maintain their customer base and their personal incomes. The peacetime governments in France, Prussia, Spain, Denmark, Russia, and Austria offered new issues of sovereign bonds that mimicked in form the British Three Per Cent Consol. With the military successes of the rebellious Spanish American colonies, government bonds issued by the new Latin American states were offered as well, followed by stocks in newly privatized mines. Many more gas-works were listed, as every community in England wanted to provide its residents and businesses with the gas lighting that was proving so successful in London. A number of insurance companies were created as the existing companies seemed especially able to profit from the ease of credit and the lack of attractive alternative assets to government debt.

But the most attractive assets offered were those from Latin America, following the success of the French 5 percent *rentes*. After the final defeat of Napoleon at Waterloo in 1815, foreign capital flowed back to the Continent from Great Britain. Foreign holdings of British debt diminished rapidly, the price of Consols rose as the supply diminished, and prices of Bank and East India stock rose in tandem. British investors accustomed to safe returns ranging between 4 and 6 percent for the past twenty years now found their options limited to yields between 3.5 and 4.5 percent. The opportunities for investment in new issues of French 5 percent *rentes* were more attractive than continuing their holdings in Consols. Figure 7.4 shows that the *rentes* maintained a

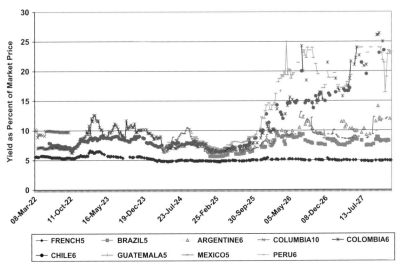

Figure 7.4 Latin American bond yields, and French _rentes_, 1822–1827 (from Castaing 1698–1908, Friday quotes)

steady return over five percent throughout the crisis period and offered a stable alternative to the British funds. Baring Brothers & Co., by its successful finance of Wellington's army in 1815, had established itself as the dominant merchant bank in England. By undertaking the flotation of the first two issues of French _rentes_ sold to pay the reparations and support Wellington's occupation forces, Barings became the "Sixth Power" in Europe, according to the Duc de Richelieu (Jenks 1927, p. 36; see also Ziegler 1988, pp. 100–111). From February to July 1817, Barings marketed three loans, the first two at a net price of 53 for 100 million francs each and the third at 65, which raised 115 million francs. Yet, according to Ziegler, no disturbance in the British trade balance or in French reserves seems to have occurred; the inflow of capital to France from Britain from the issue of _rentes_ seems to have been offset by indemnity payments and army contracts from France to Britain (Jenks 1927, p. 37)

From this success for British investors in foreign investment with the French _rentes_, it has traditionally been argued, came increased enthusiasm for other forms of investment, first in the bonds issued by the new government of Spain established in 1820, and then in the bonds issued by the new states emerging in Latin America. While the focus for foreign loans was mostly on Spain and Spanish America, Greece also received a loan and much-needed publicity for its then premature efforts to break away from Turkish rule. Over fifty years later, when the Greek government was attempting to assure the international community that it would go on a gold standard, part of its commitment was to resume payment on these initial bonds.

The collapse of Spanish control over its American empire during the Napoleonic Wars led to a variety of independent states being formed out of the former colonies by 1820. Battling one another for control over strategic transport routes, mainly rivers and ports, and over state enterprises, typically mines, each appealed to foreign investors as a source of government finance and as a means to substitute foreign expertise and technology for the vanquished Spanish. Their government bonds and their mining shares found a ready market in the London Stock Exchange, which had become the dominant market place for finance capital in the world during the Napoleonic Wars. The loan bubble of 1822–1825 ensued, eventually giving British foreign bondholders their first experience with defaults by sovereign states. None of the new Latin American states emerging from the remains of the Spanish empire (Brazil remained part of the Portuguese empire) found the means, whether by exports or taxes, to service the debts they had incurred in London. Meanwhile, they rapidly dissipated in military conflicts with neighboring states the net proceeds they received after the bonds were sold at discount and they had paid large commissions up front to the London investment houses.

From 1822, when both Chile and Colombia floated bond issues with London agents, an increasing number of Latin American governments tried to find the means for financing their transition to independence from the flush pockets of British investors. The bonds they issued, in terms of the amounts actually paid up, as distinguished from the amounts actually received by the governments, were the largest single category of new investment in the London capital market in this period (Gayer, Rostow, and Schwartz, 1975, 1, p. 189). Even so, that amount was small relative to the remaining sum of the British government's funded debt – £43 million compared to £820 million.[4]

---

[4] Gayer, Rostow, and Schwartz (1975, 1, n. 8, p. 408,) and Mitchell (1976, p. 402). These are nominal values in each case, but government debt was then trading at close to par, so its market value was roughly the same.

Figure 7.4 compares the prices of several bond issues of the emerging South American states, as given in James Wetenhall's semi-weekly *The Course of the Exchange*. At the peak of the stock market boom, there was surprising convergence in the prices of all the Latin American bonds. It was only in the ensuing two years that information on the fiscal capacity of the individual governments and their respective economic bases enabled the London market to distinguish among them. Mexico and the Andean countries were clearly marked to be disaster cases by the end of 1828, while Argentina and Brazil were already demonstrating their attractiveness to British investors, an allure that would increase until the Baring crisis of 1890. Dawson (1990) provides a readable account of this episode, but Marichal (1989) puts it into a longer-run Latin American perspective. Brazilians point with pride to the fact that their bonds never went into default, which is why their prices remained the highest among the Latin American bonds in the late 1820s. The Brazilian bonds, in fact, were the only ones issued by the Rothschilds. None of their government bond issues for Austria, Belgium, Naples, Prussia, or Russia defaulted in this period (Doubleday 1858–1859, p. 281).

The pricing pattern of foreign government bonds displayed in Figure 7.4 is a classic illustration of the so-called "lemons" problem that can occur in emerging financial markets. In this case, it appears that investors in the London market priced the Latin American bonds at a substantial discount so that the typical 5 or 6 percent yield on par value could provide a substantial risk premium compared to both the British funds and to the now-seasoned and solid French government debt. Until further information came in from newspapers or merchants' letters from the respective countries concerning their fiscal situation and credit arrangements, however, they all looked much alike and all were priced at punitively low levels. This discouraged higher-quality governments, such as Brazil, from issuing debt until the House of Rothschild had assured itself that adequate provision was forthcoming for servicing it. But it also encouraged lower-quality governments, such as Peru, to issue debt early on. Indeed, at one point in October 1822, it induced the Scottish adventurer, Gregor MacGregor, to issue bonds from an imaginary government of Poyais, presumably located around Honduras. On October 29, 1822 the official *The Course of the Exchange* quoted Poyais scrip for 6 percent bonds at 81½ percent of par, compared to Peru's 6 percent bonds at 86¾, Chile's at 84, and Colombia's at 86!

Only as more information came in or as investors began to pull out of higher-risk investments and seek safer, better-quality assets did price differences begin to show up. These differences were notable by the fall of 1825 for the new government issues from Latin America, although they did not affect the now seasoned and secure French *rente*. While the history of the various bond issues is extremely colorful, it appears that Jenks' assessment made many years ago is still fundamentally correct – their main effect was to enrich some issuing agents and impoverish or imperil others, including the redoubtable Barings. Jenks notes that the typical arrangement mimicked that devised by the Goldschmidts for the Colombian loan of 1824, whereby "[t]hey received a commission for raising the money, a commission for spending it, and a commission for paying it back" (Jenks 1927, p. 49). Ziegler (1988, pp. 102–107) argues that they lost money on the Argentina loan by buying back large amounts of it in a futile effort to maintain the market price of the bonds and lost even more on the ill-advised investments in Mexico of Francis Baring, the second son of Alexander Baring.[5] In the case of both the Rothschilds and the Barings, however, it appears that the sums risked were relatively small and the risks generally appreciated even by an inexperienced British public. We have to look elsewhere for an explanation of the 1825 speculative bubble and collapse, perhaps in the new domestic companies that were being formed.

British domestic securities

As the London stock market had proved attractive by 1824 for the new issues of debt by the restored European governments and the revolutionary Latin American governments, so a much wider variety of newly formed joint-stock corporations offered their shares as well to the London investors. In the words of a contemporary observer, "bubble schemes came out in shoals like herring from the Polar Seas" (Hunt 1936, p. 30). The success of three companies floated to exploit the

---

[5] Ziegler (1988, pp. 102–107). Ziegler quotes a fatherly reprimand from Alexander to Francis which includes the eloquent sentence, "One of your bad qualities, my dear Francis, and I do not attribute many to you, is that you are a bad taker of advice, but if, on this occasion, I administer mine rather harshly, it is because I have no time for circumlocution and because you are entitled to have from me my unequivocal sentiments."

mineral resources of Mexico – the Real del Monte Association, the United Mexican, and the Anglo-American – led to flotations of domestic projects in early 1824. In February 1824, the Barings and Rothschilds cooperated to found the Alliance British and Foreign Life and Fire Insurance Company, which immediately enjoyed enormous success (Hunt 1936, p. 32). In March 1824 there were thirty bills before Parliament to establish some kind of joint-stock enterprise, whether a private undertaking for issuing insurance or opening a mine, or a public utility such as gas- or water-works, or a canal, dock, or bridge, and in April there were 250 such bills (Hunt 1936, p. 32).

The limitation of joint-stock enterprises to these fields arose from: first, the Bubble Act of 1720, which forbade joint-stock corporations from engaging in activities other than those specifically stated in their charters; second, common law, which made stockholders in co-partnerships with transferable shares (i.e. unincorporated joint-stock enterprises) liable in unlimited amount, proportional to their shares in the equity of the company; and, third, the limited liability and ease of transfer for shareholders in mines created on the "cost-book" system (Burt 1984, pp. 74–81). Mine shareholders were subject only to calls up to the capitalization authorized by the cost-book, which required neither deed, charter, nor Act of Parliament to establish. Despite the resistance of Parliament to incorporating new companies with limited liability, the speculative mania continued, with new projects floated daily. Speculation was encouraged on the possibility that an enterprise might receive a charter, based on the connections in Parliament of its board of directors.

The extent of the speculative fervor and its lack of permanent effect were spelled out by a contemporary stockbroker, Henry English, and his analysis has remained authoritative to this day. Briefly, English listed 624 companies that were floated in the years 1824 and 1825. They had a capitalization of £372,173,100. By 1827, only 127 of these existed with a capitalization of £102,781,600, of which only £15,185,950 had been paid in, but the market value had sunk even lower to only £9,303,950 (Hunt 1936, p. 46). But even at the height of the enthusiasm for new issues, the total capital paid in had amounted to no more than £49 million (Gayer, Rostow, & Schwartz 1975, 1, p. 414). Compared to the stock of government debt available, £820 million, this was still almost as limited in scale as the investments in Latin American securities. Perhaps we have to look still further for an explanation of the events of 1825. The role of the country banks, in particular, needs to be examined.

The country banks

The expansion of the economy continued through 1823 and 1824. By April 1825 at the latest, the stock market boom reached its peak (Figure 7.5), and the resulting drop in collateral values combined with a contraction by the Bank of England in its note issue began to create jitters in the money market. By July, city bankers were beginning to be more cautious. In September, reports of difficulties by country banks in Devon and Cornwall began to appear. All country banks were then faced with the seasonal strain that occurred each autumn. Government tax revenues were required to be remitted to London in the autumn before interest payments on government debt were made in December. This caused more country banks to fail in October and November in 1825. When the major London banks of Wentworth, Chaloner, & Rishworth and Pole, Thornton & Co. failed on December 8 and 13, respectively, and forced dozens of correspondent country banks to suspend payments, a general run began on country banks. They, in turn, came to their London banks for cash, which turned to the Bank of England. Finally, the Directors of the Bank woke up to the crisis and

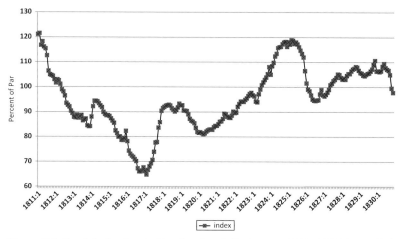

Figure 7.5 Stock Index for the London Stock Exchange, 1811–1830 (compiled by author from quotes for fifty companies in Castaing 1698–1908)

began to discount bills and notes for their customers as fast as they could with diminished staff and resources. The pressure on the Bank lasted for the rest of December, depleted its bullion reserves and forced it to issue small £1 and £2 notes again, but did not force it to suspend payments as feared.

The credit collapse led to widespread bank failures, 73 out of the 770 banks in England and even 3 out of the 36 in Scotland (Kindleberger 1984, p. 83), and a massive wave of bankruptcies in the rest of the economy, reaching an unprecedented peak in April 1826 (Gayer, Rostow & Schwartz 1975, 1, p. 205). The Bank and the London private banks joined forces for once by blaming both the speculative boom and the subsequent credit collapse on excessive note issue by the country banks. They argued that the ease of note issue had encouraged the more careless or unscrupulous partners in country banks to invest in high-risk, high-return financial ventures that were being offered on the London capital market, such as the Poyais scrip. Pressnell (1956), however, discounts this as the driving force both in the boom and in the timing of the collapse. Evidence supplied by Henry Burgess, secretary of the Committee of Country Bankers, to the Bank Charter Committee of 1832, shows that while many country banks did increase their note issue substantially between July 1824 and July 1825, their total note issue by then only restored the sharp fall that occurred between 1818 and 1822. Ultimately, the cause of the crisis of 1825 was surely the ongoing disconnect between the efforts of the Treasury and the Bank of England to cope with post-war fiscal and monetary arrangements.

The Bank of England

To understand the internal causes of the crisis of 1825, therefore, we must turn back to the role of the Bank of England, in particular, the relationship between its activities as a potential lender of last resort and the wave of bankruptcies that disrupted English commercial life for years following the crisis of 1825. The question naturally arises: could the Bank of England have prevented this financial disaster, say, by acting earlier and as a monopoly bank bearing more responsibility to the public than to its stockholders? It must bear part of the blame for the expansion of the money supply that apparently arose in 1823–1824 and especially for failing to offset the monetary expansion occurring elsewhere. But if, as Duffy (1985) suggests, it was the Bank of England's drawing account activity rather than its note issue that played the strongest role in easing or constraining the credit conditions in the London money market, then the Bank can be no more culpable than the country banks. The sums advanced from the Drawing Office plummeted after resumption of cash payments in 1821, and the Bank restricted drawings through most of 1825, and they never rose to the pre-resumption level until the first quarter of 1826. But this analysis simply casts the Bank in the role as just another bank, albeit much larger and more influential. If it was supposed to be able to combine up-to-date, authoritative information from the worlds of finance, commerce, and government policy, it might have been expected to play an earlier, more constructive role. In fact, the evidence from the minutes of the Court of Directors of the Bank indicates that the Bank was taken by surprise and responded with much too little, much too late.

The first mention of the crisis in the Directors' minutes occurs on December 8, 1825, when "The Governor [Cornelius Buller] acquainted the Court that he had with the concurrence of the Deputy Governor [John Baker Richards] and several of the Committee of Treasury afforded assistance to the banking house of Sir Peter Pole, etc."[6] On the previous Saturday, the Governor and Deputy Governor counted out £400,000 in bills personally to Henry Thornton, Jr. at the Bank without any clerks present (Forster 1956, p. 117). All this was done to keep it secret so that other large London banks would not press their claims as well. A responsible lender of last resort would have publicized the cash infusion to reassure the public in general. Instead, the run continued on Pole & Thornton unabated, causing it to fail by the end of the week. Then the deluge of demands for advances by other banks overwhelmed the Bank's Drawing Office.

Evidence on the timing and pattern of the Bank's discounts of commercial bills of exchange in the months leading up to the 1825 crisis (Neal 1998) shows that merchants dealing with South America were especially pressing in their demands for credit by June 1825. This could have given the Bank ample warning that payments of dividends on Latin American bonds and mining company stocks were in jeopardy as well. Instead of reacting to this information in a constructive way, however, the Bank decided it would be risky to advance

[6] Bank of England, TVC3/11 G4/48, fo. 150.

Table 7.1 *Report of the Bank of England's committee on branch banking, 1825–1826*

Benefits to the Bank of England:

(1) Increase circulation of Bank of England notes
(2) Increase Bank's control of whole paper circulation "and enable it to prevent a recurrence of such a convulsion as we have lately seen"
(3) Deposits would be very large
(4) Protect the Bank against competition of "large Banking Companies" if the government should encourage them.

Benefits to the general public:

(1) More secure provincial circulation
(2) "Disasters arising from the sudden expansion and contraction of the currency would not so often occur"
(3) Increase security and facility of transmission of money
(4) Provide secure places of deposit "in every quarter of the Kingdom"

---

funds on some categories of collateral, kept its rate of discount high compared to the rest of the market, and raised its rate of discount back to 5 percent in early December 1825, when demands became increasingly urgent. In the interim, the Bank chose to respond to the lack of discounting business by cutting costs. The number of clerks in the Drawing Office had fallen from seventeen to eleven by February 1825, and of these eleven, four were regularly sent to serve in other departments.[7]

The first proactive response of the Bank at the level of the Court of Directors did not appear until January 12, 1826. At that meeting the Court appointed a committee to report on the practicality and expediency of establishing branch banks (Table 7.1). The very next week, the committee reported, "Branch banks would be highly expedient." The reasons they gave, however, were quite revealing of the ruling mentality of the Bank's leadership at the time. The benefits were listed first for the Bank of England and then second for the general public. The practicality was not an issue, given the experience of Scotland for

---

[7] Bank of England, C 35/2 4783/2, No. 2, "Special Discount Committee from 12 Feb. 1811 to 26 Jan 1830 inclusive, fo. 159." Later, the Committee recommended a further reduction in the number of clerks (fos. 164–65).

eighty years, not to mention the success of the Bank of the United States, the Bank of Ireland, and the recently established Provincial Bank of Ireland.

The Bank was clearly responding belatedly to decisions already made by the government to force the Bank to open branches and to promote large, joint-stock banks. The week after this report was laid before the Court, the Governor presented to the Directors the letter he had received from Lord Liverpool, First Lord of the Treasury, and Mr. Frederick Robinson, the Chancellor of the Exchequer. The arguments laid out in the letter show that the government, in this instance, was determined to work around the Bank rather than through it. The Liverpool–Robinson letter began with the assertion, "there can be no doubt that the Principal Source of it [the recent distress] is to be found in the rash spirit of Speculation which has pervaded the Country for some time, supported, fostered, and encouraged by the Country Banks."[8] So, the letter continued, it seemed advisable to repeal the authority of the country banks to issue small notes and return to a gold circulation. This would spread pressure on the exchanges over a wider surface and make it felt earlier – a clear reference to the Bank's negligence in 1825. But this alone would not suffice. After all a similar convulsion had occurred in 1793 when there were no small notes and Scotland had "escaped all the convulsions which have occurred in the Money Market of England for the last thirty five years, though Scotland during the whole of that time has had a circulation of One Pound Notes." In the past, the Bank of England "may have been in Itself and by Itself fully equal to all the important Duties & Operations confided to it" but "the rise of country banks alone shows it is no longer up to the tasks required from the increased wealth and new wants of the Country."[9]

The government proposed two remedies: (1) the Bank should establish branches of its own; and (2) it should give up its exclusive privilege as the number of partners engaged in banking except within a certain distance from the Metropolis. The first suggestion was impracticable, in the government's view, and it was obvious that the Parliament would never agree to an extension of the Bank's privileges in London. All in all, the government's proposed legislation would remove pressure from the Bank. It would still have the government's business and

---

[8] Bank of England, TVC3/11 G4/48, fos. 201–202. [9] *Ibid.*, fo. 204.

be the only establishment at which the dividends on the national debt would be paid. With this condescending argument, the letter concluded, "so we hope the Bank will make no difficulty in giving up their privileges, in respect of the number of Partners in Banking as to any District [left blank] Miles from the Metropolis."[10]

Clearly, the Bank had failed to meet the recent challenges adequately and the government was determined to create competitive banks that might better serve the public and, presumably, the government. The Bank's response was understandably churlish, which Liverpool informed them on 25 January he regretted, but was determined to move ahead, merely asking if they had any amendments to propose to the bill pending in Parliament to permit joint-stock banking. He did then accede to encouraging them to set up their own branches as well. Thus, the Bank went ahead with establishing branches, gradually dispersing seven of them into the industrial cities of Manchester, Gloucester, Swansea, Birmingham, Liverpool, Bristol, and Leeds starting in 1828 and adding Exeter, Newcastle, Hull, and Norwich in 1829, when small note issues by the remaining country banks ceased. By the time of the Bank Charter Committee in 1832, the branches at Manchester and Birmingham were clearly the most dominant in terms of note issues and bills discounted.[11]

Conclusion

King, in his classic study of the London discount market, identified the crisis of 1825 as bringing about "changes in the banking structure which were responsible for every major influence upon market evolution in the succeeding twenty years" (King 1936, p. 35). His analysis of the crisis follows very much the discussion above, adding only the additional factor that a series of good harvests had made the country banks in agricultural districts especially flush with funds. In terms of the conditions in the money market, however, the effects were limited in duration. By June of 1826, the money market rate had fallen well below 5 percent and the Bank of England was no longer besieged with requests for re-discounting of bills. Of more interest to King were the implications for the development of the bill market in London from four changes in the financial structure that occurred in response to the

---

[10] *Ibid.*, fo. 215.   [11] Bank Charter Committee Report, Appendix No. 46, p. 47.

crisis. These were: (1) the beginnings of joint-stock banking, (2) the establishment of Bank of England branches, (3) the cessation of re-discounting by the London private banks, and (4) the assumption of some central banking functions by the Bank of England (King 1936, p. 38). We will examine these in detail in Chapter 8, leading up to the next huge shock to the international financial system – the outpouring of gold from the new state of California, added to the US' growing republic as its thirty-first state in 1850.

8 | British recovery and attempts to imitate in the US, France, and Germany, 1825–1850

Essential features of the 1825 crisis

Problems of adverse selection in the London credit markets arose in intensified form during the 1824–1825 bubble on the London stock market. Yields for the various funds comprising British national debt – EIC stock, Bank of England stock, and the various perpetual annuities mostly in the Three Percent Consols – moved apart after the pressures of war finance had abated. Especially striking is the initial convergence and then wide dispersion of yields on the various Latin American government bonds. Clearly, information asymmetry, always present in financial markets, became especially severe in the London markets in the years leading to the crash of 1825. Asymmetric information is the usual situation where borrowers know more about the actual investment projects they are carrying out than do the lenders. Lenders, knowing this, charge a premium proportional to the uncertainty they feel about the borrowers and the projects in question. Charging risk premiums on loans, however, creates the problem of adverse selection – higher-quality borrowers are reluctant to pay the high interest rates imposed by the market and withdraw while lower-quality borrowers are willing to accept higher rates and to default in case of failure. In an expanding market, which the London Stock Exchange certainly was in the boom years 1806–1807 and again in the early 1820s, the availability of loanable funds at premium rates will attract lemons to the market (e.g. Mexican mines), and discourage borrowing by sound enterprises (e.g. Brazilian diamonds). High-quality borrowers revert to internal sources of funds or to a compressed circle of lenders who know their superior quality and are willing to extend credit at lower rates.

In the case of British firms in the 1820s, the compressed circle of knowledgeable, low-interest lenders was the web of country banks that had arisen in the past three decades. The continued access of high-quality firms to credit, however, depended in each case upon the continued liquidity of the small, local financial intermediaries. Their willingness to continue lending at preferential rates was limited increasingly by the risk of withdrawals by depositors wishing to participate in the high-interest, high-risk investments available in the national financial market. A financial boom of the kind normally experienced before financial crises can discourage real investment, therefore, and intensify the lemons' problem as high-quality borrowers withdraw from the loanable funds market.[1] It can also place increasing pressure upon local financial intermediaries, specializing in monitoring credit to local enterprises. It cannot be mere coincidence that the collapse of the bubble of 1825, according to one account, was set off by the refusal of a country bank in Bristol to honor the request of a Mr. Jones to redeem in gold its notes that he presented (Doubleday 1858–1859, pp. 288–289). The *coup de grâce* happens when higher-risk borrowers have to provide collateral for additional loans just as the financial collapse decreases the value of their collateral. The outcome may be either a general wave of bankruptcies, or less formally, a widening circle of payment stops that discourages normal investment and consumption. Bankruptcies continued to occur for years after the collapse of the stock market bubble at the end of 1825, especially outside the greater London area. So, all the elements of a classic financial crisis existed in 1825 for England. How did the authorities respond?

British policy responses

Under public pressure, the Bubble Act was repealed in June 1825. In July 1826, the establishment of joint-stock banks with no limit on the number of partners (the limit had been six previously) was allowed beyond a 65-mile radius of London. Both actions were counter productive if we accept the traditional story that the entire episode was yet another example of irrational speculative bubbles derived from crowd behavior in which investors acted, first too optimistically and then too pessimistically, upon fragments of information. But if the basic problem was how to process information under the new

---

[1] Mishkin (1991, pp. 70–75), gives a detailed exposition of the various routes by which increases in asymmetric information may exacerbate adverse selection, monitoring, and moral hazard problems, especially if a banking panic limits the ability of financial intermediaries to serve a monitoring function.

peacetime conditions following a quarter century of unprecedented war effort, then both actions were constructive. Repeal of the Bubble Act sped up the Parliamentary process of granting corporate charters and limited the speculative period during which uncertainty over the prospects of passage of the proposed charter dominated price movements in the initial share offerings. Moreover, repeal did not mean that limited liability was granted to shareholders in the new joint-stock enterprises. Unlimited liability remained in principle. Supplementary legislation in 1826 specified, moreover, that Parliament could determine for each charter the extent of liability of the shareholders. With these changes, Parliament both encouraged the continuation of the corporate charter business, which must have been profitable to large number of the MPs, and discouraged overpricing of the subscription shares while the incorporation bill was in progress.

The collapse of country banks in 1826 was one of the last examples of a widespread banking panic in the British banking system. As Mishkin (1991) argues for banking panics in the US, the failure of numerous small unit banks removed from the British capital markets the principal monitors who could effectively distinguish borrowers by their quality without resorting to credit rationing or arbitrarily high prices for credit. This worsened the information problems in the British capital markets. Creating joint-stock banks within which the country banks could become branches instead of correspondents helped to restore this critical monitoring function to the British system. In the peculiarities of the 1826 Act this was done by linking the various country banks within the structure of a joint-stock bank headquartered in London. But the London headquarters performed no banking function. Its role was to process and diffuse information to the various branch offices located beyond the 65-mile radius from London.

The new joint-stock banks had to function outside London (thanks to the resistance of the Bank of England) and they had to compete with existing country banks by attracting deposits rather than issuing notes. Those joint-stock banks that began business by issuing notes gave them up after a few years because the Bank of England branches refused to do business with joint-stock banks that did issue notes.[2] Given that the

---

[2] Testimony by Henry Burgess, the Secretary of the Association of Country Banks to the Committee on Bank of England Charter, fos. 5324–5326, in Great Britain (1968, pp. 427–428).

business of the new joint-stock banks was necessarily local and that they had no notes to redeem, they kept minimum reserves and relied upon re-discounting inland bills of exchange to obtain cash when needed to meet withdrawals of deposits. Due to the reduction in yields on the outstanding national debt the joint-stock banks also greatly preferred short-term loans on inland bills of exchange rather than government securities. As the country banks wound up their small note business, they also turned increasingly toward deposits and adopted the behavior of joint-stock banks. From roughly 1830 until the 1860s or 1870s the inland bill market became the most important way in which domestic credit was distributed within Great Britain (King 1936, p. 41).

The second factor to promote the rise of the bill market was the establishment of branches by the Bank of England. While initially the Bank's branches would seem to be serious competitors to the local banks, they limited their lending activities strictly to commercial bills and then only to the very short-term and highest-quality bills, as approved in London. This effectively kept business intact for the existing local banks, save that their commissions on discounting bills were reduced by the knowledge among their customers that the Bank branches did not charge commissions. But the facility of making remittances to London and receiving credits back from London through the Bank's branches helped local bankers use the London bill market more cheaply. A bill drawn locally could now be sent directly to a bill broker in London, who would be instructed to pay the proceeds into the Bank of England for the credit of the local bank at the branch bank. Moreover, a trader in Leeds could pay or receive money in Birmingham through the medium of the Bank's branches, for the "simple charge of postage of a letter."[3] In short, the branches of the Bank of England greatly improved the payments mechanism that underlay the smooth functioning of the bill market.

The third change that helped the rise of the discount houses in London was the withdrawal of London private banks from re-discounting after the 1825 crisis. The run upon the Bank of England, as well as its obvious reluctance to hold too much reserves in gold not earning income for its stockholders, convinced the London banks

---

[3] Testimony of William Beckett to the Committee on the Bank of England Charter, fos. 1436–1438, in Great Britain (1968, p. 101).

they should not rely on the Bank exclusively for cash in times of pressure. Instead, they turned to providing call loans to bill brokers, who could, in turn, increasingly become bill dealers. Instead of delaying discounting of bills in London until a matching buyer had been found for the bills offered for sale, larger-scale firms could now purchase the bills immediately, using funds on deposit with them by the London private banks (King 1936, p. 64). Only a few firms were as yet large enough to be able to risk the next step, which was to move from brokering to dealing in bills. Even firms like Gurney's probably would not have done it then had not the market rate of discount fallen below the usury limit of 5 percent. Had it been at or above the usury limit, there would have been no possibility of making a profit from strict dealing.

The final step to complete the new structure only occurred in 1830, when the Bank opened its re-discount facilities to the bill brokers. Even this was not sufficient to overcome the informational asymmetries that could still arise in the market, and which lay at the heart of later crises when the emerging bill market was abused opportunistically. The remaining problem was the continued refusal of the Bank to discount at market rates, meaning that it was unaware of emerging imbalances in the demand and supply of bills of exchange until a large excess demand for cash showed up at the Drawing Office, as in December 1825. Only when the practice of maintaining fixed discount rates at the Bank was forsaken in the crisis of 1847 did the "bank rate" come to play its key regulating role in the British financial system (Calomiris and Haber 2014, Chapter 5). Nevertheless, information flows through the medium of the bill market enabled the London banks to keep closer tabs on the conditions of the country banks, whether they were in agricultural or industrial districts, essentially through the intermediation of the London discount houses. Further improvements in the management of information flows within the entire financial structure were elicited in response to later financial crises, caused by new, unanticipated shocks encountered as the global economy of the nineteenth century was created.

At the time, however, the reforms seemed marginal: the Treasury instituted smoother patterns of tax collection and interest disbursement, the Bank of England established branches throughout England, the remaining country banks competed with or were absorbed by joint-stock companies outside of London, and the stock market rid itself of the Bubble Act of 1720. Even the bankruptcy laws began to be re-written, starting in 1831 (Duffy 1985, Chapter 1). These disparate reforms made marginal improvements in the efficiency of information gathering and processing by the government, the central bank, the banking system, and the stock market while preserving the separation of functions among them. Maintaining these "firewalls" among the types of institutions making up the financial sector of the British economy diminished the immediate impact of the reforms, but enabled them to become increasingly effective over time. True, crises continued to arise throughout the rest of the century as the British economy was subjected to repeated shocks of wars, famines, frauds, and foreign defaults. But each crisis was surmounted with increasing confidence by the evolving financial sector of the British economy, all the while preserving these firewalls. The firewalls meant that relationships among the financial intermediaries and the financial markets had to be maintained by short-term contractual relationships set in a competitive market environment rather than by regulations imposed by centralized authority with long-term rigidity. From time to time, the Bank of England would assert its primacy among peers by acting as a lender of last resort, even as the scale of operations by the leading joint-stock banks of Britain eventually exceeded that of the Bank.

While the focal point for these new market relationships was the market for discounted commercial bills that arose rapidly in importance after the crisis of 1825 (King 1936 , Chapter 2) the London Stock Exchange also increased the scope of its activities and improved its internal organization (Davis and Neal 2006). From the beginning of its formal organization in 1801, the London Stock Exchange made a clear division between its owners (the *Proprietors*) and its operators (the *Members*) due to the long-standing practices of stockjobbers who had long been accustomed to dealing in securities at the various coffee houses in Exchange Alley. The Proprietors (individual shareholders in the corporation responsible for construction and maintenance of the physical facilities that housed the stock exchange) were limited in how much stock they could hold so group agreement had to be reached on any change in marketing strategy. Their continued fear that a competing stock exchange could arise within London if they restricted membership or raised annual subscription fees significantly restricted their profit-seeking strategies to ways to increase the total number of subscribers rather than increasing the subscription fees. The Members

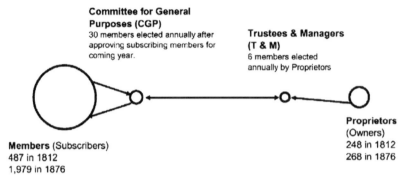

Figure 8.1 Microstructure of the London Stock Exchange, 1812–1876 (from Davis and Neal 2006, Figure 1, p. 283)

(stock brokers and dealers who paid nominal fees for annual access to the exchange if they met the approval of the Committee for General Purposes each year) sought constantly to cultivate new sources of income (see Figure 8.1). Members could use the facilities of the exchange as brokers (earning commissions), as jobbers (dealers taking the spread between bid and ask prices), or as promoters (charging underwriting fees). Given the large and growing number of members competing within the exchange for each source of income, each class of members was compelled to innovate continually. *Brokers* sought to widen their customer base, either by broadening their client pool or by increasing the variety of financial products they offered each client. Membership in the exchange, however, required that no broker offer any off-site banking services to a client. *Jobbers* likewise tried to increase the volume of their transactions rather than their spread while they were concerned jointly to minimize market volatility, because volatility would increase inventory costs for them. *Promoters*, drawn mainly from brokers who were the less well-capitalized members among the subscribers, increased the number of listings, often engaging in trade in unlisted companies while the governing committee of the exchange tried to ensure the quality of those companies that obtained formal listing.

At the meeting of subscribers on March 4, 1801, David Ricardo carried a motion "that no proprietor of the Stock Exchange shall have a right to vote for the election of new Members or any regulation respecting the Stock Subscription room unless he be elected of the Committee by the Subscribers at large." Ricardo's motion set the precedent that the powers of the Proprietors, delegated to the Trustees and Managers of the new stock exchange, were to be separated from the powers of the Subscribers, which were delegated to the Committee for General Purposes. From this initial separation of the rights and responsibilities of ownership from the rights and responsibilities of operation, the path dependency of the governance structure for the London Stock Exchange was determined for the rest of the nineteenth century.

But first the new governance structure had to establish its legitimacy. It took another thirty years before the governance structure was solidified in the face of repeated shocks to the market for securities. Discontent re-surfaced periodically among the stock traders, some of whom found supporters in Parliament. In 1810, for example, an attempt was made to form a rival stock exchange and was only defeated in the House of Lords. In response, the Committee for General Purposes and the Trustees and Managers agreed to codify the operating procedures of the new London Stock Exchange, which they did by February 1812. But it was not until 1832 that the rules and regulations finally settled into a form that persisted until 1912.

The most dramatic test of the governance structure of the formal organization of the London Stock Exchange came in 1822; its resolution set the pattern for enlargement and innovation in the membership for decades to come. It concerned the issue of dealing with the spate of defaulters among the younger, undercapitalized members of the London Stock Exchange during the volatile period of 1819–1822. Often, it appears, the defaulters had layed off their risks with option contracts made with older, better-capitalized members. The Committee for General Purposes, dominated at the time by older, more established members of the House, resolved to outlaw any dealings in options among members of the exchange. There ensued a vigorous battle within the membership of subscribers for control of the Committee at the next election.

Essentially, the battle pitched the older, better-established jobbers against the younger members, usually brokers. Abraham Montefiore, brother-in-law of Nathan Rothschild, was a leader of the "anti-optionist" or "constructionist" faction, while Jacob Ricardo, nephew of the deceased David Ricardo, was the outspoken leader of the "optionist" faction. Ricardo's arguments, reproduced in full in the minutes of the Committee for General Purposes, were obviously directed at the Proprietors and their interests in maintaining a large membership of subscribers to the exchange. He argued that options were especially necessary for the younger members of the exchange and the less wealthy members during periods of price turbulence, such as had been experienced with the resumption of the gold standard, declared by Parliament in 1819, but not taking full effect until 1821. In the event, his argument was compelling and the Managers saw to it that Ricardo and his allies dominated the Committee for General Purposes elected in 1822.[4]

The compelling interest of the Proprietors to maintain a substantial membership was even more clearly demonstrated shortly afterwards, with the rise of interest in foreign securities, especially the bonds that were issued from 1822 on by the seceding colonies of the Spanish Empire in America. For the decade comprising the boom and bust in Latin American bonds, the Committee focused on an entirely different issue – how to cope with the demands of an entirely new group of traders who wished to trade in foreign securities. The new securities included both the bonds issued by the newly independent states of Spanish America and the shares in the newly privatized mines expropriated by the rebellious colonists. Again, the Proprietors, with their eye on the possible revenues from an expanding membership who would have to engage in an extended range of activities to earn a living, were favorable to the requests of these traders for expanded, and preferably separate, facilities for carrying on this new trade. At least four of the new members of the Committee supporting the "optionists" were Proprietors. The strict constructionists, as a matter of principle, raised the objection that the Deed of Settlement only referred to dealing in "British stocks" so they feared that dealing in foreign stocks would be illegal for the London Stock Exchange. The "optionists," again with recourse to legal counsel, argued that while the Deed mentioned British funds, it did not forbid dealing in foreign stocks. Rather than resume warfare on this issue, however, the Committee compromised by referring the matter to the Trustees and Managers (Guildhall Ms. 14600/9).

---

[4] While 419 ballots were cast, all but 4 were declared ineligible by the scrutineers from the Managers. Those 4 ballots determined that the new Committee would have a majority of "optionists," headed by Jacob Ricardo.

The Trustees and Managers of the Proprietors responded quickly by renting an adjacent building, dedicating it to dealing in foreign stocks, and taking responsibility for admitting the members to the Foreign Exchange. They were careful, however, to admit these new traders on the same terms used by the Committee for General Purposes for admitting members to the British exchange. The subscription fees were the same in both exchanges, to the benefit of the Proprietors. In their report to the Committee on January 6, 1823, the Managers reassured the British exchange that they had carefully vetted the applicants and admitted no fewer than 120 with many others applying.

Trouble promptly loomed, however, when the subscribers to the Foreign Market refused to elect seven members from the fourteen names presented them by the Committee. There followed a battle of wills between a deputation from the Foreign Stock Exchange and the Committee as the Foreign Stock Exchange tried to establish its freedom from governance by the Committee and the Committee tried to maintain control of its market place by ensuring that the Foreign Stock Exchange did not usurp its premier role in determining the price of British securities. The overlapping membership of the two exchanges was a cause of concern on both sides.

As long as the boom in foreign securities lasted – that is, until the autumn of 1825 – the representatives of the Foreign Stock Market found their membership increasing, and consequently they held fast to their determination for establishing independence from the Committee for General Purposes. By the election of 1823 the Foreign Stock Market had its own governance system, the Foreign Committee. Faced with new securities devised by the London merchant banking houses eager to exploit the fabled (and much exaggerated) riches of Spanish America, the Foreign Committee proved to be the source of several innovations that were later incorporated into the rules and regulations of the London Stock Exchange. Most important were formal listing requirements for new securities to prove the legitimacy of the government or enterprise (to avoid repetition of the embarrassment of listing the bonds of the non-existent kingdom of Poyais) and a commitment not to list any new bonds from a foreign government that had defaulted on its earlier loans, which meant Greece and later a number of states in the US.

By 1827, with membership in the Foreign Exchange dwindling and the business of both Committees taken up with sorting out the claims upon numerous defaulters in both houses, the Foreign Committee proposed consolidation. The Committee for General Purposes, however, having recently increased the sureties required of their Members to three separate recommenders each posting bonds of £300, thus nearly doubling the guarantee required of new Members, had no wish to allow the members of the Foreign Exchange into the House without similar guarantees. Only if the members of the Foreign Exchange had been members for at least three years, and not failed at any time, could they be admitted on the terms that had applied previously to members of the English Exchange, namely two bonds of £250 each. This was a significant increase for the members of the Foreign Exchange and they naturally objected, but to no avail. And members of the Foreign Exchange of less than three years' standing had to come up with the new level of guaranties, three bonds of £300 each (Guildhall Ms. 14600/11, fos. 193, 197, 222, 224, 253.) On July 30, 1831, the Committee for General Purposes unanimously approved including the appropriate rules on Bargains and Quotation of Prices from the Rules and Regulations of the Foreign Market (Guildhall Ms 14600/12). With the absorption of the Foreign Market, the pre-eminence of the London Stock Exchange and the power of its Committee for General Purposes to regulate the exchange independently of government regulation were affirmed and would not be challenged for decades to come. In the years that followed, securities issued by new enterprises and governments around the globe would be welcomed to the London Stock Exchange and its customers worldwide.

To sum up: British policy reforms, both public and private, made in response to the financial crisis of 1825 proved beneficial for the British government as well as for the British economy. The government's funded debt continued to decline, after a small rise in 1827, throughout the remainder of the century with modest increases caused by the compensation to West Indies slave owners and dealing with the Irish famine in the 1840s, the Crimean War (1853–1856) and the Boer War (1899–1902). The gross income of the government remained high and comfortably above gross expenditures, save for the years 1827 and 1828, when it dropped slightly below (Mitchell 1988, pp. 392, 396, 402). The comfortable financial situation gave Britain the advantage of the lowest interest rates of any European government on its debt throughout the nineteenth century, a great advantage whenever it came to the prospect of mobilizing resources for armed conflict anywhere in the world (Neal 1990). It also laid the basis for continuing political reform in 1834, then economic reform with the repeal of the Corn Laws and the Navigation Acts in the 1840s, and ultimately promotion of limited liability joint-stock corporations in the 1850s and 1860s. Fortunately for the future of British finance, the piecemeal reforms by the government during the crisis of 1825 and its immediate aftermath proved capable of maintaining British naval superiority, financing its industrial revolution, and creating a railroad network throughout the empire and even worldwide over the following century.

Imitation and innovations in the US

The convulsions of finance in Britain in adjusting to the post-Napoleonic War environment had ripple effects across the Atlantic, affecting not only the new republics in Latin America (Chapter 7) but also the new republic in North America, the United States of America. Not only had enterprising merchants in Baltimore, New York, and New Orleans benefited from their role as neutral shippers to facilitate the provisioning of European armies during the prolonged conflicts, some had also encroached upon the Asian trade previously dominated by the English and Dutch companies (Fichter 2010). While the War of 1812, which followed from Jefferson's Embargo Act in 1808, disrupted American foreign trade, the Battle of New Orleans ensured that this port would serve as the primary outlet for American agricultural exports to the rest of the world in the future. Settlement of the rich cotton lands in Alabama and Mississippi by American planters previously confined to South Carolina and Georgia quickly followed. Finance came from local merchants with overseas connections to the European markets for cotton and tobacco. Among these was Vincent Nolte, who remained in New Orleans as a leading merchant in the cotton trade after doing his part in carrying out Ouvrard's scheme described in Chapter 7 (Nolte 1854).

The future cotton fields of Alabama and Mississippi were initially public lands held by the US Federal government, which rapidly sold them off to help offset the deficit in customs revenues caused by the Jefferson Embargo and then the War of 1812. Finance was provided by the expansion of state chartered banks, although the strains of war finance forced most to suspend convertibility of their bank notes in specie in 1814. The Second Bank of the United

States was then re-chartered in 1816, on condition that it accept state bank notes at par initially and then issue its own notes when it could sustain convertibility in specie. While the Second Bank of the United States did acquire specie through sale of its stock in Europe, its resumption happened to coincide with the maturity of the Louisiana Purchase bonds in the autumn of 1818 and early 1819. These amounted to over $4 million (out of the original $11.75 million), but they were mostly held in Europe and due to be paid in specie. With the reversal of its previous easy money policy, which had been the political condition for its re-chartering in 1816, the Second Bank of the United States brought on the "panic of 1819" (Rothbard 1962, p. 11).

Hamilton's system, which he had brilliantly constructed upon the template provided by British public finance but with noteworthy improvements, fell apart when the First Bank of the United States ceased operation in 1811 and a flurry of state banks arose to replace it. In face of the exigencies of financing the War of 1812, Hamilton's system was partially resurrected when the Second Bank of the United States was chartered on the same basis as the First Bank in 1816. This bank, however, had to cope with the political fallout caused by its obvious role in precipitating an end to the land booms that Andrew Jackson's military victory at New Orleans had set off. The monetary debates that followed were complex and often sophisticated, certainly on a par with the "Banking School" versus "Currency School" debates in Britain, but they had political consequences as a result of the animosities hardened by the heat of dispute. Moreover, the two burgeoning capitalist economies, the US and Great Britain, became mutually dependent over the course of the following century in ways that tended to coordinate their respective financial crises.

The 1825 crash in the London Stock Market had only minor effects on the US economy, however, although it created problems for Vincent Nolte's sale of his consignment of New Orleans cotton to his backers in London, the Barings merchant bank, as well as for US exporters in general (Nolte 1854, Chapter 18). Much of the resilience of the US economy in the decade of the 1820s can be traced to the effects of the massive infrastructure project, the Erie Canal, which was constructed over the period June 1817 to 1825. Already by 1821, the revenues from the tolls on the completed sections of the canal, not yet reaching its final destination on Lake Erie but traversing much of upstate New York, began rolling in and by 1825 they exceeded the interest payments on the outstanding debt by a wide margin. The initial financing of the Erie Canal was a bond issue in 1817 by the state of New York for $200,000 paying 6 percent annual interest and maturing in 1837. Two British investors took significant shares of this first of ten more bond issues that followed – David Bevan, director of the Rock Life Assurance Company ($34,000) and John Deacon, director of the Royal Exchange Assurance Company ($40,000) – to jump start the financing effort. Later bond issues, however, were typically purchased only in small amounts by New Yorkers of modest means, while their wealthier compatriots subscribed instead to the Second Bank of the United States (Miller 1962, p. 87). Only after the middle section was completed in 1819 did the Canal Fund's bonds become a favorite investment for wealthy New Yorkers and foreign capitalists, mainly from Britain. The lack of other investment opportunities in the aftermath of the panic of 1819 also helped the Canal Fund increase both the scale of borrowing at reduced interest rates and the pace of construction, which became self-financing by 1821 (Miller 1962, p. 108).

Even so, the largest single investor in the Erie Canal by 1821 was the Bank for Saving in New York City. Chartered in 1819, the Bank for Saving was the first mutual savings bank created in the US to provide a secure place for the deposits of small savings by working class men and women and offering them a secure, if modest, rate of return. It was restricted by its charter to invest only in government-backed securities, very much on the model of the first mutual savings bank founded by the Reverend Henry Duncan in Ruthwell, Scotland, in 1810. By the end of 1818, there were 465 such savings banks scattered throughout the British Isles. The Bank for Saving, unlike the attempts by Hamilton to imitate and improve on the British example, continued to flourish. Not only had it become the largest single investor in Erie Canal bond issues by 1821, by 1860 it was one of the ten largest business firms in the US, along with two other mutual savings banks in New York City (Olmstead 1976, pp. 4–6). In the second half of the nineteenth century, when financial capitalism was spreading globally, a wide range of successful imitations of cooperative credit institutions that facilitated the savings of urban and rural working classes spread first into Germany, then Austria-Hungary, Italy, and even into post-emancipation Russia (Peters 1892).

Hamilton's legacy meets Andrew Jackson

The US success with mutual savings banks was just part of the growth of the financial sector that Alexander Hamilton had initiated with his re-structuring of central government finance in 1790–1791. In the next decade, most states initiated their own banking systems, typically as joint-stock banks with varying degrees of liability for their shareholders. Corporations of all kinds arose to provide infrastructure projects such as roads, canals, bridges, and port facilities. While most corporations were closely held so that shares were not readily traded, there were organized stock markets in New York, Philadelphia, Boston, Baltimore, Richmond, Charleston, and New Orleans – seven in all compared to the one central market in London. The total capital traded on these exchanges for non-government securities in 1830 was probably about the same as that traded on the London Stock Exchange, according to Sylla (2009, p. 226). Sylla also makes the point that by 1830 US banks had attracted twice the investment capital of UK banks with only half the population of the UK (2009, p. 224). Further, US banks were much less likely to fail over this period than UK banks, as their state regulators would rather see them suspend convertibility of their banknotes into specie for a brief period than go into prolonged bankruptcy proceedings. The effect of Hamilton's financial revolution, essentially completed by the end of his one term as Secretary of the Treasury, was to launch the US immediately on a course of sustained, rapid economic growth, When Jefferson's Embargo in 1808 followed by the War of 1812–1814 cut off export opportunities for shipping and cash crops, the financial resources of the young nation were readily diverted to create an infant industrial complex in Pennsylvania and Massachusetts.

Continuation of Hamilton's financial revolutions, based solidly on imitation of the Bank of England in the form of the First and Second Banks of the United States, however, was doomed to failure thanks to the unrelenting opposition of Andrew Jackson, US President from March 1829 to March 1837. He began his war on the Second Bank of the United States in earnest at the start of his second term. In 1833, he directed the Secretary of the Treasury to withdraw all the deposits of the Federal Government from the Bank and distribute them among a range of so-called "pet banks" favored by Jackson's Democratic Party. Nicholas Biddle, an eminent Philadelphia banker who had largely restored the fortunes and influence of the Second Bank of the United States after he became president of the Bank in 1822, attempted to recover the Bank's influence, particularly in the cotton trade of the South, and acquire bullion reserves drawing on major merchant banks in England and France. Jackson countered with his Specie Circular of 1836, which required land sales by the Federal government in the western territories to be paid in specie, rather than on credit, as had been the case in the years leading up to the panic of 1819. When the Bank's charter lapsed in 1836, Biddle had it re-chartered as a state bank in Pennsylvania, re-naming it the Bank of the United States of Pennsylvania, and plotted how to restore the bank's pre-eminence by coordinating actions with banks in New York and New Orleans.

Jackson's successor as President, Martin Van Buren, refused to repeal the Specie Circular after taking office, despite pleas from Congress and a delegation of New York City banks. Further, the Secretary of the Treasury continued to make supplemental re-distributions of government deposits away from New York and to the West and Southeast, where banks quickly lost specie to would-be purchasers of Federal lands. The Panic of 1837 began in May in New York with a run on the Mechanics Bank, followed by a general suspension of payments in specie by New York banks and then spread nationwide as news of the New York suspensions reached the rest of the country. Biddle desperately tried to acquire foreign financing in Europe by offering $5 million in bonds, backed by cotton sales he had arranged from New Orleans. By 1839, however, demand for American cotton in England and France fell due to the combined effects of monetary tightness due to increased imports of grain and adequate inventories of cotton built up earlier by the leading spinners in Manchester. Biddle's bonds could not be fully redeemed by the proceeds of his cotton sales so he had to declare bankruptcy, wrapping up finally the Bank of the United States of Pennsylvania, along with its remaining branches. The most rapidly growing economy in the world was then left without a central bank for the rest of the nineteenth century. What Jackson had begun with his war on the Second Bank of the United States starting in 1832, Biddle had completed by the end of 1841 with his failed efforts to maintain a national branch banking system.

State banking, however, expanded rapidly once the constraints of a national public bank were removed, inaugurating the period of so-called "free banking" in the US from 1837 to 1860. Banking was "free" only in eight states – New York, New Jersey, Connecticut and the states linked economically to New York via the Erie Canal. Moreover, entry into banking was only free of requiring legislative assent to a new bank's charter. Instead, promoters of a new bank bought the required amount of state bonds to show their good faith, and then only issued bank notes to the market value of the bonds, which were held in trust by the state. Other states chartered banks individually, but only fourteen allowed them to have branches within the state, mostly in the South, and seventeen states gave their chartered bank a monopoly (Weber 2006a, p. 4). Of the 2,291 banks that ever existed in the US from 1782 until the end of 1860, most failed at some time. But from a total of 563 banks with 97 branches at the end of 1836, the number of banks in existence had risen to 1,371 with 213 branches by the end of 1860 (Weber 2006b, Table 1, pp. 439–444). Free banks, with their note issues backed by state bonds held in trust, proved less likely to fail over time than banks chartered by states under special conditions extracted by the legislature, and were typically smaller in size as well (Weber 2006a).

Jackson went even further to destroy the remaining elements of Hamilton's carefully constructed financial and fiscal system for the US. In addition to putting an end to the national bank, Jackson paid off the entire national debt in 1835, while distributing the surplus revenues of the Federal government to politically favored banks in the individual states. Future revenues would come mainly from land sales rather than rising customs revenues as tariffs were put aside. Keeping up land sales, in turn, would require further westward expansion backed by military efforts. Jefferson's ideal seemed to have finally been realized and Hamilton's vision put to rest, but the pressures of war finance in the future – an unintended but predictable consequence of the Jefferson–Jackson policies – would require other financial innovations.

The succeeding financial crises of 1837 and 1839 in the US, each marked by a general and short-lived suspension of convertibility of banknotes into specie as well as widespread merchant bankruptcies and bank failures, set the stage as well for a round of defaults or repudiations of debts by individual states. In 1841 and 1842, eight of the twenty-six states defaulted on their outstanding debts, dampening the enthusiasm of foreign investors who had eagerly bought their securities after their disappointment with Latin

American government bonds and mining stocks. The chronological sequence appears to confirm a general tendency for credit expansion to lead to excessive speculation, brought to collapse by freezing of short-term commercial credit, and eventually leading to defaults on long-term debts. Conspiracy, incompetence, and corruption all must have played reinforcing roles in what seems a recurring pattern in financial capitalism. Closer analysis, state by state, however, reveals a variety of patterns that are less condemning of the decision makers at the time (Wallis, Sylla, and Grinath 2004). True, sale of public lands in the southern and western states had increased tremendously in the early 1830s, and Jackson's Specie Circular and destruction of the Second Bank of the United States was intended to dampen it, while making sure that the Federal government received hard currency rather than paper money issued by banks. States responded to the closing of their branches of the Second Bank, however, by encouraging their re-organization as state-chartered banks, and Biddle did his best to encourage this, even in New York City but certainly in Mississippi, Louisiana, and Alabama.

The typical technique for replacing the defunct branches of the Second Bank was for the state to issue bonds in the amount of capital to fund the bank, which in turn issued shares to the state. The outcome was that state debt actually increased even more after the Panic of 1837 than in the years preceding. Dividends on the shares were supposed to equal interest payments on the bonds, provided, of course, that the new bank would be making profitable investments, usually in the public lands that the Federal government had granted to the state. If land prices kept rising, all would be well. Even if land prices did not rise, the public lands could be taxed once they were in private hands, so rising state revenues could easily service the bonds. Indeed, that was the case for Alabama and Ohio, where legislatures did raise taxes at the same time they issued new bonds – just as Alexander Hamilton had insisted when he created the Federal government debt, and as the state of New York had done when initiating the Erie Canal.

But states that depended on dividends from their holdings of bank stock to cover their debt obligations instead found that increasing amount of debt had to be issued just to meet current interest payments on existing debt – the case of Pennsylvania and Maryland initially. Arkansas, Florida, Louisiana, Michigan, and Mississippi also fell into this trap with bank debt, which they ended up repudiating entirely, setting a precedent for their repudiation of state debts later during the Civil War, and, in the lone case of Arkansas, even during the 1930s. The Federal government, still determined to leave internal improvements and land development to the individual states, refused to bail out any of the states, although its own debt began to rise again as receipts from both land sales and customs revenues fell sharply. States in turn began to prohibit state or local government ownership of private company stocks and in the next decade eleven states wrote new constitutions that explicitly required governments to raise taxes when bonds were issued, and obtain voter approval of such taxes. Canal projects continued, not all as successfully as the Erie Canal, and roads were improved and bridges built. Meanwhile, the Republic of Texas arose in 1836 from American settlers moving further west and became a state in 1844. The Mexican–American War of 1846–1848 followed directly, but had little impact on Federal finances, which had recovered sufficiently by then to allow the war to be fought without any increase in taxes and only a modest rise in outstanding debt. The fateful outcome for international finance worldwide, however, came as a result due to the annexation of the Mexican province of California as a territory in 1848, and admitted as a state in 1850 after the discovery of massive gold fields in 1849.

French imitations and innovations to 1849

The restoration of the Bourbon monarchy in France, abortively in 1814 and then definitively in 1816 after Napoleon's successive abdications, allowed Gabriel-Julien Ouvrard to play again a leading role in France finances. Having maintained his credibility with both leading financiers in London, the House of Baring, and in Amsterdam, the House of Hope, Ouvrard offered his services to Louis XVIII upon his return to Paris, just as he had to Napoleon, first on the Emperor's return from the disastrous campaign in Russia, and then on his triumphant return to Paris from exile in Elba in 1815. This time, however, he had a more receptive audience as Louis XVIII, doubly chastened by Napoleon's evident popularity in France and the presence of Wellington's troops as an occupation force in Paris, acceded to the British and American examples of having a representative Parliament create a national debt backed by the Parliament's taxing authority. But the imposition of reparations charges of 700 million francs and occupation charges of 150 million per year for five years by the Allies after the Battle of Waterloo proved quickly to be beyond the capacity of the fledgling monarch and Parliament. At Ouvrard's initiative, the merchant banking firms of Barings and Hope, now both controlled by Alexander Baring who had bought out the Hope & Co. partners in 1808 while keeping the name, agreed in January 1817 to provide the French government with 100 million francs in return for French bonds bought at 50 percent of par. They sold the bonds quickly at a modest profit, and in April took up another 100 million francs, this time at 55 percent of par and then a third tranche at 61.5 percent for 115 million francs (Austin 2007, p. 12). These three loans established Barings as the leading financial house of Europe but also made French *rentes* an attractive investment opportunity for returning *émigrés* from abroad. They also established a precedent for the establishment of sovereign bonds elsewhere in Europe and the Americas, provided that they were backed by legislative commitment of republican or constitutional assemblies.

The French Treasury was able to issue future *rentes* on its own initiative while Baring Brothers typically took the lead among the syndicates of banking houses that combined to take up the new securities at a favorable price. Taking no less than 89 percent of the huge issue in 1818 of 480 million francs at a price between 74 and 76 percent of par, however, turned out to be far too optimistic. The problems of 1819 forced Baring to re-schedule the purchase of the *rentes*, this time at a more reasonable price of 60 percent of par. By 1821, prices had risen to 87 and by 1823 to nearly 90, leading to the next effort by the French government to convert the outstanding *rentes* paying 5 percent to *rentes* paying only 3 percent, the same as the British Consols. By this time, however, James Rothschild was able to take the lead in organizing the conversion, relying on the resources of his older brother, Nathan, in London. Meanwhile, the internal organization of the Paris *Bourse* was permanently strengthened. While the governing body of the Paris *Bourse*, the *Compagnie des Agents de Change*, was outlawed along with all other guilds during the course of the French Revolution, Napoleon had reformed it in 1801, with eighty individuals given indefinite tenure when they provided adequate security bonds. The internal cohesion of the *Compagnie* was strengthened further when the Restoration government of Louis XVIII asked the individual agents remaining in 1816 (their number had dwindled to fifty at the end of Napoleon's reign) to put up an additional purchase price for their offices, raising it from 100,000 francs to 125,000. But in return the government made it possible for each *agent de change* to name his successor. So while the government continued to control the nomination and the disposition of the title, the current titleholder had a property right now that could be sold. Possessing heritable rights to their monopoly of the securities trade, the *agents de change* were no longer civil servants named for life but public officers with specific powers delegated to them. The same act of 1816 strengthened the self-governance of the *Compagnie*, restoring a *Chambre syndicale* that enjoyed the triple powers of recruitment, discipline, and regulation. The corporate solidarity that naturally arose within the *Compagnie des Agents de Change* enabled them always to exercise effective influence on the successive governments to maintain their privileged position within France. The power of the Minister of Finance over the operation of the *Bourse* was effectively conceded to the *Compagnie*, which kept the trading and the internal accounts of its members under tight control. Promoting new companies or government bonds was left to the informal, or bankers' market, called the *Coulisse*, which operated either immediately outside the *Bourse* or in adjacent corridors of the magnificent Palais Brongniart when it was completed in 1826. The formal exchange did its business inside around the basket located in the center of the parquet floor, hence the distinction between *Parquet* and *Coulisse* thereafter, similar to the relationship between the New York Stock Exchange and the Curb market later in the nineteenth century.

The political basis, however, for sustaining a "credible commitment" to the continued servicing of French national debt, which dominated business for the *Parquet*, was still uncertain. Charles X, who became king in 1824, tried to impose more royal authority but ended with forced abdication in 1830. The subsequent rule by Louis-Philippe proved unable to cope with the series of poor harvests and urban unrest in the 1840s, so that he was forced to abdicate as well in 1848.

Private credit markets in France also had an uneasy history after Napoleon's exile. While many of the property reforms created by the revolutionary seizures of lands and estates of the nobility and clergy were sustained after 1815, extension of the voting franchise proved to be difficult and lagged behind British reforms of 1832 and especially American reforms. The result was uncertain property rights limiting the extension of banking services to the general public. Notary publics, who had used their superior "insider" information on the properties held by their clients and the loanable funds at their disposal to provide a workable domestic capital market in Paris before the revolution of 1789, one that at times had exceeded in value the market for government securities that were always in danger of default, now found that the new property rights made their services less valuable. Notaries in the provinces, however, had improved opportunities, so much of French economic history in this period reflects more small-scale investments in farms and shops in the provinces than large-scale enterprises financed from Paris (see Hoffman *et al.* 2000, Chapter 10).

Under the *code de commerce* of Napoleon I, French business enterprises found it much more practical to organize as *sociétés en commandite* when they needed outside capital. This form of business organization was considered as a private contract among the partners, who divided themselves into active managers with unlimited liability (but typically limited resources) and passive shareholders with limited liability (but often strong voting power). With the flexibility of governance structure offered by the *sociétés en commandite* they became the typical form of French enterprises other than simple partnerships or single proprietorships. Shares of the passive partners, although transferable, were not suitable for trade in an active secondary market, much as was the case for small, closely held corporations in the US in the nineteenth century. Similarly, the Paris *Bourse*, even when reconstituted with a more limited number of members after Napoleon's exile (reduced to 60 from 100) and re-located in the fabulous building that Napoleon had begun to construct for them, had mostly the new French *rentes* to trade. The Rothschild brothers' connections to the rest of Europe, however, allowed James Rothschild in Paris to offer shares in the government debts his brothers and correspondent bankers had bought in Austria, Naples, and Prussia.

The revolutions of 1848

The cumulative effects of continued poor harvests, financial disturbances caused by the fraught relations of the two leading capitalist powers of Britain and the US, and the reluctance of political powers in general to accede to popular pressures or imitate obvious policy successes in neighboring states or countries led to the outbreak of

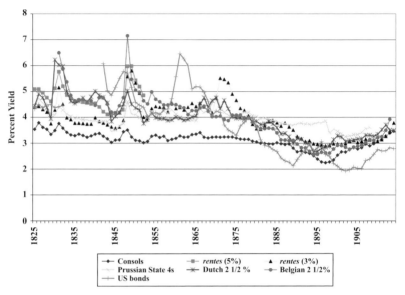

Figure 8.2 Government bond yields, industrial core nations, 1825–1913 (from Homer and Sylla 1991)

revolutions throughout continental Europe in 1848. By this time, most European countries as well as European offshoots in North and South America had created their version of the sovereign bonds that were so obviously successful in Great Britain, but with a bewildering variety of legislative commitments and taxes depending on the political prerogatives in each state (Neal 2010). Most countries had established either a silver or a bimetallic standard for their currencies. Only Britain had an unabashed commitment to a gold standard and then only from 1821 on. None of the countries in Europe, however, had yet found a comfortable political relationship between executive and legislative authorities comparable to the British example. The American example of financial diversity was still fraught with repeated conflicts between Federal and state governments that offered no persuasive lessons for would-be imitators, except possibly Russia. The American success in expanding its territory at the expense of Mexico in 1846 may have encouraged the Tsar to wrest Crimea from the weak Ottoman empire in 1854.

Figure 8.2 highlights the fragility of the political arrangements across Europe and the US made between 1815 and 1848, as well as the general convergence toward more settled affairs in the second half of the nineteenth century.

In the midst of the turmoil on the international bond markets caused by the political uncertainties throughout Europe, two bond issues by the government of Brazil, both promising 5 percent interest, nevertheless traded at different prices on the London Stock Exchange. The one underwritten by the House of Rothschild recovered first and continued to command a premium over the other issue, underwritten by a much smaller firm, Thomas & King. This confirmed the general observation made by Hiram Clarke in 1878 (Clarke 1878) and later tested rigorously by Flandreau and Flores (2009) for the period 1820–1830 when Rothschild first floated a bond for Brazil. Investors in the railroad shares and bonds issued during the railway mania of the mid 1840s also distinguished clearly between the well-established railways and the most recent ones just starting construction (Campbell and Turner 2012).

By 1850, investors accessing the London Stock Exchange from around the world knew they had entered a new era of international finance. D. Morier Evans, the chronicler of the financial crises of 1847–1848 (Evans 1848) and 1857–1859 (Evans 1859) edited the fifteenth edition of the standard reference manual for British investors, *Fortune's Epitome of the Stocks and Public Funds* in 1850. In his introduction, he observed that in the ten years since the fourteenth edition had appeared, "striking changes have occurred in the character and appearance of most of the negociable English and foreign Securities which then existed; and that others have been called into circulation, which were then not contemplated" (p. ix). Indeed, the era of global capitalism, led by innovations in international finance, had begun.

9 | Financial globalization takes off: the spread of sterling and the rise of the gold standard, 1848–1879

With hindsight, economic historians now acknowledge that 1848 divides the economic and financial history of the world into separate epochs. Before 1848, international trade was rising faster than ever before and was connecting all regions of the world into new patterns of trade. But it was only after 1848 that enough price competition arose for the same international commodities around the world that a truly global market emerged (O'Rourke and Williamson 1999; Williamson 2011). Financial innovations appeared hand in hand with the revolutionary adoption of steam power for both land and water transport systems combined with the new information technology of the telegraph. The exclamations made in the 1850 edition of *Fortune's Epitome of the Stocks and Public Funds* about the rise of securities marketed on the London Stock Exchange over the 1840s, dominated by the railroad booms in Britain and the US, were modest compared to the ecstatic remarks made by his successor, R. L. Nash, in the 1876 edition of *Fenn's Compendium of the English and Foreign Funds*:

Upon this question of indebtedness hangs a world of vitality and progress with which the future well-being of mankind is signally identified; and it would be a very narrow view of a very mighty question if we could regard it in any other light. Humanly speaking, we are only at the commencement of a new era ... [T]here can be no question – that with this modernized system of credit the world has acquired light, health, progress, and prosperity; that every man has more of the world's goods than could have been boasted of a century ago; that every man is better educated; that every man is a better citizen; and that if these are the results of indebtedness, we may fairly leave the solution of the problem to the future with that confidence which experience well earned amply justifies. (Nash 1876, p. xiv)

Essential features of the international crises, 1847–1849

The financial crisis of 1847 helped initiate a number of far-reaching policy changes in Britain especially, and then in Europe generally, with repercussions that were even more important in the future for the rest of the world as modern capitalism spread globally. Britain led the way, starting with re-institution of the income tax in 1842, followed by the "ten-hours bill" in 1844, the repeal of the Corn Laws in 1846 to end entirely in 1849, and concluding with abolition of the Navigation Acts in 1849. The last two measures opened up the period of free trade for the industrializing countries of Europe for the next quarter century. All of these policy initiatives were important for the British financial system, which responded fully, as noted above by the most eminent contemporary observer. But in the midst of the railway mania of the 1840s that was overwhelming the members of the London Stock Exchange and stimulating the rise of regional stock exchanges, the British Parliament tried to stifle the speculative fervor (which was infecting quite a few MPs at the time) by setting new terms for the operation of the Bank of England.

The Bank Charter Act of 1844 re-organized the Bank of England into an Issue Department, responsible for maintaining the convertibility of its bank notes, and a Banking Department, responsible for its commercial lending operations. The Issue Department was required to maintain enough gold reserves to cover redemption of most of its outstanding notes. The Bank's gold reserves in the Issue Department therefore limited the amount of notes it could issue, just as the Bullion Report of 1810 had recommended. The Banking Department could claim the remaining gold reserves that were not needed to cover the note issue as a buffer against possible loan defaults. By this time, of course, the Banking Department was the major source of profits for the Bank, which had vastly increased its business of lending on the basis of accepted bills of exchange. The Bank's practice was to discount at an announced rate the bills that appeared most creditworthy and were due to be paid back in full within a few months or less. The volume of this business had continued to expand with the expansion of both foreign and domestic trade after the brief interruption of the cotton trade in 1837. As the demands for cash from the Bank grew sharply after 1845 due to the combined effects of dealing with the Irish famine, harvest shortfalls on the Continent, the fall in prices of railroad securities that had been floated at the height of the railway mania in Britain, and the trade credit crisis of 1847, the Bank had to ask for waiver of the note cover for the Issue Department in order to accommodate the demands on it for cash in the Banking Department.

The number of discounts reached an all-time high in 1847, but the Bank's refusal, or inability, to meet all demands led to a large number of failures, even of joint-stock banks formed in response to the crisis of 1825. Nevertheless, the recovery from the crisis appeared satisfactory, with the lesson learned that the government should suspend the Act of 1844 upon the Bank's request, a lesson that was repeated again in response to the crises of 1857 and 1866. Bagehot's classic work on Lombard Street (1873) laid out three principles for a central bank to follow in case of a financial panic: to lend freely and early but only on good collateral and at a rate high enough to limit lending to those truly in need of liquidity. This has become canonized as "Bagehot's Rule," but he based it on his approval of the Bank's behavior in dealing with the Overend, Gurney failure in 1866 when the Bank's early actions in lending freely before asking for suspension of the Act of 1844 had effectively ended the panic before further liquidity was needed. This contrasted with the Bank's hesitancy in lending until the Act of 1844 was suspended in the previous successive crises of 1847 and 1857. He also noted that the stringencies in the money market in late 1860, a response to the problems of New York banks after Lincoln's election, had not resulted in panic in the London money market, thanks to the Bank's prompt lending from its reserves in the Banking Department. Later analysis comparing the Bank's actions in the successive crises of 1847, 1857, and 1866 shows that the Bank's success was due to canny selection of which supplicants for credit to oblige and which to deny. In the earlier crises, the Bank did not follow Bagehot's prescription to "lend freely at a high rate on good collateral" in the face of a financial panic. Instead, the Bank loaned at rates often below those prevailing in the London discount market and in limited amounts, compared to its actions in the later crises of 1857 and 1866 (Bignon, Flandreau, and Ugolini 2012, pp. 590–594). That is, the Bank rationed its credit to the London banks and discount houses that the Bank's directors felt were most worthy of support, presumably on the basis of collateral or privileged information.

Moral hazard, the risk of encouraging further risk-taking by merchant bankers if they knew their outstanding loans could be re-financed, even at higher rates of interest than normal, was not yet an issue, and the panic of 1847 was short-lived with little long-run consequences, other than to show that the note cover restriction for the Bank was easily removed in case of financial stringency in the London money market. In short order, gold shipments from the California fields came in to London, with mining equipment and expertise financed by acceptance credits offered by the leading merchant banks in London, not least of which was Barings.

The rise of gold and the spread of finance

Australian gold discoveries followed in 1851 and the combined outpouring of the monetary reserve metal overwhelmed the bimetallic regimes of Europe with their fixed mint ratios of silver to gold, averaging 15:1. The effect, however, was not to change the mint ratios, but rather to accumulate gold reserves as well as acquire the silver needed for minting the coins used especially for trade with South America and Asia. Figure 9.1 shows that the market price of silver to gold in the New York market remained remarkably stable until the 1870s, when both France and the US committed to replace their bimetallic monetary standards with a gold standard.

The explanation, according to Velde and Weber (2000), was the ability of the major international trading powers to finance their mint requirements, whether of gold for specie used to settle large accounts in international trade and to pay mercenary armies or of silver for smaller coins in Europe and for covering Europe's trade deficits with Asia, by issuing sovereign debt, the existing stocks of silver or gold serving as

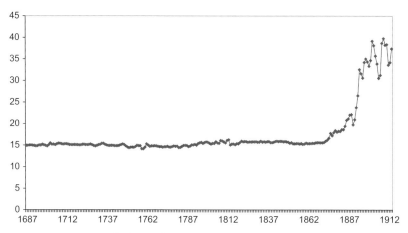

Figure 9.1 Ounces of silver to buy one ounce of gold, US market, 1687–1912 (from Warren and Pearson 1935, p. 260)

excellent collateral. Earlier, we saw how the Bank of Amsterdam provided financing to large merchant bankers in 1763 on the basis of silver coins posted as collateral after they were imported from London, presumably by selling British sovereign debt to merchant bankers in London. Indeed, the only country to adopt gold as the monetary standard after the Californian and Australian gold rushes of the 1850s was Portugal, in 1854. Like Britain in 1696, Portugal had overvalued gold compared to the rest of Continental Europe by setting its mint ratio higher than that maintained in either the Netherlands or France. Consequently, the first destination for new output of gold, whether from Brazil in the eighteenth century or California and Australia in the nineteenth century, was either Portugal or Britain. And even Portuguese imports of gold ended up mainly in Britain as the manufactured goods needed to equip mines in Brazil and clothe slaves on the sugar or cotton plantations came mainly from Britain (Reis 1996).

If either gold or silver had been necessary to finance the increase in trade and production of manufactured goods that occurred after 1850, however, modern economic growth and the global spread of capitalism would certainly have been severely constrained if not stymied entirely. What enabled the hundreds of thousands of emigrants to make their way to distant California or Australia in the decade following the gold discoveries was certainly the commercial credits extended by merchants on the basis of collateral posted in the form of new bonds, whether from sovereign states or chartered corporations, as the author of *Fenn's Compendium* enthused in 1874. Even the crisis of 1857, which affected not only Britain, but also the European trading powers and the US, did not slow down the expansion of railroads or of national territories. The Crimean War had stimulated the use of sovereign debt worldwide as well as further expansion of railroad networks globally. When it ended, with the repulsion of Russian advances against the fiscally weakened Ottoman empire, an entirely new financial framework existed internationally.

The Ottoman empire's finances were bolstered by the issue of its own sovereign bonds, packaged deliberately for sale in the European capital markets with the joint guarantee of the British and French governments. The first issue of £3 million in 1854 met with limited success. Even offering 6 percent interest, well above the yield available on either British or French sovereign bonds, the underwriting houses had to lower the market price to 80 percent of par. The next issue, £5 million in 1855, however, offered only 4 percent but was underwritten by Rothschild's in London and Paris and so was oversubscribed, bringing in £5.3 million (Tuncer 2011, p. 342). British finance of the war, despite political posturing by Gladstone, who claimed that wars had to be paid for by taxes, not loans, ended up increasing the national debt for the first time since the end of the Napoleonic Wars. Even as the income tax was doubled and a variety of new excise taxes imposed, loans still covered 46 percent of the total cost of the war to Britain. True, this was less than any preceding war, but had the war continued longer the share of loans would have risen sharply as new bond issues were in preparation (Anderson 2001, p. 318).

A side effect of the Crimean War finance was to force the promoters of the first land-grant railroad under construction in the US, the Illinois Central, to take their bonds to Amsterdam and Frankfurt instead of London for placement with European investors, which established a flow of railroad finance that continued into the twentieth century. Another side effect may have been to decide the government of Portugal, which was undergoing another round of political turmoil in 1854 due to its dynastic connections with Brazil after 1808, to resolve the confusion of its currencies, variously minted in Brazil, Portugal, and Britain, by establishing a uniform gold standard under which all the gold coins could circulate at fixed exchanges and as legal tender (Reis 1996). As the first European country to follow Britain's lead in formally establishing a gold standard for its currency, Portugal's historic decision went completely unremarked in the pages of *The Economist*, which was more interested in seeing Portugal adopt free trade (which it did not) and stop shipping slaves from its African colonies to Brazil (which it did not). Portugal also turned out to be the first country in Europe to leave the gold standard, a not-so-innocent victim of contagion from the Argentine default on its bonds in 1890, and the first Baring crisis, which will be covered in Chapter 10.

The commercial and financial crisis of 1857

The end of the turmoil created by the combination of British policy changes and the Crimean War was the financial crisis of 1857, which began in the US but quickly involved Britain and the Continent as well. One possibility is that the New York banks had become so dependent upon continued shipments of gold from California that the loss of a huge cargo of gold aboard the USS *Central America*, which sank in a hurricane off the coast of North Carolina while en route to New York, made it impossible for New York banks to meet the unusual demands for specie withdrawals that occurred in October. Withdrawals from New York banks were expected each season at harvest time, but were exacerbated in 1857 due to a shock to the previous surge of settlement into trans-Mississippi territories that had been part of the Louisiana Purchase. Political uncertainty over whether the new territories could be free or slave, however, was heightened by a Supreme Court decision (*Dred Scott* v. *Sandford*) that affirmed a slave owner's legal possession of a slave anywhere in the US, even in states or territories that outlawed slavery. Announced on March 6, 1857, just after the inauguration of President James Buchanan, the *Dred Scott* decision had far-reaching implications. In addition to making slavery enforceable everywhere in the states and territories of the US, it ruled the Missouri Compromise of 1820 unconstitutional and cast further doubt on the legitimacy of the Louisiana Purchase. The immediate consequence was to end abruptly the rise in western land prices, discourage further settlement in the new territories, and reduce the prospects of new railroads built to service them. The eventual suspension of convertibility by New York banks in October, coordinated through the Clearing House, stopped the panic from spreading in the North, while branch banking in the South, whose leaders welcomed the *Dred Scott* decision, enabled banks there to weather the crisis without suspending convertibility (Calomiris and Schweikart 1991).

For Britain, however, the consequent rise in import prices of wheat and cotton, combined with a severe blow to one of its primary export markets, created a trade cycle that had all the features of the modern business cycles that were to follow thereafter (Hughes 1956). The Bank of England responded more quickly this time than it had in 1847 to suspend the Bank Act of 1844 that restricted the use of its gold reserve for backing the note issue, but business failures were nevertheless widespread. Bagehot's rule for central bank response to financial panics, not yet formulated even by the editor of *The Economist*, came closer to realization in response to the panic of 1857, according to recent analysis of the number of firms receiving loans from the Bank and the terms on which the Bank loaned. Unlike its actions in 1847, the Bank largely charged rates at or slightly above those ruling in the market to its customers, showing only a brief period of credit rationing, just before suspending the Bank Act of 1844. While the clients using the Bank's discount facility were now restricted more narrowly to banks and discount houses, more of them used the discount facility at the height of the crisis than in 1847 and a smaller percentage of the applicants were rejected (Bignon, Flandreau, and Ugolini 2012, pp. 590–591).

The revolutions of 1848 on the European Continent

The revolutions of 1848 dominated the political and economic history of Continental Europe, and certainly the history of international finance as well. Before 1848, traditional power elites throughout Europe tried to re-create their dominance on the basis of combining a landed aristocracy with an implicit constitutional monarchy, believing that that combination was the source of British economic and military success. After 1848, all European power elites saw that some form of finance on the British model was essential if they were to sustain or regain their dominance in their country. The revolutions of 1848 also generated financial innovations throughout Europe, leading to the Second Empire in France, the economic unification of Germany under Prussian leadership, and the eventual political unification of Italy in 1862. Leading the way was France, first with the *Comptoir national d'Escompte* created by the Provisional Government of 1848 and then followed by two great institutions established under Louis Napoleon – the *Crédit Foncier* and the *Crédit Mobilier*. All three were joint-stock corporations that combined either commercial or real estate banking with investment banking. All would serve as examples for the rest of Europe in the years to come. In addition, many more banks and credit companies were created during the course of the Second Empire, including the *Crédit Industriel* (1859), the *Crédit Lyonnais* (1863), and the *Société Générale* (1864). While the activities of the House of Rothschild dominated the mobilization of French savings into public works, railways, and central government debt for the rest of the nineteenth century, one may argue (Cameron 1953, 1966) that it was the competition of the innovative Péreire brothers, who founded the *Crédit Mobilier* in 1852 with the support of Napoleon III, that drove the Rothschilds to expand and innovate their investment activities.

Railroad finance goes international

Railroad financing took pride of place as Napoleon III determined to radiate lines from Paris to each of the six borders of France after the experimental railway between Paris and Saint-Germain, jointly financed by Rothschild and the Péreire brothers, had proved its financial viability. The *Crédit Mobilier* took the lead in establishing the Eastern, Western, Southern, and Grand Central railway networks, although Rothschild took the lead in the much more profitable lines to the iron and coal fields of the north and to the Mediterranean port of Marseille. Until 1865, when internal management issues began to plague the continued operation of the *Crédit Mobilier*, it dominated the French financial system – and the initiation of French industrialization and modern economic growth.

Beyond France, Prussia responded to the revolutions of 1848 by providing more resources to its western provinces acquired after 1815 (Tilly 1967). To finance the exploitation of the Ruhr coal fields and Silesian iron, as well as the necessary railways to connect Berlin to Cologne, the *Darmstädter Bank für Handel und Industrie* was chartered in Germany in 1853. Explicitly modeled on the *Crédit Mobilier*, the success of the *Darmstädter Bank* led to imitations of universal bank adopting the joint-stock corporate form. Set up in 1851 to act purely as a discount bank for commercial bills of exchange, the *Disconto-gesellschaft* became a joint-stock company in 1856, explicitly imitating the *Darmstädter* (and the *Crédit Mobilier*). All the German "great banks" that followed, especially after 1871, were modeled on the *Darmstädter*.

The Péreire–Rothschild competition moved from France and Germany into Austria as well. The Austrian State Railway Company was created in 1854 with its board of directors dominated by the Committee of Paris, sitting in the offices of the *Crédit Mobilier*. Rothschilds countered by reasserting their presence in Vienna, creating the *Kreditanstalt für Handel und Gewerbe* in 1855. The *Kreditanstalt* then initiated the finance for six newly organized railways in Austria to the west and south into the Italian provinces. While the Péreires actively promoted another Austrian railway to the southeastern territory of the Austrian empire, their financing faltered with the financial crisis of 1857, leading to a sellout to the Rothschilds. But the competition was renewed in 1863 when the Péreires bid up the price Rothschilds had to pay for underwriting the Austrian state lottery, and then several directors of the *Crédit Mobilier* created the *Bodenkreditanstalt* in imitation of the *Crédit Foncier* in France. The Austrian *Kreditanstalt* and *Bodenanstalt* will play a central role in creating the world depression after the First World War, but the *Bodenanstalt* was able to finance Austria's payments to Prussia after the former's defeat in the war of 1866 by mortgaging the Crown lands of the Habsburg monarchy.

Spain and Italy also benefited from the Rothschild–Péreire competition by expanding their rail networks and improving access to their mines. The *Credito Mobiliario Español*, established in 1856, was the most successful of all Péreire enterprises as it continued to be controlled by the Péreire family until winding up in 1909. Both the Rothschild and Péreire families followed the dictates of Napoleon III to help finance the Spanish rail network, but mainly in competition with one another over the various routes, delaying the final connection to France over the Pyrenees until 1878. But the main problem was the constant turmoil of Spanish public finance, which kept Spanish bonds from being listed on either the Paris or London Stock Exchanges, not to mention the lack of profitable traffic between Spanish provinces. Both Rothschilds and Péreires managed to extract significant subsides from the Spanish authorities to continue their competition. By 1870, the railway network of continental Europe was essentially completed and clearly followed the lines of trade and finance that had already existed at the beginning of the eighteenth century (Figure 9.2).

Meanwhile, the British enthusiasm for railroad construction spread into Canada, Australia, and India, with a major market opening for British supplies in the US. There, arguably the most innovative approach to railroad finance was to initiate land grants to railroads, setting aside alternate sections of land along possible rights of way that would open up new possibilities for settlement and for freight traffic. First was the Illinois Central Railroad, which in 1852 received permission from the Federal government to provide land-grants in Illinois, Mississippi, and Alabama. The project, jointly sponsored by Senator Stephen Douglas of Illinois and Senator Jefferson Davis of Mississippi, was designed to connect eventually the port of Chicago on Lake Michigan with the port of Mobile, Alabama on the Gulf of Mexico. Bonds mortgaging lands assigned to the railroad along the right of way found a ready market in New England and eventually in Europe, especially on the Continent.

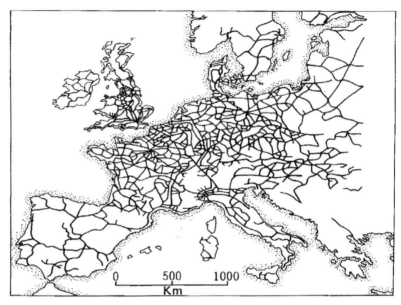

Figure 9.2 The railway network of Europe, 1880 (from Pounds 1990, p. 434)

Not only did the Illinois Central set a pattern for even larger schemes for financing the trans-continental railroads that would come to fruition only after the American Civil War, it also set a pattern for American railroad accounting practices in the future. Given the diverse sources of earnings – passenger fares, freight earnings, and land sales – all of which rose dramatically each year as new settlers poured into the lands now accessible for cultivation of wheat and cotton to export to Europe, the annual reports documented each type of freight, the population of each town (all placed at least one mile from existing settlements), and the price of land sold or still held by the company (Flesher and Previts 1999). Given the specific assets that were mortgaged to the bondholders, such detail was valuable for reassuring distant investors in Boston, New York, London, Paris, Amsterdam, and Frankfurt that their stake in what was the longest railroad in the world by 1861 was both safe and remunerative. When American railroads resumed expansion after the Civil War, each company tried to tailor its bonds and equity shares to meet the specific tastes of investors in each country as well. The railroad mortgage bond was a specific asset designed to overcome the hurdles of moving from personal to impersonal exchange, and it worked very well indeed. Unfortunately, the motivation for building railroads, whether in North America, Europe, Russia, or Asia, was never simply to expand peaceful commerce. Strategic considerations of enhanced military capability for defense or conquest were always in play as well.

War finance again

Stephen Douglas, the Illinois Senator who had made possible the Illinois Central Railroad, ran for nomination as the presidential candidate for the Republican Party in 1860 against Abraham Lincoln, the Illinois lawyer who had been the chief counsel for the Illinois Central Railroad. Lincoln won the Douglas–Lincoln debates, the nomination, and became President of the United States of America in March 1861. In April, the US descended into the long-threatened War Between the States, as it was termed then. Later, resentful Southerners would call it the War of Northern Aggression, while victorious Northerners still call it the American Civil War. Whatever one calls it, the war pitted the northern, mostly free of slavery, states against the Confederate States of America, all slaveholding states in the South that seceded from the Union. Neither side was prepared for what proved to be the bloodiest war in America's history, accumulating in barely over four years more fatalities than in all of the other wars fought before or since. As so often in history, financial innovations emerged to help both the North and South achieve their respective military objectives. The North was determined to preserve the Union and its eventual expansion to the Pacific coast and eventually (after the Emancipation Proclamation of 1863) to end slavery as well. The South was determined to secede as individual states while continuing slaveholding cultivation of commercial crops beyond the Mississippi wherever possible. The financial expedients that emerged were necessarily shaped by the respective political constraints and aspirations on each side.

President Jefferson Davis of the Confederacy, the Mississippi Senator who had helped legislate the Federal and state land-grants for the Illinois Central Railroad, had in the 1840s proudly proclaimed the sovereign right of the state of Mississippi to default on its debts. His speeches to that effect in the US Senate were promptly published and distributed by Northern emissaries throughout Europe, effectively closing off foreign capital markets. The Confederacy had no unified tax capacity for funding its debt, a problem that had plagued the original thirteen colonies between independence in 1783 and Alexander Hamilton's creation of a national debt in 1790 with national customs revenues to service it. With no tax base and no market for its debt, the Confederacy basically had no choice but to finance its war effort by printing money, which soon led to rampant inflation, which made it harder even for the individual states to find a market for their individual state debt and therefore to fund their own militias as their share of the war effort.

The one successful bond issued by the Confederacy was truly innovative. Designed by the Erlanger investment bank headquartered in Paris, the bond was a warrant convertible into a fixed price for cotton to be picked up at the buyer's expense in the South. True, the holder of the warrant had to run the Union blockade both into the South and then back again to Europe, but the price per bale became increasingly attractive as the price of cotton from alternative sources such as Egypt, India, or Brazil rose sharply in Liverpool. Effectively, the cotton bond became a call option on cotton in New Orleans and its price behaved in the waning years of the war and at the height of the "cotton famine" in Liverpool much as the Black–Scholes formula for calculating option prices would have predicted, had it been available to speculators in commodities at the time (Weidenmier 2000). Even so, the bond's net proceeds contributed only a small fraction of the South's war finance, and even that portion was only posted as collateral for the commercial credit needed to pay the British supplier of the special boats needed for running the blockade in order to pick up the cotton (Weidenmier 2005).

More significant and enduring were the financial innovations by the North. Congress, now composed only of Senators and Representatives from the non-seceding states, could and did raise taxes nationally. Measures included doubling the tariff, increasing excise taxes on a widening range of commodities, and enacting a temporary income tax. But to create a national market for US debt, Salmon P. Chase, the Secretary of the Treasury in the first Lincoln administration, had to resort to novel measures as his initial efforts to place bonds with New York banks quickly ran into liquidity constraints caused by large-scale withdrawals of specie in anticipation of the coming conflict. The success of the Philadelphia banker, Jay Cooke, in selling Pennsylvania's initial bonds for funding its contribution to the war effort, led

Chase to rely on him for selling the first major issue of US bonds domestically. Cooke used the national telegraph network to establish a broad customer base for the bonds, which were issued in various denominations as bearer bonds, which made them attractive as means of payment as well as sources of interest payments and symbols of support for the North's war effort.

Treasury Secretary Chase created the "greenback," a demand note that initially was redeemable in gold, but later issues became legal tender in 1862, with a further expansion of issues in successive acts in 1862 and 1863. The National Banking Act in 1863 allowed national banks to issue notes printed by the Treasury up to an amount determined by the US Treasury bonds they deposited with the Comptroller of the Currency. This was a new office created for the purpose of overseeing the new National Banking system, much as state comptrollers had overseen state banks chartered under free banking, as in Chase's home state of Ohio. In 1864, National Banks became chartered directly by the Comptroller and only National Banks were allowed to issue the bank notes, which were printed up to uniform standards by the Treasury.

The financing of the North's war effort was partly by export of gold from California, but mainly by the combination of printing greenbacks and issuing sovereign debt backed by the central taxing authority of the Federal government, and held mostly domestically. The greenbacks could be exchanged domestically for gold coins, still in circulation, and the exchange rate of greenbacks for gold in New York was carefully reported. Usually falling between 70 and 80 percent of a gold dollar, the greenback at times fell close to 40 percent when Union forces suffered defeat in battle. Overall, Mitchell estimated that the greenback added about one-fifth to the North's war expenditure than if it had been able to maintain full convertibility with gold (Mitchell 1903, p. 419). With Union victory in 1865, the greenback rose in value and speculation mounted that full convertibility to gold (or silver) would occur as foreign investments in the US resumed as well as domestic investments, including completion of the Union Pacific Railroad (Friedman and Schwartz 1963, Chapter 2). Full convertibility, however, was delayed until 1879. In the meantime, another war, much shorter in duration and less bloody than the American Civil War, took place, with lasting effects on the international monetary system.

War in Europe

The Austro-Prussian War of 1866 and then the decisive Franco-Prussian War of 1870 put to the acid test of war finance the possibilities created by the international market for sovereign bonds. In response to the revolutions of 1848, the Bank of Prussia had continued to finance commercial relations with West Prussia. The diverse German states included in the *Zollverein*, the customs union created in 1834 to facilitate trade between Berlin and Cologne, responded to the increase of traffic through their territories by building stretches of railway, nearly all of which were financed by state bonds. The resulting railway boom quickly linked the two centers of government and commerce in Prussia. Austria had countered with its own railway building, as described above, with the intent to separate Bavaria and the various south German states from the *Zollverein* dominated by Prussia. Prussia's decisive victory over Austria in 1866 led to its further expansion by provoking war with France in order to seize the rich iron ore fields of Alsace-Lorraine adjacent to the coal fields of the Ruhr.

Prussia's subsequent victory over France in 1870 led to the creation of a new German Reich in 1871 intended to consolidate all the German states into one economic unit with no internal tariff barriers. But to realize full benefit of trade among the industrial and agricultural areas of the empire, the Bank of Prussia was combined with the public banks in the other German states to create the *Deutschebank* as the bank of issue for the new currency, the *Reichsmark*. As most of the German states had silver-backed currencies, all that was needed was to agree on a common mint standard, much as Charles V had done for the Low Countries in the sixteenth century (Chapter 3). To overcome political squabbling among the newly united German states over setting a common mint standard for their silver coins, the decision was made to adopt a new gold standard and replace as much as possible all the former silver coins with gold coins. One motivation might have been to imitate Britain's continued success in finance and to encourage further trade with Britain. Another motivation, no doubt, was to note the success of the Northern Union's method of finance in the American Civil War, as opposed to the disparate attempts of the confederated states of the South.

To facilitate the move to a gold standard, it was important to sell off the silver reserves of the German states at a favorable price, say at the 15.5 mint ratio maintained by France since the currency reform of

Napoleon I where the Bank of France still had the largest monetary reserves of gold in the world, not having had time to deploy them effectively in the war with Prussia. To make sure the French bought the German silver, reparations were demanded – 5 billion francs, nearly one-third of French GNP (Flandreau 1996b, p. 873). German silver reserves amounted to 2 billion francs, so the French reparations would have easily covered the purchase had the French monetary authorities been willing and able to absorb this increase in their silver supplies. Flandreau argues they were able in fact to do so, even while maintaining their bimetallic ratio of silver to gold at 15.5:1 (Flandreau 1996b, p. 874). But rather than facilitate Germany's currency reform in this manner, the French monetary authorities decided to demonetize silver entirely, cutting off any potential supply from Germany. Only with this decision, made effective in August 1873 (after the successful sale of perpetual annuities called the *rentes Thiers* to cover the cost of the reparations) did the price of silver fall on the Paris market (Flandreau 1996b, p. 875). It was this decision, made to thwart the designs of the German victors to use French demand for silver to cover the costs of their currency reform for the new German empire that led to the continued collapse in the price of silver and the rise of the classical gold standard by 1880.

The French decision had international repercussions, as its decision to let the price of silver drop meant that the price of gold would rise as well, at least in France and Germany. The earlier Coinage Act of 1873 in the United States, signed into law in February of that year, however, had lowered the price of gold by setting the mint ratio between silver and gold dollars at 14.88:1, counter to the increased supplies of silver coming from the mines of Nevada and Colorado. That was the "Crime of 1873" according to the Populist movement, representing the agricultural states in the South and the mining states in the West, as it appeared to reduce prices for their outputs while raising prices for their inputs. It certainly led to shortages of silver coins produced at the US mints as the world market price for silver in terms of gold was higher and continued to rise after 1873. The Resumption Act of 1875 followed the consequences of the Coinage Act of 1873 by setting 1879 as the date when the remaining greenback dollars would be fully convertible to the gold dollar.

These government actions in the US and France, taken really for short-term political imperatives rather than for long-run economic objectives, were unexpected and unanticipated shocks to international currency markets. Among other effects, they thwarted the expectations of Jay Cooke and many others in the US that the greenback dollar would not reach par with the gold dollar for another few years, as the greenback dollar now became dearer in terms of European currencies and actually overshot the final parity set in 1879 (Mixon 2008, pp. 748–750, esp. Figure 5). One consequence of the temporarily overvalued greenback was to put another crimp in Jay Cooke's speculation on the sale of Northern Pacific Railroad bonds, which he had intended especially for German and Austrian investors who had supported him initially in constructing another transcontinental railroad to compete with the Union Pacific. With the greenback now more expensive, reduced demand by German and Austrian investors for Northern Pacific bonds, and the Northern Pacific falling behind on its payments on the bonds still held by Cooke, his company was forced to declare bankruptcy in September 1873.

As Mixon (2008) points out, Austrian investors had started to withdraw from the US railroad bond market after Austria's defeat in 1866 while German investors turned to the greatly expanded investment opportunities opened up in 1870 to take advantage of the new resources for German joint-stock companies in Alsace and Lorraine. So, while the subsequent Panic of 1873 set off a worldwide recession, the US stock market crash in September–October 1873 was not a case of contagion from the difficulties in continental Europe, as famously argued by Kindleberger (2000). His narrative of 1873 starts with the reparation payments from France that started flowing into Germany after 1870. These huge payments stimulated speculative excesses in Germany – the euphoria of the Reich's *Gründungsjahr*. In 1871 and 1872, these "spilled over" into Austria, with both Austrian and German stock market bubbles bursting in May 1873. The "cascade effect" then of irrational exuberance, now deflated in accordance with the behavioral economics theory of crowd behavior, eventually reached the US, with the signal event being the failure of America's pre-eminent investment banker, Jay Cooke.

Counter to Kindleberger's wonderful story, however, Mixon (2008) found that investors in the US securities markets behaved rationally, as evidenced in the behavior of option prices of various equities compared to the bond prices. Overall, the participants in the US securities market centered in New York assessed the relative riskiness of the various railroads sprawling across the North American continent depending on their earnings from passenger and freight traffic, or land sales in the case of land-grant railroads such as the Union Pacific. Much of the investment in US railroads came from Europe, but after the Civil War it appeared that British investors kept to the proven railroads in the East while Dutch and German investors stayed with the higher-yield, riskier railroads shunned by British investors relying on their proven investment bankers such as the Rothschilds and Barings. Neal and Weidenmier (2003) determined that if contagion had spread from Germany into Austria and then the US, as predicated in the Kindleberger story, then the coefficient of variation among the markets for short-term commercial credit in the financial centers of those countries would have increased during and after the panic of 1873. Increases in the volatility of short-term interest rates during a financial crisis in one country should raise the volatility of interest rates in trading partners as well. This didn't happen in 1873, as most countries took steps to inoculate their domestic credit markets from the infection spreading from the US and newly unified Germany. On the contrary, each crisis had local determinants.

True, the financial panic in the US, which followed a few months after the stock market declines in Vienna and Berlin, led to a world depression in trade and industrial production, a depression that lasted until the end of the 1870s or even 1881 in the case of US industrial production. The depression encompassed both France and Russia, neither of which had financial panics but both of which were increasingly involved in the global markets in agricultural commodities, especially grains, and precious metals that emerged after 1850 and continued to expand thereafter. The cases of Austria and the US show that even in the absence of an international lender of last resort, countries on the periphery of the international financial system could insulate themselves from panics in the center, Germany in the case of 1873. The Bank of England had limited its role as a lender of last resort by 1866 when it let the major discount house of Overend–Gurney fail. In 1873, it did not respond to failures of various joint-stock banks, perhaps because they were in Scotland.

Conclusion

We cannot overlook the dire consequences outside of Europe that arose with the expansion of global capitalism after 1850, however.

The Taiping Rebellion in China (1850–1864) was even more deadly in terms of total casualties than the American Civil War, with perhaps 20 million deaths occurring before the Qing government managed to quell the last remnants of the revolt. While motivated by religious fanatics (Christian in this case), the main support for the rebellion came from the south of China, which had the closest contact with western capitalism and resented the imposition of treaty ports by the western powers after the First Opium War in 1842. Nor should we overlook the Sepoy Rebellion in India in 1857, which ended with the British government taking over direct control of India as a colony from the East India Company. In 1853, an American naval commander, Matthew Perry, visited the port of Edo in Japan (modern Tokyo) with the object of opening Japan to American trade. The presence of four warships help convince the emperor to sign the treaty opening Japan to American and then western trade generally. British, French, American, and German adventurers made various claims over the islands of the South Seas over the remainder of the nineteenth century. The division of Africa by European colonial powers came next.

One example of how intimately related trade finance became with government finance in this transition period of global finance is the case of Peru. Even late in the nineteenth century, Peru was still trying to stabilize its borders with the various Andean countries that arose from the breakup of the Viceroyalty of Peru after 1808. To finance Peru's military efforts against its neighbors, a succession of bonds were issued in London during the "guano boom" (1850–1875). They performed very well over this period, despite continued political instability – fourteen different governments, ten of which came after a civil war or revolution (Vizcarra 2009, p. 359). Indeed, Peru became the largest Latin American debtor nation in this period, enjoying high prices for its bonds issued successively to finance wars with its neighbors or specu-lative railroads. The key to their success, however, was that a British merchant banking firm, the House of Gibbs, took responsibility for marketing the bonds in London, and then making the interest pay-ments and redemptions from the revenues of the guano sales world-wide, for which the Gibbs firm also had a monopoly (Vizcarra 2009). The technique was similar to that developed by the Dutch merchant banks in Amsterdam for handling the sovereign debt of the Danish crown in the eighteenth century (Chapter 3). Before this arrangement to tie the finance of its primary export good to its "sovereign" bonds,

Peru's government bonds traded at huge discounts, reaching 20 percent of par. After the arrangement ended with the collapse of the guano boom, Peru defaulted on all its bonds again in 1875.

But our attention must now focus on the financial underpinnings of the subsequent expansion by the emerging capitalist powers of the Atlantic economy, all of which had adopted the gold standard by 1879, creating the classic gold standard period of January 1880–July 1914. In retrospect, the adoption of the gold standard by the most advanced countries of the world may seem to have been a response to Great Britain's economic success. In one respect, that perception is correct, but the various ways that countries adopted the gold standard had more to do with the attraction of a common gold standard to provide fixed exchange rates for British investors in overseas enterprises and governments than in the inherent economic virtues of gold as a metallic standard, or even the value of fixed exchange rates, for that matter. Variety is the spice of life, and the variety of experiments made by countries responding to the spread of financial capitalism in the latter nineteenth century are fascinating for revealing the challenges of coordinating financial innovations among banks, markets, and governments.

10 | The first global financial market and the classical gold standard, 1880–1914

All the industrial core of the Atlantic economy and much of the European periphery were joined financially in the classical gold standard, 1880–1914. The US formally adopted the gold standard in 1879, but already in fact had kept the Civil War greenback dollar at par since 1873. Germany and the Scandinavian Monetary Union had switched from silver to gold in 1871. France and the other members of the Latin Monetary Union soon joined as well. Even the Ottoman empire declared its commitment in 1881. The standard justification for general adoption of the gold standard at the time was that it facilitated the expansion of international trade. Commitment to a gold standard implied as well a commitment to fixed exchange rate with the other countries on the gold standard, which in turn promoted a multilateral settlement of trade imbalances: a country's bilateral trade deficit with one trading partner could be offset by its surplus with a third trading partner.

But international trade had already expanded rapidly in the thirty years before the widespread adoption of the gold standard. In response to the free trade initiatives of Great Britain in 1849 and the continued drop in freight rates, due to the application of steam power both on land and sea, trade had grown globally in all basic commodities. Further, commodity prices had converged across the trading world as had never before been possible (O'Rourke and Williamson 2005). The Anglo-French Commercial Treaty of 1860 with its most-favored nation clause had promulgated a general round of tariff reductions throughout Europe. Each succeeding negotiation between any pair of countries that included a reduction in tariffs had to include the same reduction with the countries whose previous treaties had included the proviso that their future tariff barriers would never be higher than that of the "most favored nation." The free trade movement, however, started to lose momentum just when the gold standard spread within Europe and eventually beyond to Russia and Japan in 1895.

There was a general rise in tariff barriers, led initially by the US and Germany and eventually even France, the major countries responsible for moving from bimetallism or silver to a gold standard in the first place. A "golden paradox" emerged in which one policy that promoted the expansion of trade (the gold standard) accompanied a policy designed to protect domestic producers from foreign competition (protective tariffs). The resulting "golden paradox" is resolved, however, once we recognize the importance of foreign capital flows to finance industrialization by countries trying to follow the lead of Great Britain and the US.

Adopting the gold standard confirmed a country's commitment to a liberal economic policy in support of its commercial and industrial sectors as they entered into the competition of international trade. It also meant that a country could issue its sovereign debt on more favorable terms than before. Figure 10.1 shows the general reduction in yields that countries had to offer on their national debts, even as they increased the size of their national debt relative to their national product. The access to foreign capital markets, especially in London and Paris after 1848, and then Amsterdam and Berlin after 1879,

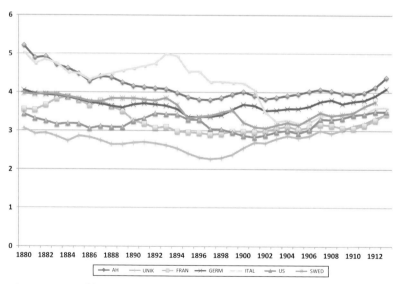

Figure 10.1 Yields on sovereign bonds, major European countries, 1880–1914 (from Flandreau *et al.*, *Global Finance Database*, http://eh.net/database/global-finance/)

meant that governments could guarantee the bonds floated by their own railway companies and other corporations committed to the construction and operation of the infrastructure needed to participate competitively in a global market that kept expanding. Access to foreign savings through the issuance of sovereign bonds meant that new liberal governments could make their investments in infrastructure without taxing or expropriating the traditional landed elite. Eventually, most of them did increase their taxes, but they did so gradually and only when the benefits of industrialization had appeared (Cardoso and Lains 2010)

The bond yields in Figure 10.1 are percent of par in nominal terms; the general downward trend in most of them reflects the general deflation in commodity prices that also set in from 1873 until 1897, as shown in Figure 10.2. The easiest explanation for the quarter century of falling prices among the gold standard countries is that their combined efforts to accumulate the gold stocks they felt necessary to maintain convertibility of their national currencies increased the world demand for gold just as the supplies from Australia and California were petering out. Given a commitment to keep the price of gold fixed in terms of national currencies, the only way to meet the increase in demand for gold was to decrease the price of all other goods exchanged

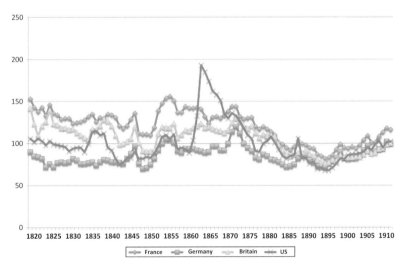

Figure 10.2 Wholesale price indices for industrial core countries during the gold standard, 1820–1910 (from Mitchell 1978)

for gold. Eventually, the increase in the real price of gold led to efforts to explore fresh sources of gold, which were found in South Africa and Alaska by the turn of the century. The subsequent rise in prices of all other commodities then reflected, at least in part, the increasing supply of gold coming into the gold standard countries, all of whom kept the price of gold fixed as long as they remained on the gold standard.

The trend break in 1897 is evident in both graphs, but there was considerable variation among the leading industrial countries, both during the quarter century of deflation and the nearly twenty years of subsequent, mild, inflation. Financial crises help to explain most of the individual blips in both the wholesale price indices and the nominal bond yields over the entire period of the gold standard. The Barings crisis in 1890 provides the most general and powerful explanation for the interruption of the deflationary trend up to 1897, while the 1907 panic in New York explains much of the interruption to the inflationary trend up to the First World War. But in addition to the disturbances in trade and economic activity created by these two major financial crises, the long period of deflation stimulated financial innovations and government regulations that were to have longer-run consequences for economic growth based on new technology. Only some of the implications of electricity, automobiles, airplanes, chemicals, and plastics that were beginning to appear before the First World War changed the trajectory of finance and technology. Before examining how financial innovations interacted with new technologies, however, we need to review the international financial crises that punctuated the gold standard period.

Financial crises during deflation and the lessons learned

The Baring crisis in 1890 proved to be the defining moment of the gold standard system and of effective action by the regulatory authorities, especially the Bank of England. After the Bank let Overend, Gurney, the largest discount brokerage firm in Britain at the time, fail in 1866, the British financial system recovered quickly. Finance of international trade through London acceptance houses continued and overseas investment by British savers resumed and, importantly, the danger of moral hazard – the belief the Bank would always step in to rescue an overextended financial firm if its risky loans turned sour or toxic – had been put to rest. Thereafter, Bagehot's Rule for the Bank, to lend freely (but only on really good collateral) at a penalty rate, whenever a liquidity crisis struck the London money market, seemed to be working nicely. Raising the Bank rate brought gold to the Bank or to British firms while lowering it induced more trade financing. And, thereafter, the Bank moved its rate much more frequently in response to movements in the market. The "light touch" regulation of the British financial system was also helped by the continued expansion of the joint-stock banks as they absorbed country banks into their national network of branches. The major joint-stock banks also realized that the gold reserves of the Bank were not expanding as fast as the liabilities of the banking system overall, or even as fast as the gold reserves of the other countries that had now committed to the gold standard, so they took other measures to protect themselves from liquidity shocks.

On the other side of the Channel, moreover, there was the vast accumulation of gold reserves by the *Banque de France*, determined as the French authorities were not to be outdone by the *Reichsbank*'s accumulating war chest of gold reserves (Figure 10.3). It seemed to many observers at the time that the *Banque de France* had the "big bazooka" in its pocket for assuring the stability of the French financial system, which meant that it did not have to keep altering its re-discount rate in response to fluctuations in seasonal and cyclical demands for trade finance, which the Bank of England began to do with increasing frequency. The *Banque de France* did fulfill, however, the central bank function of a "lender of last resort" in several cases during the classic gold standard period. The first occurred in 1882 after the "*krach*" of the Union Générale, a new joint-stock bank founded in 1878 that was modeled on the defunct *Crédit Mobilier*. The *Union Générale* had invested lavishly in new infrastructure projects in central and eastern Europe and had generated a stock market bubble fed by excessive leverage. When it collapsed in January 1882, the share prices of the companies it had created also plummeted, bringing down fourteen of the sixty stockbroking firms that comprised the *Bourse* in Paris. The common fund that the *agents de change* had created to cover obligations of failed member firms was exhausted and only a major loan by the *Banque de France* kept the Paris Stock Exchange open (White 2007). During the following decade the loan had to be repaid and the remaining stockbroking firms kept a low profile, while the stock exchanges of London, New York, Berlin, and even Amsterdam flourished.

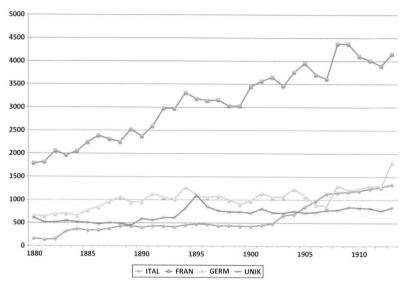

Figure 10.3 Gold reserves of the major European public banks, 1880–1914 (million French francs) (from Flandreau *et al.*, *Global Finance Database*, http://eh.net/database/global-finance/)

In 1889, another joint-stock bank in France, the *Comptoir d'Escompte*, failed and elicited a much stronger intervention by the *Banque de France*. This time, the *Banque*'s concern was to protect the other private and joint-stock banks in Paris from the consequences of the payments stoppages by the *Comptoir*, then the largest bank by far in France. A "lifeboat" was created by the *Banque* explicitly to cover the losses of individual firms from the bad loans they had made to the *Comptoir*. But each banking firm had to post good collateral before it was allowed to access the *Banque*'s emergency fund, or "lifeboat" (Hautcoeur, Riva, and White 2014). The success of this operation in France served as the model for the Bank of England's subsequent intervention on behalf of the leading investment bank, Barings, in November 1890.

Barings' problems grew during 1890 after Argentina bonds, some issued to finance construction of water-works for the city of Buenos Aires, stopped payment. In short order, problems with bonds issued by Brazil's new government appeared, and given the importance of Brazilian remittances for maintaining Portugal's commitment to the gold standard, the Bank of Portugal suspended convertibility.

The contagion among these three countries could have infected London as well, had the Bank of England not intervened to "rescue" Barings with a fund it cobbled together from the other leading banks in London, supplemented by a major loan from the *Banque de France*, and a commitment by the Russian government to withhold its demands for gold on its deposits with Barings.

The story is well-known: the Bank of England under the leadership of its Governor, William Lidderdale, organized a bail-out financed by an ad hoc consortium of leading London bankers. Perhaps less well known is the reaction of the Members of the London Stock Exchange to the episode. At their meeting on December 22, 1890, the Committee for General Purposes of the London Stock Exchange formally addressed the Governor of the Bank to praise him for his actions in the Baring Crisis. The Chair of the Committee, Mr. H. Rokeby Price, stated:

Being from their position necessarily well acquainted with the unexampled character of this crisis, the Committee are fully able to estimate the magnitude of the disaster which at one time threatened to disorganize, if not to overwhelm, the vast financial and commercial interests of this and other countries, and they are convinced that it was almost entirely owing to the masterly ability with which the measures of yourself and the Court of Directors were carried out in the negotiations in this country and abroad, and more especially to the firm and decisive manner in which your great influence, as governor, was so wisely and courageously exercised, that a panic of unparalleled dimensions was averted. (Guildhall Library, Manuscripts 14600, "Minutes")

Governor Lidderdale was very pleased to receive these plaudits from the Members of the London Stock Exchange, and responded by stating that he appreciated their opinion all the more,

as coming from a body peculiarly well able to judge of the magnitude of the crisis, and of the consequences that would have followed the suspension of Messrs. Baring Brothers & Co., with liabilities to the extent of £21,000,000. What these consequences might have been I hardly dare to think. What security would have been saleable: What bills could have been discounted, if so great a disaster had really come to pass ... When you thank the Bank of England it is very important to bear in mind the willing and cheerful assistance that we have received from others. In the first place, from Lord Rothschild, whose influence with the Bank of France was of such assistance to us in obtaining those means, without which we could not have rendered the aid we were enabled to give. Secondly, the help of Her Majesty's Government in the assurance of support if required, a support which it has happily not been necessary to claim. Equally valuable was the prompt assistance of those who subscribed to the Guarantee Fund, without which it would have been impossible even for the Bank of England to have undertaken so enormous a responsibility. (Guildhall Library, Manuscripts 14600, "Minutes")

Lidderdale's response to Baring crisis demonstrated the government's commitment to maintaining a regulatory and monetary environment within which the securities business could continue to flourish even as pressures mounted due to the continued deflation in commodity prices and the continued declines in yields on prime securities, especially for sovereign bonds and railroad securities. Starting with the Baring crisis of 1890 in London and ending with the passage of the Gold Standard Act of 1900 in the US, the stock exchanges that created the first global market in financial capital responded in different ways to a series of financial crises after enduring a quarter century of deflation. The internal reforms in market microstructure or regulations by government in each of the major exchanges of the world – London, New York, Paris, and Berlin – changed fundamentally the operations of the global market of the time.

Government regulation vs. self-regulation

Comparing four of the core industrial countries of the time – Great Britain, France, Germany, and the US – one finds that each differed from the others in at least one important political or legal respect. Great Britain and France had centralized political systems with the financial power and the major capital market located in London and Paris, while Germany and the US were more fragmented politically so that financial power and capital markets were more dispersed. There were also dramatic differences in their legal systems: Britain and the US functioned on the basis of precedent-driven, judge-decided, common law, overridden by statutory law of the central government when it was applicable. France and Germany both relied on the statutory laws written explicitly in their respective commercial codes. The four countries provide us with a separate experiments in combining different legal systems with distinct political systems: Britain with central government and common law; the US with federal government and common law: Germany with federal government and civil law; and France with both central government and civil law.

London

The effects of continued deflation upon bond prices and market returns affected the London Stock Exchange largely through the repercussions that the economic difficulties in the US, South America, and Australia posed for British investors – investors who had increasingly diversified their holdings of securities in the global capital market that British merchant bankers had created in the middle of the nineteenth century. There followed a continued expansion of both the business of the London Stock Exchange and the size of its membership. Between 1893 and 1913, commercial and industrial shares were the largest gainers in the number of listings. The impetus to their expansion came first in the form of so-called debenture shares that permitted breweries to pledge the incomes they received from their tied public houses toward payment of the dividends on new capital – new capital that had been issued precisely to purchase the exclusive vending rights to beverages sold in previously independent, free, pubs (Watson 1996).

These new activities, however, clearly bore higher risks for the members undertaking them. To confront the problems raised by the increasing number and severity of failures among the members despite the absence of banking or financial crises, a series of protective measures were taken by the London Stock Exchange. Over time, especially after 1882 when each new member had to become a proprietor as well, the main increase in number of members came from brokers, as opposed to dealers (jobbers). Consequently, new rules tended to favor brokers and to restrict the range of activities available to dealers so they could not undercut brokers' commissions by shunting trades to other exchanges. As the membership continued to increase over the following years, the interests of the Proprietors and Members tended to converge, but as most Members were brokers, the convergence was toward the interests of the brokers. Eventually in 1904, the Members voted to require that any new member purchase a nomination from a retiring member so that total membership would be capped at the existing level. The number of members then peaked at 5,481 in 1905. That enabled the brokers then to establish minimum commissions in 1912 for the first time in the history of the Stock Exchange in London.

But the needs of the small partnerships that made up the bulk of the membership meant that new listings were encouraged, regardless of size, so there was an effort to increase the number of corporations.

Even more effort was devoted to increasing the size of the existing stocks or bonds that were in greatest demand by investors, whether they were British or foreign. Consequently, the number of corporations listed was much larger than that for any other exchange in the world, although the average size was lower than on the New York, Berlin, or Paris exchanges. A high proportion of the securities were foreign as well.

New York

In the US, the continued effect of deflation upon the values of the huge stock of railroad bonds motivated the innovative responses of the New York Stock Exchange in the 1890s (Snowden 1987). Persistent deflation in the US raised the real price of railroad bonds, which first increased the wealth of existing bondholders, but then decreased the interest rate on bonds purchased by new investors. Because the US railroad companies were private enterprises that lacked financial backing from the Federal or state governments, they had originally offered very favorable terms to bondholders – terms that included not only high nominal interest rates but also a guarantee that the bonds would not be called or redeemed if their market price rose above par. As the price of more and more bonds did rise above par, railroads found themselves in the unpleasant position of having to continue to lay out high fixed nominal interest payments while, at the same time, facing falling prices for their freight and passenger services. Moreover, they could not take advantage of the falling market yields to replace high-interest debt with new low-interest bonds, because they would have to buy the existing bonds at market prices. They could not turn to the money markets to cover those costs, because the value of the collateral available to back new bonds was declining due to the general deflation.

The management of the American railroads responded in a variety of ways to this financial dilemma. Ultimately, however, their best recourse was to declare bankruptcy and to throw themselves on the mercy of a judge's decision about the appropriate method for settling creditors' claims. At the time, there was no Federal bankruptcy law. Therefore, railroads declaring bankruptcy not only had the advantage of suspending interest payments while continuing normal operations during the time that they were in the hands of a receiver, but also had some discretion in picking the judge or, at a minimum, the state that had jurisdiction over the legal proceedings and that would decide the terms of reorganization (Campbell 1938). By the end of 1895, the series of competitive bankruptcies had put 25 percent of the total US railroad mileage into the hands of receivers.

The suspension of interest payments to bondholders brought investment houses into the center of the re-organization schemes that were proposed in the series of attempts that were made to restore the long-run viability of American railroads. Three interrelated courses of action were developed and deployed: first, to replace the outstanding bonds with new bonds bearing a lower coupon rate; second, to write down the principal of outstanding bonds at the same coupon rate (essentially a partial default); and, third, to substitute contingent income claims, usually in the form of preferred stock, for the existing bonds. Across the board, the net result was to restore the profitability of American railroads and profitability led to a new surge of investment in the period 1897–1907 – investment that was focused on double-tracking, rail yards, and stations rather than on new routes (Neal 1969).

While new technologies were emerging rapidly in the US at the end of the nineteenth century, the accumulated effects of deflation on the secondary market for securities in the US were leading to a series of innovative initiatives by businessmen engaged in stockbroking, especially those fortunate enough to be members of the club called the New York Stock Exchange. Driven primarily by the goal of restoring their incomes – incomes that had declined because of the loss of business as their wealthiest customers abandoned the stock market – the brokers took steps both to retain their traditional customers and to attract a wider customer base. To compensate for the disappointing returns now available in the dominant securities – railroad stocks and bonds – they widened the range of products available. Not only industrial and utility stocks in the new sectors, but also new forms of railroad securities – securities such as warrants, preferred stocks, and bond issues backed by specific forms of new capital – were promoted by the New York Stock Exchange. To re-assure their clients, they imposed listing requirements that, over time, steadily became more detailed and demanding. In order to reduce the costs of operating the exchange they finally created a clearing house for completing transfers of stocks. To limit the threat of competition from competing exchanges, both within and without New York, they tightened their control over access to the ticker tape that provided up-to-date price information.

Meanwhile, regional exchanges, especially in Chicago and Cleveland, brought shares to market of new companies in the emerging technologies (Deere, McCormick, Dow, Standard Oil) as well as in local electrical utilities and urban transport systems. The nation's unit banks vied in providing finance to local auto dealers so they could pay in advance for orders from Detroit's auto manufacturers. In short, a range of financing techniques became available for different technologies at different stages of their respective developments.

Throughout the nineteenth century, the central governments in both Britain and the US restrained themselves from any direct regulation of the stock exchanges, only imposing temporary rules at the outbreak of the First World War. While the self-regulating governance of the London and New York stock exchanges could have led to opportunistic behavior at the expense of the investing public, competition among brokers and jobbers was strictly enforced within the London Stock Exchange, while in New York the existence of the Consolidated Exchange in New York, as well as literally dozens of regional specialized exchanges throughout the US, forced the New York Stock Exchange to stay competitive. The informal Curb market allowed shares in new firms to be traded until they became large enough to move to the "big board" on the Stock Exchange.

Berlin

In Germany, the explosion of incorporations that occurred both before and after the founding of the *Reich* in 1871 and the receipt of 5 billion francs in reparations from the defeated French nation led to speculative manias that ended in the *gründerkrach* of 1873. That explosion was certainly aided and abetted by a law passed on June 11, 1870 – a law that made it much easier to create a corporation. The passage of that piece of legislation was the high point of a series of attempts to liberalize the marketing of corporate shares, and it sealed the structural interdependence of the German nation's banks and industry – an interdependence that still exists to this day. The rise of new joint-stock banks after the passage of the law is particularly noteworthy. In the first two years of the new German *Reich*, 107 joint-stock banks were founded – banks with a total capital of 740 million marks. By the end of 1873, seventy-three of the newly chartered banks were in liquidation (Gömmel 1992, pp. 154–156).

Faced with a crisis, and in an attempt to protect the earnings of the remaining corporations, the government's initial reaction was to raise customs barriers. In the longer term, however, as it tried to improve the economic robustness of the nation's business organizations, the government moved to restructure the internal organization of the nation's corporations. In 1884, a new law redefined the framework of governance of German corporations. Each corporation was required to adopt an institutional decision making structure that consisted of three distinct boards, with each committee serving a different function. The managing board of directors (*Vorstand*) and a general assembly of stockholders (*Generalversammlung*) were features that were common to corporations in all four countries. The German law, however, added a third oversight board, the *Aufsichtsrat* – a board with a large majority of its members drawn from outside the firm. Those members represented not owners and managers, but labor, the government, the general public, and the banks. The *Aufsichtsrat* was peculiar to Germany.

The stock market crises of the early 1890s led to further major reforms in Germany. As occurred in other Continental countries at this time, the German reforms outlawed the informal exchanges – the so-called *Winkelbörsen* – that had sprung up around the formal exchange; and they specified that only transfers validated on the formal exchange would have standing in legal disputes. The new law went further, however, by outlawing uncovered, or short selling, of securities. As a result, trading in corporate securities tended to move, not merely out of Berlin, but out of all of Germany, to the more friendly purviews of the Amsterdam and London Stock Exchanges (Michie 1988). In retrospect, it seems that the formation in 1892 of the *Börsenenquetekommission* – a commission that included only token representation from members of the London Stock Exchange and a commission that was heavily weighted with representatives of agricultural interests eager to do anything to raise prices of farm products – was responsible for this outcome. But, given that the concerns of a wide range of potential interest groups had been represented in the composition of the *Aufsichtsraten* – one of the three committees charged with overseeing the governance of a corporation – the broad composition of the commission reflected political reality, if not economic rationality.

As a result of the legal changes, trading on the German stock exchanges quickly became concentrated on public securities issued by German state and city authorities. At the same time, the great banks continued their efforts to develop new private sector business in adjacent, politically friendly, countries. Both Austria and Italy were initial beneficiaries of the legal changes and the response of German investment banks to those changes. According to Cohen (1992) and Good and Ma (1999), the initial outcomes have been deemed beneficial for both Italy and Austria, although additional analyses of the financial sectors in each country (Fohlin 1998; Tilly 1998) suggest that there may have been few long-run benefits.

Paris

In France, the government's regulatory role varied with changes in the political regime, but even these rules affected the role of the *Coulisse*, the informal or bankers' exchange dominated by dealers and speculators, more than the role of the *Parquet*, the formal exchange that enjoyed government protection and regulation. Inhabited exclusively by a small number of bonded brokers with life tenure and the right to name their successors, the *Parquet*'s microstructure was overseen by its *Compagnie des Agents de Change*. The *agents de change* were more than civil servants named for life, but public–private officers with specific powers. In 1816, the government also strengthened the *Compagnie*'s self-governance by restoring the *Chambre syndicale* – an organization that enjoyed the triple powers of recruitment, discipline, and regulation. The corporate solidarity that naturally arose within the *Compagnie* enabled them effectively to influence the government's policies, and, thus, to maintain their privileged position within France. For the remainder of the long nineteenth century, the power that the Minister of Finance had exercised over the operation of the *Bourse* was effectively conceded to the *Compagnie*.

The *Coulisse* originally served a complementary function to the official *Parquet*. It provided counterparties to agents of the *Parquet* who were seeking matching buy or sell orders, but who were unable to serve as dealers themselves. During the Second Empire (1852–1870), the *coulissiers* expanded their business rapidly. They organized two separate markets: one for dealing in government *rentes* and the other for trading in securities that were not yet listed on the official exchange. The *coulissiers* were mainly bankers who were dealing on behalf of the large joint-stock banks and the customers of those banks. By the 1890s, the volume of business on the *Coulisse* was more than 50 percent greater than that done in the official market, a fact only discovered when returns from the transactions tax on sales in both the *Parquet* and the *Coulisse* imposed in 1888 came to light. In 1898 legislation raised the number of *agents de change* from sixty to seventy and allowed each *agent* to employ a larger staff, especially *remisiers* or shunters. These individuals directed business from the *Coulisse* or foreign or provincial exchanges to the *agent de change* that employed them. The majority of the *remisiers*, or shunters, were traders on the *Coulisse*, who were put back in their place as subordinates of the *agents de change* by the legislation of 1898. Thus, like the Curb market in New York, the *Coulisse* ended as a complement, rather than as a competitor, to the official exchange, the *Parquet*. Not only did the *Parquet* remain the official market, but the redesigned *Coulisse* was reorganized as rigidly as the *Parquet* – re-organized with a limited membership and similar internal rules of conduct. Further, it was limited in scope to the forward business of stock trading and to the same, mostly government, government-backed, or government-sanctioned securities. In the case of *dirigiste* France, therefore, the risk taking in response to diminished nominal returns on their traditional *rentes* was taken by the French investing public, rather than by the members of the organized stock exchanges, as was the case of New York and, to a lesser extent, in London.

Summary

Whether the continued deflation in world commodity prices was the fundamental cause of the repeated and increasingly severe financial crises, it was certainly the basic cause of the search for new financial products. New forms of assets appear on each of the major exchanges, with reverberations in the lesser and provincial exchanges. As interest yields fell on high-quality bonds, whether government gilts in London and Paris or railroad bonds in New York and Berlin, traders produced new assets for investors who were searching for higher returns. From brewery and mining stocks in London to industrial securities in

New York, specialized securities appeared in each exchange. Financial crises often, but not always, followed that fell most heavily on the newest, most speculative securities. The government inquiries that followed resulted in different reforms for each exchange.

The internal structure of the London Stock Exchange changed, reflecting more and more the self-interests of the growing majority of the traders who were specialized as brokers, rather than dealers, while banking consolidation proceeded more rapidly. The New York Stock Exchange consolidated its pre-eminence among the American markets with its dealer specialists, while the banking sector fragmented and became increasingly vulnerable to payments crises. The Paris *Bourse*, backed by government fiat, took over control of trading in foreign securities from the informal market, while ceding control of its settlement procedures to the *Banque de France*. Berlin was forced by government decree to put its forward trading operations into Amsterdam and London while the great banks expanded their operations into central and southern Europe.

Financial innovations and technological breakthroughs

Financial crises did occur, of course, but both banks and markets responded, as well as governments, to minimize the economic consequences, as described above. More consequential in the long run were the financial innovations that proliferated in the gold standard period along with the technological advances that we now identify as the Second Industrial Revolution (Neal and Davis 2007). In the last quarter of the nineteenth century and the first decade of the twentieth, the separate worlds of technology and finance were both transformed, much as they were in the last decade of the twentieth and continue to be in the first decade of the twenty-first. In technology, historians of science now regard the scientific breakthroughs that occurred in this period as defining the research agenda that spawned the scientific miracles of the twentieth century and continue to transform our daily lives to the present. Concentrated in this short time span were inventions of electric generators, dynamite, photographic film, light bulbs, electric motors, internal combustion engines, steam turbines, aluminum, pre-stressed concrete, and all this even before the turn of the century. The pre-First World War surge of invention culminated with airplanes, tractors, radio, plastics, neon lights, and synthetic fertilizers in the first decade of the twentieth century – the Second Industrial Revolution.

Financial historians label the same period either the classical gold standard or the spread of finance capitalism. The years 1880–1913 saw the spread of the gold standard throughout the industrialized world, the rise of joint-stock banks in the US and Germany to compete internationally with the great merchant banks of Britain, the explosion of new corporations whose shares were traded on the stock exchanges of London, New York, Paris, and Berlin, futures markets in organized commodity and currency exchanges, holding companies, and trust companies. It seemed apparent to observers of events at the turn of the previous century as well that the rapid spread of new technology in electricity, telephony, wireless, and petroleum owed much to the concurrent rise of finance capitalism. Indeed, Joseph Schumpeter built his entire theory of business cycles and the internal dynamic of capitalism on the interaction of the worlds of finance and technology, based on his observations of developments in Europe and the US in the late nineteenth and early twentieth centuries (Schumpeter 1939).

The leading country in innovations both in finance and technology during the 1890s was the US. Why this was so at the turn of the nineteenth century lies in major part in the particular features of the American financial system, with its complementary array of financial intermediaries and capital markets. The US stood apart from the other leading industrial nations in the fragmentation and diversity of its banking system. The repeated banking crises under the National Banking System of the late nineteenth century did lead eventually to the formation of the Federal Reserve System, beginning its operations just as the First World War was breaking out in Europe in 1914. While most financial histories focus on the policy responses to the banking crises, especially that of 1907, which led to the creation of the Federal Reserve System, and the damages to the real economy they caused, it is more enlightening (and encouraging) to focus on the competitive responses that occurred in the capital markets spread across the US, which had become the leading industrial nation of the world by 1900.

In the 1890s, new financial intermediaries – trust companies – arose that invested directly in securities traded on competing stock exchanges throughout the country. The competitive quality of American capital markets as well as American banking fragmentation contrasts with the financial sectors in other leading industrial nations. While much of the theoretical literature of finance finds it useful to regard financial institutions and capital markets as substitute forms of financial intermediation, the historical experience described in earlier chapters highlights their complementarity in the long run, and this proved especially to be the case for the US in the 1890s.

Moreover, these distinctive features of the American financial sector meshed well with the peculiarities of the emerging technologies. Studies of new technology show that some of them require privileged information to become effectively operable, while others need open access to other innovators and potential users to become commercially viable. Privileged information technology requires personal finance such as that provided by relationship bankers; open access technology requires impersonal finance available through open capital markets. When a new technology becomes commercially profitable it then attracts the attention of talented scientists and technical experts. In the US case, continued innovations and advances in productivity then followed as each new technology diffused rapidly throughout the economy after 1900.

Liquid and deep capital markets are especially important for the finance of "loose coupling" or "non-linear" technologies. Electricity was such a technology at the end of the nineteenth century, as was information technology at the end of the twentieth. The earlier technologies derived from iron and steel and industrial chemicals were "tight coupling" or "linear" in nature (Perrow, Reiss, and Wilensky 1986). Lending officers in banks could see clearly what a proposed innovation in the production processes of iron, steel, soda, and sulfur could accomplish at the level of an individual plant or firm. To realize the commercial prospects for electricity, telephony, or the internet, by contrast, a firm needs complementary inputs from a social infrastructure. Financing the infrastructure of transmission lines or fiber optic cables needed to make the new technology commercially viable requires access to large, liquid capital markets. A financial system concentrated excessively on either capital markets or on banks cannot respond effectively to the financing needs of developing technologies. As technologies emerge from breakthrough scientific concepts to diffusion of generally useful applications, their financing needs to evolve as well – from the personal or relationship finance of privileged technical knowledge to the impersonal, capital market finance of networks of varied applications of the new technology. The US and Germany took the lead in developing the technology of the Second Industrial Revolution, due in large part to the diverse and competitive financial systems within each country as well as the expansionary goals of their governments.

The end of the first global financial market

The pressures of persistent and widespread deflation culminated in the decade of the 1890s, as every country adhering to the gold standard experienced directly or indirectly the effects of a series of financial shocks. After 1897, by contrast, a combination of gold discoveries, improved technology for exploiting known gold reserves, and the withdrawal of certain countries (first Argentina, Brazil, and Portugal, then Italy and Austria-Hungary) from the competition for gold reserves relieved deflationary pressures. Only the systemic crisis of 1907–1908 and the pressures of preparation for potential war, which did break out in 1914, marred the persistent expansion of the global financial system over the period 1897–1914. This period of gold inflation also spurred rapid economic growth in the core industrial countries and a continued outpouring of technical progress and rising productivity.

True, there were occasional wars engaged by each of the leading industrial and financial powers, but each one – the general European "Scramble for Africa" (1884–1914); the Spanish–American War (1898); the Boxer Rebellion in China (1898–1900); Britain's Boer War (1899–1902) – was easily financed and handily won by the various leading industrial powers. Japan entered the gold standard club in 1895, using the gold it demanded from China as reparations after a brief naval war. The treaty obligation to allow imports of western manufactured products also expired in 1895 so Japan raised its tariff as well. Soon, Japan used its commitment to the gold standard to float railroad bond issues in New York, rather than London. Russia, with the encouragement of France and chastened by repeated defeats in wars with China and the Ottoman empire, first raised a tariff in 1891 and then joined the gold standard in 1897 to aid foreign financing of its coal and iron industry in modern Ukraine and the Trans-Siberian Railway. Even the US ramped up its combination of high tariffs and commitment to fixed exchange rates with the Dingley Tariff of 1897 and the Gold Standard Act of 1900.

The Panic of 1907, however, showed that the mutual advantages of the gold standard for each participating country were coming to an end, as was the leading role of London in the global money market. Beginning in the US with the failure of the largest trust company in the country, Knickerbocker Trust, in October 1907, the repercussions of the liquidity crisis in New York quickly affected London, Paris, Berlin, and even Milan. Contagion, not just interdependence, spread from the money market of New York to France, then Berlin, and even into Italy in 1907 in contrast to the earlier crises of 1825, 1847, 1857, 1873, 1882, 1889 and 1890, and 1893 (Neal and Weidenmier 2003). The reason was that the Bank of England found that it could not deal effectively with a severe and prolonged external drain of its gold reserves in late 1906 by using its traditional tool of raising its discount rate.

The high rate hurt London's ability to finance trade while gold continued to flow out in response to insurance claims on British companies due to the fires caused by the San Francisco earthquake in April 1906 (Odell and Weidenmier 2004). As an alternative policy, the Bank lowered its discount rate, but imposed an embargo on discounting any American paper. Trust companies in the US had been taking advantage of their regulatory freedom to borrow extensively on the London discount market during their growth spurt starting in 1896 (Neal 1971). Working around the London embargo, which took effect at the end of 1906, American finance houses turned to Berlin and Paris, which in turn put pressure on their correspondents in central and southern Europe. Hence the evidence of contagion, once the serious panic began in New York with the failure of the Knickerbocker Trust Company.

A series of ad hoc measures were taken in the US that eventually quelled the panic. First, the Secretary of the Treasury tried to ease problems for New York banks with an infusion of government deposits. But it took the leading international banker, J. P. Morgan, to coordinate a clearinghouse arrangement among the leading investment bankers, much as had been done in France with the *Comptoir d'Escompte* case and in Britain with the Baring failure. Further, Morgan identified a way to induce the *Banque de France* to release gold on hand to pay for cotton imports from the US, which also helped relieve the liquidity crisis in New York (Rodgers and Payne 2014). To avoid such ad hoc measures in the future, Congress created the

National Monetary Commission in 1908 to study why the US dollar was so little used in financing international trade compared to the pound sterling, French franc, and German mark. The Commission produced thirty reports during its existence from 1909 to 1912, many of which remain classics in monetary and financial history. The main outcome was to recommend the creation of the Federal Reserve System, which Congress duly enacted in 1913, to take effect by the end of 1914.

Alas, the Great War, as it came to be known, disrupted the start up of this major innovation in government regulation. The First World War changed everything about the way international finance could be conducted in the future as well.

11 | *The Thirty Years War and the disruption of international finance, 1914–1944*

The outbreak of the Great War in the summer of 1914 created a whirlpool of financial disturbances that disrupted completely the global financial market. Until then, international finance, operating both through banks with foreign branches and correspondents and securities markets open to corporations and customers both domestic and foreign, had been expanding worldwide. When Austria declared war on Serbia on Tuesday July 28, stock exchanges in Montreal, Toronto and Madrid closed, followed on Wednesday July 29, by the closure of exchanges in Vienna, Budapest, Brussels, Antwerp, Berlin, and Rome. On July 30, St. Petersburg and all South American countries closed, as did the Paris *Bourse*; first on the *Coulisse* (the bankers' market) and then on the *Parquet* (the official exchange). When even the London Stock Exchange shut down on Friday morning July 31, only the exchanges in New York remained as markets where the world's panic could vent. All this happened before the Great Powers themselves got around to declaring war.

As with the outbreak of wars in the past, there was an immediate scramble for liquidity and the pound sterling rose sharply on the foreign exchanges (Keynes 1914). The shock of universal sell orders on all the world's stock exchanges was completely predictable, but two aspects were new and cause for future concern whenever the hostilities ended. First was the extent to which foreigners with open positions on the London Stock Exchange and with the London discount houses were unable to meet their obligations. The importance of the London money market for the finance of international trade meant that the outbreak of general hostilities inflicted what we now call "counterparty risk" upon the entire financial community of London. As the bulk of the world's international trade at the time was then financed through the London money market, whether a British firm was actually involved in the trade or not, counterparty risk reverberated throughout the world.

The second problem encountered in London was the pusillanimity with which the London banking community met the systemic liquidity crisis (Keynes 1914, pp. 461–462). Wednesday July 29, happened to be Settlement Day for the London Stock Exchange, when the past two weeks of transactions among the members of the exchange had to be settled, either by completing a transaction with delivery of the security or by prolonging the duration of the loan made on the collateral of a given security. Given that Austria had already declared war and that the exchanges on the continent were in the process of closing that day, it was clear that a systemic crisis was looming. The banks responded by refusing to renew loans and by calling up additional collateral from the stockbrokers. In the following three days, they made massive demands on the discount houses, which in turn borrowed in large quantities from the Bank of England, whose gold reserves plummeted in response to a massive internal drain. Belatedly, government regulators stepped in, first to use pressures on the Bank of England by allowing it to enter gold ready to be shipped but still in South Africa, Canada, or the US as part of its reserves, and second to forestall further pressures from the panic sales of securities on the London Stock Exchange by imposing a set of "Temporary Regulations" (which lasted until 1922).

The subsequent responses of the financial systems of the four major powers to the pressing demands of war finance over the next five years changed the relationships of banks, markets, and governments in each country in ways that no one could have foreseen based on previous history or economic theory. France and Germany each responded by the central government demanding, and receiving, immediate finance from their respective central banks to mobilize their armies for the coming conflict while Great Britain, and eventually the US when it entered the war, went to their respective capital markets to raise the money for their war efforts. It was the New York Stock Exchange, and the US stock markets in general, that proved most helpful in financing the war effort, first of Britain, then that of the British allies, and eventually that of the US itself. US finance for the war in Europe was decisive for bringing victory to the Allies by the end of 1918. Not far behind, however, was the London Stock Exchange, which provided a market for the massive issuance of British government debt throughout the conflict. Under the watchful eyes of government officials from both the US and UK, a massive repatriation of the bonds and stocks of American corporations held in London took place to New York.

On the London Stock Exchange, the foreign securities were replaced increasingly with British government debt as the war continued (Burk 1985). The Paris *Bourse* lagged far behind in helping the French government, while the Berlin *Effectenbörse* was really hopeless as far as sustaining the military efforts of Germany and the Austro-Hungarian empire.

How the Great Powers financed the First World War

From its establishment in 1871, the German *Reich* had only limited taxing powers, basically from the customs revenues collected from the imperial tariff. By design, Prussia, as the largest and most prosperous part of the German empire, kept control over its finances and refused to raise taxes even as revenues from customs fell off as Britain imposed an effective blockade on Germany's overseas trade. Consequently, nearly 98 percent of Germany's war expenses were met by issuing debt, as shown in Table 11.1. The successive issues of German debt were forced on the joint-stock banks through the *Reichsbank*, which led to increased issues of bank deposits and bank notes, the cause of persistent wartime inflation in Germany. France kept its issues of debt down to around 80 percent of total expenditure, as did Great Britain. The US fared best, at just over 71 percent.

On the first problem of dealing with open positions that could not be covered due to trade in securities within the global (or at least Atlantic) capital market of 1914, New York clearly was the most successful of

Table 11.1 *First World War expenditures and debt, the Great Powers*

	Total (million $)	War debt (million $)	Percent debt financed
Great Britain	41,887	34,056	81.3
US	32,261	23,042	71.4
France	32,617	26,031	79.8
Germany	48,616	47,426	97.6

Note: The sources for Russia's finance of the First World War and the White Russian fight against the Bolshevik regime after the October 1917 revolution have only recently been calculated, as the sources were not available to western researchers until after 1979. For more recent calculations, see Broadberry and Harrison (2009) and Siegel (2014).

the three exchanges, while Paris was the least successful. London fell somewhere in the middle, mainly because its settlement periods were halfway between the daily settlements in New York and the monthly settlements in Paris. New York met the problem of frozen payments by agreeing that the last price quoted on the New York Stock Exchange would be the price for any security posted as collateral to a bank lender. This expedient resolved the problem in New York due to its practice of making daily settlements and the relatively small proportion of foreign dealings carried on at the time, certainly in comparison with both London and Paris. The London situation was complicated because of the complex web of loans and time bargains made among the members in addition to the loans owed to London banks. London soon adopted the same procedure as New York, but only for the main securities used for collateral (which rapidly became government debt). The Paris *Bourse* never did resolve these problems until after the war ended. Its problems were worse than either New York or London because of the varying length of contracts, most at least one month and many even longer, which made pricing any collateral that had been posted nearly impossible. The Bank of France stepped in, as on the previous occasions of stock market distress, to provide liquidity for trading in new issues of government debt.

The second feature common to all three Allied exchanges was to resume trading, but only for cash, in a select set of securities, which were gradually broadened. This meant that existing open positions were frozen and had to be worked down gradually, not exacerbated by taking on fresh commitments to deliver more of a security at some time in the future when perhaps prices would have recovered. This prevented the problem of frozen balances becoming worse over time. Both features were very congenial to the war finance needs of the respective governments as well. Because the main financial asset available for collateral was British government debt, the temporary rules of the London Stock Exchange maintained reasonable prices for existing debt and the new issues of debt. The Bank of England stood ready to make loans on the basis of government debt offered as collateral, which meant that it effectively came under the control of the Treasury for the duration of hostilities. But as government debt was very useful to be held by the private sector for purposes of collateral, the Bank's guarantee did not imply the kind of inflation in Germany that direct purchase of the new government debt by banks created there.

Restricting stock exchange business in London to cash dealings cut off the possibility that the enemy could obtain finance from the London Stock Exchange by liquidating foreign securities on the market. Proof that title to the security was in the name of a British national before the outbreak of the war had to be given by each seller as well. If, however, an owner of an American security wished to sell, he or she could do so in exchange for new British government debt. So, while the lucrative business for the London Stock Exchange of trading among foreigners in foreign stocks was drastically curtailed, a new business in the dispersal of fresh government debt rose rapidly to take its place. The British Treasury then sold the American securities acquired from sellers in London in the New York Stock Exchange. The huge increase in repatriated US railroad securities that arose out of the London sell off of American securities created a boom in trading business for members of the New York Stock Exchange.

The self-regulating organization of both the New York and London exchanges was strengthened as a result. The existing microstructure was reaffirmed in New York, but in London business was permanently shifted in favor of government securities so there the interests of commission brokers increasingly prevailed over those of jobbers and promoters on the London Stock Exchange. For Paris, the tight control of the *Chambre Syndicale* over its members was strengthened by its ability to buy into the *commandite* companies of the *agents de change* who were in difficulty with their partners, thanks to the *Chambre's* cooperation with the *Banque de France* and the Minister of Finance throughout the war. But role of the Paris *Bourse* as an international exchange of first standing was permanently reduced, especially given the difficulties created by the political confusion of post-war finance.

Post-war problems

With the armistice agreement of November 11, 1918, military action ceased and hostilities moved to the conference tables around Paris – Versailles, Saint Germain-en-Laye, Neuilly-sur-Seine, Trianon, and Sèvres – to work out treaties between the Allied powers and Germany, Austria, Bulgaria, Hungary, and the Ottoman empire over the course of the next two years. The Allies demanded reparations from Germany, Austria, Hungary, and Bulgaria, while also dismantling the existing empires in Europe, creating new nation-states with hastily drawn boundaries. The economic adjustments required to validate the new borders were left to the League of Nations, which all the new nation-states and the remains of the Russian, German, Ottoman, and Austro-Hungarian empires were required to join. The US, however, failed to join the League so the subsequent efforts of the League's Financial Commission to manage the economic transitions from wartime conflict to peacetime cooperation lacked the economic clout of the largest economy in the world.

That did not prevent the British empire from taking initiatives under the leadership of Montagu Norman, who first became Governor of the Bank of England in 1920 after having been a director of the Bank in 1907 and Deputy Governor in 1917. Every Governor of the Bank of England since its founding in 1694 had served at most two terms of two years, but under the circumstances following the end of wartime dominance of the Bank by the Treasury, Norman's efforts to restore the pre-eminence of the Bank in managing the London money market and in international finance were so appreciated by the shareholders of the Bank, still a private institution, that he was re-elected again and again, and only retired in 1944 as the Second World War was ending. As Governor of the Bank of England from 1920 through 1944, Norman was the chief architect of the cooperative efforts of central banks in Europe and across the British empire to restore the primacy of public banks in the new nation-states against the possible domination of central government treasuries headed by ministers of finance.

The Brussels Conference of 1920 was organized by the Financial Commission of the League of Nations with the express goal of coordinating restoration of financial stability and attempting to set the basis for restoring a system of fixed exchange rates, a system that had been so successful in expanding trade and economic output before 1914. Special attention was paid to government expenditures so they would not exceed current revenues, so that government debt would not be increased or even reduced. Most countries, however, faced new demands for expenditures to recover from wartime damages while their revenues were reduced, whether from the loss of territory in the case of the defeated Central Powers or from the loss of trade flows in the case of the new countries created out of the remains of former empires. Consequently, a follow-up conference in Genoa in 1922 was initiated by the UK and the US in order to define the role of central banks in the general financial reconstruction needed to return to pre-war levels of trade and output.

The new countries were urged to establish national banks of issue with a monopoly on the new national currency. The new banks would eventually commit to maintain fixed exchange rates with the key currencies used in international trade, now the US dollar and, anticipating a return to pre-war conditions, the British pound sterling. The US dollar had never left the gold standard throughout the First World War and indeed had accumulated huge reserves of gold as payment for supplies to the Allies in Europe. The UK pound had suspended convertibility during the war, but as had been the case after the Napoleonic Wars in 1815, was committed to return to the pre-war gold standard as soon as possible. To mobilize long-term capital movements into the European countries recovering from over four years of intensive warfare, some guarantee of repayment in terms of key currencies generally used in the finance of international trade was needed. That meant that each national bank of issue in a country receiving foreign capital had to commit to make its new currency convertible in either gold or a foreign currency that was on the gold standard. The new system, designed to restore a system of fixed exchange rates in order to facilitate long-term capital movements needed for reconstruction, while economizing on the supply of gold available for making international payments, became known as the "gold-exchange standard." It was also called the gold bullion standard as only the US was still able to convert its paper currency into coins for domestic payments. All other countries could only supply gold bullion from their bank of issue in exchange for large-scale demands upon its domestic currency.

The gold-exchange standard system clearly sprang from the way the Bank of England and major joint-stock banks in Great Britain had offered payment services to countries belonging to, or shadowing, the gold standard before 1914. The Bank of England, or any London bank doing regular business with a foreign country, could make transfers among accounts without actually transferring gold or even give short-term advances to regular customers, such as the Bank of Portugal. The Bank of England had even met the extraordinary liquidity demands placed upon it in July 1914 by giving credits on gold held on its account in Canada, Australia, or especially South Africa. That way, gold belonging to the Bank of England stayed in the country

where it had been produced and only legal claims to it were transferred. The system before the First World War of using the pound
sterling as a key currency depended on the hegemonic position of
London in the finance of international trade and capital movements.
To make it work in the period after the First World War, however,
required some further innovations in cooperation with the Bank of
England and Montagu Norman.

The inter-Allied war debts

First, was the problem how to work off the huge stocks of wartime
debts that the Allied powers had accumulated over the course of
the war. Figure 11.1 is the classic portrayal of the situation from the
French point of view.

All the Allied powers at one time or another had floated loans in the
US, Britain especially with a total of $4.7 billion. But Britain had also
provided financing for many of the Allies, $3.0 billion to France and
$3.2 billion to "Other Countries," which meant mainly Tsarist
Russia before the Bolshevik Revolution of 1917. France had also
loaned $3.5 billion, mainly to Russia, while borrowing $3.0 billion
from Britain and $4.0 billion from the US. Sorting out the repayments
was complicated by the default of Russia, as the Communist revolu-
tionaries were not about to honor the debts accumulated by the Tsarist
regime they had overthrown. The US insisted upon full repayment of
the debts owed to it, depending on the ability of its debtors. Britain
suggested that it would forgive its debtors but only to the extent that
the US might write off the debt it owed there. This left France with only
reparations from the defeated Central Powers, especially Germany, as
its main recourse. Just as France had paid reparations to Germany at
the end of the Franco-Prussian War in 1870–1871, so it now
demanded comparable reparations from Germany.

Weimar Germany's new government, struggling to establish its
legitimacy in the wake of having accepted defeat, the loss of substantial
territory, its entire navy, and much of its merchant marine, had not yet
established a unified tax structure for what remained of the former
German empire. Consequently, it failed repeatedly to make good
on the reparations payments that were finally established by a
Reparations Commission in 1922. In frustration, France and Belgium
sent troops in to the Ruhr industrial heartland of Germany to enforce

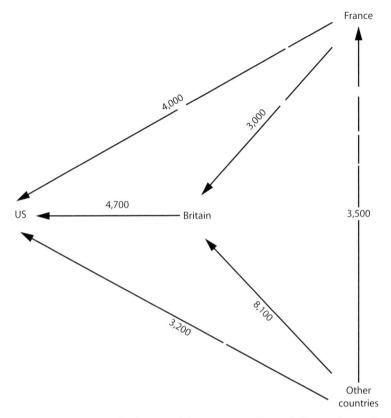

Figure 11.1 Inter-Allied war debts,1919 (million dollars) (from Sauvy 1965–1967, p. 169)

Note: The sources for Russia's finance of the First World War and the White Russian fight against the Bolshevik regime after the October 1917 revolution have only recently been calculated, as the sources were not available to western researchers until after 1979. For more recent calculations, see Broadberry and Harrison (2009) and Siegel (2014).

payments in kind of coal, steel, and assorted materials for restoring the railroads of Alsace-Lorraine, which had been returned to France. The Weimar government responded by paying workers in the Ruhr to remain at their respective mines, mills, and plants but without working – a general sit-down strike. As the occupation by French troops continued in 1923 while German workers were paid to not produce anything, the famous German hyperinflation ensued, ending only in November 1923.

The end came when a new government took office that was willing to admit defeat, while also bringing the US back into the settlement process. The Dawes Loan of 1924 provided 800 million marks (with the new mark defined in gold and US dollars at 4 marks to the dollar) but on account with the *Reichsbank*, which was re-organized under the directorship of Hjalmar Schacht, whose earlier career with the *Dresdener Bank* had brought him contacts with J. P. Morgan in the US and Montagu Norman in the UK. By injecting private investment funds from the US into Germany through the *Reichsbank*, the Dawes Plan allowed Germany to pay regular reparations to France, which allowed France to make regular repayments to both the US and UK governments, while ignoring the debts of "other countries" for the rest of the twentieth century until the collapse of the Soviet Union in 1991. The Dawes Plan effectively solved the problem of inter-allied war debts, the "toxic assets" of the 1920s, by taking them out of the payments networks that financed international trade.

Soon after Germany was put back on the gold standard via the Dawes Plan, Britain re-established the gold standard for the pound sterling in April 1925 at its pre-war parity, as Montagu Norman had committed when he urged new national banks in Europe to accept the pound sterling as a key currency. By the end of 1926, France was able as well to re-establish the gold standard. By the end of 1928, then, the gold-exchange standard had four key currencies – the US dollar, the German mark, the UK pound, and the French franc. Moreover, the new countries created from the dismantling of the empires on the European continent had all joined the gold exchange standard by 1930.

Again, the reconstruction loans developed for the new countries emerging from the aftermath of the First World War in Europe were another financial innovation that can be mostly attributed to the leadership of Montagu Norman at the Bank of England. Starting in 1922, Austria became the first example of a central bank joining the gold-exchange standard on the basis of a reconstruction loan that, while lodged on the books of the central bank, was overseen by an outside authority. The Financial Commission of the League of Nations appointed a commissioner to monitor the revenue sources of Austria's central government to make sure they were committed to making the regular interest payments and amortization of the reconstruction loan by the national bank of Austria. The success of this innovation in revitalizing the moribund Austria economy led to its imitation in

Hungary in 1923. The examples of Austria and Hungary gave the impetus for the Dawes Plan to establish a Reparations Agent in the offices of the *Reichsbank* to monitor the revenues of the Weimar Republic that had to be committed first toward interest and amortization of the Dawes Loan. Parker Gilbert, a partner in J. P. Morgan's investment bank, was the Reparations Agent and exercised due diligence while Germany benefited from a rash of foreign investments that came pouring in for German corporations and municipalities as well.

There followed the "five good years" (1924–1928) of expanding international trade and prosperity worldwide (Lewis 1949), as the new sovereign bonds issued by the twelve new countries that had been created in Europe after the First World War found favor in the revitalized capital markets of New York and London. There were frictions, however, as the Commissioners overseeing the reconstruction loans in Austria and Hungary bowed out in 1926 and 1927 while the Reparations Agent continued to oversee the Dawes Loan and the reparations payments of Germany, much to the distaste of Schacht. In 1930, with the fervent support of Montagu Norman, the Bank for International Settlements (BIS) was created as an alternative to the Reparations Agent. The founding central banks of the UK, the US, France, Germany, Belgium, Italy, and Japan located the BIS in Basel, Switzerland, as a neutral site with excellent rail connections to the rest of Europe. The Young Plan then replaced the Dawes Plan with the BIS taking over the responsibility of monitoring the transfers among the respective central banks, which came to include the rest of the countries still committed to the gold-exchange standard.

The end of the gold-exchange standard, France, and the Great Depression

By 1929, it was clear that the gold-exchange standard was in trouble. Cooperation among the central banks of the four Great Powers was essential to maintain its credibility. The personal ties among Montagu Norman (Governor of the Bank of England), Hjalmar Schacht (President of the *Reichsbank* (1924–1930; 1933–1937), and Benjamin Strong (Governor of the Federal Reserve Bank of New York (1914–1928) kept it going during the five good years, but when Benjamin Strong became ill and died in October 1928, a leadership vacuum was created. Making continued cooperation more difficult was the role of the new governor of the _Banque de France_, Émile Moreau (1926–1930), who was determined to restore the gold standard for France on the same basis as France had experienced from 1880 through 1913. That meant building up a huge stockpile of gold reserves to be loaned out as needed to maintain financial stability in France as before, but now also to maintain stability and allegiance to France among the restructured nation-states of Europe.

To do this, he began building up reserves surreptitiously by insisting that bills of exchange drawn on London be redeemed in gold rather than re-exchanged for credits in French francs. By 1928, Moreau had accumulated enough gold to declare formally that France was once again on the gold standard, and the _Banque de France_ was capable of redeeming any banknotes presented to it in gold. On this basis, moreover, France could now replace the British, Americans, or Germans in establishing reconstruction loans to the new nation-states as well. First off was Romania, as it happened the last country in Europe to join the gold-exchange standard. It turned out that France's rising gold hoard, once again as it had in the last quarter of the nineteenth century, created worldwide deflation by driving down the prices of all internationally traded commodities in the world (Johnson 1997).

Because France was constantly increasing the world demand for gold faster than the supply from the world's mines, and the spread of the gold-exchange standard had fixed the price of gold in terms of any national currency, including those of the leading gold producing countries, the only price adjustment that could take place was in the price of "all other goods" that could be exchanged for gold in international markets. In agricultural goods, especially grains harvested by family farms, the response to falling prices was to increase output, which exacerbated the fall in prices. In cases where cartels could regulate supply, such as tin and rubber, stockpiles could accumulate for a while before the price declines began. For a country like Austria, which had to export agricultural goods to earn foreign exchange needed to pay the interest and amortization on its outstanding reconstruction loans, the problem became more and more severe as France continued to accumulate more gold reserves (Figure 11.2).

The League of Nations report, _Economic Stability in the Post-war World_, only published after the Second World War, to help anticipate and forestall the problems that had arisen after the First World War, noted that prices of primary commodities all began to decline

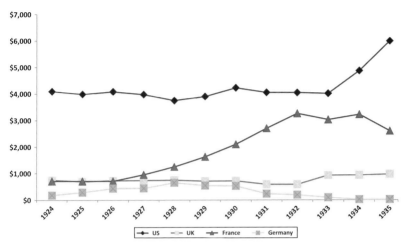

Figure 11.2 Gold reserves of the leading powers, 1924–1935 (from Flandreau *et al.*, *Global Finance Database*, http://eh.net/database/global-finance/)

worldwide, starting in 1926 and only started to recover after 1932 (1945, p. 85). The authors of that study blamed overproduction in general, but examining the timing and size of the buildup of gold reserves by France over the same period, clearly identified French monetary policy as the source of difficulty, ending what had been the beneficial effects of the financial innovation by central banks – the gold-exchange standard. More recent work has quantified that both the US and France were responsible for the worldwide deflation set off by their accumulations of gold, but the *Banque de France* much more so than the Federal Reserve System of the US, especially after 1930 (Irwin 2011).

The immediate cause of the financial collapse caused by the accumulated price deflation on the sovereign debt liabilities amassed after the First World War was the failure in May 1931of the *Kreditanstalt*, the largest bank in Austria (Schubert 1991). The previous year it had been forced to absorb the *Bodenanstalt*, essentially the land bank of Austria. Saddled with mortgages on agricultural land that was now producing products at increasing losses as prices fell, the *Bodenanstalt* was supposed to weather the downturn with the resources of the *Kreditanstalt*. But as the mortgages held by the *Bodenanstalt* continued to default with the continued decline in agricultural prices and the loans of the *Kreditanstalt* in turn began to default, the foreign exchange reserves of the Austrian National Bank ran out and all payments abroad had to stop (Schubert 1991). When even German banks followed the example of Austrian banks by stopping all foreign payments in June 1931, the monetary and financial crisis became truly international. While this sequence of stoppages from Austria to Germany has all the appearance of contagion, possibly reflecting psychological unease by foreign investors, it appears that the German banks managed to overextend their loans quite independently of events in Austria. Moreover, the *Reichsbank* was unable to serve as a traditional lender of last resort under the existing rules of the gold-exchange standard, given its minimal gold and dollar reserves. The German crisis, therefore, became a classic "twin crisis," combining both a banking crisis from massive withdrawal of deposits and a currency crisis from exchange of marks into foreign currencies (James 1984, 1986; Schnabel 2004).

The German government then declared a stop to foreign payments, including reparations to France. While Montagu Norman frantically tried to provide financing to the *Reichsbank*, the British joint-stock banks that had been financing trade with Germany and central Europe were now forced to default as well. On September 21, while Norman was still returning by ocean liner from a trip to Canada, the Bank of England left the gold standard, this time for good. Bank officials had alerted Norman while he was at sea by sending him a cryptic telegram, "The Old Lady goes off on Monday," which Norman reportedly mistook to mean that his mother would be leaving for her holidays before he returned.

The collapse of the gold exchange standard became definitive, despite the attempt by the League of Nations in 1932 at Stresa, Italy, to analyze the source of the problem and to suggest a united effort to re-allocate the world's limited supplies of monetary gold (League of Nations 1932). The diverse responses by the banking systems of the Great Powers to their individual domestic banking problems simply restricted international payments further, leading to a continued fall in international trade, which made repayment of foreign loans ever more difficult, which led to more intensive responses by national authorities to isolate their economies from the Great Depression. The debt–deflation problems of Austria, debts remaining fixed in nominal terms while income fell with the worldwide fall in commodity prices, proved to be a general problem. Merchant banks in Britain that had borrowed in London to loan to exporters in central Europe began to fail even before the Bank of England ran short of gold (Accomminotti 2012). Unit banks throughout the US, which had been failing in wheat producing states with the fall of grain prices starting in the mid 1920s, really began to fail at the end of the 1920s from the defaults on residential mortgages as well (Postel-Vinay 2014).

Later analysis by financial historians and economists confirms that the sooner a country stopped foreign payments based on adherence to the fixed exchange rate they had committed to observing when joining the gold-exchange standard, the less severe was the subsequent depression for their domestic economy (Figure 11.3). It took a presidential election in the US in 1932 and a belated devaluation of the US dollar of 50 percent, from $24.60 to the Troy ounce of gold to $35.00, to begin the recovery in the US. France held on until the election of a Socialist government, the Popular Front, in 1936 gave it the political will to abandon the gold standard. The rise of the Nazi party in Germany, led by Adolf Hitler, led to his accession to power by declaring a state of emergency in 1933.

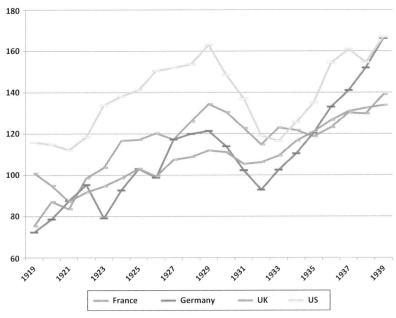

Figure 11.3 The course of GDP for the major powers, 1919–1939 (from Maddison 1995, Table C-16a, pp. 180–183)

Depression can stimulate financial innovation: Nazi Germany and imperial Britain

Upon assuming power in 1932, Adolf Hitler wisely induced Hjalmar Schacht to return from retirement and take economic leadership as President of the *Reichsbank* in March 1933. Schacht, having resigned in disgust at the previous German government's acceptance of even the reduced reparations under the Young Plan as to be administered by the BIS, took the independence of the German central bank to new extremes. Shortly after taking office in 1933, Schacht announced a "New Plan" for the German economy. Domestically, he underwrote finance of new investment by using the cover of a dummy corporation, the *Metallurgische Forschungsgesellschaft*, whose "Mefo" bills were guaranteed by the *Reichsbank*, which redeemed them at face value. These were explicitly designed to provide covert financing of Germany's re-armament, in direct violation of the Versailles Peace Treaty. For foreign trade, Schacht undertook bilateral exchange agreements with adjacent and then with traditional trading partners. These all took the form of agreeing on fixed amounts of goods imported by Germany from the partner in exchange for a fixed amount of goods exported by Germany to the same partner country. Payments by Germany for the imports were made by crediting the central bank of the partner country with blocked marks in an account at the *Reichsbank*. These "*sperrmarks*" could only be withdrawn by paying for the goods that Germany had agreed to export to the partner country.

The resulting system of finance looked very much like the early modern use of bills of exchange between leading merchant bankers across the European capitals, only now the bills were explicitly passed through the respective central banks that had been created across Europe after the First World War. The amounts credited to any one country in the books of the trading partner could only be drawn down by payment for goods previously agreed upon. Naturally, these agreements were most easily drawn up with Germany's closest and most active trading partners, which meant countries like Austria, Hungary, and then Sweden and the Baltic countries. Eventually, they spread to Romania and Brazil. Given the large market that Germany represented for each of these countries, the natural assumption by Anglo-American economists was that Germany took advantage of its size to extract very favorable terms for itself, whether in the terms of trade, or in the goods it allowed to be exported in exchange for vital raw materials.

Later analysis of how the trading worked out in practice, however, shows that Schacht's financial innovations worked very well to stimulate the rebound of the German economy while the pressures of increased demand for inputs in German industry actually gave more bargaining power to partner countries that had essential materials for German industry – Swedish iron, Hungarian chrome, Brazilian cotton, and Romanian oil were prime examples. Only if the country withheld further exports to Germany by waiting until it was satisfied with the goods Germany had sent in return would it not ride along with the economic expansion of the German economy. This proved to be the case for Romania, still laboring under the influence of its French advisers who had induced Romania to join the gold-exchange standard in 1930. Hungary, by contrast, adopted a policy of paying its exporters immediately for the goods they send to Germany without waiting for any German imports to show up (Neal 1979; Ritschl 2001). The problem with Schacht's successful financial innovation, however, was that it enabled Hitler to finance his plans to re-arm Germany in order to restore and even expand Germany's pre-war empire. When Schacht objected, he was dismissed from office in 1937 and sidelined for the remainder of the war.

After abandoning convertibility in September 1931, Britain took the initiative to increase its trade with the British Commonwealth and Empire countries with the Ottowa Conference meetings in 1932. All the British colonies and dominions had kept fixed exchange rates to the pound sterling, meaning they all devalued at the same rate as Britain. "Imperial preference," agreed upon in Ottawa, reduced tariffs among the sterling bloc countries while raising tariffs against the rest of the world. This served as an additional impetus to increase trade financed by the use of sterling bills of exchange intermediated through London. The World Economic Conference held in London in 1933 after Roosevelt took office as president in March 1933, failed to achieve anything other than to encourage the US to stimulate trade with its own colonies (the Philippines and Puerto Rico) while using the US dollar and encouraging Central American countries to do likewise under reciprocal trade agreements.

Depression can stymie financial innovation: France and the US

France maintained its commitment to the gold standard and compen-
sated for the effect of its now overvalued currency by raising tariffs, an
expedient easily reciprocated by the other gold bloc countries around it
in Europe. The net result was to stifle the expansion of trade among the
gold bloc countries as well as with the rest of the world (Eichengreen
and Irwin 1995). When France did abandon gold convertibility in
1936 with the election of the Popular Front government, it did agree
with the UK and the US to maintain fixed exchange rates among
the three currencies in the Tripartite Agreement in September 1936.
The other gold bloc countries of Europe acceded to it as well. This
effectively acknowledged that all three countries had overvalued their
currencies when setting up the gold-exchange standard in the 1920s,
and was an attempt to write down the size of the inter-Allied war debts
still being paid off from the agreements of the early 1920s. Neither
trade nor capital flows responded positively, however, as each country
focused on restoring its own domestic economy.

The US recovery had begun shortly after Roosevelt took office, most
likely when he temporarily suspended the gold convertibility of the US
dollar in 1933. When Roosevelt did restore convertibility of the dollar
in gold, it was only for gold bullion, not gold coins, and it was at a
50 percent devaluation of the dollar, raising the price of an ounce of
gold from $24.00 to $35.00, where it was to remain until August 1971.
While Roosevelt's initiative was by executive order, Congress took it
upon itself to deal with the financial collapse as Congressional leaders
saw the problems. In the House of Representatives, Rep. Henry Steagall
from Alabama was a staunch proponent of deposit insurance to protect
the savings of small investors. In the US Senate, Carter Glass of Virginia
had long wanted to separate trust companies from National Banks, in
the belief that speculation on new securities by trust companies endan-
gered the depositors in the state and national banks that had acquired
trust companies as affiliates in response to the Federal Reserve Act of
1913. The two Congressional leaders combined deposit insurance with
a mandatory separation of investment banking from commercial banks
that joined the Federal deposit insurance scheme into the legislation
called the Glass–Steagall Act, the Banking Act of 1933.

The consensus of later analysis by historians and economists is that
trust companies before the First World War, when they were

independent of commercial banks, and even after the First World War, when many became affiliates of National or state banks, helped finance widespread innovation in the new technologies of the twentieth century (Neal 1971; White 1983). Especially marked was their role in financing small and medium-sized companies, including especially the startup firms in the automobile industry. Then as now, these firms were the main source of new employment. By protecting small depositors at the expense of financing for small and medium business, the unintended consequences of the Glass–Steagall Act were to stifle further technological innovation and prolong the levels of high unemployment that peaked in 1933 (Neal and White 2012).

From the collapse of the gold standard to the Second World War

The political consequences of the industrial powers of the world attempting to restore the economic health of their domestic economies by imposing trade restrictions on the rest of the world, whether by tariffs, exchange controls, or bilateral barter all had the effect of moving toward self-sufficiency economically and strengthening domestic political control of the party in power. The economies of the US, the British empire, and the Communist regime of the Soviet Union were all large enough to enable self-sufficiency without further territorial expansion. Smaller European countries with overseas colonies – France, Italy, Spain, Portugal, Belgium, the Netherlands – all tried to extract more resources from their overseas possessions while excluding outsiders. But both Germany and Japan, late industrializers with a strong military tradition, found that their growing industrialization was limited by the need to import vital commodities from abroad. Both countries became militarily aggressive, Germany first re-occupying the Ruhr and re-assimilating the Saarland before moving into the industrial resources of Czechoslovakia and the mineral resources of Poland, while Japan was occupying the iron ore fields of Manchuria and eventually the oil wells of Indonesia.

 Both countries facilitated their exploitations of their conquered territories by seizing control of the victim's central bank. The captive country's bank of issue was then forced to issue local currency to the occupation authority to maintain its troops and extract resources needed in the homeland or the battlefronts. The extraction of resources by the Nazi occupation of France through control of the *Banque de France* was significantly larger and less troublesome for the German troops than had been the case for France and Belgium when they tried to seize resources in kind from the occupied Rhineland in 1923 (Milward 1970). Aware of the dire consequences of excessive note issue, however, Nazi occupation forces, wherever they appeared in Europe over the course of the Second World War, kept strict control over the accounts of the occupied country's central bank, while continuing the use of blocked accounts with the *Reichsbank* to pay for resources extracted, as in the case of Belgium (Berger and Ritschl 1995).

Britain countered the Nazi economic strategy by a similar tactic, crediting members of the sterling bloc for what they supplied to Britain and to British forces wherever they were fighting, with blocked sterling balances held to their account in the Bank of England (Pressnell 1986; Schenk 1994). It was to take decades after the end of the Second World War for these blocked accounts and the capital controls to enforce them to end. As had been the case for financing the First World War, however, it was the US that eventually provided the finances for Britain and the Soviet Union to obtain military victory in Europe. Lessons learned from the confusion created by both the inter-Allied war debts and the volatile exchange rates that had made the five years following the First World War so miserable for the economies of both defeated and victorious countries led to a new strategy by the US – Lend-Lease Agreements.

Lend-Lease Agreements between the US and the Allies were a financial innovation in war finance that succeeded in avoiding the uncertainty over repayment of loans that had dragged on for so long after the First World War. A total of $50 billion of aid was extended by the US to the Allies: $ 31.4 billion to the UK, $11.3 billion to the Soviet Union, $3.2 billion to France, $1.6 billion to China, and $2.6 billion to other Allies (Figure 11.4). The terms were that the equipment would be loaned until the end of the war when it would be either returned to the US or bought at reduced prices by the recipients, the only condition being that the recipient had to agree to work with the US on constructing a multilateral world trading system after the Second World War.

For Britain, this meant putting an end to imperial preference, the operation of which had upset both the US and Canada in the 1930s. For France, the Soviet Union, and China it was not clear what this meant

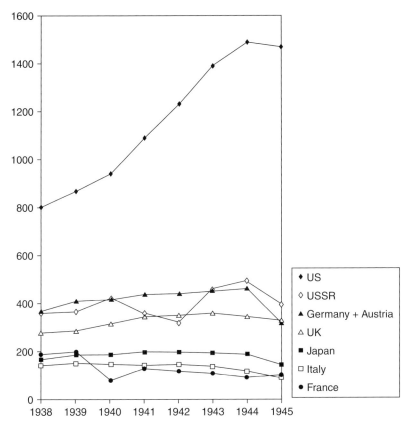

Figure 11.4 Real GDPs of the Great Powers, 1938–1945 (billion dollars at 1990 prices) (from Harrison 1998, p. 11)

as the course of the war took turns that were unanticipated from the First World War experience. Nevertheless, during the darkest periods of the war from the perspective of the US and Britain, as losses in the North Atlantic shipping lanes from German submarine attacks were at their highest, American and British officials were negotiating the outlines of the post-war monetary system. The British–American negotiations, essentially between Lord John Maynard Keynes representing Britain and Harry Dexter White, representing the US, laid out the terms of the Bretton Woods Agreement eventually signed at the Mount Washington Hotel in Bretton Woods, New Hampshire on July 22, 1944.

While the war was still raging in both Europe and the Pacific, the overwhelming power of the US overshadowed the economies of all the belligerents at the time, enabling it to dictate the terms of the post-war world to the forty-four nations represented at the Bretton Woods conference. From 1945 until 1973, international finance was split among those countries that adhered to the Bretton Woods System, dominated by the US, and those that did not, whether opposed to the US in the Cold War or non-aligned. The global financial system of the gold standard era seemed safely buried and it became fashionable to regard the gold standard as a barbarous relic.

12 | *The Bretton Woods era and the re-emergence of global finance, 1945–1973*

The Bretton Woods Conference in 1944 was an ambitious initiative by the US to reshape the post-war international economy in ways that would avoid the confusion and obvious mistakes that had been made after the First World War. This time, instead of withdrawing into isolation from the problems of post-war adjustments and inadvertently making them worse by setting unrealistic goals, the Roosevelt administration was determined to maintain in peacetime the leadership it had acquired during the war. A piece of doggerel on a scrap of paper found after one of the meetings, "Said Lord Halifax to Lord Keynes, they have the money bags, but we have the brains!" expressed another view. From the British perspective, the US would benefit from the imperial experience of the mother country on how to use its economic hegemony constructively. For Keynes, this meant providing international liquidity in a structured way rather than the ad hoc procedures that had eventually been cobbled together after the First World War. But even that fragile structure had then led to five good years of international prosperity, so it seemed worth constructing something similar but sooner and more solidly.

In Keynes' view, countries could commit to fixed exchange rates with each other by buying into the capital stock of an international bank, set up to issue its own currency, the *bancor*, which would have a fixed value in terms of gold. Each country with accounts denominated in *bancor* could use them to settle international accounts with each other. (Readers of Chapter 3 will recall how the *Wisselbank* in Amsterdam created just such a system for financing European international trade in the seventeenth and eighteenth centuries with its *schellingen banco* defined in terms of silver and gold.) The US negotiators in Washington from the Treasury were suitably impressed by this vision (Harry Dexter White, Assistant Secretary of the Treasury, had written his PhD thesis on the French experience with the gold standard in the nineteenth century), but they insisted that the US, which necessarily would be the largest shareholder with the largest existing stock of gold on hand and with the US dollar still fixed at $35.00 per ounce of gold, would have to keep control of the purse strings. Out of the negotiations came the compromise of an International Monetary Fund (IMF), which would lend short-term to countries with temporary balance of payments deficits. For the transition period of reconstruction following the war, member countries could borrow long-term from the International Bank for Reconstruction and Development (IBRD). The two international organizations were generously funded by the US, initially 40 percent later reduced to 25 percent of the capital of each, but both were housed in Washington, DC and together they were responsible for operating the Bretton Woods System. These idealistic ambitions to learn effectively from the mishaps that had plagued economic recoveries after the First World War were soon altered, however, as they confronted unforeseen problems in the implementation of post-war policies.

German inflation: again?

To avoid the problem of a recalcitrant and weak German government that had confounded the payment of reparations after the First World War, the Allies had early agreed to fight on until the Axis governments acknowledged complete defeat with "unconditional surrender." Further, the Allied forces would continue military operations until all of Germany was occupied by their troops and divided up into occupation zones. The common objective was to make sure that Germany would never re-arm or even have the industrial capacity to compete economically with its neighbors in Europe. Problems in reaching these goals quickly arose as each ally took a different approach to achieve the common objective within its particular zone. Initially, the occupying powers all used a common occupation currency but allowed the re-organized *Reichsbank* to issue the currency under Allied supervision. Inflation quickly appeared in terms of the occupation currency, which spiraled out of control. The Russians used the currency to buy materials to replenish their losses farther east; Americans used it to cope with huge influxes of refugees from the other zones where the final battles of the war had been waged; the British and French used the currency to reconstruct their own economies with supplies taken from their zones in occupied Germany.

Cooperation between the British and American zones evolved naturally as supplies to house and feed the refugees who ended up over-
whelmingly in the American zone came through the British zone. The
Americans and British agreed to coordinate policies in their occupation
zones, which they combined as Bizonia. Currency reform that would
prevent further Russia purchases of goods in the western occupation
zones, while stabilizing the economic situation for the western occupying powers finally came in June 1948 after France agreed in March
1948 to merge its zone with Bizonia, briefly creating Trizonia. The new
currency, the *Deutsche Mark*, was issued by the state banks already
existing in the individual *Länder* in Trizonia under the general supervision of the *Bank deutsche Länder*, located in Frankfurt, the main
base for American troops. The setup obviously imitated the Federal
Reserve System of the US and it was intended to keep intact the
strong regional differences among the separate German states. Like
the Federal Reserve System, the German central bank of issue was
independent from the German finance ministry and simply obliged to
maintain price stability in West Germany. The new German central
bank, renamed the *Bundesbank* in 1957, succeeded in ending the post-
war inflation, which never reached the levels of hyperinflation that had
occurred after the First World War, and did it in just three years
instead of the six that were needed after 1918. In retrospect, its success
was due to the immediate assertion of Allied authority over possible
objections by various interest groups within occupied Germany and
the explicit assumption of political responsibility for the success of the
currency reform by the western occupying powers. (The Dawes Plan in
1924 was based on a private loan made on strict commercial terms.)
In East Germany, by contrast, the Russian occupiers set up a new
central bank to issue its separate currency there, the *Ostmark*. This
was on the model of Soviet banks that simply financed the implementation of the government's central plan. The contrast between the strict
control of finance in East Germany to enable exploitation by the
occupying power and the light touch regulation in West Germany by
the western allies to facilitate economic recovery in the rest of Europe
as well as in Germany would last until reunification in October 1990.

While the respective currency reforms set off a Russian blockade of
land routes into Berlin and the Berlin airlift by the Allies, lasting until
May 1949, the long-run difference between West Germany (BRD,
Bundesrepublik Deutschland) and East Germany (DDR, *Deutsche*

Demokratische Republik) arose from their differences in dealing with price controls left from the Second World War. These had been set up by the Nazis during the period of re-armament in the mid 1930s, and then enforced rigorously through the war and still adhered to during the initial occupation. By lifting price controls on most consumer items in West Germany, pent-up consumer demand ignited the economic miracle there. By keeping price and wage controls in place in East Germany, the occupying Russian army was able to continue repressing consumer demand just as the Nazis had in preparation for war in the 1930s and especially during the war. The accumulated differences in economic responses to market-driven prices in West Germany and to central government fixed prices in East Germany would be the source of huge problems when reunification finally occurred.

With the new currency in the western zones replacing the former *Reichsmark* (at a ratio of 10 *Reichsmark* to 1 *Deutsche Mark*), West Germany's economic miracle began. A similar resurgence of growth had occurred in Italy after the currency reform there the year before. Much was made of the lifting of price controls, but prices of housing, food, and coal remained fixed even in West Germany, which kept down the cost of raw materials and labor so that firms could expand production easily to meet rising consumer demand. Construction materials, especially cement, became the focus of limited Marshall Plan aid when it began shortly after the currency reform (Kindleberger 1993, Chapter 22).

Financial innovations to deal with the dollar shortage

Perhaps the greatest influence of the war on the post-war European economies was to alter their trading relationships, both with each other and with the rest of the world. The lack of a multilateral trading system after the collapse of the gold-exchange standard in 1931 saddled Europe with a serious balance-of-payments disequilibrium. Europe's problems in 1945 stemmed from several different sources. The war had witnessed the liquidation or destruction of foreign property holdings. In 1950–1951, earnings from this source were, in real terms, less than a quarter what they had been in 1938, and even that was a substantial improvement over the previous years. Besides this, countries were rapidly incurring new debts to finance reconstruction. For example, the UK incurred debts to the US and

Canada of $1 billion at the end of the war and in 1947 borrowed $4.4 billion from the US and $1.25 billion from Canada. France borrowed $1.9 billion the same year.

To service these debts, the borrowers had to export commodities as the post-war disruptions to services such as tourism, shipping, insurance, or finance had cut off those sources of earnings from foreigners that had been so important to Britain and Western Europe before the Second World War. But they could not sell to just any foreign customer. The absence of domestic supplies or of imports from traditional European sources, especially Eastern Europe and West Germany, increased their dependence on the dollar area. The dollar deficit increased enormously compared with their pre-war experience and it could not be offset by export to colonies or Eastern Europe as in the interwar period. The scarcity of earnings in hard (convertible to dollar) currencies forced the European countries to restrict imports and to control trade through bilateral agreements, augmented with quantitative restrictions and exchange controls.

The dollar shortage that emerged after 1945 can be understood most clearly in terms of a standard supply–demand portrayal of the foreign exchange market. The European need for imports from the US translates then into a demand curve for dollars in the foreign exchange market where dollars are bought and sold. The European demand curve for dollars had been shifted out for every country thanks to wartime destruction and military diversion of civilian production. The supply curve of dollars, in turn, was based on the US demand for imports from Europe. Thanks to the high tariffs in the US and the plentiful supply of domestic products available as substitutes for European goods, not to mention the unavailability of European consumption goods in any case, the supply curve of dollars had been shifted inward. Both situations could be expected to change as conversion occurred on both sides of the Atlantic from a war economy to a civilian economy.

A complication had been added, however, by the Bretton Woods Agreement, signed in July 1944, which committed all the signatories to fixed exchange rates with the dollar, defined in terms of gold at $35 per ounce of pure gold. Each country joining the IMF had to pay in its share of the capital stock that gave the IMF its initial supply of operating funds. Part of each country's share could be paid in terms of the country's own currency, but part had to be paid as well in either gold or dollars. To minimize the cost of acquiring the necessary gold and dollars, each country naturally tended to overvalue its own currency, which it could produce at will, in terms of the dollar. This also had the advantage of decreasing the cost to a country of acquiring dollars in the foreign exchange markets in order to pay for imports from any other country, as the dollar was clearly the currency preferred for payment by any exporter in the world. The fixed exchange rate set at this time acted as a price ceiling that kept the price of dollars in terms of, say, pounds sterling, from rising high enough to equilibrate supply and demand. Each European nation joining the IMF was trapped in a situation of continued excess demand for dollars.

The resulting situation is portrayed in Figure 12.1, where the solid lines for the supply curve of dollars, the demand curve for dollars, and the price ceiling set for dollars in terms of a European currency depict the situation in 1945. The dotted lines show how the situation could have looked in 1950, after a substantial amount of recovery had taken place in Europe, Marshall Plan aid had been distributed in large quantities, and all the European currencies had devalued, most by the same 30.5 percent that the British pound had been devalued in 1949, and the European Payments Union (EPU) established in 1950. Each program – the Marshall Plan, IMF-approved devaluations, and the EPU – was an attack on the problem from one of the three possibilities:

(1) Increase the supply of dollars,
(2) Remove or at least raise the price ceiling on dollars, or,
(3) Decrease the demand for dollars.

Any one approach could have solved the problem on its own if pursued vigorously enough. All three were used, in fact, and each approach proved effective so the dollar shortage could have been eliminated by 1950 using any of the strategies. In fact, the dollar shortage in western Europe was eliminated some time between 1950 and 1952. Policy makers in both the US and Europe, however, continued to act as though a dollar shortage existed until 1958. Consequently, the shortage rather quickly turned into an increasing dollar surplus, thanks to the continued use of the same strategies to eliminate the dollar shortage that were initiated after 1945. By 1971, the dollar surplus was so overwhelming that the US abandoned its commitment to convert

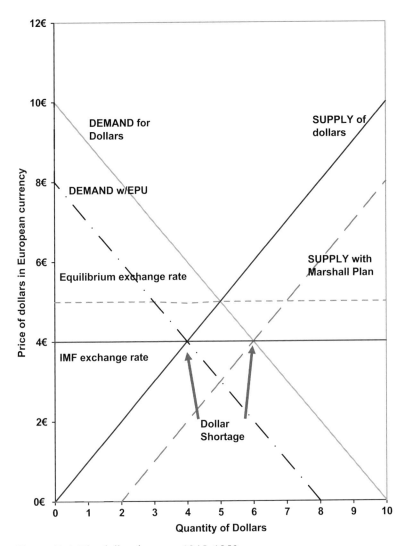

Figure 12.1 The dollar shortage, 1945–1950

dollars into gold, and in 1973 all the IMF countries abandoned their commitment to fixed exchange rates as well. Whenever and however the shortage was eliminated, it is useful to think of the programs described below as attacks on the problem of the dollar shortage using one of the three basic approaches.

1 Increase the supply of dollars: the Marshall Plan, 1948–1952

First, the US made major efforts to increase the supply of dollars. Under this heading, one can count the US contribution of nearly $4 billion to the United Nations Relief and Rehabilitation Administration's expenditures in Europe, 1945–1947, as well as the expenses of US military occupation forces in Germany and bases established in Italy, France, and Britain, at least to the extent they were spent on local supplies and services. The US made a loan of $5 billion in 1945 to Great Britain to compensate the British for terminating the Lend-Lease program at the end of the war. The major condition for this loan, however, was that the British should restore convertibility of the pound sterling at the end of two years. When the British did this in July 1947, unfortunately, their reserves of dollars and gold were almost immediately paid out to foreign holders of claims on sterling, claims that had been made on a large scale during the war to finance Britain's overseas military and naval efforts.

All these dollar expenditures by the US were not enough to fund the immediate needs of European governments to restore law and order, convert military manpower and production to civilian uses while also providing housing and jobs for their people. In June 1947, in his commencement address at Harvard University, US Secretary of State George Marshall announced to the world what came to be known as the Marshall Plan for Europe. The Marshall Plan transferred about $12.5 billion to Europe in grants, loans, and conditional aid, distributed mainly in the first two years of the program (1948–1950). Grants accounted for $9,199.4 million, loans for $1,139.7 million. Conditional aid was awarded as backing the intra-western European payments agreement of 1948 and came to $1,542.9 million (Milward 1970, p. 95). Marshall Plan funds were administered by the Economic Cooperation Administration (ECA) on the American side and by the Committee for European Economic Cooperation (CEEC) and its successor, the Organization for European Economic Cooperation (OEEC), on the European side.

2 Raise the price of the dollar: the devaluations of 1949

While the Marshall Plan was rightly hailed as an unprecedented act of generosity by a victorious military power, it was not sufficient to overcome the dollar shortage overall, and especially not for Britain. In September 1949, the second strategy for solving a dollar shortage was initiated by the British government as it devalued the pound sterling relative to the US dollar by 30.5 percent (from $4.03 to $2.80). Most European governments followed suit, so that Britain's exchange rates with most of the European currencies remained relatively unchanged. Overall, the price ceiling for the dollar in European currencies was raised by an average of about 20 percent. For an economist, it is clear that this was the single simplest and most effective way to solve the dollar shortage. For policy makers at the time, however, it was already evident, given the variety of exchange rate changes among the European states elicited by the British initiative, that political considerations would always make coordinated devaluations difficult to arrange. Consequently, the third strategy was undertaken: help the Europeans reduce permanently their demand for dollars. The system devised to accomplish this was the EPU, mainly a US initiative given that the infusion of Marshall Plan dollars was coming to an end.

3 Reduce the demand for dollars: the European Payments Union,1950–1958

Responding to these problems, and under American pressure, the OEEC European members established the EPU on September 19, 1950, and applied retroactively to July 1, 1950. It was to facilitate trade and establish a multilateral payments system by helping to clear country imbalances and establishing fully convertible currencies. A country's balance of payments on current account within the EPU was determined by its debts to or from all the other members with respect to trade carried on free of quantitative restrictions or bilateral trade agreements. To participate fully in the clearing system, therefore, a country had to replace its quantitative trade restrictions with tariffs. Tariffs could be high enough to keep trade at previous levels at first, but they did allow exporters to increase their exports by cutting prices.

Debits were paid by central banks to the BIS, which administered the EPU, at first in domestic currency and then in increasing amounts in hard currency, either dollars or gold, up to an initial quota. After the quota was reached, payments had to be entirely in dollars or gold, unless some special arrangement was made. The quotas totaled

$3,950 million and were calculated for individual countries on the basis of 15 percent of the value of their total merchandise trade. Originally the largest quotas were the UK, 27 percent of total; France, 13 percent; Belgium and Luxembourg, 9 percent; the Netherlands, 8 percent; and West Germany, 8 percent. The US provided $350 million, some of which was given to countries with "structural" problems, leaving the initial capital of the EPU at $271.6 million.

According to the original agreement, by the time a country had reached its quota limit, it would have paid 40 percent in gold and 60 percent in domestic currency. The system of increasing gold payments improved the incentives from the former agreements: gold or dollar losses would motivate countries to cure persistent deficits, while growing credits would lead surplus countries to reduce their surpluses. The exact distribution of credit to gold as either debt or credit increased for a member country was as shown in Table 12.1.

The 60:40 ratio was subsequently altered because it seemed too "soft" on debtors and because the skewed operation of the system (whereby debtors paid in gold at a lower rate than creditors who were paid out for the first 80 percent of the quotas) increased its costs. In mid 1954, the coverage was changed to 50:50 and in 1955 to only 25:75.

Already by 1953, a number of members permitted multilateral currency arbitrage: currency transactions that could be carried out on ordinary foreign exchange markets, not just by central banks as before. In addition, eight EPU members agreed to standardize the spreads between the official buying and selling limits of their currencies at about 0.75 percent on either side of parity and to permit banks to deal

Table 12.1 *Increasing gold payments with the European Payments Union*

Percent of quota		Payments by debtors		Payments to creditors	
		Credit	Gold	Credit	Gold
1st	20	20	0	20	0
2nd	20	16	4	10	10
3rd	20	12	8	10	10
4th	20	8	12	10	10
5th	20	4	16	10	10
	100	60	40	60	40

with each other in any of the eight currencies. These measures, in addition to the increased dollar/gold requirement to settle payments, moved the members closer to convertibility. In 1955 the EPU members further agreed that when sufficient members so decided (the members so deciding had to hold at least half of the EPU quotas) they could make their currencies fully convertible. On December 27, 1958, this moment finally arrived. Belgium and Luxembourg, France, Germany, Italy, the Netherlands, and the UK, who combined held more than the required one-half of all EPU quotas, announced that they would make their currencies externally convertible. Sixteen non-EPU members announced that they would follow and allow convertibility of their currencies as well. The EPU had completed its mission of establishing a working multilateral trade and payments system for Europe and the wider world.

The Bretton Woods System at work, 1958–1971/3

With full convertibility of the European currencies at least on current account payments, the Bretton Woods System finally took full effect. Basically, it dealt with the trilemma of open economies by keeping fixed exchange rates among members of the IMF, allowing the central banks of each country to have monetary independence to deal with domestic inflation or unemployment as it saw fit, and allowing each country to enforce capital controls. British governments saw capital controls as essential, especially after seeing how quickly their 1947 loan from the US had been sucked out by demands from the sterling area. Imperial preference, which seemed to have worked reasonably well in the 1930s, and had helped finance Britain's war effort, was clearly not working in the new post-war economic environment. The long-run problem for the future, however, was that the capital controls imposed to protect the dollar and gold reserves for a country also discouraged foreign investors from helping to finance either reconstruction or new industries, as they had in the classical gold standard period.

As long as the US had both the means and the will to invest abroad, however, the disincentives of capital controls might be overcome by enticing the US government to establish and maintain military bases or, better, allowing US corporations to establish manufacturing plants inside tariff barriers. US military bases were placed around the world at least in the northern hemisphere as part of US strategic policy of

264 Introduction to International Finance

containment against the Soviet Union or Communist China. US corporations saw the need to put their manufacturing plants inside the
customs union created by the European Economic Community (EEC)
after 1958. There followed what economic historians now see as the
Golden Age of Economic Growth, from 1950 to 1973. The economic
miracles that began in Italy and West Germany carried along the
Benelux countries from the beginning, while France joined in after
shedding both Algeria and Vietnam as expensive colonies. The UK
also did better, but mainly after eliminating capital controls as part of
the widespread reforms made by Margaret Thatcher at the end of
the 1970s.

Figure 12.2 shows how the various measures undertaken by both the
US and the Europeans worked to redistribute gold from the US to the
central banks of the other IMF member countries. Initially, the US
accumulated more gold as countries wishing to join the IMF bought up
gold or dollars to make their capital contribution. As Marshall Plan aid

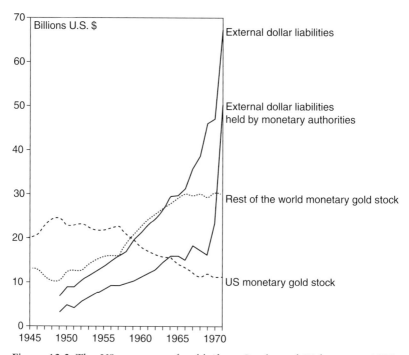

Figure 12.2 The US runs out of gold (from Bordo and Eichengreen 1993,
p. 39)

and, especially, the general devaluation of European currencies in 1949 cut in, gold started to move out of the US and into other countries. By 1958, monetary gold stocks were roughly equally divided between the US and the rest of the IMF countries. Full convertibility of the European currencies, at least on current account for trade in goods and services, took place then and the EPU was formally wound up. Capital controls remained, however, so each that country could exercise control over its money stock independently of the need to keep its exchange rate fixed to the US dollar.

Britain and France both found it difficult to meet the IMF requirements and re-assert control over their colonies that had been either left to their own devices during the war or actually occupied by German or Japanese forces. The responses of the two countries to their monetary difficulties were strikingly different, however.

Britain's past financial history proved to be a seedbed for financial innovations that helped it deal with US dominance and the gradual loss of its colonies until the final collapse of the Bretton Woods System in 1973. France's past reliance on its central bank for finance of its military and colonial enterprises, by contrast, took it down a different path of continued inflation, economic malaise, and reluctant decolonization. Both countries played a role in bringing about the demise of the Bretton Woods System, Britain by facilitating the rapid growth of external dollar liabilities that continued to expand after the end of the EPU in 1958, and France by inducing many of those dollar liabilities held in private hands to be turned in to the *Banque de France* during the height of US expenditures on the war in Vietnam at the end of the 1960s. It was the sudden conversion of private dollar liabilities abroad into central bank-held dollar liabilities that made the dwindled US gold reserves in 1971 unable to cope with a run on the dollar led by the *Banque de France*.

Britain's financial innovations: euro-dollars and offshore accounts

The idea of inducing American companies to put their dollar earnings into accounts held in London banks apparently came in 1955, during one of the recurrent attempts by the Bank of England to ease pressure on its dollar and gold reserves by raising its discount rate above going market rates. The Midland Bank, one of the smallest of Britain's joint-stock banks but a dutiful member of the implicit cartel agreement among the five major banks to keep its lending rates in line with each other, responded by offering higher interest rates on US dollars held in its accounts than US banks could offer in the US. The Midland Bank could do this because from 1933 on, Regulation Q of the Federal Reserve System had required US banks that enjoyed deposit insurance under the Glass–Steagall Act to limit the interest they could pay on either demand or time deposits. It didn't take much, therefore, for the Midland to attract substantial deposits of US dollars, but then the Midland used the dollars to buy sterling in the forward exchange market, ending up with borrowing sterling at a combined interest rate (the rate offered on US dollars on deposit + the forward premium on the sterling/dollar exchange) less than it would have had to pay the Bank of England. The Bank of England, wanting to keep sterling accounts from being paid out, but also eager to see foreign money coming in to the City of London's financial sector, chose to let the Midland continue – a case of regulatory forbearance, which would become the hallmark of Bank of England policy thereafter (Schenk 1998).

The Midland Bank's foray into attracting US dollar deposits with minimal interest rates was easily imitated and quickly spread among the banks in London. It was probably the initiatives of Siegmund Warburg, however, that led to the euro-dollars on deposit in London becoming euro-bonds denominated in US dollars, but held anywhere in the world, with interest credited to the euro-dollar accounts held in London (Ferguson 2009). Warburg, related distantly to the Warburg banking dynasty in Hamburg, had migrated to London in 1933 when Hitler's persecution of German Jews was just beginning, but he had met frequently with Schacht in Switzerland at meetings of the BIS, reporting back to the British intelligence services. Meanwhile, the Warburg merchant bank in Hamburg had remained under Max War-burg until he left Germany in 1938. His descendants, however, returned after the war to restore the bank as M. M. Warburg & Co., a private universal bank that contributed to the reconstruction of West Germany in the years that followed. Siegmund Warburg also had close ties with New York, where Paul Warburg had been one of the founders of the Federal Reserve System in 1913 and a partner in the Kuhn, Loeb investment bank. Through these and other contacts in western Europe, Siegmund's firm specialized in giving financial advice to firms trying to adapt to the Bretton Woods world, which meant among other things devising ways to circumvent capital account restrictions on repatriating profits.

The Bank of England, nationalized in 1945 by the Labour government and thereafter permanently under the control of the Treasury, just as it had been informally during both the First and Second World War, was charged with enforcing the restrictions on capital movements out of the blocked sterling accounts it held for the government. But, managed by bankers trained under Montagu Norman, the Bank was also interested in restoring London's central role in international finance. The opportunity of overseeing investment of euro-dollars in euro-bonds, with payments of interest into euro-dollar deposits, while maintaining restrictions on the use of sterling deposits for foreign payments, provided a way for the Bank of England to reconcile its conflicting goals. In practice, stamp taxes and withholding taxes were levied on sterling accounts and sterling-denominated bonds but were excused from dollar-denominated accounts and bonds.

The first euro-bond placed in London was by an Italian company set up to construct the first Italian toll road, the *Autostrade*. Warburgs had worked with the Italian steel company, Finsider, which did the construction of the super-highway, but the bonds were issued in the name of *Autostrade* so that interest could be paid on the bonds without the Italian authorities deducting taxes. Avoidance of local taxes as well as British taxes in London set the basis for further growth of the euro-bond market. Just to make the regulatory arbitrage really effective, the US passed an Interest Equalization Tax bill in July 1963 to deter US citizens and institutions from investing in Europe. Afterwards, New York was cut off from handling investments in Europe and London restored its previous standing as the leading center for international finance with the subsequent explosion of the euro-bond market. From 1962 to the end of 1971 when the Bretton Woods System ended, $15.7 billion Euro-bonds were issued, most on the London market and denominated in euro-dollars. Growth continued while the US maintained Regulation Q in force, even with the Interest Equalization Tax applied to keep US funds out of the market. With interest rates higher in Germany, however, a buildup of *Deutsche Mark* (DM) bonds began to appear (Figure 12.3).

These financial innovations in the euro-dollar and euro-DM bonds helped sustain the rapid growth of western European economies as

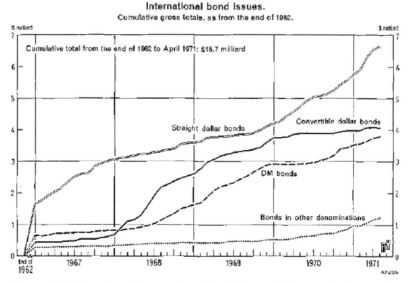

Figure 12.3 The rise of international bond issues during capital controls, 1963–1971 (from Bank for International Settlements, *Forty-First Annual Report*, Basel 1971, p. 54)

they caught up to US technology with high rates of capital formation. Among those countries, however, Germany, the Netherlands, and Austria were able to continue export-led growth thanks to the competitive advantage they enjoyed from falling real exchange rates with their trading partners. The *Bundesbank* could keep strict control over domestic inflation in Germany, thanks to its legal independence from the central government, while the central banks in their main trading partners (Britain, France, and Italy) all had to meet the political demands of their respective governments so domestic inflation there always exceeded that in Germany. With fixed exchange rates, the real exchange rate of Germany kept falling with respect to the other four major countries in Europe.

Pressures kept showing up as political stresses in Britain, France and Italy led to widespread strikes followed by significant wage concessions, all leading to economists advising policy makers to do something about "wage-push inflation," which essentially required central bank independence as in Germany. While the Federal Reserve System in the US had been the role model for the establishment of the *Bundesbank*, it came under increasing pressure to help finance the overseas military

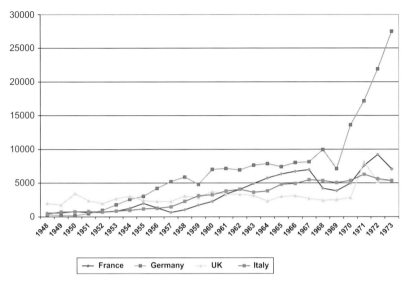

Figure 12.4 International reserves of the major European powers, 1948–1973 (million SDRs) (from International Monetary Fund 1978)

expenditures required to continue the US war effort in Vietnam. US dollars spent in Asia somehow ended up in the central banks of Japan and France, Japan because of its role in the supply chain between the US and Vietnam and France because of the flight capital of expatriate South Vietnamese (*viz.* Madame Nhu). With fixed exchange rates with respect to their trading partners who had committed to the IMF, but whose central banks were subject to domestic political pressures to accommodate government deficits, the low-inflation countries built up export surpluses. If they were not used to expand the domestic money supply, the central bank would build up its stock of international reserves.

Figure 12.4 shows how Germany built up its international reserves especially after the EPU was established in 1950. Meanwhile, Great Britain found that its stock of international reserves was constantly under pressure from trade deficits rising every time the economy expanded to maintain full employment. By 1960, its reserves were below those of Germany, France, and even Italy. To maintain continued stability of prices in Germany, the *Bundesbank* was forced to keep interest rates high, which attracted more short-term capital flows in the late 1960s, as explained above. As most of the reserves accumulated were in US dollars, and the US gold stock was still declining, it was only a matter of time before the French demands for gold as reserves would force the US to stop payments to central banks demanding gold in place of their dollars. When the *Bundesbank* actually succumbed to the French pressure by asking for some gold in place of its rapidly mounting dollar reserves, the US was forced to end the Bretton Woods era.

By closing the gold window at the Federal Reserve Bank of New York on August 15, 1971, US President Nixon unilaterally abrogated the Bretton Woods Treaty. On that date, 300 years after the birth of John Law in Scotland, his vision of a central government-controlled fiat currency as the basis for exchanges in the international financial system was finally realized. Chaos ensued for the rest of the 1970s, as each country's government exercised its national sovereignty to do the best it could for itself. The first thing to go was the price of gold, as it was clear the US dollar could not sustain fixed parity at $35.00 per ounce. This meant a general devaluation of the dollar holdings in central banks and private deposits around the world. If sorting out the various exchange rates took time when Britain devalued in 1949, sorting out the much broader array of exchange rates across the world when the US dollar effectively floated in 1971 would take much longer and require more fundamental changes than simply creating the EPU for countries in Western Europe.

Negotiations conducted within the framework of the IMF ensued in Washington and various European capitals until December 1971. When the Smithsonian Agreement was signed in Washington that month by the finance ministers of the G-10 countries, US President Nixon proclaimed it was "the greatest monetary agreement in the history of the world." All it did, however, was to set off more speculation against the dollar and in favor of gold. The attempt to re-align exchange rates and keep them fixed at the new rates without an anchor in an internationally accepted medium of exchange such as gold (or silver, or cowrie shells, or *bancor*) was doomed to failure. The basic problem with the Bretton Woods structure, identified early on by the Belgian–American economist Robert Triffin, was the conflict between the need of the international trading system for financial liquidity and the need of even a dominant economy such as the US to maintain domestic price stability. The "Triffin dilemma," as it became known, finally became unresolvable when the US committed to fund its war in

Vietnam by expanding its money supply rather than increasing taxes or getting other countries to contribute. The stopgap arrangement of the Smithsonian Agreement had the US agree to raise the price of gold to $38.00 an ounce, devaluing the dollar by 8.5 percent, while the remaining G-10 countries agreed to re-value their currencies at varying rates so that the average devaluation of the US dollar came to over 10 percent. This arrangement lasted until February 12, 1973 when the US devalued the dollar another 10 percent to $42 an ounce of gold. But the market price of gold had already risen to $90 an ounce, so both Germany and Japan simply let their currencies float, abandoning any further attempt to salvage the dollar as the anchor currency in the international financial system, while staving off further inflation in their own economies. So ended definitively the Bretton Woods System and the Bretton Woods era.

13 | *From turmoil to the "Great Moderation," 1973–2007*

The end of the Bretton Woods era had long been predicted. In 1958, the Belgian–American economist, Robert Triffin, had spelled out what became known as the "Triffin dilemma." The dilemma was that as international demand for a reserve currency rose with the expansion of world trade, the nation supplying the reserve currency would have to keep running balance of payments deficits on current account, which would make its currency worth less (Triffin 1958). The death throes of the Bretton Woods System over the period from August 15, 1971 to February 12, 1973 foreshadowed two monetary phenomena that became permanent parts of the international financial system thereafter:

(1) flexible exchange rates, with the US dollar sometimes falling and occasionally rising against all other currencies, and
(2) rising prices of gold internationally, accompanied by rising rates of inflation for most countries.

Both phenomena were natural outcomes of the Triffin dilemma, and various economists had predicted that the dilemma would eventually be resolved either by flexible exchange rates or by international agreement to raise the price of gold. What was not analyzed and could not have been foreseen were the effects of the successive oil shocks in 1973 and 1979. Especially remarkable was the resurgence of financial globalization that mimicked in many ways the earlier period of globalization during the classical gold standard of the late nineteenth century. How did the three phenomena – floating exchange rates, rising price of gold, and sudden increases in oil prices – interact to create financial globalization again, but under quite different background conditions than under the classical gold standard? The answer lies in the various ways that the trilemma of open macroeconomics can be resolved. One of the three desirable policies for a country open to foreign trade has to be given up, whether it is fixed exchange rates, monetary independence, or access to foreign capital. The classical gold standard resolved the trilemma by each participating country forfeiting monetary independence. The central banks were left to do whatever was needed to maintain fixed exchange rates with the other countries on the gold standard. This led to an unprecedented surge of international capital flows at the time (Obstfeld and Taylor 2004). The Bretton Woods System resolved the trilemma by letting governments forfeit commercial access to foreign capital while they kept fixed exchange rates and their monetary independence, which meant keeping their central banks under control to meet the government's priorities, as they had during the Second World War. The post-Bretton Woods System turns out, by and large, to forfeit fixed exchange rates in favor of keeping both monetary independence (to respond to domestic political imperatives) and access to foreign capital. The post-Bretton Woods System took a while to fall into place, but when it did cohere by the end of the 1990s it seemed to work well, until the crisis of 2007.

Emergence of the post-Bretton Woods System

Already in 1970, one could see emerging differences in the independent monetary policies pursued by the leading economies in the Bretton Woods System. The central banks in Germany, Japan, and Switzerland had all pursued policies to keep domestic inflation in check, at least relative to the US. The result was a slight appreciation of their currencies relative to the dollar as the system began to collapse. By contrast, the central banks in France, Italy, and Britain all followed the political directives of their respective governments to meet the wage demands of union-led workers to get their share of the gains from continued economy growth during the Golden Age of Growth, 1950–1993. Once in place, these national differences quickly exacerbated the differences in exchange rates with the US dollar as the Bretton Woods System collapsed in 1971–1973 (Figure 13.1). Meanwhile, the price of gold in terms of dollars just kept rising, with each oil shock, peaking in 1980 at $615 per Troy ounce.

The gold prices reflect nicely the sequence of three successive shocks to the international financial system: (1) the first oil shock in 1973, when the Organisation of Petroleum Exporting Countries (OPEC) quadrupled the price of oil in US dollars; (2) second oil shock in 1979 when OPEC doubled the price of oil again; and (3) the "Volcker shock" in 1980 when Paul Volcker, chair of the US Federal Reserve System, radically changed

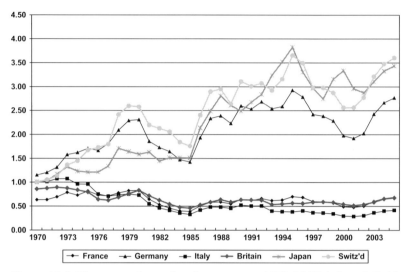

Figure 13.1 The uncertainty of exchange rates, 1970–2005 (selected G-10 countries against the US dollar, 1960) (from Organisation for Economic Cooperation and Development. 1996 and 2005)

US monetary policy to reduce the supply of dollars on foreign exchange markets (Figure 13.2). Only after the Volcker "shock" took effect through international financial markets did the period subsequently dubbed the "Great Moderation" begin, the result of renewed international cooperation among the major industrial economies belonging to the IMF (the Plaza Accord in 1985 started devaluing the dollar, followed by the Louvre Accord in 1987 to stabilize the dollar).

Each of the three shocks had different effects upon national economies, depending on their idiosyncratic policy responses. To sort out the lessons that could have been learned from the various national policy experiments in this period, it is useful to take a closer look at the European Union (EU) countries. Over the period of the three successive shocks to the international financial system, the Common Market added four new countries: the UK, Ireland, and Denmark in 1973 and Greece in 1979.

The European response to the 1970s shocks

The reaction of the EU countries to the first stage in the breakup of the Bretton Woods System, the Smithsonian Agreement in December

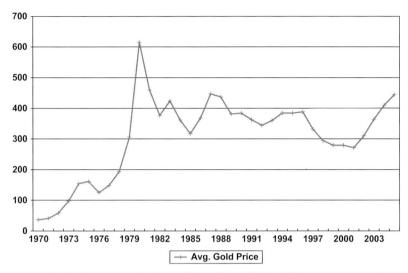

Figure 13.2 The price of gold in US dollars, 1970–2005 (average per Troy ounce) (from Timothy E. Green, historical gold price table, www.nma.org/pdf/gold/his_gold_prices.pdf)

1971, was to agree that their currencies would maintain fluctuations with a 2.25 (+/–) percent band with respect to one another, but not with respect to US or Canadian dollars. A bit later, in March 1972, they determined to maintain margins with respect to each other that were only +/– 1.125 percent from the agreed central rates (the "snake"), while keeping within the +/– 2.25 percent margins with respect to the other currencies in the Smithsonian Agreement (the "tunnel"). These were known as the G-10 at the time and consisted of the US, the UK, Japan, West Germany, France, Italy, Canada, Belgium, the Netherlands, and Sweden, with Switzerland as an observer. Britain joined the snake in the tunnel agreement only briefly (May to June 1972) as a token gesture of its commitment to membership in the European Community (EC), which was to begin formally in 1973, but the pound sterling then floated from June 1972 on. Italy left the arrangement in February 1973, just before the entire Smithsonian Agreement broke down and generalized floating began in March 1973.

This ended the tunnel, but the snake continued to float, although with a varying membership (dubbed "snake in the lake" by some). By January 1974, France had dropped out of the arrangement, rejoining briefly from July 1975 to March 1976. While Norway and Sweden

participated from time to time, the joint float ended up being conducted by Germany, the Netherlands, Belgium, Luxembourg, and
Denmark. Obviously, it was the German *Bundesbank* that was orches-
trating this arrangement (Neal 2007, Chapter 5).

While each major country in the EC pursued its own national policy
to respond to the first oil shock, the German economy and those linked
most closely to it in the snake had the most success. This can be
attributed in large part to the effect of Germany's tight money policy
in absorbing a large part of the oil shock through an appreciation of
the *Deutsche Mark* relative to the dollar. The oil shock consisted
of the OPEC countries quadrupling the price of crude oil in dollars.
When the *Deutsche Mark* and the currencies pegged to it appreciated
by 30–40 percent relative to the dollar (Figure 13.1), they wiped out
that much of the price increase for imported oil. Meanwhile, France
and Italy continued to depreciate their currencies relative to the dollar
and thus magnified the oil (dollar) shock for their economies. Recognizing their failure relative to the strong currency policies of West
Germany and the Netherlands, the central banks of France and
Italy renewed their efforts to imitate the German policy when they
were confronted with the second oil shock. This started in late 1978,
and lasted through 1979 into 1980. To gain the necessary independence from their governments, the central banks in France and Italy
supported the formation of the European Monetary System (EMS),
which committed them by treaty to peg their currencies to the
Deutsche Mark.

The European Monetary System, 1979–1992

The inclusion of France and Italy in the joint float with Germany
against the dollar and yen was launched at the July 1978 meeting of
the heads of government of the member countries (the European
Council) although operation of the EMS did not begin formally until
March 13, 1979 (Ungerer 1983). Great Britain opted out for a variety
of reasons, pragmatic and political. Its previous effort at floating with
the rest of the EC had aborted after only one month in 1972; as yet its
trade with the rest of the Community had not expanded to the extent
hoped for when it had joined; and, most important, its commitment to
development of its offshore oil resources in the North Sea was coming
to fruition, foretelling the emergence of Britain as a net oil exporter

rather than oil importer, unlike the rest of the EC. The importance of this was that the price of oil was then (and still is) set in US dollars by the OPEC cartel. Germany's tight money policies during the first oil shock of 1973–1974 had meant the *Deutsche Mark* appreciated relative to the dollar, so the price of oil, while still rising in terms of *Deutsche Marks*, did not rise as much as it did in dollars. This was a definite advantage for a net importer like Germany and the rest of the EC, but it was a definite disadvantage for a net exporter such as Britain, which has kept the pound sterling closely tied to the US dollar ever since.

In the event, the British decision proved right: almost immediately with the launching of the EMS came the second oil shock of 1979–1980, set off by the revolution in Iran. This redoubled the price of oil, which had already quadrupled in response to the power of the OPEC cartel in 1973–1974. The British decision to stay out of the EMS forced Ireland and Denmark, two small open economies whose major trading partner had traditionally been Great Britain before they entered the Common Market in 1973, to decide where their future lay. Both opted to stick with Germany and to take their chances on trade with Britain. That proved costly as the pound floated with respect to the *Deutsche Mark* and fell sharply in terms of the latter and even relative to the US dollar. In the short run, the decision to peg the Irish punt to the *Deutsche Mark* proved especially painful for Ireland, as it found itself priced out of much of its traditional British market and not yet competitive in the rest of the EC. No doubt the Irish government judged the economic costs worth bearing for the political independence from Britain it gained by committing its future to Continental Europe.

More important than the short-run costs for these two small countries, however, was the effect of the second oil shock on the stability of the newly created system. The first oil shock had destroyed permanently the Bretton Woods System of fixed exchange rates, set with adjustable pegs to the US dollar, despite the best efforts to re-align rates in the Smithsonian Agreement of December 1971. Would the second oil shock destroy the more modest effort of the Europeans to have a limited area of exchange rate stability within the confines of their customs union? Surprisingly, the EMS survived, expanded in membership, strengthened in effectiveness, and eventually induced even Britain to join in late 1990.

There were two keys to the survival of the EMS in face of the second oil shock, which reduced economic growth, greatly increased unemployment, and increased political turnover in most of the participating countries. One key was the flexibility of the EMS compared to the Bretton Woods System, manifested in the frequent re-alignments of exchange rates among the participants. These usually allowed France or Italy to depreciate a bit more relative to the German *Deutsche Mark* and the Dutch guilder. The more significant key to the success of the EMS, however, was the good fortune of having two favorable shocks in the 1980s. First was the Volcker "shock," which sharply appreciated the US dollar in the early 1980s and gave a boost to the export competitiveness of all the EMS currencies. Second was the "third oil shock" in the late 1980s, which collapsed the price of oil in dollars. These two felicitous shocks were far more important to preserving the EMS than the flexibility of the EMS members because all the European currencies, whether they were in the EMS or not, had the same experience. Each European currency had depreciated against the US dollar from 1980 to 1985, which improved each country's balance of trade even as the depreciation made the second oil shock more severe, save for Britain and Norway, who had just become oil exporters. After 1985 each oil importing country benefited from the collapse in the price of oil during the Iraq–Iran war at the end of the 1980s.

Even so, re-alignments were frequent in the first few years of the EMS system under the duress of the Volcker "shock" – twice in 1979, 1981, and 1982, then once in 1983 and finally in July 1985. After 1985, the remaining re-alignments, until the breakaway of Britain and Italy in September 1992, occurred in the context of new entrants coming into the Exchange Rate Mechanism (ERM) of the EMS, or existing members narrowing their bands from 6 percent (Italy and Ireland initially, and then Spain, Britain, and Portugal as they entered the ERM) to 2.25 percent. The "third oil shock," the collapse of crude oil prices at the end of 1985, inaugurated a period of relatively cheap energy that was only briefly interrupted during the Gulf War of 1990–1991. Moreover, the US dollar fell relative to the other OECD currencies after the Louvre Accord in 1987, making oil prices even cheaper for the European economies. With this fortuitous combination of falling oil prices and a falling dollar, small wonder that the participating currencies in the EMS had no further need for re-alignment. Europeans congratulated themselves on having made the necessary adjustments in central par rates during the shakedown part of the cruise toward achieving a common currency, one that might challenge the all-mighty dollar for pre-eminence in international finance.

The euro-dollar market re-cycles petro-dollars

While the Continental Europeans were negotiating among themselves how to restore the economic miracles they had enjoyed during the heyday of the Bretton Woods System, the euro-dollar market, already well-established in London during the 1960s, enabled the UK to re-cycle "petro-dollars" through its financial system. Given the inelastic demand for oil by importing countries, huge surpluses in dollars were quickly accumulated by the OPEC countries, $68 billion in 1974, completely swamping their limited demand for imports. Estimates by the BIS are that most of the OPEC surpluses, $56.3 billion, were invested abroad. The IMF quickly established an "Oil Import Facility" so it could borrow dollars from OPEC countries and lend them on to oil importing developing countries. But the IMF's conduit played only a very small part in the overall process of re-cycling petro-dollars, $3.5 billion in 1974 and $4.0 billion in 1975 before dwindling and dropping out of existence in 1979 (IMF 2006, p. 85).

"Deposits in foreign currency markets" (the euro-dollar markets that had sprung up by 1971) came to $22.8 billion in 1974 and surged again to $31.2 billion in 1979 when the second oil shock hit. A special bilateral arrangement between particular oil exporters and important importers (e.g. Libya and Italy; Iraq and France) were the second most important conduit. Sterling deposits in the UK or dollar deposits in the US remained minor parts of the re-cycling of petro-dollars throughout both oil shocks. The international banks that attracted petro-dollar deposits in turn sought out borrowers in oil importing developing countries, mostly in Latin America, to help them cover the cost of oil imports. The subsequent loans set the stage for the various Latin American debt crises of the 1980s when the Volcker "shock" hit.

The efficacy of the private and bilateral official conduits for re-cycling petro-dollars during the two successive oil shocks of the 1970s did teach a permanent lesson for policy makers – capital controls had to go. The initial import of petro-dollars after the shocks in 1973 and 1979 had been in short-term bank deposits or money market investments before moving into higher-yielding longer-term investments. But short-term capital movements were discouraged if capital controls limited the possibility of repatriating investments, so it was important to remove capital controls in general so that countries could have access to international finance, whatever the source, in case of need. As European countries on the Continent moved toward establishing a common currency while Britain, Norway, and the Netherlands tried to develop their own sources of fuels they all realized that domestic capital controls had to be removed. Even if the EU members of the EMS were trying to maintain fixed exchange rates with each other, as under the Bretton Woods System, they understood from the pressures of financing the repeated oil shocks that capital controls had to go so they could access the petro-dollars needed to pay for oil imports. The process started with Britain under US-led pressure on the IMF in 1976 and was completed by monetary reforms under Margaret Thatcher, who became Prime Minister in 1979.

London finance finally unfettered: the end of exchange controls, 1976–1979

Despite hosting more and more foreign banks in the euro-dollar market to circumvent the capital controls deployed worldwide under the watchful eye of the IMF, London as a financial center had to deal with disarray within the British government's policy responses to the end of fixed exchange rates and the end of its special relationship with the US in managing the international financial system. Just as a new Labour Party government in Britain faced the task of adapting its relationship with the sterling bloc countries to the requirements of coordinating policies with the Member States of the EEC as negotiated by the Conservative Party, the first oil shock struck in 1973. In the confusion of economic policy that followed, the pound floated, inflation soared, and the Labour Party committed to encouraging massive foreign investment in developing the oil fields under the North Sea. Having decimalized the pound so that the 240 pence that made up the pound sterling, now became 100 new pence, Britain also set the exchange rate at $2.40 to make the old pence now worth just one American cent (Neal 2007, Chapter 14).

The Labour Party, now in power, created inflation in Britain to compensate workers for the higher cost of food under the Common Agricultural Policy (CAP) of the Common Market. The inflation, however, quickly made the new exchange rate overvalued. At one point late in 1976 (Thursday October 28), the pound sank to $1.555, marking the nadir of British economic woes (Capie 2010, p. 752). While the government apparently wanted sterling to fall to around $2.00, international banks clearly felt more comfortable placing deposits in Germany, and massive interventions by the Bank of England did nothing to staunch the continued downward pressure on the pound. Eventually, in December 1976, the IMF agreed to make £2.3 billion available for two years, the first such arrangement by the IMF. The IMF loan came with conditions, however, reminiscent of the bondholders' committees of the late nineteenth century and the League of Nations Financial Commission oversights of the Austrian and Hungarian loans after the First World War. Government borrowing had to be cut substantially by reducing expenditures and selling off some shares in British Petroleum that the government had acquired earlier. IMF conditionality, which became a hallmark of its future efforts when dealing with the Latin American debt crises in the 1980s, was not accepted gracefully the first time, especially not by Britain.

Using the connections established with the BIS, however, an unconditional loan was arranged in Basel for a $3 billion facility to enable Britain to convert the remaining sterling balances into convertible currencies. The Bank of England succeeded in selling bonds to the sterling bloc countries, mainly India, for a total of £395 million, half in US dollars and the rest in *Deutsche Mark*, Japanese yen, and Swiss francs (Capie 2010, p. 758). While this took care of the remaining sterling balances, the remaining exchange controls seemed increasingly picayune and irrelevant, especially in the context of a floating pound, which began to rise in value in 1977 after the announcement of the IMF loan.

According to the official history of the Bank of England, however, the final resistance to eliminating exchange controls ended in August 1979 when Bank officials read an account in the German business newspaper of a foreign exchange swap arranged between pounds and dollars by Continental Illinois, an American bank (which later failed dramatically in 1984, the largest bank failure in US history – at least until the failure of Washington Mutual in 2008). In 1979, however, Continental Illinois had received a deposit of sterling worth $25 million by the British firm, Consolidated Goldfields, while it also received a deposit of $25 million by an American firm wishing to have access to the sterling over a period of ten years. The American firm paid 2 percent annually to the British firm to compensate for the higher interest rates in Britain on sterling accounts, and all this, according to the German paper, was an innovation that did not violate UK exchange controls (Capie 2010, p. 767). With the new Conservative government under Margaret Thatcher taking office in May 1979, the Bank's staff could stop enforcing exchange controls altogether. Reducing over 700 staff through a voluntary severance scheme, the Bank was also able to help the new government meet the IMF's conditions for reduced government spending (Capie 2010, p. 770).

The Latin American debt crisis, 150 years after the first one (in 1825)

The recycling of petro-dollars in the 1970s took advantage of the euro-dollar market that had arisen from private initiatives to circumvent the capital controls that had been practiced by all the IMF member countries. In the case of Latin American countries, the best bet for the international banks exploiting the euro-dollar market in London was to lend to Latin American governments by underwriting new issues of their sovereign bonds. Given the uncertainties of the par rates of the dollar with the main convertible currencies in the G-10 countries, however, the bonds had to be denominated primarily in US dollars, which after all were needed to pay for oil imports. The second oil shock simply exacerbated the dependence of oil importing countries in Latin America on external debt. In one case, the pressures did lead Chile to liberalize its capital account controls in 1975, with all that implied for eventual deregulation of Chile's domestic financial sector. The relative success of Chile's experiment in opening up its financial sector to the rest of the world led eventually to other Latin American countries attempting to adopt "*apertura*" policies as well, in order to tap in more effectively to international capital markets. The earlier success of Spain's *apertura* policies in the 1960s was also a positive example for finance ministers throughout Latin America.

The increased international debt incurred throughout Latin America was accompanied by many other policy changes in response, including tariff reductions, fiscal reforms, and a general replacement of the "import substitution industrialization" model that most had pursued since insulating themselves from the shocks of the 1930s. All these reforms were very much encouraged by the two international agencies based in Washington, the IMF and the World Bank. In light of European experience in recovering from the Second World War, much was made of the need for Latin American governments to free up trade restrictions as well so that new export earnings could be generated to pay the interest on external debt. The Volcker "shock" in 1980, however, caught the Latin American countries in an unforeseen vise of liabilities in one currency, US dollars, and assets in their domestic currency, which fell sharply relative to the dollar. Country after country began to default or, at least, begin negotiations for re-financing of existing debt or outright forgiveness with the individual banks that held their debt, while the original lending banks tried to reduce their exposure to such troubled borrowers.

As private individuals began to intermediate among the debtor countries and the various international banks, it became clear that some kind of collective action was needed to coordinate the various creditors holding sovereign bonds issued by countries facing more than short-term liquidity problems. Nicholas Brady, US Secretary of the Treasury, proposed in 1989 the creation of new, tradable financial assets with backing by US sovereign debt (thirty-year, zero coupon, US Treasury bonds) by each debtor country. The Brady Plan had three essential features: (1) the bank creditors granted some debt relief in exchange for greater assurance of future payments of principal and interest; (2) debt relief was granted in exchange for commitments to economic reform by the country; and (3) the new form of debt would be standardized and therefore tradable in secondary markets. Banks previously stuck with bad loans made to defaulting countries could now re-finance them into securities that might be profitable investments for the international financial community. The new bond issues took many different forms, depending on the specific situation for each defaulting sovereign, but a total of $160 billion at face value were issued by Argentina, Brazil, Bulgarian, Costa Rica, the Dominican Republic, Ecuador, Ivory Coast, Jordan, Nigeria, Panama, Peru, the Philippines, Poland, Russia, Uruguay, Venezuela, and Vietnam (EMTA 2014).

In 1994, trading in Brady bonds accounted for 61 percent of trading in emerging markets debt trading, but by 2005 had dropped to only about 2 percent. Most Brady bonds had been paid off by then and replaced with a wide variety of other forms of sovereign debt. Most notable were issues in domestic currencies by many countries that had enjoyed success in making fiscal and monetary reforms domestically while improving their access to international commodity markets through tariff reductions and removal of non-tariff barriers (NTBs). These countries had overcome the "original sin" problem of facing exchange rate risk for their external debt when they had to denominate their sovereign debt in the preferred currency of their foreign creditors, whether American, German, or Japanese. From now on, they could issue sovereign debt in their own currency and let foreign investors take on whatever exchange risks might develop in the future.

Another shock to the European financial system: German reunification

The successive oil shocks of the 1970s that quadrupled, then doubled again, the price of oil in dollars had apparently not affected at all the centrally planned economies of the Soviet Union and Communist China, committed as they were to self-sufficiency within their respective domains. While the Soviet Russia was an oil exporting country, it was not a member of OPEC and, furthermore, was committed to long-term barter arrangements with the Eastern European economies it dominated. Russian oil or gas was bartered for specific items needed to fulfill the objectives of each Five-Year Plan. Consequently, Russia did not benefit from the oil shocks the way the other oil exporting countries could and did, while its satellite countries in eastern Europe were protected from the shocks that had hurt oil importing countries in Asia and Latin America. China's leaders already understood by the time of the second oil shock that they had to adopt an export-led model of growth for their future, which they began to implement in 1978.

When the third oil shock occurred in the mid 1980s, however, the Soviet model of bartering Russian oil for industrial imports from Eastern Europe looked less appealing to Russia's European satellites unable to take advantage of the fall in the price of oil. The collapse of the Soviet barter model of trade within the Eurasian empire Russia had created after the Second World War came soon after, symbolized by the fall of the Berlin wall in November 1989. German reunification followed quickly, taking place officially in October 1990. Reunification was prompt and politically popular on both sides, as all that had to be done was to add five new states to the existing Federal Republic of Germany, with appropriate political representation in the expanded German Parliament. The only glitch was that the West German Chancellor, Helmut Kohl, had promised the East Germans that their holdings of *Ostmark*s, the East German currency, would be exchanged 1:1 up to one month's average salary, and then 2:1 thereafter. These exchange rates were a huge overvaluation of the East German *Ostmark*, which had been trading at levels up to 12:1 at the time. This financial windfall made it easy for East German voters to approve overwhelmingly for reunification with West Germany immediately.

The windfall for East Germans, however, proved to be a serious economic problem for West Germany and the tradition of price stability that had been carefully sustained by the *Bundesbank* ever since the currency reform of 1948. To mop up the excess *Ostmark*s that the East German government had created in its death throes after the fall of the Berlin wall, the *Bundesbank* raised interest rates, which strengthened the *Deutsche Mark* against the dollar while also strengthening all the EMS currencies that were pegged to the *Deutsche Mark* as well. The resulting pressure on the foreign reserves of the other European central banks proved too much for Italy and Great Britain. Italy had recently tightened its peg to the *Deutsche Mark* to limit fluctuations to within +/– 2.25 percent instead of 6 percent, while Britain had finally joined the EMS in October 1990 at the same time that German reunification was completed. Both countries had to leave the EMS in September 1992 as their foreign reserves were running out. The remaining countries, led by France, nevertheless stuck it out with Germany to commit to establish a common currency, the euro, by the end of the 1990s. They were able to do this by temporarily allowing huge swings in their exchange rates, +/– 15 percent, to take place instead of using up foreign reserves to intervene in foreign exchange markets.

Figure 13.3 shows the wide disparity in European exchange rates in 1960 when the Bretton Woods System of fixed exchange rates with the US dollar took full effect. The breakup of stable exchange rates in the 1970s showed the disparity in central bank policies among even western European countries as they exercised monetary independence with the protection of capital controls. Some, like Germany, the Netherlands, and Austria, continued to strengthen against the US dollar, which mitigated the first oil shock for their economies. Others,

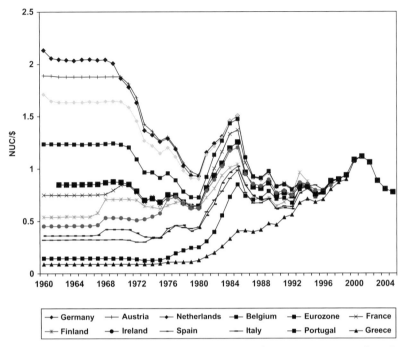

Figure 13.3 Leading up to the euro, European exchange rates against the US dollar, 1960–2004 (from International Monetary Fund, *International Financial Statistics, Supplement* (for 1950–1959) 1966; and from Organisation for Economic Cooperation and Development 1996 and 2005)

like France and Italy, continued to weaken against the US dollar, making the first oil shock worse, until their central banks followed the lead of the *Bundesbank* after 1978 and strengthened their currencies against the US dollar to help mitigate the second oil shock on their economies. The Volcker "shock," however, weakened all the currencies against the US dollar, but the EMS managed to keep most of the currencies moving together, finally achieving the long-desired goal of a common currency by 1998 (Neal 2007, Chapter 5).

Given the evident difficulties of maintaining fixed exchange rates worldwide, which had eventually undermined the structure of the Bretton Woods System, and the turmoil that the German reunification had created in 1990–1992 when the *Bundesbank* was determining monetary policy for the entire EMS, one wonders why the other countries stuck with the common currency plan and then one wonders why Germany went along with it. The most convincing answer to the skeptical Anglo-American economist to this conundrum lies in the effect that the commitment to fixed exchange rates with the German *Deutsche Mark* had on the pricing of sovereign bonds for the other countries. All of them had to increase their national debts in response to the oil shocks, and most had been increasing their government indebtedness even before in anticipation of continued economic growth during the Golden Age of Economic Growth. Countries with weak fiscal systems, however, found that international investors demanded a risk premium in the form of higher interest rates on the bonds they bought, a risk premium that kept rising as the ratio of outstanding debt to GDP rose for a country.

Figure 13.4 depicts the course of events for the initial group of European countries that adopted the euro as their common currency by 1998 (Greece finally joined in 2002 just as euro coins and notes were issued to replace the former currencies). German monetary policy and fiscal restraint enabled German sovereign bonds to have consistently the lowest yield, even after the reunification shock took hold in 1991. When the other countries joined the German model of monetary

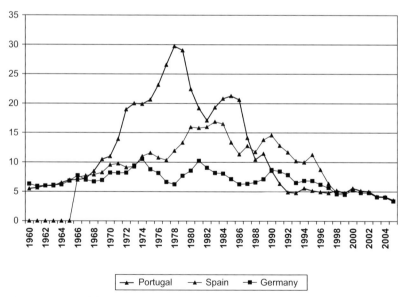

Figure 13.4 Yields on government debt for euro-zone countries, 1960–2004 (from Organisation for Economic Cooperation and Development 1996 and 2005)

discipline and fiscal restraint by proving they could meet the "Maastricht criteria" that Germany had insisted on putting in the Treaty of European Monetary Union signed in the Dutch city of Maastricht in 1992, they enjoyed a reduction in interest expenditures on their stock of accumulated debt. The reduction amounted to nearly 1 percent of GDP for the countries on average, and clearly more for countries like Greece and Italy that had built up very high ratios of government debt to GDP over the previous decades.

So much for the motivation of the follower countries, but why would Germany accept giving up its strong, stable currency for an uncertain future with a common European currency governed by the newly established European Central Bank (ECB)? The answer at the time was that Germany insisted that each country adopting the currency imitate the essential features of the German monetary and fiscal system at the time. These were identified as five specific quantitative measures that each country had to maintain for at least two years before it would be allowed to join the European Monetary Union (EMU):

(1) inflation within 1 percent of the average of the three lowest inflation rates within the European Union;
(2) interest rates within 1 percent of the average of the three lowest rates of interest on long-term government bonds in the European Union;
(3) exchange rate within 2 percent of parity with the euro for two years;
(4) government deficits under 3 percent of GDP;
(5) government debt under 60 percent of GDP.

The first three criteria dealt with monetary discipline, and were purposefully redundant to guard against an applicant country using some form of the currency controls allowed under the Bretton Woods System to manipulate the exchange rate or the rate of inflation. The last two were intended to guard against governments of the applicant country putting pressure on the central bank to monetize its debt, as the deficit of 3 percent and debt stock of 60 percent seemed acceptable from West German experience in the 1960s. Each applicant, moreover, had to pass formal legislation to make the national central bank independent from the central government. The mandate of the ECB would be to maintain price stability within the Member Countries. All in all, Germans could be satisfied that the structure of the ECB made it even more reliable as a guardian of the stability of currency than had been the case with the *Bundesbank*. The final steps to make all bank accounts denominated in euros were completed in 1998, taking full effect on January 1, 1999. All seemed to have gone much more smoothly than feared by some Europeans or foretold by many Americans.

International repercussions

As usual, the annual report of the BIS noted the importance of the fiscal constraints on the member governments joining the EMU and the long-run importance of taking advantage of the low interest rates on government debt to make structural reforms in the labor markets (BIS, *Annual Report* 1999). These were needed to restore international competitiveness because the ECB was not going to tamper with interventions in the foreign exchange markets. The Maastricht Treaty bound the ECB to confine its efforts to maintaining domestic price stability, nothing else. If it succeeded in doing that, everything else would work out fine, as long as governments acted responsibly in terms of national fiscal policies. Later, historians would learn that the central bankers working on recommendations for making the ECB work effectively under the sponsorship of the BIS had argued strenuously against putting the scheme into operation without stronger safeguards against political interference from member governments and the Commission of the European Union (James 2012).

The Asian financial crises, 1997–1998

Meanwhile, the international financial system had to deal with the ripple effect of financial crises in Asia. These began in Thailand as Thai banks that had borrowed short-term loans in Japanese yen to invest in long-term mortgages to finance the property boom in Bangkok and coastal resorts found they could not renew their loans except at higher interest rates. When the central bank stopped convertibility of the Thai baht on July 2, 1997, the exchange rate rapidly depreciated, which meant that Thai banks found that their assets, denominated in Thai baht, became less and less valuable relative to their liabilities, denominated in US dollars or Japanese yen. In retrospect, the Thai crisis was a classic example of how countries pursuing an export-led growth model with fixed exchange rates could run into financial difficulties, whether runaway domestic inflation – as had been the case with Latin American countries in the 1960s and again especially in the 1970s – or property bubbles – as had been the case in Japan in the 1980s. Economists came to call this the "Balassa–Samuelson effect," after the two economists, Béla Belassa, who had identified the empirical evidence for the phenomenon in Latin America (Belassa 1964), and Paul Samuelson, who formulated it in mathematical terms to persuade the rest of the economics profession of its validity (Samuelson 1964).

The effect happens when a country that has been pursuing economic and political policies to come as close as possible to self-sufficiency, as was the case for most of Latin America in the 1930s through the 1950s, decides to open up to the possibilities of international trade. Prices of tradable goods in the previously autarkic economy now rise to the common level they have in the international economy. Firms and workers taking advantage of the higher prices now available to them from exporting goods or services in which the country has a comparative advantage then begin to drive up prices of non-tradable goods and services in the economy. The ultimate non-tradable, of course, is land, and speculative bubbles in property especially suitable for export-oriented activity are a common feature of the transition from autarkic to open economies. Letting the nominal exchange rate appreciate runs counter to the export-led model of economic growth, so the central bank usually restricts the domestic money supply by raising interest rates or credit rationing. If an essential part of opening up the economy to the rest of the world is to allow capital imports, however, speculation can be funded by borrowing abroad, which was the case for Thailand in the 1990s.

It was also the case for Indonesia, South Korea, the Philippines, Malaysia, Hong Kong, and Taiwan, all of which had pegged their currencies to the US dollar as part of their export-led growth strategies, and which had been wildly successful for each of them in the 1980s and early 1990s. When the Thai baht floated, however, financial panic set in and continued to make the economic situation worse in Thailand with cascading defaults on mortgages and bank loans. The devalued Thai currency made life more difficult for exporters in the other Asian economies, which began to contract as well. Interesting experiments in economic policy then followed as some countries took on IMF advice and others resisted. The IMF was willing to make loans to the governments of each country (save Taiwan or Hong Kong), but only on the standard conditions that had been developed in previous decades dealing with the Latin American cases. Conditions required governments to work toward balanced budgets, whether by raising taxes, cutting subsidies, or privatizing state-owned assets. When the IMF was satisfied with a country making good faith efforts to meet its conditions for an immediate loan, it was usually the case that more loans would be forthcoming from the Paris Club of government lenders. The Paris Club was created in 1956 to deal with the first Argentina default and has met regularly ever since. By 2014, the Paris Club had reached 420 agreements dealing with 90 debtor countries. The London Club of commercial international banks (formed in 1970) is less formal and meets at the initiative of a debtor nation, but usually coordinates its actions with those previously taken by the IMF and the Paris Club.

The cases of Thailand and Indonesia trying to meet IMF conditions, however, led to a series of political difficulties in subsequent years even as some economic recovery began in the twenty-first century. The subsequent international financial crisis of 2007, moreover, set both countries back economically and renewed their domestic political difficulties. South Korea did meet IMF conditions and enjoyed significant support subsequently from American banks as a result, but was again running into the danger of a property bubble when the international crisis of 2007 hit. Malaysia spurned IMF help and set its own policies, which meant instituting capital controls against IMF advice. Malaysia's capital controls were directed against banks in Singapore, which had the most exposure to the Malaysian property bubble (of which the Petronas Twin Towers in Kuala Lumpur, the tallest buildings in the world from 1998 to 2004 were the most egregious symbol). As the Malaysian economy recovered, capital controls were gradually removed and the ringgit was allowed to float against the US dollar. Chastened by the relatively better outcomes for Malaysia than for Thailand or Indonesia, the IMF orthodoxy has changed. Now, IMF conditions for loans allow for floating exchange rates although they still require open capital accounts. They still aim for macroeconomic stability, but only after recovery has taken hold in the economy. Nevertheless, the problem remains for each country how to manage its domestic currency while reaping the advantages of an undervalued currency to support export-led growth.

Mainland China was the prime role model for all the "newly industrializing countries" (NICs) after 1998, as its central bank was able to
maintain an undervalued fixed exchange rate with the US dollar that
enabled China's industries to continue exporting massive amounts of
goods to both the US and the European Union. The central bank kept
domestic inflation under control by sterilizing the US dollars that
Chinese exporters had to deposit, refusing to grant them full value in
yuan. In turn, the central bank bought increasing amounts of US
Treasury bonds, indirectly helping to finance the US war on terror
after September 11, 2001. The other Asian economies seemed to
imitate the Chinese example to an increasing extent up to 2007 as
well. Foreign reserves rose substantially for all of them in the ten years
after July 2, 1997 (*Economist* 2007). But reserves had also risen in the
case of Britain when it floated the pound in 1976 and eliminated
capital controls, so the buildup of reserves took place in the rest of
Asia without other countries having to imitate China by undervaluing
their exchange rates or keeping capital controls in place.

The consequence of China building up a huge reserve of US dollars
while the US continued to run huge deficits on current account (mainly
with China, but also with most of the other Asian economies) and to
incur rising government deficits while pursuing its war on terror was
foreseen by one economist by 2005. Ramchuran Rajan, chief economist for the IMF at the time and now governor of the Bank of India,
was the only speaker that year at the annual conference held by the
Federal Reserve System each summer in Jackson Hole, Wyoming to
foresee that a terrible financial crisis internationally was just waiting
to happen (Rajan 2005). All other speakers, including the new chair of
the Federal Reserve System, Ben Bernanke, and the former Secretary
of the Treasury, Lawrence Summers, thought the US financial situation
was fine. Moreover, the American policy makers took pride in the
"Great Moderation" of inflation and exchange rate fluctuations that
had occurred since the Asian financial crises and the stock market
collapse of the dot.com bubble in 2000. This was due, in their opinions, to an excess of savings available in international capital markets
for a limited amount of new investment opportunities. Rajan argued,
by contrast, that a widening fault line was opening up in international
finance and it was continuing to deepen thanks to misguided economic
policies in both China and the US, an argument he later spelled out in
detail (Rajan 2010). On one side of the fault line, China was keeping its

working classes from consuming while working at low wages to produce cheap exports for the rest of the world's consumers. On the other side, the US was compensating its undereducated workers for their lack of competitiveness in the global labor market by encouraging them to increase their personal debt with credit cards and second mortgages on their homes. Rajan predicted a massive financial crisis would come if neither government changed course – and he was right!

14 | The sub-prime crisis and the aftermath, 2007–2014

With the Great Recession of 2007–2014 (and counting), the US appeared once again to be the epicenter of global financial crises as it was in the Great Depression of 1929–1933. Just as the stock market panic in New York on October 29, 1929 is a convenient marker for the start of the Great Depression worldwide, so the bankruptcy of Lehman Brothers investment bank on September 15, 2008 marks when the crisis in pricing sub-prime mortgages in the US caused global financial turmoil. It is natural in both cases to blame the US and the failures of its policy makers for the global economic difficulties that followed. Later analyses of the sequence of events leading up to and following the stock market crash of 1929, however, have painted quite a different picture of the Great Depression. As noted in previous chapters, Britain, France, and Germany all had important roles to play in initiating the Great Depression as well as prolonging it. Subsequent analysis of the sub-prime crisis that brought down Lehman Brothers in 2008 and caused worldwide financial panic may also identify other, deeper causes than simply a series of missteps by US policy makers.

For example, the first signs of trouble in the international financial system in 2007 showed up in Germany, just as they had with the Great Depression of 1929–1933. In early August 2007, IKB *Deutsche Industriebank* in Germany had to get a capital injection of $4.8 billion from a consortium of German banks. IKB's Special Investment Vehicle (SIV) had invested in an exotic Collateralized Debt Obligation (CDO) created by Goldman Sachs in the US, which it now found was worthless. (Eventually, the Goldman Sachs trader who had sold the CDO to IKB, Fabrice Tourre, was convicted of fraudulent felonies, barred from the securities industry, and fined $825,000 for his misdeeds. Avoiding a prison sentence somehow, he decided to work on a PhD at the University of Chicago as of August 2014.)

The exotic financial product that Tourre had put together to appeal to European investors like IKB combined high yields with certification by a reputable intermediary. IKB, coping with the new financial market created by the EMU, was searching for higher-yielding investments than were available in the European markets. Low interest rates throughout Europe reflected the price stability policy pursued by the ECB, as well as its acceptance of all member countries' sovereign bonds on equal terms as collateral for loans to the national central banks of Member States. Unbeknown to IKB, however, the product created by Goldman Sachs had been deliberately constructed to fail so that John Paulson, major hedge fund investor in the US, could bet against it by buying a credit default swap (CDS) against it, also from Goldman Sachs. Paulson, like most people observing the housing bubble taking place in the US after 2001, figured that mortgages that had been sold to residential property buyers in the "sand" states of southern California, Nevada, and Arizona were bound to default in the near future. Constructing a package of mortgages from these states that had been sold most recently would certainly fail in the near future in Paulson's opinion, which proved to be the case. Handpicking the diciest-looking mortgages from the most vulnerable states that would be packaged in the new CDO, Paulson only needed Tourre to get some reputable credit rating firm to approve the package as a sound investment for at least the top parts of the obligation that would be the last to fail – the so-called AAA tranches.

IKB was not alone among investors thinking that the US investment banks were selling high-yielding, safe securities even if they did not know exactly what were the underlying assets that were supposed to generate these returns. BNP Paribas, one of the largest banks in France, also ran into difficulties in August 2007. Later that month, Sachsen LB, a savings bank in Leipzig, was forced into a merger with Landesbank Baden-Württemburg (Atack and Neal 2009, p. 8). Then, the center of international finance was struck on September 17, 2007 by the first run on a London bank in over 140 years. Northern Rock bank had received a $4.4 billion line of credit from the Bank of England and depositors worried about the safety of their deposits as the bank was clearly in trouble. British deposit insurance only covered the first £2000 and then 90 percent of the balance up to a cap of £35,000. The run on branches of Northern Rock throughout the UK ended only when the British Chancellor of the Exchequer promised unlimited 100 percent coverage to all depositors who remained as of midnight on Wednesday September 19, 2007 for the duration of the crisis.

Other British banks were in similar difficulties, however, also caused
by their exposure to mortgage-backed securities of all kinds from the
UK and the US as well as other countries. They ended up being
nationalized, the UK government investing fresh capital but with voting
power to re-organize and re-structure Lloyds TSB and the venerable
Royal Bank of Scotland, whose origins go back to John Law's ideas for
creating such a national bank in his home country (Chapter 2). True,
the bankruptcy of Lehman did set off even more financial crises in the
rest of the world. Fortis, a financial conglomerate that had recently
absorbed the Dutch bank, ABN AMRO, along with the Dutch marine
insurance company that had been created in Rotterdam during the
bubble year of 1720, suffered a run on September 26, 2007, and
the governments of Belgium, Netherlands, and Luxembourg quickly
offered support. Combined they invested €11.2 billion in return for
two-thirds ownership and then split up the conglomerate into separate
pieces controlled within each country. The Belgian bank, Dexia, got
both a capital injection and a guarantee of its liabilities a few days later,
all part of the repercussions from the failure of Lehman and the complexities of bankruptcy proceedings that slowly were put into place,
first in the US and then in its various affiliates around the world.

Maybe the US was the problem

The problems of major international banks in Europe from investments in US securities going sour should have alerted US regulators
that things might not be going well for its own financial institutions.
It should have led them to take a closer look at the kinds of securities
being packaged and sold to financial institutions eager to find high
yields. In retrospect, the proliferation of new financial firms and new
financial products simply overwhelmed the US regulators. These
underpaid and overworked individuals were busy proliferating their
own bureaucracies and expanding their regulatory domains. Typically,
Federal regulators were pre-empting state regulators as part of a general policy to reciprocate for European banks the access to financial
markets in the European Union that the Single Market Act of 1985 had
created for US banks and financial firms in Europe. Further, the new
Federal agencies competed to expand their regulatory domains by
promising light touch regulations within them. Among the new financial firms taking advantage of the dismantling of previous regulatory

regimes were the misleadingly named "hedge funds," which were really speculators with "other people's money" on high-risk, short-term investment plays that could provide high yields – or go bust. New financial products arose to provide assets for SIVs that traditional financial firms could create to keep their regular loans off their balance sheets. Chief among these were residential mortgage-backed securities (RMBS) as a special category of CDO.

In retrospect, it is amazing that tranches of the RMBS became as acceptable as collateral for the short-term loans to hedge funds as had been the case for long-term US Treasury bonds. Underlying the drive for higher yields worldwide in the global financial marketplace was an increasing demand for acceptable collateral for short-term loans to the investment firms taking advantage of the increased demands for access to international capital. The information communications technology revolution of the 1970s had created a new international capital market in response to the breakup of the Bretton Woods System. The ECB eventually did its job in helping to encourage a new source of collateral by accepting the sovereign bonds of member countries in the EMU on the same basis, regardless of the fiscal balance of the individual country. But that did not happen until 1999, while in the 1990s the US government had undercut the stock of collateral for the global financial market by re-financing its stock of outstanding bonds, replacing the traditional thirty-year Treasury bond with lower-yielding ten-year Treasury bonds. The Clinton administration then ran budget surpluses, which further reduced the stock of collateral available to global financiers. After the Asian financial crisis of 1997–1998, China's insistence on building up its foreign reserves, mainly by stockpiling US Treasury securities, further reduced the stock of collateral in financial markets. Small wonder that the new assets created from mortgage-backed securities with their AAA ratings were eagerly picked up as supplementary forms of collateral for use in the burgeoning "repo" markets for short-term credit in the money market centers of the world, chiefly New York and London (Figure 14.1).

On this interpretation, then, financial innovations made to provide additional collateral to use in the international repo market that had blossomed after 1971 led to the housing bubbles that began to emerge after 2001. While the housing bubble in the US clearly was the most important, both in size and timing, similar bubbles in real estate began to appear elsewhere as well, especially in places with close connections

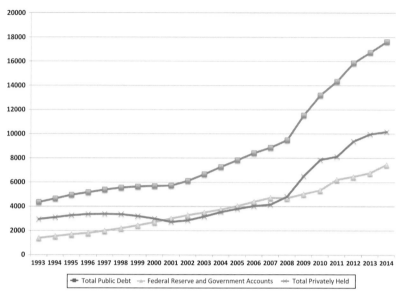

Figure 14.1 US sovereign debt, 1993–2014 (million US dollars) (from US Treasury, *Treasury Bulletin* September 2014; December 2004, Tables OFS-2, "Estimated Ownership of US Treasury Securities")

to the world's financial centers such as Britain, Ireland, Portugal, and Spain. "Securitization" of standard mortgages sold to potential home-owners was the key financial innovation that stimulated the housing booms, first in the US and then elsewhere. Securitization of mortgages in the US took time to develop and can be traced back to the New Deal programs in 1933 to provide government assistance for homeowners (White, Snowden, and Fishback 2014). But the acceleration in mort-gage securitization only took place after the mid 1990s, when the two dominant Government Sponsored Enterprises (GSEs) holding US resi-dential mortgages, Fannie Mae and Freddie Mac, were both charged to broaden their base of insured mortgages by including lower-income households. Their common goal was to increase homeownership in the US from 64 percent to a higher level, which eventually topped out at over 69 percent in 2006. The stock of mortgage debt increased sharply in response, aided by increased competition from the private lending associations that entered the mortgage market.

Neither the shares nor the bonds of the GSEs were guaranteed by the Federal government, but investors assumed that the US government

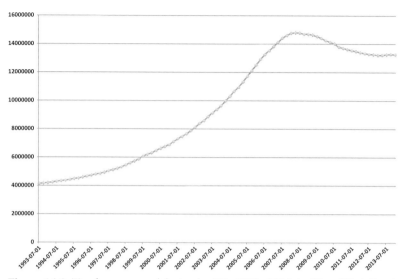

Figure 14.2 Total mortgage debt in the US, 1993–2014 (million US dollars) (from http://research.stlouisfed.org/fred2)

would not let any of them fail. Their implicit government guarantee gave GSE liabilities an extra margin of security when competing with private mortgage bundlers. Moreover, as the stock of US sovereign debt available for collateral purposes fell in the global "repo" finance markets, the GSE bonds began to take their place (Ambrose and King 2002). In addition to the bonds and preferred equity of the two GSEs, Fannie Mae and Freddie Mac, private liability versions of their mortgage-backed securities began to appear, now tapping the previously underexploited sub-prime market that had been ignored by the government until the mid 1990s. The combined result was a sharp uptick in the total of mortgage debt incurred by US households, starting in the 1990s (Figure 14.2).

As much of the rise in mortgage debt was, frankly, less than worthy for posting as collateral by third-party investors, the next innovation was to slice up the mortgages into a number of tranches that varied by seniority in terms of continuing to be serviced out of the combined payments made by the respective mortgagees. Herein lay the seeds of the disaster that eventually unfolded across the international financial markets in 2007.

Slicing and dicing the accumulated sub-prime mortgages into new financial products imitating the previously marketed CDOs looked

Sample Subprime RMBS Structure

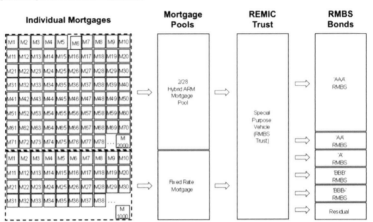

Figure 14.3 How toxic assets were created (from www.fitchratings.com/web_
content/sectors/subprime/Basis_in_ABX_TABX_Bespoke_SF_CDOs.ppt, as cited
in Gorton 2010)

good in theory – the US housing market had blossomed after the
Second World War, and in the mild business cycles during the Bretton
Woods era, housing investment had been a stabilizing, counter cyclical,
element in aggregate demand. As the dot.com bubble of the late 1990s
collapsed, it seemed historically plausible that housing would once
again be the source of new investment demand that would bring the
economy back to full employment. Pouring the combined monthly
payments on a thousand mortgages bundled into a new CDO, but
making sure that the top tranches got preference for payouts before the
rest of the payments trickled down to the bottom, riskiest layers,
enabled bundlers to claim that the top several tranches would qualify
as AAA securities, and so could be eligible as collateral in the burgeoning repo market. Figure 14.3 shows how a typical "residential mortgage backed security" could be packaged and then sold through a
REMIC (real estate mortgage investment conduit).

     The problem with the financial innovations that stimulated new
housing construction was, basically, that they broke the connection
of personal ties with impersonal exchange. In this case, the personal
connection that had existed between local neighborhood homeowners
and local savings and loan firms was broken permanently during the
disintermediation shocks of the 1970s. Worse, further steps were taken

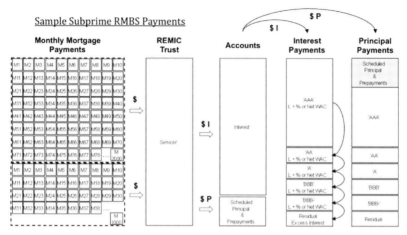

Figure 14.4 How RMBS assets used for collateral became toxic (from www.fitchratings.com/web_content/sectors/subprime/Basis_in_ABX_TABX_Bespoke_SF_CDOs.ppt, as cited in Gorton 2010)

to make sure the personal connections with the ultimate homeowner responsible for making monthly payments on each mortgage in the package were irretrievable. Figure 14.4 shows how the new securities available for collateral became toxic, in the sense that failed mortgage payments on a few mortgages from the original package would contaminate all the subsequent CDOs that were created. When the mortgage payments were separated further into interest and principal, it became impossible for a third-party holder of a tranche of such an RMBS to identify the original defaulting mortgage or to insure against it – other than by buying a CDS against the entire set of RMBS bonds. This turned out to be a service that a section of the insurance giant, AIG, was happy to provide for major investment banks and their wealthy customers. JPMorgan Chase and Goldman Sachs, among others, were quick to take advantage of the CDSs offered by the largest insurance company in the world, thinking there was no risk from a company like AIG, whose bonds were always rated AAA. Through egregious mismanagement and miscalculations at AIG, however, the commitments the company made to insure against default of AAA rated tranches of the mortgage-backed securities proved disastrous when Lehman Brothers was allowed to fail on September 15, 2008. Every counterparty in the interconnected web of international finance had to scramble for safety.

Future historians of the shambles left by the Lehman failure will argue for decades to come whether the moral hazards accumulated exponentially as various governments and central banks interceded to bail out the financial firms caught short of funds when payments stopped coming in on the CDOs they held. Moral hazard started with the German banks and government in early 2007, then the French government in mid 2007, the British government in late 2007, the US coming to the rescue of first commercial banks, then mortgage providers, and then the investment bank of Bear Stearns in March 2008. The UK followed up by nationalizing not only Northern Rock but also Lloyds TSB and the Royal Bank of Scotland. The US followed the UK example by taking over in August 2008 the two GSEs responsible for generating so many sub-prime mortgages in the first place. The repercussions from failing to bail out Lehman Brothers were so extensive, however, that the US Treasury asked for, and eventually received, authority from Congress to put $700 billion in play to bail out troubled firms with the Troubled (toxic) Asset Recovery Program (TARP).

To bail out or not to bail out: that was the question

Initially, the idea of TARP was to buy up the toxic assets that were no longer acceptable as collateral, taking them out of the US and global financial system entirely. When implemented by the US Treasury, however, the funds were used instead to inject fresh capital into hundreds of firms, not all of which were banks or even shadow banks. Oddly, considering the initial motive of the TARP funds, the largest sums of money went to the largest banks and industrial corporations in the US. While those sums were eventually paid back to the US Treasury, and even made a small profit for the government (and the US taxpayer), hundreds of smaller banks still kept the government's investment. Monitoring the use of these funds with an eye toward eventual repayment was the job of a Special Inspector General who regularly reports cases of fraud and abuse of the TARP funds by small banks and their financial officers (www.sigtarp.gov). While no senior executives of any of the firms involved in the creation and distribution of the faulty securities that were at the heart of the sub-prime crisis of 2007–2008 were ever charged, much less convicted of wrongdoing, the Special Inspector General of TARP regularly reports minor officials of smaller financial firms who have been indicted and occasionally convicted of felony offenses against the TARP program.

The original purpose of the TARP bailout fund was very much in line with successful historical examples of recovery from financial crises, namely to re-finance the toxic assets that were the crux of the initial breakdown of trust in the financial innovation that had created a speculative frenzy, and then remove them from the ongoing circuit of finance for traditional purposes. Earlier chapters have shown how such initiatives could restore the normal functioning of an economy after a financial crisis had occurred, and even propel the economy to better economic performance afterwards. So why didn't the TARP program simply re-finance the toxic assets created by the sub-prime mortgage-backed securities and their derivatives? The answer appears to lie in the lack of accountability that had been created, purposefully by many accounts, in the complex structure of the financial products at issue. What were any of the exotic products worth now, and what would any of them be worth in the foreseeable future? Continuity of contract had been broken repeatedly while creating each part of final products offered for sale in the global financial markets (e.g. the extensive discussion in Blinder 2014).

Ultimately, the decision was made to focus on what was most easily identifiable as a cause of concern in the financial markets and that proved to be to simply add capital injections to existing banks and bank holding companies. By re-capitalizing the AIG insurance company in particular, TARP funds enabled that company to settle the credit default swaps it had written for major investment banks during the housing bubble. These included Goldman Sachs and JPMorgan Chase among the US banks but also Deutsche Bank and Credit Suisse in Europe. While those payments took these banks off the hook for their commitments, they still left indeterminate who would buy the outstanding mortgage-backed securities and whether a market would ever develop for them. Consequently, these properties remain on the books of the initiating banks as "non-performing loans" or as "real estate owned" if the bank has managed to foreclose and take possession of the property. The overhang of these distressed properties keeps down both new construction and the market for existing housing as individual households go through their life cycle demands for residential facilities. The longer these issues remain unresolved, the worse are the prospects for long-term recovery of both the US housing market and the overall economy.

The contrast with the explicit funding and mission of the Resolution Trust Corporation (RTC) that was set up in 1988 to deal with the defaulting mortgages accumulated by the individual savings and loan offices across the US is dismaying, but instructive. The RTC basically nationalized the individual failed thrifts (1,043 firms from 1986 through mid 1995) and then began selling off their assets as quickly as possible. The RTC formally wound up its business in 1995, although aspects of the cleanup process continue to the present. When the RTC ceased operation in 1995, it did so by selling off the remaining portfolios of the failed thrifts to private asset management firms, but retaining a significant equity stake in the firms. In this way, as property values rose under expert management by the firms that acquired them, the RTC also shared in the rise in values. The latest analysis of the cost-recovery of the RTC through 2005 concludes that while the initial distress sales of thrift properties did reduce the value of their real estate assets to less than 50 percent of their book value in 1990–1991, the remaining sales by the asset management firms showed steady recovery rates around 75 percent. Bergstresser and Peiser (2014) conclude that TARP funds, by contrast, are simply delaying resolution of the problem It was left up to the central bank of the US, the Fed, to take up the challenge of quarantining the toxic assets created in the sub-prime mortgage bubble.

From lender of last resort to investor of last resort: the US Fed, 2008–2014

When the Federal Reserve System finally did get around to dealing with the sub-prime crisis in 2008 (after ignoring its manifestations that had really begun back in 2006 when even AIG's adventurous sales group stopped selling credit default swaps to investment banks and hedge funds), it did so in dramatic and effective fashion. Using the obscure clause from Section 13(3) of the original Federal Reserve Act of 1913 that allowed it to make emergency loans to anyone "under unusual and exigent circumstances," Ben Bernanke's Board of Governors approved lending $13 billion to Bear Stearns to get it through at least to the weekend following March 14, 2008. From there, the Fed could in good conscience extend more and more short-term lending to more and more firms as the crisis continued to explode through September 2008. From opening up new repo facilities for the vital conduit of commercial paper financing to guaranteeing JPMorgan Chase's purchase of toxic assets from Bear Stearns to the Term Asset-Backed Securities Loan Facility (TALF) and its Term Auction Facility (TAF), the Fed's balance sheet tripled in size to nearly $1.5 billion at the end of 2008.

Banks were saved as were major US corporations, including AIG as well as General Motors and Chrysler, but the economy was still in serious recession, with unemployment rising sharply and the stock market continuing to fall until the Dow Jones index hit bottom on March 9, 2009 (6,547.05), having lost nearly 54 percent from its high of 14,164.53 back on October 9, 2007. More financing was needed and no help was forthcoming from fiscal stimulus or further disbursements of TARP funds by the US Treasury. The Federal Funds rate set by the Fed was very close to zero, 0.20 percent, effectively ending that tool's usefulness for stimulating the financial markets. So the Bernanke Fed launched the first of several Quantitative Easing (QE) programs that eventually increased the Fed's balance sheet even further, reaching $4.407 trillion on July 30, 2014. This represented yet another tripling of the Fed's balance sheet from the end of 2008. From being a belated "lender of last resort" in September of 2008, the US Fed became from then on the "investor of last resort" (Mehrling 2011).

Once embarked on its new role, essentially taking over the responsibility originally intended for the TARP program, the Fed could take satisfaction from seeing that the relative rebound of the US economy from the crisis of 2008 was correspondingly stronger than that in either the UK or the rest of the European Union using the euro. When the Fed had tripled its balance sheet by 2010, the Bank of England had merely doubled its balance sheet, and the ECB had only raised its assets by 50 percent, before losing heart and actually raising short-term interest rates. Despite the apparent relative success of the Fed's QE in maintaining the economic recovery in the US, concerns were raised about when and how and with what consequences the Fed's balance sheet would be unwound.

Before he stepped down as Chair of the Board of Governors of the Federal Reserve System of the United States in 2013, Bernanke laid out both the justification for his QE exercises and a couple of reassurances about when and how the Fed could exit from the program. The justification was that they were holding down long-term interest rates as well and that the economy was recovering, albeit more slowly than desired. The reassurance was that the balance sheet could be wound down gradually with yet another innovation, "reverse repo" operations. A few "reverse repo" operations were done as test cases to show they could work. The Fed borrowed cash by posting some of its accumulated collateral and then defaulted, leaving the lender to take full possession of the collateral. This worked well enough with the long-term Treasury bonds that the Fed had accumulated and continued to accumulate through 2014 ($2.42 trillion on July 30, 2014). But could it work with the mortgage-backed securities that it had accumulated and continued to accumulate ($1.674 trillion on July 30, 2014)? That depended on whether that market had recovered by the time the Fed decided to wind down its balance sheet. Some grounds for optimism were that the toxic assets that the Fed had acquired from Bear Stearns as part of its guarantees to JPMorgan Chase in March 2008 had risen in value to $1.7 billion by July 30, 2014. The Fed continues to earn interest on these assets, which had amounted to $765 million by the end of July 2014 (Board of Governors 2014). The experience to date warrants optimism that the Fed's QE program will create that same gradual rise in value of its mortgage-backed securities. These are the toxic assets that it has taken off the balance sheets of private sector firms in the US and international financial system, essentially quarantining them until they are no longer toxic. But the Fed could, in principle if not expressly forbidden by Congress, quarantine them permanently.

Critics will point out, however, that the counterpart to the Fed's massive accumulation of financial assets is an equally massive accumulation of excess reserves held on account of depositary institutions (banks and bank holding companies) that are members of the Federal Reserve System. A similar buildup of excess reserves in the mid 1930s led the Governors at the time to worry about possible inflation and a depreciation of the dollar in terms of gold and foreign currencies if the member banks used their excess reserves to make new loans on a large scale. Now it would appear that such a move by US banks would help bring back the economy toward its full employment potential, and if inflation did pick up, the US dollar would simply lose value in terms of foreign exchange and gold. Many US policy makers would welcome this outcome – at least those who are more concerned about maintaining high employment figures than with keeping high executive bonuses in place. The rest of the world, however, might not be so happy with the way US policy makers use their control over the US dollar, still the primary unit for invoicing international trade globally, and over the supply of US Treasuries, still the primary source of "pristine collateral" for the world's international financial markets.

International alternatives: the test case of the euro

Already in September 2009, concerns were raised in a UN report on how to reform the international monetary and financial system (United Nations 2009). Explicitly, the experts, led by Joseph Stiglitz from the US, agreed that:

The increases in the US national debt and the size of the balance sheet of the US Federal Reserve have led to concerns in those countries holding large dollar reserves [China, Japan] about the stability of the dollar as a store of value. In addition, the low (near zero) return on dollar holdings means that they are receiving virtually no return in exchange for the foreign exchange rate risk which they bear. However, any attempt to reduce dollar holdings will produce the Triffin dilemma noted above, provoking the collapse in the value of their dollar holdings that they fear.

These are among the reasons to adopt a truly global reserve currency. Such a global reserve currency can also reduce global risks, since confidence in and stability of the reserve currency would not depend on the vagaries of the economy and politics of a single country. (United Nations 2009, p. 115, paras. 29 and 30)

The Stiglitz Report, as it came to be called, went on to suggest several ways such a reserve currency might be introduced. In increasing order of feasibility, they were:

(1) A system of worldwide "swaps" among central banks. Countries would exchange their own currencies for the new currency, International Currency Certificates (ICCs) according to their current or revised IMF quotas.
(2) An international agency that would simply issue the global currency, with no backing other than the commitment of the central banks to accept it in exchange for their own currencies.
(3) Simply broaden existing SDR [Special Drawing Rights] arrangements within the IMF, but provide that they be issued countercyclically, enabling the IMF to play a more constructive role as a lender of last resort in crises.

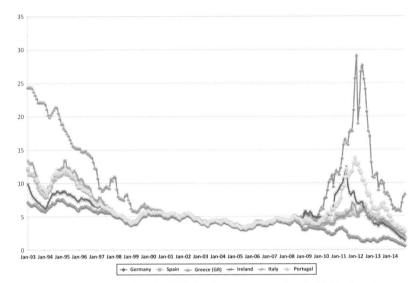

Figure 14.5 Sovereign bond yields in the euro-zone, 1993–2014 (from European Central Bank, http://sdw.ecb.europa.eu/browse.do?node=bbn4864, accessed May 13, 2014)

(4) Before such a global agreement could be reached, rely on evolutionary approaches taken regionally as "a regional reserve system ... could be established without the agreement of all countries." (United Nations 2009, p. 119, para. 54)

Indeed, such "a regional reserve system" was then already in existence, the European System of Central Banks (ESCB) established within the European Union in successive stages over a period of nearly ten years from 1992 to 2002.

Each stage was carefully prepared for one to three years beforehand to ensure its success when, first, exchange rates among the candidate currencies were fixed, then when the ECB began operation in 1999, and finally when physical coins and notes were introduced throughout the Member Countries in 2002. In terms of the economic motivation for creation of the common currency, namely to reduce the rate of interest that highly indebted European governments had to pay on their sovereign debt (Neal 2007, pp. 112–113), the European reserve system was an undoubted success. But, as shown in Figure 14.5, success lasted only ten years, from 1999 to the end of 2008.

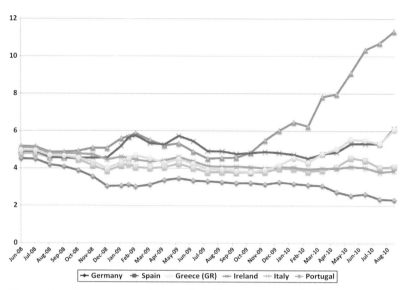

Figure 14.6 Ten-year sovereign bond yields for Greece, Ireland, Portugal, and Spain compared to Germany, January 2008–January 2012 (from European Central Bank, http://sdw.ecb.europa.eu/browse.do?node=bbn4864, accessed May 13, 2014)

Figure 14.5 highlights why countries with the weakest fiscal systems in the European Union were always the most eager to join the EMS in the 1980s and then the EMU starting in January 1999. Greece stands out even at the beginning of the EMU as the last to join just as the actual euro-currency was being distributed at the beginning of 1999. For ten years, all five of the countries that later became the focus of the euro-zone crisis enjoyed low interest rates on their ten-year government bonds, apparently because the global financial markets took it for granted that the ECB was bound to accept any member government's bonds as collateral for loans to banks in the euro-zone. The bankruptcy of Lehman Brothers investment bank on September 15, 2008 clearly had repercussions on this situation and the ECB responded quickly and effectively to inoculate its member banks from possible contagion. But a closer look at the pricing of sovereign bonds in the crisis response period reveals an apparent anomaly, given what markets later learned about the dire straits of Greek government finances (Figure 14.6).

An interesting phenomenon appeared in 2009 as the yields on all euro-zone sovereigns fell for a time, which apparently reassured

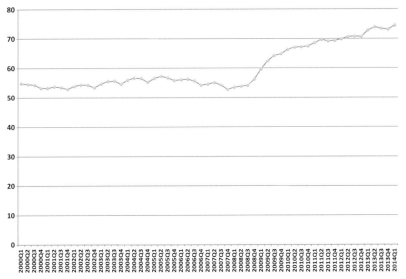

Figure 14.7 Total marketable sovereign debt in euros, as percent of GDP, 2000–2014 (from European Central Bank, series GST.Q.I7.N.B0X13.BBT. B1300.SA.Q, http://sdw.ecb.europa.eu/browse.do?node=bbn4864)

EU policy makers that the bold actions undertaken by the ECB initially in 2007 had de-coupled the European banking system from the travails of their Anglo-American cousins.

It appears now, however, that this episode was merely the initial stage of a general process of de-leveraging by European banks, a process that has continued through 2014. In the initial scramble for de-leveraging among euro-zone banks as the wholesale market for interbank short-term lending dried up with the collapse of Lehman Brothers, the first step for banks was to increase their holdings of sovereign bonds with zero risk weights, as allowed by the regulations under the Basel II accords. As some euro-zone sovereign bonds began to show signs of risk, banks had to shift from the risky government bonds to the government bonds that maintained high ratings, especially German bonds. General pressures for European governments to reduce their level of debt, moreover, put strict limits on the extent to which banks could continue to de-leverage in this manner (Figure 14.7).

The problem of changing collateral space is that banks in general, and so-called "shadow banks" in particular, must find substitutes for sovereign bonds posted as collateral for their short-debt debts as fewer sovereign bonds become acceptable to lenders such as US money market funds. Failing to find such substitutes for sovereign bonds means that both formal and shadow banks face higher costs of borrowing. Singh (2013) shows how the problem has evolved as central banks and governments have responded to the initial financial crisis in 2008. He highlights the negative effect of the central banks in the US, EU, UK, and Switzerland that have removed good collateral from financial markets to their balance sheets where it remains inaccessible (or "silo-ed" in finance jargon). Further, the regulatory demands on banks arising from the 2010 Dodd–Frank bill in the US, the Basel III regulations coming on stream for international banks, and the European Market Infrastructure Regulation (EMIR) requirements for the European Union all require financial institutions to keep more collateral as buffers on their balance sheets, making it inaccessible to the repo markets (for the full terms of the regulations agreed on internationally by the world's leading central banks, see www.bis. org/bcbs). Finally, there is the diminished issuance of debt by AAA/AA rated issuers, whether sovereign governments or multinational firms. Collateral custodians, such as JPMorgan Chase and Bank of New York Mellon, who are responsible for the tri-party repo market in the US, and Euroclear and Clearstream, who deal with the repo markets in Europe, continue trying to find ways to release collateral from the various silos that have been created (Singh 2013, p. 7).

As the future of the global financial system depends very much on the outcome of these conflicting efforts to recover from the ongoing crisis, perhaps the historical perspective on the role of sovereign bonds as collateral in the development of financial systems in this book will be useful. To repeat the lessons of history highlighted in the preceding chapters: secondary markets turn out to be essential, as well as specialist intermediaries in those markets. Transparent flows of information combined with regulatory oversight of the continuity of contracts, however, are needed to sustain a long-run balance between the "gullible and the guileful" in the financial system. Ultimately, the recurring challenge is how to coordinate effectively private financial organizations (banks), public access secondary markets for securities (stock exchanges), and government oversight (regulators) to create a beneficial financial system for an economy. Sustainable and marketable sovereign debt turns out to have been the critical linchpin for the continued operation of successful financial systems in the past. Creating, marketing, and sustaining some form of comparable collateral for the global financial markets of the twenty-first century is the ongoing challenge.

Robert Lucas Nash, chronicler of the global debt market that had sprung up after 1848, writing at the bottom of the worldwide financial crisis that began in 1873, still managed to write optimistically, "that with this modernized system of credit the world has acquired light, health, progress, and prosperity; that every man has more of the world's goods than could have been boasted of a century ago; that every man is better educated; that every man is a better citizen; and that if these are the results of indebtedness, we may fairly leave the solution of the problem to the future with confidence which experience well earned amply justifies" (Nash 1876, p. xiv). It took a century and a half to prove him right, but his optimism was, with misadventures along the way as described in previous chapters, eventually validated. It would be churlish for us in the current toils of financial reckonings at the start of the twenty-first century to be less optimistic that somehow, somewhere, people will figure how to make our financial systems work well once again.

References

Accominotti, Olivier 2012. "London Merchant Banks, the Central European Panic and the Sterling Crisis of 1931," *Journal of Economic History*, 72:1 (March), 1–43.

Marc Flandreau, Riad Rezzik, and Frederic Zumer 2010. *The Global Finance database*, http://eh.net/database/global-finance/.

Acemoglu, Deron and James A. Robinson 2012. *Why Nations Fail: The Origins of Power, Prosperity, and Poverty*. New York: Crown Publishers.

Ambrose, Brent and Tao-Hsien Dolly King 2002. "GSE Debt and the Decline in the Treasury Debt Market," *Journal of Money, Credit, and Banking*, 34:3 (August), 812–839.

Anderson, Fred 2001. *Crucible of War: The Seven Years' War and the Fate of Empire in British North America, 1754–1766*. New York: Vintage Books.

Anderson, Olive 1963. "Loans versus Taxes: British Financial Policy in the Crimean War," *Economic History Review*, 16:2 (December), 314–327.

Andreades, A. M. 1933. *A History of Greek Public Finance*, vol. 1, rev. and enlarged edn., trans Carroll N. Brown. Cambridge, MA: Harvard University Press.

Arnaud, Pascal 2011. "Ancient Sailing Routes and Trade Patterns: The Impact of Human Factors," in Damian Robinson and Andrew Wilson, eds., *Maritime Archaeology and Ancient Trade in the Mediterranean*. Oxford Centre for Maritime Archaeology, 61–80.

Ashley, M. 1934. *Financial and Commercial Policy under the Cromwellian Protectorate*, repr. 1966. New York: A. M. Kelley.

Ashton, T. S. 1959. *Economic Fluctuations in England, 1700–1800*. Oxford: Clarendon Press.

Atack, Jeremy and Larry Neal, eds. 2009. *The Origins and Development of Financial Markets and Institutions: From the Seventeenth Century to the Present*. Cambridge and New York: Cambridge University Press.

Austin, Peter E. 2007. *Baring Brothers and the Birth of Modern Finance*. London: Pickering & Chatto.

Baack, Ben 2001. "Forging a Nation State: The Continental Congress and the Financing of the War of American Independence," *Economic History Review*, 54:4 (December), 639–656.

2008. "America's First Monetary Policy: Inflation and Seigniorage during the Revolutionary War," *Financial History Review*, 15:2 (March), 107–121.

Bagehot, Walter 1873. *Lombard Street: A Description of the Money Market*. New York: Scribner, Armstrong & Co.

Bank for International Settlements (1931–present). *Annual Report*, www.bis.org/publ/arpdf/archive/index.htm and www.bis.org/publ/arpdf/ar2014e.htm.

Belassa, Béla 1964. "The Purchasing Power Parity Doctrine: A Reappraisal," *Journal of Political Economy*, 72:6 (December), 584–596.

Bell, Adrian R., Chris Brooks, and Tony K. Moore 2013. "The 'Buying and Selling of Money for Time': Exchange and Interest Rates in Medieval Europe," Unpublished Working Paper, University of Reading.

Berger, Helge and Albrecht Ritschl 1995. "Germany and the Political Economy of the Marshall Plan, 1947–52: A Re-Revisionist View," Chapter 8 in Barry Eichengreen, ed., *Europe's Post-War Recovery*. Cambridge University Press, 199–245.

Bergstresser, Daniel and Richard Peiser 2014. "Recovery Ratios in the Savings and Loan Crisis: Evidence from the Resolution Trust Corporation's Sale of Bank-Owned Real Estate," *Cityscape: A Journal of Policy Development and Research*, 16:1, 310–337.

Berman, Harold 1983. *Law and Revolution: The Formation of the Western Legal Tradition*. Cambridge, MA: Harvard University Press.

Bignon, Vincent, Marc Flandreau, and Stefano Ugolini 2012. "Bagehot for Beginners: The Making of Lender-of-Last-Resort Operations in the Mid-Nineteenth Century," *Economic History Review*, 65:2 (May), 580–608.

Blinder, Alan S. 2014. *After the Music Stopped: The Financial Crisis, the Response, and the Work Ahead*. New York: Penguin.

Board of Governors of the Federal Reserve System 2014. *Quarterly Report on Federal Reserve Balance Sheet Developments, August 2014*. Washington, DC: Federal Reserve System.

Bolles, Alfred S. 1886–1892. *The Financial History of the United States, from 1774 to 1885*, 3 vols. New York: D. Appleton & Co.

Bordo, Michael 1993. "The Bretton Woods International Monetary System: A Historical Overview," in Michael Bordo and Barry Eichengreen, eds., *A Retrospective on the Bretton Woods System: Lessons for International Monetary Reform*. University of Chicago Press, 3–98.

Bordo, Michael D. and Barry Eichengreen, eds. 1993. *Retrospective on the Bretton Woods System: Lessons for International Monetary Reform*. University of Chicago Press.

Borio, Claudio 2014. "The International Monetary and Financial System: Its Achilles Heel and What to do About It," BIS Working Papers, No. 456.

Borio, Claudio, Harold James, and Hyun Song Shin 2014. "The International Monetary and Financial System: A Capital Account Historical Perspective," BIS Working Papers, No. 457.

Boyer-Xambeu, Marie-Thérèse, Ghislain Deleplace, and Lucien Gillard 1994. *Private Money & Public Currencies, the 16th Century Challenge,* trans. Azizeh Azodi. Armonk, NY and London: M. E. Sharpe.

Braddick, Michael J. 1996. *The Nerves of State: Taxation and the Financing of the English State, 1558–1714.* Manchester and New York: Manchester University Press.

Broadberry, Stephen and Mark Harrison, eds. 2009. *The Economics of World War I.* Cambridge University Press.

Buist, Marten 1974. *At Spes non fracta: Hope & Co. 1770-1815: Merchant Bankers and Diplomats at Work.* The Hague: Martinus Nijhoff.

Bullock, Charles J. 1895. *The Finances of the United States from 1775 to 1789, with Special Reference to the Budget,* repr. 1979. Philadelphia, PA: Porcupine Press.

Burk, Kathleen 1985. *Britain, America and the Sinews of War, 1914–1918.* London: George Allen & Unwin.

Burt, Roger 1984. *The British Lead Mining Industry,* Exeter: A Wheaton & Co.

Calomiris, Charles W. 1988. "Institutional Failure, Monetary Scarcity, and the Depreciation of the Continental," *Journal of Economic History,* 48:1 (January), 47–68.

Calomiris, Charles W. and Stephen Haber 2014. *Fragile by Design: The Political Origins of Banking Crises and Scarce Credit.* Princeton University Press.

Calomiris, Charles W. and Larry Schweikart 1991. "The Panic of 1857: Origins, Transmissions, and Containment," *Journal of Economic History,* 51:4 (December), 807–834.

Cameron, Rondo E. 1953. "The Credit Mobilier and the Economic Development of Europe," *Journal of Political Economy,* 61 (December), 461–488.

1966. *France and the Economic Development of Europe, 1800–1914: Conquests of Peace and Seeds of War.* Chicago, IL: Rand McNally.

Campbell, E. 1938. *The Reorganization of the American Railroad System, 1893–1900.* New York: Columbia University Press.

Campbell, Gareth and John D. Turner 2012. "Dispelling the Myth of the Naïve Investor during the British Railway Mania, 1845–1846," *Business History Review,* 86:1 (Spring), 3–41.

Capie, Forrest 2010. *The Bank of England: 1950s to 1979.* Cambridge and New York: Cambridge University Press.

Cardoso, José Luís and Pedro Lains, eds. 2010. *Paying for the Liberal State: The Rise of Public Finance in Nineteenth-Century Europe.* Cambridge and New York: Cambridge University Press.

Carlos, Ann, J. Key, and J. Dupree 1998. "Learning and the Creation of Stock-Market Institutions: Evidence from the Hudson's Bay and Royal African Companies, 1670–1700," *Journal of Economic History*, 58:2 (June), 318–344.

Carlos, Ann and Frank Lewis 2010. *Commerce by a Frozen Sea: Native Americans and the European Fur Trade*. University of Pennsylvania Press.

Carlos, Ann and Larry Neal 2006. "The Microstructure of the Early London Capital Market: Bank of England Shareholders during and after the South Sea Bubble, 1720–1725," *Economic History Review*, 59:3 (September), 498–538.

Carlos, Ann and Larry Neal 2011. "Amsterdam and London as Financial Centers in the Eighteenth Century," *Financial History Review*, 18:1 (April), 21–46.

Carlos, Ann, Erin Fletcher, Larry Neal, and Kirsten Wandschneider 2013. "Financing and Refinancing the War of the Spanish Succession, and then Refinancing the South Sea Company," in Adrian Leonard, D'Maris Coffman, and Larry Neal, *Questioning Credible Commitment: New Perspectives on the Glorious Revolution and the Rise of Financial Capitalism*. Cambridge University Press, 147–168.

Carter, Alice 1953. "Dutch Foreign Investment, 1738–1800," *Economica*, New Series, 20:80 (November), 322–340.

Caselli, Fausto Piola 2013. "Papal Finance, 1348–1848," in Gerard Caprio, ed., *The Handbook of Key Global Financial Markets, Institutions, and Infrastructure*, vol. I. Oxford: Elsevier, 207–220.

ed. 2008. *Government Debts and Financial Markets in Europe*. London: Pickering & Chatto.

Castaing, John 1698–1908. *The Course of the Exchange & Other Things*. London: James Wetenhall.

Cauwès, P. 1896. "Commencements du crédit public en France: Les rentes sur l'Hôtel de Ville de Paris au XVIe siècle (1561–1588)," *Revue d'économie publique*, X, 407–479.

Chandaman, C. D. 1975. *The English Public Revenue, 1660–1688*. Oxford: Clarendon Press.

Charpin, Dominique 2010. *Writing, Law, and Kingship in Old Babylonian Mesopotamia*, trans. Jane Marie Todd. University of Chicago Press.

Charpin, Dominique 2012. *Hammurabi of Babylon*. London: I. B. Tauris.

Clapham, Sir John 1945a. *The Bank of England, A History*, vol. 1, "1694–1797." New York: Macmillan.

1945b. *The Bank of England, A History*, vol. 2, "1797–1914." New York: Macmillan.

Clarke, Hiram 1878. "On the Debts of Sovereign and Quasi-Sovereign States, Owing by Foreign Countries," *Journal of the Statistical Society of London*, 41:2 (June), 299–347.

Coffman, D'Maris 2008. *The Fiscal Revolution of the Interregnum: Excise Taxation in the British Isles, 1643–1663*. PhD thesis, University of Pennsylvania.

2013. "Credibility, Transparency, Accountability, and the Public Credit Under the Long Parliament and Commonwealth, 1643–53," in D'Maris Coffman, Adrian Leonard, and Larry Neal, *Questioning Credible Commitment: New Perspectives on the Glorious Revolution and the Rise of Financial Capitalism*. Cambridge University Press, 1643–1653.

Cohen, Edward E. 1992, *Athenian Economy & Society, A Banking Perspective*. Princeton University Press.

Cohen, Jon S. 1992. "Financing Industrialization in Italy, 1894–1914: The Partial Transformation of a Late Comer," in Jon S. Cohen, *Financing Industrialization*, vol. 2. Brookfield, VT: Edward Elgar, 57–76.

Condillac, Abbé de 1776. *Le Commerce et le Gouvernment, considérés l'un à l'autre*. Amsterdam and Paris: Chez Jombert & Cellot.

Courtois, Alphonse 1877. *Tableaux des Cours des Principales Valeurs Négociées et Cotées aux Bourses des Effets Publics de Paris, Lyon et Marseille du 17 Janvier 1797 (28 Nivose an V) à Nos Jours Relevés sur les Documents Officiels et Authentiques*, 3rd edn. Paris: Garnier Frères; Guillaumin & Cie.

Cribb, Joe 2004. "The Origins of Money, Evidence from the Ancient Near East and Egypt," in Guido Crapanzano, ed., *La Banca Premonetale*. Milan: Art Valley Association, 79–122.

Davis, Lance E. and Larry Neal 2006. "The Evolution of the Structure and Performance of the London Stock Exchange in the First Global Financial Market, 1812–1914," *European Review of Economic History*, 10:3 (December), 279–300.

Dawson, Frank Griffin 1990. *The First Latin American Debt Crisis: The City of London and the 1822–25 Loan Bubble*. New Haven, CT: Yale University Press.

Dehing, P. and M. t' Hart. 1997. "Linking the Fortunes: Currency and Banking, 1550–1800," in M. 't Hart, J. Jonker, and J. Luiten van Zanden, *A Financial History of the Netherlands*. New York: Cambridge University Press, 37–63.

De la Vaissière, Etienne 2005. *The Sogdian Traders: A History*, trans. James Ward. Leiden: Brill.

De Pinto, Isaac 1771. *Traité de la circulation et du credit: Contenant une analyse raisonné des fonds d'Angleterre, & de ce qu'on appelle commerce ou jeu d'actions*. Amsterdam: Chez Marc Michel Rey.

De Roover, Raymond 1963. *The Rise and Fall of the Medici Bank, 1397–1494*. Cambridge, MA: Harvard University Press.

De Vries, Jan 2006. *European Urbanization, 1500–1800*. London: Routledge.

Dickson, P. G. M. 1967. *The Financial Revolution in England: A Study in the Development of Public Credit, 1688–1756*. New York: Macmillan.

Diebold, William, Jr. 1952. *Trade and Payments in Western Europe: A Study in Economic Cooperation 1947–51*. New York: Harper.

Dooley, Michael P., David Folkerts-Landau, and Peter Garber 2003. "An Essay on the Revived Bretton Woods System," NBER Working Paper, No. 9971.

2009. "Bretton Woods II Still Defines the International Monetary System," *Pacific Economic Review*, 14:3 (August), 297–311.

Doubleday, Thomas 1858–1859. *A Financial, Monetary and Statistical History of England, from the Revolution of 1688 to the Present*, 2nd edn. London: Effingham Wilson.

Drelichman, Mauricio and Hans-Joachim Voth 2014. *Lending to the Borrower from Hell: Debt, Taxes, and Default in the Age of Philip II*. Princeton University Press.

Duffy, Ian P. H. 1985. *Bankruptcy and Insolvency in London During the Industrial Revolution*. New York: Garland Publishing.

Eagly, Robert and V. Kerry Smith. 1976. "Domestic and International Integration of the London Money Market, 1731–1789," *Journal of Economic History*, 36:2 (March), 198–212.

Economist, July 4, 2007. "Ten Years On: How Asia Shrugged off its Economic Crisis," www.economist.com/node/9432495/print, accessed August 29, 2014.

Eichengreen, Barry and Douglas A. Irwin 1995. "Trade Blocs, Currency Blocs and the Reorientation of World Trade in the 1930s," *Journal of International Economics*, 38:1–2 (February), 1–24.

Emerging Markets Trading Association (EMTA) 2014. "The Brady Plan," accessed at: www.emta.org.

Epstein, S.R. 2000. *Freedom and Growth: The Rise of States and Markets in Europe, 1300–1750*. London and New York: Routledge.

European Central Bank 1999–present. Statistical Data Warehouse, www.ecb.europa.eu/stats/html/index.en.html.

Evans, David Morier 1848. *The Commercial Crisis 1847–48 being facts and figures illustrative of that important period …* London: Letts, Son, & Steer.

1850. *Fortune's Epitome of the Stocks & Public Funds. English, Foreign, and American*, 15th edn. London: Letts, Son, & Steer.

1859. *The History of the Commercial Crisis, 1857–1858 and the Stock Exchange Panic of 1859*. London: Groombridge.

Faure, Edgar 1977. *La Banqueroute de Law: 17 juillet 1720*. Paris: Gallimard.

Felloni, Guiseppe 2006. *A Series of Firsts*. Genoa: Brigati Glauco.

Felloni, Guiseppe and Guido Laura 2004. *Genova e la storia della finanza*. Genoa: Brigati.

Ferguson, Niall 1998. *The House of Rothschild*, vol. 1 "Money's Prophets, 1798–1848." New York: Penguin Putnam.

2009. "Siegmund Warburg, the City of London and the Financial Roots of European Integration," *Business History*, 51:3 (April), 364–382.

Fichter, J. R. 2010. *So Great a Proffit: How the East Indies Trade Transformed Anglo-American Capitalism*. Cambridge, MA: Harvard University Press.

Financial Crisis Inquiry Commission 2011. *The Financial Crisis Inquiry Report*. Washington, DC: Government Printing Office, www.gpo.gov/fdsys/pkg/GPO-FCIC/pdf/GPO-FCIC.pdf.

Flandreau, Marc 1996a. "Adjusting the Gold Rush: Endogenous Bullion Points and the French Balance of Payments, 1846–1870," *Explorations in Economic Explorations in Economic History*, 33:4 (December), 417–439.

1996b. "The French Crime of 1873: An Essay on the Emergence of the International Gold Standard, 1870–1880," *Journal of Economic History*, 56:4 (December), 862–897.

2004. *The Glitter of Gold: France, Bimetallism, and the Emergence of the International Gold Standard, 1848–1873*. Oxford University Press.

Flandreau, Marc and Juan H. Flores 2009. "Bonds and Brands: Foundations of Sovereign Debt Markets, 1820–1830," *Journal of Economic History*, 69:3 (September), 646–684.

Flandreau, Marc, Christophe Galimard, Clemens Jobst, and Pilar Nogués-Marco 2009a. "The Bell Jar: Commercial Interest Rates between Two Revolutions, 1688–1789," in Jeremy Atack and Larry Neal, eds., *The Origins and Development of Financial Markets and Institutions: From the Seventeenth Century to the Present*. Cambridge and New York: Cambridge University Press, 161–208.

2009b. "Monetary Geography before the Industrial Revolution," *Cambridge Journal of Regions, Economy and Society*, 2:2 (July), 149–171.

Flesher, Dale and Gary John Previts 1999. "The Virtue of Economic Development: Accounting and Reporting for the Illinois Central Railroad, 1851–61," *Business and Economic History*, 28:1 (Fall), 181–192.

Fohlin, Caroline 1998. "Fiduciary and Firm Liquidity Constraints: The Italian Experience with German-Style Universal Banking," *Explorations in Economic History*, 35:1 (January), 83–107.

Forster, E. M. 1956. *Marianne Thornton: A Domestic Biography*. New York: Harcourt, Brace & Co.

Fratianni, Michele and Franco Spinelli 2006. "Italian City-States and Financial Evolution," *European Review of Economic History*, 10:3 (December), 257–278.

Frehen, Rik G. P., William N. Goetzmann, and K. Geert Rouwenhorst 2013. "New Evidence on the First Financial Bubble," *Journal of Financial Economics*, 108 (February), 585–607.

Friedman, Milton and Anna J. Schwartz 1963. *A Monetary History of the United States, 1867–1960*. Princeton University Press.

Fritschy, Wantje 2003. "A 'Financial Revolution' Reconsidered: Public Finance in Holland during the Dutch Revolt," *Economic History Review*, 56:1 (February), 57–89.

Garber, Peter (1989). "Tulipmania," *Journal of Political Economy*, 97:3 (June), 535–557.

(2000), *Famous First Bubbles: The Fundamentals of Early Manias*. Cambridge, MA: MIT Press.

Gayer, Arthur D., W. W. Rostow, and Anna J. Schwartz 1975. *The Growth and Fluctuation of the British Economy, 1790–1850*, 2 vols. New York: Harper & Row.

Gelderblom, Oscar (2003). "The Governance of Early Modern Trade: The Case of Hans Thijs (1556–1611)," *Enterprise and Society*, 4:4 (December), 606–639.

Gelderblom, Oscar and Joost Jonker (2004). "Completing a Financial Revolution: The Finance of the Dutch East India Trade and the Rise of the Amsterdam Capital Market, 1595–1612," *The Journal of Economic History*, 64:3 (September), 641–672.

2013. "Low Countries Finance, 1348–1700," in Gerard Caprio, ed., *The Handbook of Key Global Financial Markets, Institutions, and Infrastructure*, vol. I. Oxford: Elsevier, 175–184.

Gelderblom, Oscar, Abe de Jong, and Joost Jonker (2013). "The Formative Years of the Modern Corporation: The Dutch East India Company VOC, 1602–1623," *The Journal of Economic History*, 73:4 (December), 1050–1076.

Gervaise, Isaac 1720. *The System or Theory of the Trade of the World. Treating of the Different Kinds of Companies. And Shewing the Pernicious Consequences of Credit …* London: printed by H. Woodfall.

Gilbert, Felix (1980). *The Pope, his Banker, and Venice*. Cambridge, MA: Harvard University Press.

Glausiusz, Josie 2008. "Trading Bronze Age Technology," *Nature*, 456 (December), 709.

Gömmel, Rainer 1992. "Entstehung und Entwicklung der Effektenbörse im 19. Jahrhundert bis 1914," in Hans Pohl, ed., *Deutsche Börsengeschichte*. Frankfurt am Main: Fritz Knapp Verlag.

Goetzmann, William N. (2010), *Financing Civilization*, work in progress accessed at: http://viking.som.yale.edu/will/finciv/chapter1.htm#wall street.

Goetzmann, William N. and Elizabeth Köll 2005. "Paying in Paper: A Government Voucher from the Southern Song," in William N. Goetzmann and K. Geert Rouwenhorst, eds., *The Origins of Value: The Financial Innovations that Created Modern Capital Markets*. New York: Oxford University Press.

Goetzmann, Willam N., Catherine Labio, K. Geert Rouwenhorst, and Timothy Young, eds., 2014. *The Great Mirror of Folly: Finance, Culture, and the Crash of 1720*. New Haven CT: Yale University Press.

Goetzmann William N. and K. Geert Rouwenhorst, eds., 2005. *The Origins of Value: The Financial Innovations that Created Modern Capital Markets*. New York: Oxford University Press.

Goitein, S. D. 1967. *A Mediterranean Society: The Jewish Communities of the World as Portrayed in the Document of the Cairo Geniza*, vol. 1, "Economic Foundations." Berkeley, CA: University of California Press.

Goldgar, Anne 2007. *Tulipmania: Money, Honor, and Knowledge in the Dutch Golden Age*. Chicago, IL and London: University of Chicago Press.

Good, David F. and Tongshu Ma 1999. "The Economic Growth of Central and Eastern Europe in Comparative Perspective, 1870–1989," *European Review of Economic History*, 3 (August), 103–137.

Gorton, Gary 2010. *Slapped by the Invisible Hand: The Subprime Panic of 2007*. New York: Oxford University Press.

Great Britain. 1968. *British Parliamentary Papers. Monetary Policy. General*, vol. 4, "Session 1831–32," Report from the Committee of Secrecy on the Bank of England Charter." Shannon: Irish University Press.

Groeneveld, F. P. 1940. *Economische Crisis van het jaar 1720*. Gröningen: Noordhof.

Grossman, Ronald P. 1965. *The Financing of the Crusades*. PhD thesis, Department of History, University of Chicago.

Grubb, Farley 2013. "The Continental Dollar: The American Revolution was Financed with Paper Money – Initial Design and Ideal Performance," NBER Working Paper, No. 19577.

Guildhall Library, Manuscripts 14600. "Minutes of the Committee for General Purposes of the London Stock Exchange."

Guildhall Library, Manuscripts 19297. "Minutes of the Trustees and Managers of the London Stock Exchange."

Hale, J. R. 2009. *Lords of the Sea: The Epic Story of the Athenian Navy and the Birth of Democracy*. New York: Viking Press.

Hancock, David 1995. *Citizens of the World: London Merchants and the Integration of the British Atlantic Community.* Cambridge University Press.

Hardy, Charles O. 1936. *Is There enough Gold?* Washington, DC: Brookings Institution.

Harris, Ron 2000. *Industrializing English Law: Entrepreneurship and Businesss Organization, 1720–1844.* Cambridge University Press.

  2013. "Could the Crown Credibly Commit to Respect its Charters? England 1558–1640," in D'Maris Coffman, Adrian Leonard, and Larry Neal, *Questioning Credible Commitment: New Perspectives on the Glorious Revolution and the Rise of Financial Capitalism.* Cambridge University Press, 21–47.

Harrison, Mark, ed. 1998. *The Economics of World War II: Six Great Powers in International Comparison.* Cambridge University Press.

Hautcoeur, Pierre-Cyrille, Angelo Riva, and Eugene N. White 2014. "Floating a 'Lifeboat': The Banque de France and the Crisis of 1889," *Journal of Monetary Economics*, http://dx.doi.org/10.1016/j.jmoneco.2014.04.015.

Healey, Edna 1992. *Coutts & Co. 1692–1992: The Portrait of a Private Bank.* London: Hodder & Stoughton.

Henderson, W. O. 1962. "The Berlin Commercial Crisis of 1763," *Economic History Review*, 15:1 (January), 89–102.

Hidy, Ralph 1949. *The House of Baring in American Trade and Finance: English Merchant Bankers at Work, 1763–1861.* Cambridge, MA: Harvard University Press.

Hilton, Boyd 1977. *Corn, Cash, and Commerce: The Economic Policies of the Tory Governments 1815–1830.* Oxford University Press.

Hoffman, Philip, Gilles Postel-Vinay, and Jean-Laurent Rosenthal 2000. *Priceless Markets: The Political Economy of Credit in Paris, 1660–1870.* University of Chicago Press.

Homer, Sidney and Richard Sylla 1991. *A History of Interest Rates*, 3rd edn. New Brunswick, NJ and London: Rutgers University Press.

Hoppit, Julian 2000. *A Land of Liberty? England, 1689–1727.* Oxford University Press.

Horsefield, J. Keith 1960. *British Monetary Experiments, 1650–1710.* London: G. Bell & Sons.

Hughes, J. R. T. 1956. "The Commercial Crisis of 1857," *Oxford Economic Papers*, 8:2 (June), 194–222.

Hunt, Bishop Carleton 1936. *The Development of the Business Corporation in England, 1800–1867.* Cambridge, MA: Harvard University Press.

International Monetary Fund 1978. *International Financial Statistics. 1978 Supplement, Annual Data 1953–1977.* Washington, DC: International Monetary Fund.

1980–present. *World Economic Outlook*. Washington, DC: International Monetary Fund.

2002–present. *Global Financial Stability Report, A Report by the Monetary and Capital Markets Department on Market Developments and Issues*, Semi-annual. Washington, DC: International Monetary Fund.

2006. *World Economic Outlook* (April), Chapter 2, "Oil Prices and Global Imbalances." Washington, DC, 71–96.

Irwin, Douglas A. 2011. "Did France Cause the Great Depression?," NBER Working Paper, No. 16350.

Israel, Jonathan I. 1989. *Dutch Primacy in World Trade, 1585–1740*. New York: Oxford University Press.

James, Harold 1984. "The Causes of the German Banking Crisis of 1931," *Economic History Review*, 38:1 (February), 68–87.

1986. *The German Slump: Politics and Economics 1924–1936*. Oxford University Press.

2012. *Making the European Monetary Union*. Cambridge, MA: The Belknap Press of Harvard University Press.

Jenks, Leland H. 1927. *The Migration of British Capital to 1875*. New York: Barnes & Noble.

Johnson, H. Clark 1997. *Gold, France, and the Great Depression, 1919–1932*. New Haven, CT: Yale University Press.

Johnson, Noel D. 2006. "Banking on the King: The Evolution of the Royal Revenue Farms in Old Regime France," *Journal of Economic History*, 66:4 (December), 963–991.

Johnson, Paul 1991. *The Birth of the Modern: World Society 1815–1830*. London: Weidenfeld & Nicolson.

Jones, D. W. 1988. *War and Economy in the Age of William III and Marlborough*. Oxford: Basil Blackwell.

Jonker, Joost and Keetie Sluyterman 2001. *At Home on the World Markets: Dutch International Trading Companies from the 16th Century Until the Present*. Montreal: McGill–Queen's University Press.

Jursa, Michael 2010. *Aspects of the Economic History of Babylonia in the First Millennium BC: Economic Geography, Economic Mentalities, Agriculture, the Use of Money and the Problem of Economic Growth*. Münster: Ugarit-Verlag.

Justice, Alexander 1707. *A General Treatise of Monies and Exchanges …* London: printed for S. & J. Sprint, and J. Nicholson & R. Smith.

Kaplan, Herbert H. 2006. *Nathan Mayer Rothschild and the Creation of a Dynasty: The Critical Years, 1806–1816*. Stanford University Press.

Kerridge, Eric 1988. *Trade and Banking in Early Modern England*. Manchester University Press.

Keynes, John Maynard 1914. "War and the Financial System, August, 1914," *Economic Journal*, 24 (September), 460–486.

Kindleberger, Charles P. 1984. *A Financial History of Western Europe*. London: George Allen & Unwin.

1993. *A Financial History of Western Europe*, 2nd edn. New York and Oxford: Oxford University Press.

2000. *Manias, Panics, and Crashes: A History of Financial Crises*, 4th edn. New York: John Wiley.

Kindleberger, Charles P. and Robert Z. Aliber 2011. *Manias, Panics, and Crashes: A History of Financial Crises*, 6th edn. New York: Palgrave Macmillan.

King, W. T. C. (1936). *History of the London Discount Market*. London: George Routledge & Sons.

Kleer, Richard 2015. "Riding a Wave: The Company's Role in the South Sea Bubble," *Economic History Review*, 68:1 (February), 264–285.

Kosmetatos, Paul 2014. "The Winding-Up of the Ayr Bank, 1772–1827," *Financial History Review*, 21:2 (August), 165–190.

Kuznets, Simon 1966. *Modern Economic Growth: Rate, Structure, and Spread*. New Haven, CT: Yale University Press.

Lane, Frederic and Reinhold C. Mueller. 1985. *Money and Banking in Medieval and Renaissance Venice*. Baltimore, MD: Johns Hopkins University Press.

Law, John, 1705. *Money and Trade Considered; with a proposal for supplying the nation with money*. London: Lewis.

League of Nations 1932. *Report by the Stresa Conference for the Economic Restoration of Central and Eastern Europe: Submitted to the Commission of Enquiry for European Union*. Geneva: League of Nations.

1945. *Economic Stability in the Post-War World: The Conditions of Prosperity After the Transition From War to Peace*. Geneva: League of Nations.

Lesger, Cle 2006. *The Rise of the Amsterdam Market and Information Exchange: Merchants, Commercial Expansion and Change in the Spatial Economy of the Low Countries, c. 1550–1630*. Aldershot: Ashgate.

Lewis, W. Arthur 1949. *Economic Survey, 1919–1939*. London: George Allen & Unwin.

Lo, Andrew 2012. "Reading about the Financial Crisis: A Twenty-One-Book Review," *Journal of Economic Literature*, 50:1 (March), 151–178.

Lowndes, William 1695, *A Report Containing an Essay for the Amendment of the Silver Coin*. London: printed for W. Whitlock.

Luca, Giuseppe de 2008. "Government Debt and Financial Markets: Exploring Pro-Cyclical Effects in Northern Italy during the Sixteenth and the Seventeenth Centuries," in Fausto Piola Caselli, ed., *Government Debts and Financial Markets in Europe*. London: Pickering & Chatto, 45–66.

Lunt, William E. 1934. *Papal Revenues in the Middle Ages*, 2 vols. New York: Columbia University Press.

McKee, Samuel, Jr. 1934. *Papers on Public Credit, Commerce, and Finance by Alexander Hamilton*. New York: Columbia University Press.

McLean, Bethany and Joe Nocera 2010. *All the Devils are Here: The Hidden History of the Financial Crisis*. London: Penguin.

Maddison, Angus 1995. *Monitoring the World Economy, 1820–1992*. Paris: OECD.

Marchant, Jo 2012. "Underwater Archaeology: Hunt for the Ancient Mariner," *Nature*, 481:7382, 426–428.

Marichal, Carlos. 1989. *A Century of Debt Crises in Latin America: From Independence to the Great Depression, 1820–1930*. Princeton University Press.

2007. *Bankruptcy of Empire: Mexican Silver and the Wars between Spain, Britain and France, 1760–1810*. Cambridge University Press.

Marsilio, Claudio 2013. "European State Finance, Genoa, 1348–1700," in Gerard Caprio, ed., *The Handbook of Key Global Financial Markets, Institutions, and Infrastructure*, vol. I. Oxford: Elsevier, 235–249.

Mehrling, Perry 2011. *The New Lombard Street: How the Fed Became the Dealer of Last Resort*. Princeton, NJ and Oxford: Princeton University Press.

Michie, Ranald 1988. "Different in Name Only? The London Stock Exchange and Foreign Bourses, c. 1850–1914," *Business History*, 30:1, 46–68.

Miller, Nathan 1962. *The Enterprise of a Free People: Aspects of Economic Development in New York State during the Canal Period, 1792–1838*. Ithaca, NY: Cornell University Press.

Millett, Paul 1991. *Lending and Borrowing in Ancient Athens*. Cambridge University Press.

Milward, Alan S. 1970. *The New Order and the French Economy*. Oxford: Clarendon Press.

Mishkin, Frederic 1991. "Asymmetric Information and Financial Crises: A Historical Perspective," in R. Glenn Hubbard, ed., *Financial Markets and Financial Crises*. Chicago, IL and London: University of Chicago Press, 69–108.

Mitchell, Brian R. 1976. *Abstract of British Historical Statistics*. Cambridge University Press.

1978. *European Historical Statistics*. New York: Columbia University Press.

1988. *British Historical Statistics*. Cambridge University Press.

Mitchell, Wesley C. 1903. *A History of the Greenbacks, With Special Reference to the Economic Consequences of their Issue: 1862–65.* University of Chicago Press.

Mixon, Scott 2008. "The Crisis of 1873: Perspectives from Multiple Asset Classes," *Journal of Economic History*, 68:3 (September), 722–757.

Morris, Robert, 1782. "Report on Public Credit," repr. in Robert Morris, John Catanzariti, and James E. Ferguson, *The Papers of Robert Morris, 1781–1784*, vol. 6. University of Pittsburgh Press, 1973–1988.

Morris, Robert, John Catanzariti, and James E. Ferguson 1973–1988. *The Papers of Robert Morris, 1781–1784*. University of Pittsburgh Press.

Mortimer, Thomas 1761. *Every Man his own Broker: or, a Guide to Exchange-Alley* . . ., 4th edn. London: printed for S. Hooper.

Mueller, Reinhold C. 1997. *The Venetian Money Market: Banks, Panics, and the Public Debt, 1200–1500.* Baltimore, MD: Johns Hopkins University Press.

Munro, John H. 2003. "The Medieval Origins of the Financial Revolution: Usury, Rentes, and Negotiability," *The International History Review*, 25:3 (September), 505–562.

2013. " 'Rentes' and the European Financial Revolution," in Gerard Caprio, ed., *The Handbook of Key Global Financial Markets, Institutions, and Infrastructure*, vol. I. Oxford: Elsevier, 235–249.

Murphy, Anne L. 2009. *The Origins of English Financial Markets: Investment and Speculation before the South Sea Bubble.* Cambridge University Press.

Murphy, Antoin E. 1997. *John Law: Economic Theorist and Policy-Maker.* New York: Oxford University Press.

Nash, Robert Lucas 1876. *Fenn's Compendium of the English and Foreign Funds, Debts and Revenues of All Nations*, 12th edn., re-written. London: Effingham Wilson, Royal Exchange.

Neal, Larry. 1969. "Investment Behavior by American Railroads: 1897–1914," *Review of Economics and Statistics*, 51 (May), 126–135.

1971. "Trust Companies and Financial Innovation," *Business History Review*, 45:1 (Spring), 35–51.

1979. "The Economics and Finance of Bilateral Clearing Agreements: Germany, 1934–1938," *Economic History Review*, 32 (August), 391–404.

1990. *The Rise of Financial Capitalism: International Capital Markets in the Age of Reason.* Cambridge and New York: Cambridge University Press.

1991. "A Tale of Two Revolutions: International Capital Flows 1789–1819," *Bulletin of Economic Research*, 43:1 (January), 57–92.

1998. "The Bank of England's First Return to Gold and the Stock Market Crash of 1825," *Federal Reserve Bank of St. Louis Review* (May–June), 53–76.

2000. "How it all Began: The Monetary and Financial Architecture of Europe from 1648 to 1815," *Financial History Review*, 7:2 (October), 117–140.

2005. "Venture Shares in the Dutch East India Company," in William N. Goetzmann and K. Geert Rouwenhorst, eds., *The Origins of Value: The Financial Innovations that Created Modern Capital Markets*. New York: Oxford University Press, 165–175.

2007. *The Economics of Europe and the European Union*. Cambridge University Press.

2010. "Conclusion: The Monetary, Fiscal, and Political Architecture of Europe, 1815–1914," in José Luis Cardoso and Pedro Lains, eds., *Paying for the Liberal State: The Rise of Public Finance in Nineteenth Century Europe*. Cambridge University Press, 279–301.

2011a. "The Evolution of Self- and State Regulation of the London Stock Exchange, 1688–1878," in Debin Ma and Jan Luiten van Zanden, eds., *Law and Long-Term Economic Change: A Eurasian Perspective*. Stanford University Press, 300–322.

2011b. "A Reading List for Economic Historians on the Great Recession of 2007–2009: Its Causes and Consequences. Review Article," *Journal of Economic History*, 71:4 (December), 1099–1106.

2012. *"I am not master of events": The Speculations of John Law and Lord Londonderry in the Mississippi and South Sea Bubbles*. New Haven, CT: Yale University Press.

Neal, Larry and Lance E. Davis 2006. "The Evolution of the Structure and Performance of the London Stock Exchange in the First Global Financial Market, 1812–1914," *European Review of Economic History*, 10:3 (December), 279–300.

2007. "Why Did Finance Capitalism and the Second Industrial Revolution Arise in the 1890s?," Chapter 3 in Naomi Lamoreaux and Kenneth Sokoloff, eds., *Financing Innovation in the United States, 1870 to the Present*. Cambridge, MA: MIT Press, 129–161.

Neal, Larry and Maria Concepción Garcia-Iglesias 2013. "The Economy of Spain in the Euro-Zone before and after the Crisis of 2008," *Quarterly Review of Economics and Finance*, 53:4 (November), 336–344.

Neal, Larry and Stephen Quinn 2001. "Networks of Information, Markets, and Institutions in the Rise of London as a Financial Centre," *Financial History Review*, 8:1 (April), 7–26.

Neal, Larry and Marc Weidenmier 2003. "Crises in the Global Economy from Tulips to Today: Contagion and Consequences," Chapter 10 in

Michael D. Bordo, Alan M. Taylor, and Jeffrey G. Williamson, eds., *Globalization in Historical Perspective*. Chicago, IL and London: University of Chicago Press, 473–574.

Neal, Larry and Eugene N. White 2012. "The Glass–Steagall Act in Historical Perspective," *Quarterly Review of Economics and Finance*, 52:2 (May), 104–113.

North, Douglass C. and Barry Weingast 1989. "Constitutions and Commitments: Evolution of Institutions Governing Public Choice in Seventeenth Century England," *Journal of Economic History* , 49:4 (December), 803–822.

Nolte, Vincent 1854. *Fifty Years in both Hemispheres, or, Reminiscences of the Life of a Former Merchant*. New York: Redfield.

Obstfeld, Maurice and Alan M. Taylor 2004. *Global Capital Markets: Integration, Crisis, and Growth*. Cambridge and New York: Cambridge University Press.

Odell, Kerry A. and Marc D. Weidenmier 2004. "Real Shock, Monetary Aftershock: The 1906 Earthquake and the Panic of 1907," *The Journal of Economic History*, 64:4 (December), 1002–1027.

Officer, Lawrence H. 1996. *Between the Dollar–Sterling Gold Points: Exchange Rates, Parity, and Market Behaviour*. Cambridge University Press.

Olmstead, Alan L. 1976. *New York City Mutual Savings Banks, 1819–1861*. Chapel Hill, NC: University of North Carolina Press.

Organisation for Economic Cooperation and Development 1996. *OECD Economic Outlook*, No. 60 (data CD).

2002–present. *OECD Journal: Financial Market Trends*, Semi-annual. Paris: OECD.

2005. *OECD Economic Outlook*, No. 77 (data CD).

O'Rourke, Kevin H. and Jeffrey G. Williamson 1999. *Globalization and History: The Evolution of a 19th Century Atlantic Economy*. Cambridge, MA: MIT Press.

O'Rourke, Kevin H. 2005. "From Malthus to Ohlin: Trade, Industrialisation, and Distribution Since 1500," *Journal of Economic Growth*, 10:1 (January), 5-34.

Padgett, John F. 2012. "Early Capitalism and State Formation," in John F. Padgett and Woody Powell, eds., *The Emergence of Organizations and Markets*. Princeton University Press, 115–266.

Parthasarathi, Parsannan 2011. *Why Europe Grew Rich and Asia Did Not: Global Economic Divergence, 1600–1850*. New York: Cambridge University Press.

Pearce, Adrian J. 2009. "The Hope–Barings Contract: Finance and Trade Between Europe and the Americas, 1805–1808," *English Historical Review*, 124:511 (December), 1324–1352.

Perrow, Charles, Albert J. Reiss, and Harold L. Wilensky 1986. *Complex Organizations: A Critical Essay*. New York: Random House.

Peters, Edward T. 1892. *Co-Operative Credit Associations in Certain European Countries*. Washington, DC: US Government Printing Office.

Peters, Madison C. 1911. *Haym Solomon: The Financier of the American Revolution*. New York: The Trow Press.

Petram, Lodewijk 2011. *The World's First Stock Exchange: How the Amsterdam Market for Dutch East India Company Shares Became a Modern Securities Market, 1602–1700*. Unpublished PhD dissertation, University of Amsterdam, http://dare.uva.nl/document/201694.

Pezzolo, Luciano 2013a. "Sovereign Debts, Political Structure, and Institutional Commitments in Italy, 1350–1700," in D'Maris Coffman, Adrian Leonard, and Larry Neal, eds., *Questioning Credible Commitment: New Perspectives on the Glorious Revolution and the Rise of Financial Capitalism*. Cambridge University Press, 169–198.

2013b. "Venetian Finance, 1400–1797," in Gerard Caprio, ed., *The Handbook of Key Financial Markets, Institutions, and Infrastructure*, vol. I. Oxford: Elsevier, 301–317.

2014. "The *via italiana* to Capitalism," in Larry Neal and Jeffrey G. Williamson, eds., *The Cambridge History of Capitalism*, vol. 1, "The Rise of Capitalism: From Ancient Origins to 1848." Cambridge University Press, 267–313.

Pezzolo, Luciano and Guiseppe Tattara 2008. " 'Una fiera senza luogo': Was Bisenzone an International Capital Market in Sixteenth-Century Italy?," *Journal of Economic History*, 68:4 (December), 1098–1122.

Postel-Vinay, Natacha 2014. *Commercial Bank Mortgage Lending and the Great Depression in Chicago, 1913–33*. PhD dissertation, London School of Economics and Political Science.

Posthumus, N. W. 1926. "De Speculatie in Tulpen in de Jaren 1636 en 1637," I. *Economisch-Historisch Jaarboek*. Gravenhage: Martinus Nijhoff.

1927. "De Speculatie in Tulpen in de Jaren 1636 en 1637," II. *Economisch-Historisch Jaarboek*. Gravenhage: Martinus Nijhoff.

1929. "The Tulipmania in Holland in the Years 1636 and 1637," *Journal of Economic and Business History*, 1 (May), 441–442.

1934. "De Speculatie in Tulpen in de Jaren 1636 en 1637," III. *Economisch-Historisch Jaarboek*. Gravenhage: Martinus Nijhoff.

Postlethwayt, Malachi 1971 (1774). *The Universal Dictionary of Trade and Commerce*, 4th edn., London, repr. New York: Augustus M. Kelley.

Pounds, Norman J. G. 1990. *An Historical Geography of Europe*. Cambridge University Press.

Pressnell, Leslie S. 1956. *Country Banking in the Industrial Revolution*. Oxford: Clarendon Press.

1986. *External Economic Policy since the War*. London: HMSO.

Quinn, Stephen. 1994. *Banking before the Bank: London's Unregulated Goldsmith-Bankers, 1660–1694*. PhD dissertation, University of Illinois.

——— 1996. "Gold, Silver, and the Glorious Revolution: Arbitrage between Bills of Exchange and Bullion," *Economic History Review*, 49:3 (August), 473–490.

——— 1997. "Goldsmith-Banking: Mutual Acceptance and Interbanker Clearing in Restoration London," *Explorations in Economic History*, 34:4 (December), 411–432.

——— 2001. "The Glorious Revolution's Effect on English Private Finance: A Microhistory, 1680–1705," *Journal of Economic History*, 61:3 (September), 593–614.

Quinn, Stephen and Will Roberds 2012. "Responding to a Shadow Banking Crisis: The Lessons of 1763," Federal Bank of Atlanta, Working Paper, 2012-8, 28.

Rajan, Ramchuran 2005. "Has Financial Development made the World Riskier?," *The Greenspan Era: Lessons for the Future, a Symposium Sponsored by the Federal Reserve Bank of Kansas City, Jackson Hole, Wyoming, August 25–27, 2005*, 313–369, www.kansascityfed.org/pub licat/sympos/2005/pdf/rajan2005.pdf.

——— 2010. *Fault Lines: How Hidden Fractures Still Threaten the World Economy*, Princeton University Press.

Rappleye, Charles 2010. *Robert Morris: Financier of the American Revolution*. New York: Simon & Schuster.

Redish, Angela 2000. *Bimetallism: An Economic and Historical Analysis*. Cambridge University Press.

Redlich, Fritz 1959. "Contributions in the Thirty Years' War," *Economic History Review*, 12:2 (December), 247–254.

Reinhart, Carmen and Kenneth Rogoff 2009. *This Time is Different: Eight Centuries of Financial Folly*. Princeton University Press.

Reis, Jaime 1996. "First to Join the Gold Standard: 1854," in Jorge Braga de Macedo, Barry J. Eichengreen, and Jaime Reis, eds., *Currency Convertibility: The Gold Standard and Beyond*. London: Routledge, 159–181.

Richards, R. D. 1929. *The Early History of Banking in England*. London: P. S. King & Staples Ltd.

Riley, James C. 1980. *International Government Finance and the Amsterdam Capital Market, 1740–1815*. Cambridge University Press.

Ritschl, Albrecht 2001. "Nazi Economic Imperialism and the Exploitation of the Small: Evidence From Germany's Secret Foreign Exchange Balances, 1938–1940," *Economic History Review*, 54:2 (May), 324–345.

Robinson, Damian and Andrew Wilson, eds., 2011. *Maritime Archaeology and Ancient Trade in the Mediterranean*. Oxford Centre for Maritime Archaeology.

Rockoff, Hugh 2009. "Upon Daedalian Wings of Paper Money: Adam Smith and the Crisis of 1772," NBER Working Paper, No. 15594.

Rodgers, Mary Tone and James E. Payne. 2014. "How the Bank of France Changed US Equity Expectations and Ended the Panic of 1907," *Journal of Economic History*, 74:2 (June), 420–448.

Roseveare, Henry 1991. *The Financial Revolution, 1660–1760*. London: Longman.

Rothbard, Murray 1962. *The Panic of 1819: Reactions and Policies*. New York: Columbia University Press.

Rousseau, Peter and Richard Sylla 2005. "Emerging Financial Markets and Early US Growth," *Explorations in Economic History*, 42:1 (January), 1–26.

Samuelson, Paul A. 1964. "Theoretical Notes on Trade Problems," *Review of Economic and Statistics*, 46:2 (May), 145–154.

Sapori, Armando 1970. *The Italian Merchant in the Middle Ages*. New York: Norton.

Sargent, Thomas J. and François R. Velde 2002. *The Big Problem of Small Change*. Princeton University Press.

Sauvy, A. 1965–1967. *Histoire économique de la France entre les deux guerres, t. I: 1918–1931*. Paris: Fayard.

Schenk, Catherine R. 1994. *Britain and the Sterling Area: From Devaluation to Convertibility in the 1950s*. London and New York: Routledge.

   1998. "The Origins of the Eurodollar Market in London: 1955–1963," *Explorations in Economic History*, 35:3 (April), 221–238.

Schnabel, Isabel 2004. "The German Twin Crisis of 1931," *Journal of Economic History*, 64:3 (September), 822–871.

Schnabel, Isabel and Hyun Song Shin 2004. "Liquidity and Contagion: The Crisis of 1763," *Journal of the European Economic Association*, 2:6 (December), 929–968.

Schramm, Percy Ernst 1949. *Kaufleute zu Haus und über See: Hamburgische Zeugnisse des 17., 18. und 19. Jahrhunderts*. Hamburg: Hoffmann und Campe Verlag.

Schubert, Aurel 1991. *The Credit-Anstalt Crisis of 1931*. Cambridge and New York: Cambridge University Press.

Schumpeter, Joseph 1939. *Business Cycles: A Theoretical, Historical, and Statistical Analysis of the Capitalist Process*, New York: McGraw-Hill.

Scott, W. R. 1912. *The Constitution and Finance of English, Scottish and Irish Joint-Stock Companies to 1729*, 3 vols. Cambridge University Press, repr. Gloucester, MA: Peter Smith, 1968.

Seligman, Edward R. A. 1919. "The Cost of the War and How It Was Met," *American Economic Review*, 9 (December), 739–770.

Siegel, Jennifer 2014. *For Peace and Money: French and British Finance in the Service of Tsars and Commissars*. Oxford University Press.

Singh, Manmohan 2013. "The Changing Collateral Space," IMF Working Paper, No. WP/13/25.

Skalweit, Stephan 1937. *Die Berliner Wirtschaftskrise von 1763 und ihre Hintergründe*. Stuttgart & Berlin: Von W. Kohlhammer.

Slotsky, Alice Louise 1997. *The Bourse of Babylon: Market Quotations in the Astronomical Diaries of Babylonia*. Bethesda, MD: CDL Press.

Smith, Adam 1776. *An Inquiry into the Nature and Causes of The Wealth of Nations*, 2 vols. London: printed for W. Strahan, and T. Cadell.

Snowden, Kenneth 1987. "American Stock Market Development and Performance, 1871–1929," *Explorations in Economic History*, 24:3 (October), 327–353.

Sperling, J. 1962. "The International Payments Mechanism in the Seventeenth and Eighteenth Centuries," *Economic History Review*, 14:3 (September), 446–468.

Spufford, Peter 2003. *Power and Profit: The Merchant in Medieval Europe*. London: Thames & Hudson.

Stasavage, David 2003. *Public Debt and the Birth of the Democratic State: France and Great Britain, 1688–1789*. New York: Cambridge University Press.

    2011. *States of Credit: Size, Power, and the Development of European Polities*. Princeton University Press.

Stein, Stanley J. and Barbara H. Stein 2000. *Silver, Trade, and War: Spain and America in the Making of Early Modern Europe*. Baltimore, MD: Johns Hopkins University Press.

Stolper, Matthew W. 1985. *Entrepreneurs and Empire: The Murašû Archive, the Murašû Firm, and Persian rule in Babylonia*. Istanbul: Nederlands Historisch-Archaeologisch Instituut te Istanbul.

Studenski, Paul and Herman E. Krooss 1963. *Financial History of the United States: Fiscal, Monetary, Banking and Tariff, including Financial Administration and State and Local Finance*, 2nd edn. New York: Macmillan.

Sumner, William 1891. *The Financier and the Finances of the American Revolution*. New York: Dodd, Mead & Co, repr. Augustus M. Kelley, 1968.

Sussman, Nathan and Yishay Yafeh 2006. "Institutional Reforms, Financial Development, and Sovereign Debt: Britain, 1690–1790," *Journal of Economic History*, 66:4 (December), 906–935.

Sylla, Richard 2009. "Comparing the UK and US Financial Systems, 1790–1830," in Jeremy Atack and Larry Neal, eds., *The Development* of Financial Markets and Institutions from the Seventeenth Century to the Present. Cambridge and New York: Cambridge University Press.

Temin, Peter 2004. "Financial Intermediation in the Early Roman Empire," *Journal of Economic History*, 64:3 (September), 705–733.

2013. "Roman Finance, Private and Public," in G. Caprio, ed., *Handbook of Key Global Financial Markets, Institutions, and Infrastructure*, vol. I. London: Elsevier.

T' Hart, Marjolein 1991. "'The Devil or the Dutch': Holland's Impact on the Financial Revolution in England, 1643–1694," *Parliaments, Estates and Representation*, 2:1 (June), 39–52.

Thompson, Earl A. 2007. "The Tulipmania: Fact or Artifact?," *Public Choice*, 130:1/2 (January), 99–114.

Tilly, Richard 1967. "The Political Economy of Public Finance and the Industrialization of Prussia, 1815–1866," *Journal of Economic History*, 26:4 (December), 484–497.

1998. "Universal Banking in Historical Perspective," *Journal of Institutional and Theoretical Economics*, 54:2 (March), 7–32.

Timothy Green's Historical Gold Price Table 2015, www.nma.org/pdf/gold/his_gold_prices.pdf.

Tracy, James 1985. *A Financial Revolution in the Habsburg Netherlands: renten and renteniers in the County of Holland, 1515–1565.* Berkeley, CA: University of California Press.

Triffin, Robert 1957. *Europe and the Money Muddle.* New Haven, CT: Yale University Press.

1958. *Gold and the Dollar Crisis.* New Haven, CT: Yale University Press.

Tuncer, Ali Coşkun 2011. *Fiscal Autonomy, Monetary Regime and Sovereign Risk: Foreign Borrowing and International Financial Control in the Ottoman Empire, Greece and Egypt During the Classical Gold Standard Era.* PhD thesis, The London School of Economics and Political Science.

Ungerer, Horst 1983. *The European Monetary System: The Experience, 1971–1982.* Washington, DC: International Monetary Fund.

United Nations 2009. *Report of the Commission of Experts of the President of the United Nations General Assembly on Reforms of the International Monetary and Financial System.* New York: United Nations.

Vam Malle Sabouret, Camille 2008. "De la naissance de la dette publique au plafond souverain: Rôle des gouvernements régionaux dans l'évolution de la dette publique." Unpublished doctoral thesis, Finances Internationales, Institut d'Études Politiques de Paris.

Van der Mierop, Marcus 1992. *Society and Enterprise in Old Babylonian Ur.* Berlin: Dietrich Reimer Verlag.

2005. "The Invention of Interest," in William N. Goetzmann and K. Geert, Rouwenhorst, eds., *Origins of Value: The Financial Innovations that Created Modern Capital Markets*. New York: Oxford University Press.

Van Dillen, J. G. 1925. "De Amsterdamsche Wisselbank," *Economisch Historisch Jaarboek*, 11, 245–249.

1930. "Isaac Le Maire en de handel in action der Oost-Indische Compagnie," *Economisch Historisch jaarboek*, 16, 1–165.

Van Dillen, J. G., Geoffrey Poitras, and Asha Majithia 2006. "Isaac Le Maire and Dutch East India Company Shares," in Geoffrey Poitras, ed., *Pioneers in Financial Economics*, vol. I. Cheltenham: Edward Elgar, 45–63.

Veenhof, K. R. 2010. "Ancient Assur: Its Traders, and its Commercial Network," *The Journal of the Economic and Social History of the Orient*, 53, 39–82.

Velde, François R. 2009. "John Law's System and its Aftermath, 1718–1725," in Jeremy Atack and Larry Neal, eds., *The Origins and Development of Financial Markets and Institutions: From the Seventeenth Century to the Present*. New York and Cambridge: Cambridge University Press, 99–120.

Velde, François R. and Warren E. Weber 2000. "A Model of Bimetallism," *Journal of Political Economy*, 108:6 (December), 1210–1234.

Vizcarra, Catalina 2009. "Guano, Credible Commitments, and Sovereign Debt Repayment in the Nineteenth Century, *Journal of Economic History*, 69:2 (June), 358–387.

Wallis, John, Richard Sylla, and Arthur Grinath, III 2004. "Sovereign Debt and Repudiation: The Emerging-Market Debt Crisis in the US States, 1839–43," NBER Working Paper, No. 10753.

Warren, George F. and Frank A. Pearson 1935. *Gold and Prices*. New York: John Wiley.

Watson, Katherine 1996. "Banks and Industrial Finance: The Experience of Brewers, 1880–1913", *Economic History Review*, 49:1 (February), 58–81.

Weber, Warren 2006a. "New Evidence on State Banking Before the Civil War," Research Department, Federal Reserve Bank of Minneapolis, Working Paper, No. 642.

2006b. "Early State Banks in the United States: How Many Were There and When Did They Exist?," *Journal of Economic History*, 66:2 (June), 433–455.

Wee, Herman van der 1977. "Money, Credit and Banking Systems," Chapter V in E. E. Rich and Charles H. Wilson, eds., *The Cambridge Economic History of Europe*, vol. V, "The Economic Organization of Early Modern Europe." Cambridge University Press. 290–392.

1993. "Antwerp and the New Financial Methods of the 16th and 17th Centuries," Chapter 8 in Herman van der Wee, *The Low Countries in the Modern World*, trans. Lizabeth Fackelman. Aldershot: Ashgate. 145–166.

Weidenmier, Marc 2000. "The Market for Confederate Cotton Bonds," *Explorations in Economic History*, 37:1 (January), 76–97.

2005. "Gunboats, Reputation, and Sovereign Repayment: Lessons from the Southern Confederacy," *Journal of International Economics*, 66:2, 407–422.

Wells, John and Douglas Willis 2000. "Revolution, Restoration, and Debt Repudiation: The Jacobite Threat to England's Institutions and Economic Growth," *Journal of Economic History*, 60:2 (June), 418–441.

Wessel, David 2009. *In Fed We Trust: Ben Bernanke's War on the Great Panic*. New York: Crown Business.

White, Eugene N. 1983. *The Regulation and Reform of the American Banking System, 1900–1929*. Princeton University Press.

2007. "The Crash of 1882 and the Bailout of the Paris Bourse," *Cliometrica*, 1:2 (July), 115–144.

White, Eugene N., Kenneth Snowden, and Price Fishback, eds. 2014. *Housing and Mortgage Markets in Historical Perspective*. University of Chicago Press.

Wilkins, Mira 1989. *The History of Foreign Investment in the United States to 1914*. Cambridge, MA: Harvard University Press.

Williamson, Jeffrey G. 2011. *Trade and Poverty: When the Third World Fell Behind*. Cambridge, MA: MIT Press.

Wilson, Charles 1941. *Anglo-Dutch Commerce and Finance in the Eighteenth Century*. Cambridge University Press.

Wolf, O. 1932. *Ouvrard, Speculator of Genius, 1770–1846*, first published in German, 1932; London: Barrie & Rockliff, 1962.

Wright, Robert 1996. "Thomas Willing (1731–1821): Philadelphia Financier and Forgotten Founding Father," *Pennsylvania History*, 63:4 (Autumn), 525–560.

Ziegler, Philip. 1988. *The Sixth Great Power: A History of One of the Greatest of All Banking Families, The House of Barings, 1762–1929*. New York: Alfred A. Knopf.

Index

Index

United States (US) (cont.)
  movement of gold to IMF member
    countries 264–265
  railroad bond market 206–207
  recovery from Great Depression
    248
  regional stock exchanges 221
  repayment of war debts by Allies
    238
  stock market crash (1873) 206–207
  war on terror, finance for 292
Ur
  contract negotiations 18
Uruk
  beginnings of finance 15–16
US dollar, and gold standard 237
  devaluation of 245, 248
USS Central America, loss of gold cargo
    196
usury
  and heritable annuities 53
  laws 86
  limits, and British merchants 107
  religious prohibition of 28
  see also exchange dealers *per arte*;
    pactum di recorsa

Vam Malle Sabouret, Camille
    44–45
van Buren, President Martin, and Panic
    of 1837 181
van de Mieroop, M., establishment of
    Uruk 15–16, 18
van der Wee, Herman 76
  transmission of financial innovations
    77
Van Dillen, J.G. 57, 98
Velde, F.R. 78, 92, 193
Venice 28, 38
  Banco di Rialto 40
  Monte, consolidated debt 39
  and War of the League of Cambrai
    40
Verona, and self-government 38
Vicenza, and self-government 38
Vietnam, US war finance for 268
  and Triffin dilemma 270–271
Vizcarra, C. 208
VOC (Verenigde Oost-Indische
    Compagnie)

corporate governance structure
    55–56, 62, 83
  creation of 63
  and English financial revolution 74
  investment in 56–57, 62
  development of secondary market
    57–58
  long-term debt 60
  regulation of 59
  shares, options on 104
  see also Hans Thijs; stock exchange
Volcker, Paul 273
  and Volcker "shock" 273, 278–279,
    286
Voth, H.-J. 46–47
voorcompagnien 55
  see also VOC

wage-push inflation 268
Wall St Journal 6
Wallis, Sylla and Grinath III 183
Walpole, Robert, and South Sea bubble
    84–85, 96–97
Wandschneider, K. 84–85
war debt, of Allied powers after World
    War I 238
  Russian communist default on 238
  see also Dawes Loan; Weimar
    Germany
war finance
  18th century financial systems 109
  Britain's success in 18th century
    72–73
  driver for financial innovation
    43–45
  pressures on Italian city-states 28
  responses of financial system (1914)
    232–233
  self-regulation of exchanges (1914)
    235
  see also François I; individual stock
    exchanges; individual wars
War of American Independence
    (1775–83) 128
  American alliance with France 130
  British defeat at Battle of Saratoga
    (1777) 130
War of the Austrian Succession 73
  finance for 97
  British finance for 109–111, 125